The Purifying Knife

THE PURIFYING KNIFE

THE TROUBLING HISTORY OF EUGENICS IN TEXAS

BY MICHAEL PHILLIPS AND
BETSY FRIAUF

UNIVERSITY OF OKLAHOMA PRESS : NORMAN

Published in Cooperation with the William P. Clements Center for Southwest Studies, Southern Methodist University.

Library of Congress Cataloging-in-Publication Data
Names: Phillips, Michael, 1960– author. | Friauf, Betsy, 1955– author.
Title: The purifying knife : the troubling history of eugenics in Texas /
    by Michael Phillips and Betsy Friauf.
Description: Norman : University of Oklahoma Press, 2025. |
    Includes bibliographical references and index. | Summary: "Explores
    the roles of eugenics and eugenacists in Texas and their impact on
    the state's attitudes towards race, immigration, religion, education,
    and politics"—Provided by publisher.
Identifiers: LCCN 2024038402 | ISBN 9780806195360 (hardcover ;
    alk. paper)
Subjects: LCSH: Eugenics—Texas—History. | Involuntary sterilization—
    Texas—History. | Reproductive rights—Texas—History. | Eugenics—
    Political aspects—Texas—History.
Classification: LCC HQ755.5.U5 P45 2025 | DDC 363.9/209764—
    dc23/eng/20241214
LC record available at https://lccn.loc.gov/2024038402

The paper in this book meets the guidelines for permanence and durability of the Committee on Production Guidelines for Book Longevity of the Council on Library Resources, Inc. ∞

Contents

Acknowledgments / vii

Prologue: Sex, Eugenics, and a Forgotten Episode
in Texas History / 1

1 A Brief Prehistory of Texas Eugenics, 1853–1874 / 28

2 Regulating Reproduction in Texas, 1883–1914 / 39

3 Eugenics, Disability, and Anti-Democratic Discourse
in Texas, 1890–1925 / 74

4 Eugenics, the IQ Panic, and Immigration, 1915–1940 / 126

5 Texas Eugenics From 1931 On / 170

Notes / 213
Select Bibliography / 257
Index / 271

Acknowledgments

THE OBSCURE HISTORY of eugenics in Texas first fascinated one of the authors, Michael Phillips, almost three decades ago while he researched his dissertation, later published as his first book, *White Metropolis: Race, Ethnicity, and Religion in Dallas, 1841–2001* (2006). One day, he encountered news coverage of a better baby contest at Dallas's Fair Park in 1914. Such contests, held across the country, encouraged those judged biologically superior to have large families in order to save the human race from other people thought to be dangerously fertile and "unfit." Better baby and fitter family contests represented one of the most visible public outreach programs of the worldwide eugenics movement, which sought to upgrade the human race and eliminate supposed biological "defects" through a variety of means, including selective breeding, compulsory birth control, and (at its most extreme) euthanasia and genocide.

Texas barely merited mention in the few works Phillips read about the history of the eugenics movement in the United States. He discovered that better baby and fitter family contests provided entertainment and dubious education for years at the always-popular State Fair of Texas, but that the eugenics movement cast a much larger shadow on Texas culture than just those quirky sideshows.

A University of Texas (UT) professor, Alexander Caswell Ellis, spoke at that 1914 Dallas contest to promote selective human breeding. This particularly intrigued Phillips, who as a graduate student at UT researched the evolving definitions of whiteness in Dallas. Already aware that previous generations of academics at the University of Texas had defended the state's history of slavery, as well as segregation and Black disenfranchisement, he soon realized that his academic home had also played a role in the early twentieth-century American eugenics debate. Phillips spent years on other scholarly projects, but a desire to uncover the history of this particularly malign and dangerous idea in the Lone Star State became an obsession that eventually flowered into the volume you are reading now.

His research on Texas eugenics began in earnest in 2014. Progress was slow, but Phillips got a substantial boost when he received a Mellon Foundation/American Council of Learned Societies Community College Faculty Fellowship for 2019–20. This excellent program, which unfortunately ended in 2023, provided financial support for research conducted by professors working at two-year colleges who typically do not receive sabbaticals or other forms of institutional backing. Phillips and his wife and coauthor, Betsy Friauf, used the funds from the fellowship for multiple trips for archival research in New York, Michigan, and across Texas.

This book was born in hardship. A significant part of the research and much of the writing took place during the COVID-19 pandemic, a time when many archives shut down and airline travel became impossible or dangerous. Phillips also became involved in a major First Amendment battle with his employer, Collin College, on matters ranging from the removal of Confederate monuments in Dallas to whether faculty should be allowed to recommend that students wear masks while the lethal coronavirus slew thousands of Texans. That struggle for free speech, draining and difficult, proved a painful distraction from this important research. It nevertheless did not deter the authors from completing their work.

At one of the lowest points in his adult life, Phillips got a phone call from Andrew Graybill, the director of the Clements Center for Southwest Studies at Southern Methodist University, who had heard of Phillips's ordeal and believed in his book project. Graybill offered him a senior research fellowship at the Clements Center, a position that provided a generous stipend, travel funds, and a subvention grant. This gave Phillips the chance to work full-time on the manuscript.

One of the best gifts provided by the Clements Center is the opportunity to have manuscripts reviewed by top scholars in a particular field. In this case, two of the world's foremost authorities on the history of eugenics, Edward Larson, author of *Sex, Race, and Science: Eugenics in the Deep South* (1996) and Diane B. Paul, one of the editors of *Eugenics at the Edges of Empire: New Zealand, Australia, Canada and South Africa* (2017) provided invaluable insights that immeasurably improved an unwieldy early draft. With their direction, Phillips and Friauf were able to apply their own purifying knife and reduce the proposed book to a publishable length. The authors thank both Larson and Paul for their wisdom and their sharp eye, and hope they are pleased with the result.

Larson and Paul were joined by Neil Foley, who had been Phillips's dissertation director at the University of Texas, in a vigorous manuscript workshop. Foley has always been demanding but an enthusiastic supporter, an intellectual polestar throughout Phillips's career. That amazing workshop included a remarkable group of young scholars who undoubtedly will be the movers and shakers in their respective areas of expertise, including one of the authors' best friends, Chad Person, a groundbreaking labor historian, as well as Kimberly Hill, who specializes in the social justice work of African American religious leaders, and the other talented members of the 2022–23 fellowship cohort at SMU: Tiffany González, Nicholas Myers, and Katherine Bynum. The flow of ideas from so many top-notch minds was of incalculable value. The authors also want to express gratitude to the remarkable Ruth Ann Elmore, the Clements Center's assistant director and the person who does more than anyone to make the place a welcoming home for up-and-coming and even crusty old historians.

Both Phillips and Friauf received abundant help from colleagues, librarians, archivists, and friends over a decade. Staff provided excellent guidance at the Dolph Briscoe Center for American History and the Nettie Lee Benson Latin American Collection, both at the University of Texas. Kathryn Kenefick in particular has always been a great guide to the Briscoe Center's vast holdings. Clare Bunce, the archivist at the Cold Spring Harbor Laboratory, the former home of the Eugenics Record Office (ERO) on Long Island, New York, patiently guided Phillips through the available materials on Texas, particularly those pertaining to Hermann Joseph Muller, a one-time University of Texas professor who advocated eugenics but became an important anti-racist dissident in the movement. The Cold Spring Harbor Library provided Phillips with a comfortable and affordable dormitory room as he dug through the ERO records during a lovely, marvelously mild midsummer.

This book also could not have been finished without the help of the Woodson Research Center Special Collections staff at Rice University's Fondren Library (who helped the authors explore the Julian Huxley papers) and the sharp minds at the University of Texas at Arlington Special Collections division, who gathered material on E. E. Davis, the eugenicist dean of the school from the 1920s to the 1940s, when it was known as North Texas Agricultural College. Librarians also made visits to the Texas State Library and Archives in Austin and the Southwest Collection/Special Collection Archive at Texas Tech University in Lubbock pleasant and enlightening.

Phillips and Friauf want to express appreciation to David O'Donald Cullen, a friend who authored a detailed, thoughtful historiographical essay on the history of eugenics in the United States, which provided an excellent roadmap for research, and who generously read several drafts of this manuscript. They also want to express gratitude to another colleague and friend, Kyle Wilkison, for his knowledge of labor history in Texas and his nomination of Phillips for the East Texas Historical Association's 2021 Ottis Lock Educator of the Year Award. Meanwhile, John Mckiernan-González gave extensive suggestions for revisions that have greatly improved this work.

The authors owe much to Rachel Gunter for her kindness, her help with all things technological, and for her insights into early twentieth-century politics in Texas. With this book, they also celebrate the bonds forged in a fight for justice with their fellow free-speech warriors, Lora Burnett, Audra Heaslip, and particularly Suzanne Jones, who showed a bravery rare and inspiring to all lucky enough to meet her. Another former colleague at Collin College, Kim Parker Nyman, became an eloquent ally. She may have differed from Phillips and Friauf on many political issues, but she shared their love of higher education and the belief that a free people thrive only if they are allowed to speak freely. There also have been no greater fellow crusaders for the truth than the brave Lorena Rodríguez, Adrian Tan, and Linda Wee Swee Lian.

The authors' work would not have gotten off the ground without the support of longtime friends who opened their homes to the weary travelers, afforded them every comfort, and fed them like royalty. In Houston, these beloved friends were Charles "Chuck" Luke and the late Lory Garrett; in New Rochelle, New York, they were Amy and Mike Csenge.

The writers also extend gratitude to the following for organizing and participating in rallies held in support of Phillips as he fought for his job: Leslie "Les" Cunningham, Charles Hermes, Andrew Kirk, Susie Curts, and Ben Wright. Les became an incomparable comrade-in-arms. Deep appreciation is further extended to the East Texas Historical Association (ETHA) and the members who form the heart of the organization: Executive Director Scott Sosebee as well as Mary Jo O'Rear, Bernadette Pruitt, Deborah Liles, and Jeffrey Littlejohn. The ETHA became one of the first organizations to draft a resolution supporting Phillips's free-speech cause. Meanwhile, Cary Wintz, an esteemed historian of the African American experience in Texas, was always ready to write a kind and fulsome letter of recommendation during Phillips's sometimes tumultuous career, even as Sharon Kowalski at Texas A&M University at Commerce and Jennifer Wallach at the University of North Texas gave him a chance to teach again. Phillips and Friauf also owe a deep debt to the American Historical Association, the Academic Freedom Alliance, and the American Association of University Professors, all of which took a stand against the suppression of faculty rights.

The authors are proud to have been represented by the best legal team in the country, the attorneys from the Foundation for Individual Rights and Expression (FIRE). Bob Schmidt, Joshua Bleisch, Katlyn Patton, J. T. Morris, Kelly Bregenzer, and especially the relentless Greg Greubel prepared an excellent case and worked tirelessly, around the clock. Greg was much more than a lawyer and became a cherished friend. We enjoyed talking about sports and parenthood with him and will always treasure our time together, through good times and bad.

Each day of our First Amendment trial, cherished supporters Cunningham, Jim Frisinger, and the world-acclaimed photographer Byrd Williams showed up to help Phillips and Friauf get through difficult times. Jerry Hawkins and the team at Dallas Truth, Racial Healing, and Transformation, podcaster Ed Gray, and world-class scholars Erich Freiberger and Brandon Jett kept Phillips's work in the public eye, as did gifted documentarian Quin Mathews, who asked Phillips to appear in and serve as historical consultant on his documentary about the sixtieth anniversary of the Kennedy assassination, *City of Hate*. Remarkable journalists Simone Carter, Steve Monacelli, Jobin Panicker, and Bill Zeeble gave Phillips and Friauf repeated chances to tell their story to the world.

Stephanie Drenka taught the authors about the history of Asian Americans in Dallas and created a beautiful personal website for Phillips (https://drmichaelphillipsphd.com). Helen Juliette Muller granted permission for the use of a photo of her father in the famous "Fly Room" at UT Austin, where he conducted Nobel Prize-winning research that proved exposure to x-rays caused mutations in fruit flies. Margarita Birnbaum provided invaluable help with translating Spanish-language newspaper articles on eugenics. The wonderful Michael and Judy Botson provided the fantastic photograph of the Francis Galton bas-relief at Rice University, and lifelong friend Susanne York created the moody, symbolic picture of eugenicist Lewis Meriwether Dabney's Dallas gravesite.

During the often chaotic nine years it took to gestate this book, Phillips and Friauf also had the privilege to participate in one of the greatest and most successful protest movements in Dallas history, the effort to remove Confederate monuments and rename schools, roads, and other sites designated in honor of traitors and enslavers. Ed Gray, the Reverend Michael W. Waters, the Reverend Eric Folkerth, Sarah Mokuria, Ed Sebesta, and lifelong justice warrior John Fullinwider became not just friends but heroes to the authors during the campaign. The authors also had the honor and privilege to fight alongside our cherished colleagues, Benjamin Johnson, Leah LaGrone, and John Lundberg as we resisted a right-wing takeover of the Texas State Historical Association, exposed the removal of books about racism and slavery from the sites of former slave labor camps in Texas, and helped create a new statewide historical organization. Johnson in particular helped Phillips in many ways, providing a recommendation for the Clements fellowship and starting a petition drive on his behalf.

Susan Krasnow and Linda Abramson Evans have been at the writers' side, literally or metaphorically, through the best and the worst. Mary Shomon is the type of friend you only get once in a lifetime. Her love has been constant and she reminds the authors always that they are never alone in the darkest of hours.

The authors thank J. Kent Calder, then the acquisitions editor for the University of Oklahoma Press, for offering a contract after hearing them make a presentation about eugenics in Texas, and Andrew Berzanskis, who picked up the reins and steered the book toward what hopefully will be great success.

Betsy Friauf extends very belated thanks to the late Pauline Smith Burdick, her third-grade teacher whose words endured across the decades: "When you publish your first book, send me an autographed copy."

Mrs. Burdick was the special kind of teacher who inspires young people to follow their passion. It is the authors' hope that the country holds a future in which all sincere educators may speak openly as they light the way for inquiring minds.

Most of all, the authors dedicate this work to their children. Dominic Shehan Phillips was born when Michael Phillips was forty-three and has been the unexpected treasure of his life ever since. The years spent writing this book saw Dominic earn a junior black belt in taekwondo, act, travel the world as a cellist and angelic singer, immerse himself in Chinese, become part (on his own initiative) of a US State Department program in which he spent a summer in South Korea with a local family as he began learning Korean, and win a scholarship at prestigious Yonsei University in Seoul. With his Sicilian, northern Italian, French, Welsh, Irish, Mvskoke, Ashkenazic, Moroccan, and Turkish ancestry, Dominic is a eugenicist's nightmare. But he has been not only brilliant, but also kind-hearted and, best, of all, has found happiness learning about everything all the time all at once.

Friauf also dedicates this volume to her children, Sarah Elizabeth Swallow and Aaron Benjamin Swallow. These beautiful human beings are, and for more than three decades have been, Friauf's guiding light.

Finally, in addition to their children, the authors want to dedicate this work, to borrow a phrase from Bob Dylan, to "each unharmful, gentle soul" who fights racism, sexism, misogyny, homophobia, transphobia, or economic injustice with no certainty of victory but only with the assuredness that they stand for the right. The struggle is worth it. It is better to stand for principle than for whatever tainted and quickly tarnished trinkets others foolishly treasure.

Parts of this book were published as "A Serviceable Villain: Eugenics, The Fear of the 'Underman,' and Anti-Democratic Discourse in Texas Thought and Culture, 1900–1940," Betsy Friauf and Michael Phillips, *East Texas Historical Journal* 55 (Fall 2017): 7–46. The authors wish to extend our appreciation to the journal's editor, M. Scott Sosebee, for permission to use this material.

Prologue

Sex, Eugenics, and a Forgotten Episode in Texas History

MONSTERS HAUNTED THE IMAGINATIONS of some of the most educated white Texans from the 1850s to the dawn of World War II. Many of the presumed best and brightest in the state imagined a future when murderers, rapists, and sexual deviants would run amuck, ripping asunder the delicate web of civilization.

Versed in the latest "race science," these well-read Texans pictured a host of those they demeaned as inferiors (immigrants, poor whites, African Americans, and Tejanos, as well as the mentally ill and disabled) banding together to overthrow elite rule. The state would collapse into a war of all against all, they warned. In such a twilight struggle, by sheer numbers those they despised as mentally and culturally "inferior" might one day overwhelm their presumed betters, all for the privilege of ruling over ruins.

Ambivalent about the modern age, many members of the state's intelligentsia pored worriedly over immigration numbers and crime statistics in rapidly growing cities. Molded by intense xenophobia, they recoiled at an unwelcome babel of tongues in urban neighborhoods and thought wistfully of the day when only English was heard during a city stroll. They fretted over climbing admissions to the state's threadbare mental health institutions and the escalating population in its prisons. They measured skulls and IQs to detect signs that human evolution had been thrown into reverse. They saw a collapse of the American identity and a crumbling of law and order. As their state changed, many in the Texas professional and political class saw portents of an impending biological Armageddon.

Beginning in the 1850s, a loud and often privileged circle feared that Texas stood at the precipice of biological degeneracy. Nineteenth- and early twentieth-century Texas doctors like Gideon Lincecum and F. E. Daniel, psychologists such as Alexander Caswell Ellis and Clarence Stone Yoakum, as well as social reformers and educators like Carrie Weaver Smith and Edward Everett Davis debated how best to prevent what they described as an ongoing devolution of Homo sapiens. Lincecum and Daniel sought to go a step further, devising plans to breed a "master race" marked by physical perfection and universal genius.

Before the Civil War, Lincecum, a surgeon from Central Texas, lobbied the state legislature to allow forced castrations, which he promised would eliminate criminality, alcohol dependency, and other "defects." He hoped that through surgery and planned reproduction over the coming millennia doctors might fashion a tribe of real-life Olympians. Daniel, editor of the *Texas Medical Journal* from the 1880s to just before World War I, called for state-mandated vasectomies and hysterectomies to ensure that the those he designated as Anglo-Saxons ruled over the state in perpetuity.

Yoakum, a University of Texas psychologist, saw any effort to sterilize millions of those accused of being "defectives" as impractical and bound to meet resistance. Instead, he called for establishing massive walled colonies detaining and sexually segregating those he found undesirable. Meanwhile, Daniel, North Texas Agricultural College[1] president Edward Davis, United States representative John Box, and Dallas writer and attorney Lewis Meriwether Dabney cautioned that the interbreeding of "pure" whites with Jewish, Slavic, and other immigrants might derail the progress of American civilization.[2] All these doctors, activists, and politicians assumed the fragility of the modern social order. They split over if and how the state government should regulate sexual reproduction to thwart the descent into anarchy. Many Texans who feared for the future of the human race coalesced by the late nineteenth century into what came to be known as the eugenics movement.

The history of eugenics in Texas provides a window on the two schools of thought that deeply divided southern capitalists from the 1880s to the 1930s over how to manage the transition from an overwhelmingly agricultural society to an urban, more industrial one while suppressing working-class radicalism. Examining Texas uncovers what happens when scientific ideas, whether well-considered or ill-conceived, collide with the economic priorities of the wealthy and those with deeply held religious beliefs. Unearthing the historical legacy of the eugenics movement in Texas shows how deeply this purported science transformed American notions of racial and gender identity, as well as definitions of health and illness, physical and mental normality and abnormality, and intelligence and idiocy, even where it failed. This story, an important chapter in the history of a disturbing national movement, however, has not been fully told until now.

Texas and Southern Eugenics

Eugenics drew on ancient ideas, many derived from animal breeding, but the "science" itself could be understood as fully formed only at the fin de siècle. By the start of the twentieth century an array of respected authorities, including biologists, naturalists, psychologists, anthropologists, and dilettantes, haphazardly collected statistics and stretched to the breaking point the just-discovered and still poorly understood principles of heredity to "encourage healthy and discourage unhealthy reproduction," as humanities scholar Philippa Levine put it: "Eugenics hoped to improve the genetic quality of human stock and reduce human suffering by focusing on ways to control and improve reproduction."[3]

The movement gained an uncertain foothold in the Lone Star State. Texas eugenicists resembled their peers in the Deep South. The premier historian of eugenics in that region, Edward J. Larson, identified four chief characteristics of southern eugenicists. They obsessed over preventing sexual relations between so-called whites and other racial groups and preventing the birth of mixed-race children. Using harsh and dehumanizing language, eugenicists believed that those they categorized as unfit caused most violence, crime, and social disorder. They advocated laws restricting who could marry based on eugenical definitions of biological worth and empowering the government to sterilize those they believed did not measure up. Finally, across the Deep South, leadership of the eugenics movement rested in the hands of the region's small population of educated professionals such as doctors and scholars.[4]

The Texas eugenics movement shared all these traits. However, to a degree not seen in the rest of the former Confederacy, a combination of the state's shared border with Mexico and the demands by wealthy landowners for Mexican labor complicated the movement's efforts to implement legislation. Nevertheless, beginning in the first two decades of the twentieth century, Texas eugenicists made a profound impact on local public opinion. They reinforced white supremacist politics, provided a scientific rationale for voting restrictions imposed from 1903–05, and intensified intolerance of outsiders, thus shaping the state's culture and intellectual life to a previously unacknowledged degree.

An Apocalyptic Discourse

As the twentieth century unfolded, Texas eugenicists sank into gloom. They worried that humanity faced extinction or might regress to an earlier, more primitive stage of development. Eugenicist fears fit comfortably into a wider zeitgeist. Seeking signs of an impending apocalypse became a popular pastime in Texas by the early 1900s. As a result of Dallas Congregationalist pastor Cyrus Scofield's influence and the vast popularity of his 1909 *Reference Bible* at pulpits from Amarillo in the north to Laredo in the south, from Nacogdoches in the east to Lubbock in the west, preachers thundered that the world faced impending divine judgment. Soon, clergy declared, the wrath of God would obliterate all earthly principalities. The end of times ever lurked around the corner. Such prophets of divine rage told their congregations that a divinely promised millennium free of tears and pain would dawn only after years of excruciating global plagues, famines, and wars drowning the earth in blood.[5]

If they differed on the details, Texas's scientists reinforced this impending sense of catastrophe. Parallel to the spread of end-time theology, numerous Texas opinionmakers in the late nineteenth and early twentieth centuries embraced a secular analog to that grim eschatology, one that evoked terror even as it dangled the hope of a happier world tomorrow. As their religious counterparts read ominous signs of coming heavenly retribution in the biblical books of Daniel and Revelation, secular doomsday oracles in the state trembled as they parsed passages by leading American eugenicists, such as Charles Davenport, and heard warnings from health experts that the population of supposed defectives might soon grow beyond control. To believers, eugenics offered a hint at two possible paths for humanity: one leading to the rise of supermen and another to total oblivion. If many clergy proclaimed the coming judgment of God and insisted that only the Second Coming of Jesus could save a wayward humanity from doom, more worldly thinkers believed that the species could be spared only through the ruthless, unsentimental intervention of science.

Texas eugenicists never spoke with one voice. Many eugenicists (such as Daniel, the editor of the state's most important medical journal in the late nineteenth and early twentieth century), aligned with the Progressive movement. They embraced an expansive government that could wipe away sins like child labor and deadly workplaces. They also wanted to extend government power over the human body, allowing the state to parcel out the right to reproduce. Many eugenicists in the Progressive movement sought to mitigate the harshness of the winner-take-all American economy of the late 1800s and early 1900s because they feared the Gilded Age's cruel wealth gap could lead to revolution. To most eugenicists in Texas, however, inequality derived from nature. Dabney and E. E. Davis believed any effort to completely level the economic and political playing field was as fantastical as suspending the laws of gravity. Some, eugenicists said, were rich and others poor, some powerful and others weak, some civilized and some savage because of their innate biological gifts or deficits. Extending help to those at the economic bottom and opening political participation to the disenfranchised only punished innovators, wealth creators, and those with a born talent for self-government.

The opportunities created by such initiatives, in any case, would soon be squandered by the improvident masses, argued eugenicists like Daniel. According to him, democracy was suicidal because expanded voting rights placed power in the hands of a mob ill-equipped to manage their own lives, much less to run a functioning society. With exceptions noted later, those who supported eugenics in Texas fought to disenfranchise those they ranked as inferior, not just African Americans and Mexican Americans, but also poor whites. In this effort, the state's eugenicists provided a scholarly patina to the less scientific concerns of businessmen panicked by the reformist challenges to laissez-faire capitalism posed by the state's Populist movement. Texas eugenicists obsessed over the unfitness of the white underclass, and some measured the poor as not fully human. Denying the poverty stricken the franchise, however, provided only an expedient. Erasing the unfit entirely from the human family provided the only final solution, some in the medical community said.

Eugenics in its Many Forms

In the late 1800s and early 1900s, eugenical ideas swept the globe and found expression through harsh and sometimes violent government actions across North and South America, Europe, Asia, and Australia. Francis Galton, cousin of the British naturalist Charles Darwin, coined the term eugenics (derived from a Greek phrase meaning "good in birth") in 1883. A mathematician and an obsessive statistician, Galton defined eugenics as "the science of improving stock . . . [that aimed] to give the more suitable races or strains of blood a better chance of prevailing speedily over the less suitable than they otherwise would have had."[6]

Nations around the world, from Great Britain to the United States, from Nazi Germany to Japan, from Mexico to Brazil, adopted eugenical policies, experimenting with various means of giving "more suitable races or strains" the upper hand in the cold and impartial struggle for survival. In different times and places, eugenical practices encompassed providing counseling on ancestry for prospective marital partners, imprisoning or sterilizing those categorized as unfit, and euthanizing newborns with disabilities. Eugenics thinking evolved in unpredictable directions in different national and cultural settings. In Brazil, eugenics thinkers believed that, with education on heredity, over time the fittest would willingly choose ever-whiter and allegedly more biologically advanced partners. This government-encouraged natural selection, eugenicists there dreamed, would eventually erase Blackness and every perceived disfigurement. Elsewhere, eugenicists saw coercion as the only method guaranteed to ensure human improvement. In its most nightmarish expression, eugenical ideas undergirded the mass murder in the Third Reich's death camps.[7]

A Texas Eugenics Pioneer

Elements of eugenical thinking could be found in Texas decades before the movement jelled elsewhere. The Georgia-born Gideon Lincecum (1793–1874) argued after he moved to Texas in 1848 that criminality and work habits were inborn human traits.[8] A gifted botanist and surgeon who believed in natural remedies for his clients' ills, Lincecum one day in the 1850s took it upon himself to castrate an alcohol-dependent patient in

Texas, an assault he said cured his involuntary test subject's addiction. Three decades before Galton gave eugenics its name and almost six decades before Indiana in 1907 became the first state in the union to pass a mandatory sterilization law aimed at inmates confined in mental institutions, Lincecum became perhaps the first advocate of selective human breeding in the United States. After surgically "curing" his patient—applying what he called "the knife of purification"—he began lobbying the Texas legislature in favor of a bill allowing the forced castration of criminals.[9]

Castration had served as a method of criminal punishment since ancient times but had not been seen primarily as a method for culling the human herd.[10] Larson observed that the nineteenth century saw a revival of hereditarian explanations for criminality, sparking revived interest in castration though "the primary arguments for such a penalty still focused on the direct deterrent effects rather than its indirect eugenic benefits."[11] Lincecum, however, had a much bigger agenda. A prolific letter writer, Lincecum made it clear over the decades that he wanted the state to encourage those he saw as the most fit to couple. In one note, Lincecum confessed his tendency to get ahead of himself and to indulge in fanciful visions of the wonderful world that would be created if only the feckless politicians of his time would accept his radical ideas.

> I occasionally . . . work myself up to a clairvoyant condition, and, dashing 10,000 or 15,000 years ahead, I find myself in the society of . . . progressionists, possessing perfect knowledge of individual rights. Like honey bees, they have perfected their government: everyone knows their duty, and will perform it or die . . . There they stand, knife in hand, ready and by the authority of right are promptly willing to trim and prune, emasculate and purify the genus *homo* of every unclean thing.[12]

Lincecum's dreams extended beyond criminal deterrence or healing sick individuals. He hoped to reengineer the human race. Like later eugenicists, Lincecum concluded that characteristics both negative and positive were products of biological heritage and not the environment in which a person was reared. Lincecum believed that personality and talent stemmed from biology. In the decades after his death, eugenicists concluded that individuals inherited not just height, hair color, and other physical traits.

"Shiftlessness, religiosity, courage, patriotism, a sense of humor, love of beauty, taste for philosophy, trustful nature, and a tendency to wander were only a few of the traits ascribed to good or bad blood," as historian of eugenics Diane B. Paul put it. Lincecum foreshadowed that mindset. Radical surgery, and not greater economic opportunity or education, would make crime vanish, Lincecum believed. He compared castrating criminals to "the crushing of an ant egg" to prevent bites and saw medical mutilation as more compassionate than executing convicts by hanging. He was ahead of his time. Lincecum met only frustration, and frequent derision, in his campaign for a mandatory sterilization law, but in the following decades other Texans would march under his banner.[13]

Lincecum in some ways represented a prescient, one-off oddity. He won some followers but exerted no influence on what later became (at least for a time) an internationally respected science. As will be outlined later, however, his early advocacy of coerced sterilization provides a window on the political and racial anxieties already present in antebellum Texas that fueled the eugenics movement four decades later.

The Popularity of Eugenics in Texas

For almost a century after Lincecum's experimental castration, politicians, surgeons, university professors, public school teachers, experts in juvenile delinquency, psychiatrists, and newspaper editorialists fretted about how they could eliminate socialism, anarchism, insanity, mental and physical defects, and marginalized sexual behaviors by controlling who could mate or immigrate into the state. Only stringent eugenic measures could save Texas from social collapse and bloodletting comparable to the French Revolution, these experts counseled. Eugenics sank wide but shallow roots in the Texas soil. As the nineteenth century shaded into the twentieth, the gospel of selective breeding won both converts and critics. In the pages of his journal, F. E. Daniel trumpeted eugenics and the salvation of humanity that could be delivered at the point of a surgeon's knife.[14] Physicians in Texas were "the earliest advocates of coerced sterilization," noted medical historian Mark A. Largent.[15]

During public lectures, often at popular venues such as the State Fair of Texas held each year in Dallas, eugenicists warned that the fertility of criminals and others deemed undesirable posed a risk to society. Clocks calculated how often "a mentally deficient person" destined to be a tax burden came into the world. Sterilization would not suffice. The healthy and the intelligent would have to accept childbearing as a civic duty, audiences were told at better baby and fitter family contests. During special presentations sponsored by local YMCAs and YWCAs, experts encouraged audiences to see the fit and unfit as competing in a race that would determine the fate of humanity.[16]

As the twentieth century progressed, eugenics theory was also spoonfed to high school and college students and was employed to terrify the general population into carefully considering whom they should marry if they cared about the future of the human race. The eugenics movement in Texas, however, never held the intellectual sway or received the government support seen in other places such as California, where eugenicists influenced policy to horrifying effect.[17]

The eugenic movement hit significant headwinds, including a populist distrust of elites that extended to suspicion of or even hostility to higher education and the rise of politicized fundamentalism that achieved hegemony in Texas in the 1920s, just as it seemed eugenics neared its peak. In 1912 the president of Rice Institute (later known as Rice University), Edgar Odell Lovett, hoped to make Houston's newly established institution of higher learning an epicenter of eugenics research. As will be discussed below, he considered eugenics a "foundational science" that would reshape human destiny. Hoping Rice would quickly gain renown as a research institution, he added two gifted scientists, Julian Huxley and Hermann Joseph Muller, later to become prominent eugenics advocates, to the faculty. Yet, Lovett's dream of making Rice an international fulcrum of eugenics research withered. Even the presence of these two acknowledged geniuses left little to no mark regarding the success of the movement in the state. Despite their fame, both remained marginal, even within the eugenics movement itself. At the same time, the state legislature looked askance at scholars in general, and no eugenicist in Texas achieved the influence and power of their peers like Paul Popenoe, the editor of the *Journal of Heredity*, in other states.[18]

By one narrow measure, the eugenics movement in Texas represented an abject failure. Even as nations all over the planet and thirty-two American states passed forced sterilization measures, Texas stood apart.[19] All but one eugenics measures proposed in the Texas legislature met with defeat. In Austin, twice in the 1850s and in 1907, 1913, 1935, and 1937 the state house or senate considered bills that called for the coerced sterilization of the unfit. Each one failed. The legislature also voted down a law deemed essential to the state's future by University of Texas eugenicist Clarence Stone Yoakum to establish a colony for the "feebleminded" in 1913, though a similar bill passed in 1915. Another unsuccessful piece of legislation in 1915 would have banned "unsightly" people with disabilities from public spaces. A bill introduced in 1923 that would have required engaged couples to receive a certificate of health from "a reputable physician" before they could receive a marriage license met with rejection. In all, nine of ten laws favored by eugenicists in the state met defeat. On the other hand, in the thirty-two states that passed sterilization laws between 1907 and 1937, at least 63,841 victims went under the knife without their consent at state hospitals, asylums, and at the hands of individual doctors. Most scholars are confident the number is much higher. California led the way in forced sterilization, with an estimated 20,108 victims.[20] Although a violent and white supremacist place, Texas remained on the sideline during this particular American carnage.

Save for occasional references to Huxley and Muller's sojourns there, Texas has been mostly ignored in the exponentially growing history of what author Elof Axel Carlson called "a bad idea."[21] This gap is unfortunate because it obscures the tale of a vibrant and determined Texas movement that was shaped by, and in some ways shaped, the nation. A Texas eugenicist, for instance, played a profound role in the national debate that unfolded in the early twentieth century over immigration. Yoakum, the head of the Department of Philosophy and Psychology at the University of Texas from 1908–19, coauthored a report on US Army IQ tests that convinced much of the American public that the nation's average intelligence had declined as a result of immigration from eastern and southern Europe. In this climate, Congress passed the 1924 Johnson-Reed or National Origins Act, the most restrictive immigration law in American history.[22]

Though other historians contend that the army IQ tests had no impact on the Congress's actions in 1924, one scholar, Kenneth Ludmerer, has argued that "[p]assage of that law required popular sentiment in its behalf; the genetic arguments advanced by members of the eugenics movement helped organize and direct that sentiment." Texas congressman John Box, credited as playing a major role in the passage of the 1924 bill, certainly rallied support for immigration restriction based on what he saw as the intellectual shortcomings of the newest Americans and in the process received a national following.[23]

The lack of a state sterilization law, however, led many scholars to incorrectly conclude that Texas stood silent in one of the most important national debates from the Gilded Age to World War II. To fully illustrate the unusual trajectory of eugenic thought in Texas and its impact, it is necessary to first place that state in a global context by demonstrating how pervasive the idea of selective breeding and forced sterilization became on the worldwide stage. Then the presence of many of the social, political, and economic conditions that should have favored the success of eugenics in the state must be considered. Only when the international and local contexts are fully explained can the strange career of eugenics in Texas be fully understood as well as its failures and its unacknowledged successes.

Ideology and Eugenics

In the United States, the idea of selective human breeding would be promoted by elites across the political spectrum. Wealthy arch-conservatives, uncomfortable with change in general, perceived that increasing American diversity wrought by immigration endangered their cultural and religious hegemony. The right wing saw the Jews, eastern Europeans, and Italians who filled the passenger ships heading to US processing centers as particularly prone to dangerous, revolutionary politics. It is little wonder that in the United States eugenics would rise at a time of mass immigration, urbanization, and industrialization. "The growth of the cities and of democracy caused conservatives to worry about the future of society and caused a romantic yearning for the past," historian Donald K. Pickens wrote. "The past with its feudal social order and agrarian economy offered security to the conservative mind." With the slave economy still a fresh memory, this nostalgia for agrarian hierarchy proved particularly appealing to a segment of the Texas ruling class in the late nineteenth and early twentieth centuries.[24]

Writing of the movement in late nineteenth- and early twentieth-century Great Britain and the United States, Paul observed, "Many eugenicists were racist and reactionary, even by the standard of their own times. For some of them, the individual counted for nothing, the larger community for all;

only the 'fit' had the right to survive, or at least reproduce." However, it is impossible to pin blame for the horrors of forced sterilizations and other abuses of the eugenics movement on just one side of the political spectrum. The Progressive movement of the late nineteenth and early twentieth centuries provided some of the most enthusiastic supporters of eugenics. Progressives did not share identical motives or propose the exact same solutions to society's problems but, as Martin S. Pernick documented, they "did share a faith in the methods of modern science to produce efficient technical solutions for social problems [and] ... [a]mong the sciences [they] ... most admired were medicine and public health." Such progressives formed the American Social Hygiene Association, one of the most effective eugenics advocacy groups in the United States in the early twentieth century. Some of the biggest supporters of eugenics in the 1930s in Georgia would be liberal New Dealers who also supported free school textbooks, health clinics for indigent children, and pensions for the elderly along with mandatory sterilization for those accused of "unfitness." In the United States, eugenics thus appealed not only to far-right, aristocratic opponents of democracy like naturalist Madison Grant, but also to Progressives like President Theodore Roosevelt, who warned, in an argument similar to his friend Grant, that low birthrates among affluent whites and immigration of undesirable and prolific newcomers would result in American "race suicide."[25]

Texas fit the national pattern. Political reactionaries such as Davis at North Texas Agricultural College lobbied politicians to back eugenics, but several of the state's Progressives did as well. A generally affluent, white, and well-educated group, Progressives in Texas and elsewhere saw government not as a "necessary evil" but a positive good. Progressives waxed optimistic about the human capacity to solve problems: alcohol abuse (through Prohibition), crime (via scientific policing), urban overcrowding (by means of more rational city planning), and poverty (with the establishment of better schools and enhanced business regulation, among other measures). Progressives believed in expertise and that the "hard" sciences provided a model for structuring a better society. While differences of viewpoint commonly divided them, Progressives in the state's suffrage movement and notable public figures like Daniel and Carrie Weaver Smith shared the idea that if traffic can be better managed, so can human heredity.[26]

The idea even enchanted leftists like University of Texas professor Hermann Muller. He became convinced that scientific breeding, combined with the elimination of poverty, malnutrition and other ills engendered by capitalism, could result in "the positive biological improvement of mankind." Such a new age, he insisted, could be achieved "*provided* the social reconstruction occurs first," a reality he thought in the 1930s only the Soviet Union could nurture.[27]

As Progressivism rose, sterilization laws swept the land. Indiana passed its first-in-the nation sterilization law in 1907. By 1937, thirty-two states had enacted such statutes, and sterilizations had been carried out absent legal authorization in five other states (in Texas, at the behest of Lincecum and likely others, as well as in Colorado, Illinois, Pennsylvania, and Ohio).[28] In 1903, a member of the Michigan legislature introduced a bill allowing for the electrocution of infants with mental disabilities. The Iowa and Ohio state legislatures even debated bills, which ultimately languished, allowing euthanasia to relieve the suffering of the "hideously deformed" as well as children born with mental disabilities, while a Chicago physician called for fatally gassing all diagnosed as suffering from severe intellectual limitations.[29] Nothing came of the euthanasia proposals, but sterilization laws became a national norm. Texas eugenicists, fearing their state was falling behind in advanced science, could only look on in dismay.

Eugenics Propaganda and Funding in the Early Twentieth Century

Industrialization produced not only much of the turmoil that inspired calls for eugenics, but also the profits that funded the propagation of that gospel north of the Red River. In 1902, the newborn Carnegie Institution, endowed by steel magnate and infamous robber baron Andrew Carnegie, provided $32,000 (just under $1 million today when adjusted for inflation) in seed money for a "Biological Experiment Station" in Cold Spring Harbor, New York. Zoologist Charles Davenport established the center for the "analytic and experimental study of . . . race change." Davenport recruited supporters who promoted eugenical ideas through "popular magazines, in public lectures . . . in circular letters to physicians, teachers, the clergy, and legislators." With the Carnegie endowment and the support of luminaries such as Alexander Graham Bell, Davenport devoted himself to creating what ultimately proved to be a scientifically useless database based on "Family Record Questionnaires." He built a vast library of cards collected from interview subjects across the country recording instances of criminality, blindness, deafness, epilepsy, drunkenness, and other signs of supposed biological imperfection. He used his database to lobby legislators at the state and national level to adopt eugenics measures such as sterilization laws. His efforts made an impact even where such political efforts came to naught. Davenport's Eugenics Record Office not only lobbied for legislation, it published the *Eugenical News*, which provided a national platform for the theories about juvenile delinquency formulated by Smith, the controversial eugenicist first director of the Gainesville State School for Girls in Texas. Davenport assigned the Gainesville school a "field eugenicist" in 1919 to aid Smith's research.[30]

Nordics, Alpines, and Mediterraneans

Americans found no more famous or effective advocates for eugenics than two authors who wrote a pair of influential bestsellers in the second decade of the twentieth century, Madison Grant and Lothrop Stoddard. Both writers heavily influenced Texas eugenicists. Neither was a biologist. Grant, chair of the New York Zoological Society, earned a law degree from Columbia University while Stoddard, also briefly a lawyer, held a Harvard history doctorate and worked mostly as a journalist. In *The Passing of the Great Race, or the Racial Basis of European History* (1916), Grant warned of the pernicious impact of immigration to the United States by eastern and southern Europeans, Mexicans, and other supposedly retrograde subsets of humanity. Stoddard obsessed over the global threat he said was posed by the lower birthrate of superior whites compared to that of the "Underman," the label he applied those originating in sub-Saharan Africa, Asia, the Pacific islands, and Latin America. In *The Rising Tide of Color Against White World Supremacy* (1920) and *The Revolt Against Civilization: The Menace of the Underman* (1922), Stoddard predicted doom for humanity unless whites increased their reproduction versus the dangerously fertile people of color. Though they spun slightly different doomsday scenarios, the "names of Grant and Stoddard were naturally linked together by the reading public, which hailed Grant as the prophet and Stoddard as the apostle of scientific racism," as Grant biographer Jonathan Spiro wrote.[31]

Believing that humanity could be divided into clearly defined sub-categories, Grant placed "blond-haired, blue-eyed Nordics on the top of the ethnological pyramid . . . [with] other, less-worthy races falling into place beneath the master race. " He even categorized African Americans as being a separate species.[32] He declared that three distinct races populated Europe. Grant dramatically narrowed the definition of true whiteness to include only Nordics from northern and western Europe, a group he described as "a race of soldiers, sailors, adventurers and explorers, but above all, rulers . . . and jealous of their personal freedom." Nordics differed vastly from their continental neighbors, whom Grant labeled "Alpines" (southern Germans, northern Italians, and eastern Europeans) and "Mediterraneans" (southern Italians and Sicilians, Spaniards, Greeks, and Middle Easterners). Such marked biological differences separated these European races, Grant believed, that these groups constituted human "subspecies." Alpines represented "a race of peasants and . . . tend toward democracy [to Grant a bad thing], although they are submissive to authority . . . [T]he type is mediocre and bourgeois." He described "pure" Mediterraneans as excelling in art but lagging behind Nordics in literature and science. Mediterraneans, he contended, had unfortunately succumbed to race-mixing to such an extent that this "sub-species" were "so far from being purely European, it is equally African and Asiatic."[33]

To Grant and his following, "miscegenation," even between different European "races," produced bad results. "The cross between a white man and an Indian is an Indian; the cross between a white man and a Negro is a Negro; the cross between a white man and a Hindu is a Hindu; and the cross between any of the European races and a Jew is a Jew," he wrote. Grant embraced particularly virulent antisemitism. He declared that Jewish people were by nature political radicals pushing for democracy, an agenda that would wrest political rule from "the higher to the lower races."[34]

Grant openly supported euthanasia and even genocide to preserve racial purity. "Mistaken regard for what are believed to be divine laws and sentimental belief in the sanctity of human life tend to prevent both the elimination of defective infants and the sterilization of such adults as are of no value to the community," Grant wrote in *Passing of the Great Race*. "The laws of nature require the obliteration of the unfit and human life is valuable only when it is of use to the community or race."[35]

Publication of Grant's and Stoddard's books rank as key moments in the history of eugenics. *Passing of the Great Race* appeared during the first big wave of state sterilization laws passed across the country. Grant's Nordicism became a much-discussed idea in Texas, influencing the racial ideology of the reborn Ku Klux Klan of the 1920s as it became a dominant force in Texas politics. Dallas eugenicist lawyer Lewis Meriwether Dabney essentially paraphrased Grant in a speech to the influential Dallas Critic Club in which he decried "promiscuous immigration" by Asians and eastern and southern Europeans. Edward Davis, who served from 1925 to 1946 as dean of North Texas Agricultural College, derived most of the ideas animating his eugenicist novel *The White Scourge* from Grant and Stoddard. Davis encouraged xenophobic Texas congressman John Box to extend federal immigration quotas to Mexicans recruited in large numbers as farm labor by the state's cotton growers. Davis sent Box a copy of Stoddard's *Rising Tide of Color.* The college dean emphasized the critical need for Texas to exclude "lower races" from the state.[36]

Regardless of the popularity of Grant and Stoddard's books, the authors failed to move the policy needle in one regard. Congress and the White House made it increasingly difficult for immigrants from Asia and eastern and southern Europe to enter the United States, via such laws as the 1882 Chinese Exclusion Act, the so-called Gentleman's Agreement with Japan in 1907–08, and a series of ever more severe immigration restrictions aimed at Jews, Italians, and other from outside northern and western Europe in 1917, 1921, and 1924. Hoping to ride this xenophobic wave, Box and the rest of the Texas eugenicist movement, however, battled in vain to close the state's border with Mexico.[37]

Davis and Box both used Grant's and Stoddard's racial theories as justification for choking off the flow of migrants from south of the Rio Grande. But, as will be explored in greater detail later, on this issue the Texas eugenics movement ran headlong into the economic interests of the state's powerful agricultural industry. With the loss of underpaid immigrant labor from other lands, American business interests in Texas and beyond had too much to gain from leaving the door open to Mexican migrants. "Employers began to look longingly toward Mexico as a source of labor for their steadily increasing needs," said historian George J. Sánchez. "Not surprisingly, immigration restrictions directed against Mexicans were at first consistently deferred under pressure by southwestern employers and then, when finally enacted, were mostly ignored by officials at the border." The owners of Texas's large cotton plantations and other colossal farming operations, "factories in the field," sought "a large, mobile, and seasonal labor force" less likely to organize unions and, the growers hoped, too vulnerable to fight for better working conditions. For a time, at the Mexican border migrants avoided paying the head tax required under the 1917 immigration law because the federal government barely provided staff to monitor checkpoints. In spite of statutes prohibiting the recruitment of foreign-born workers overseas before their arrival in the United States, labor recruiters traveled by rail from border cities like El Paso to find farm and factory labor deep within the Mexican interior. Until the massive expulsion of Mexicans from the United States at the start of the Great Depression in the 1930s, workers moved with relative ease back and forth across the Texas frontier. The pursuit of profit margins by a still-racist Texas business community outweighed their concerns about the preservation of white racial purity. The state's eugenics movement could never shut down the border. Instead, the "Southwest became another kind of racial frontier where Mexicans were welcomed as cheap and disposable labor but not as members of the polity," a reality that still horrified Texas eugenicists but one they found themselves powerless to change.[38]

As Texas eugenicists floundered in their attempts to achieve their goals, their peers exercised power and influence across the world. From the beginning of the twentieth century, Finland, France, Germany, Italy, Japan, and Turkey paid bonuses to promote high birth rates among the supposedly fit, while Poland, seeing itself in a reproductive race with its German and Russian neighbors, debated tax breaks as a reward for larger families. Medals were awarded to fertile mothers in Finland, France, Germany, Japan, and the Soviet Union. Statutes restricting marriage became commonplace outside the United States, with laws requiring tests for syphilis and mandating health certifications put into effect between 1907 and the 1940s in Switzerland, Turkey, Japan, Mexico, France, the Soviet Union, and across Scandinavia. Switzerland began sterilizing "violent" patients in the late nineteenth century, while Finland implemented sterilization for inmates of mental institutions in the early twentieth century.[39] As a 1913 cover for the American humor magazine *Puck* put it, eugenics made the world go around.[40]

All the social, economic, and political predicates that led to eugenics measures from Argentina to the Soviet Union existed in Texas. However, Texas, along with a handful of other states scattered across the nation, remained a stubborn exception to the eugenic tide in spite of the state's movement enjoying what should have been substantial advantages in achieving their political objectives.

Whatever Happened in Texas?

The geography of Texas seemed designed to provoke the demographic anxieties for eugenicists. Texas sits astride a racial and national borderland where identities clashed, splintered, and reformulated. Geographer Terry Jordan memorably dubbed the state a "shatterbelt." Texas fits comfortably within the American West, the South, and the borderlands of the American Southwest and northern Mexico. The state's shared border with Mexico has loomed large in the Texas imagination from its independence in 1836 until the present day. As the historian Andrew Torget put it, "the regions known as 'Texas' were never controlled or dominated by any single people or nation. Texas was, instead, a territory defined by the crashing together of numerous forces and people coming from multiple directions . . . a central crossroads for overlap, collusion, and conflict between various powers—not only Mexico and the United States, but also Indian nations and European countries."[41]

The dominance of the international cotton trade in the early nineteenth-century global economy drew Anglos to what was then northeastern Mexico. White migrants sought land cheaper than what was available in the United States in hopes of turning that real estate into slave labor camps. At the same time, the "rise of lucrative markets for horses and mules created by the expanding U.S. cotton industry" also attracted Comanche and Apache raiders. Enslavers in the United States provided a lucrative market for the draft animals Comanche and Apache horsemen seized in Texas and neighboring territories. Military conflict between Anglos and their Native Americans rivals ensued throughout the history of the Texas Republic, lasting beyond its absorption by the United States in 1845. Anglos dreaded that a rising tide of color, red and brown, would drown them.

The sense of demographic menace that animated later eugenicist sentiment shaped Texas's racial politics from its earliest days. Early Anglo political leaders depicted the survival of the white population in Texas as dependent on the mass murder of Native Americans and Mexicans. From 1750 to 1850, as the historian Pekka Hämäläinen has noted, a Comanche Empire "manipulated and exploited colonial outposts in New Mexico, Texas, Louisiana, and Northern Mexico...[extracting] resources and labor from their European and Indian neighbors through thievery and tribute and incorporated foreign ethnicities into their ranks as adopted kinspeople, slaves, workers, dependents, and vassals." The power of the Comanches created among whites a sense of genocidal urgency. The Comanches built a highly flexible political system and a sophisticated commercial network and became a vast military power-house. Through "a creative blending of violence, diplomacy, extortion, trade, and kinship politics .. they imposed their will upon neighboring polities, harnessed the economic potential of other societies for their own use, and persuaded their rivals to adopt and accept their customs and norms." In so doing, they successfully thwarted the expansionist dreams of the Spanish, Mexicans, and (for a time) Anglo newcomers.[42] Anglos reacted to this threat with fear and fury that turned murderous.

Before eugenics and racist, classist, and ableist surgical sterilizations, Anglo Texans already had engaged in decades of battlefield slaughter that did not spare the old, those with disabilities, unarmed civilians, or even children. "The word 'extermination' was consistently creeping into the vocabulary of Texas officials," as historian Gary Clayton Anderson wrote. Anglo Texans ethnically cleansed indigenous people from the 1830s through the closing years of Reconstruction.[43] Meanwhile, myths of "savage war" supposedly waged by Native Americans and later by Mexicans resisting the Anglo invasion of the region reinforced in the Anglo mind the need for demographic dominance by any means necessary as a matter of survival.[44]

Anglo-Saxonism in Mid-Nineteenth-Century Texas

Decades before eugenicists expressed similar forebodings, the white Texas leadership believed that the pollution of white bloodlines spelled doom for the advanced but fragile society they built on the plains. In the antebellum period, much of the southern ruling caste identified itself as "Anglo-Saxon." Historical Anglo-Saxons came from varied peoples. However, many white Texans bragged of their "pure" blood. "By the late 1840s, most Americans either thought of themselves as the descendants of English immigrants, speaking English, bound together by a common culture and a talent for government, or they thought of themselves as a superior, distinct 'American' race, drawn from the very best of the stocks of Northern and Western Europe," as historian Reginald Horsman wrote. This concocted Anglo-Saxon identity, historian L. D. Burnett observed, signified "purported racial and intellectual superiority [that] . . . not only entitled them to rule, but actually destined them to conquer and occupy the whole continent of North America after forcefully subduing all other races."[45]

Prominent figures like Sam Houston, military leader of the Texas Revolution, attributed his success in the war of independence from Mexico to his army's Anglo-Saxon heritage. "Tell the civilized world that a little band of patriots, animated by the daring spirit and unconquerable love of freedom, which distinguished the Anglo-Saxon race, had battled successfully with an empire so powerful, had burst the bonds of tyranny, and sprung full grown into a nation."[46] Presaging the eugenicist belief that the capacity for not just battlefield valor but also democracy and self-government was a racial trait, Texan Anglo-Saxonists like Houston proclaimed that Mexicans, enslaved African Americans, and others lacked these qualities and could not equally participate in a republican society. In spite of his racial beliefs, Houston generally sought kinder, gentler treatment of Native Americans. He proved an exception. Over the course of the coming decades, Anglo-Saxonism in Texas provided justification for, respectively, Indian displacement and liquidation, anti-Mexican pogroms, and Black enslavement, without contradicting the purported white love of liberty. When blended with the race science of the late nineteenth century, similar white supremacist attitudes provided a rationale for eugenical assaults on non-whites or those of European heritage considered biologically tainted.

Anglos assumed that their constructed racial identity gave them a license to kill. Texans began their program of biological "purification" with the implements of war. Conquering Anglos like Henderson Yoakum wrote joyfully of an 1839 white assault on an indigenous village along the San Saba River in which Texas Rangers "opened the doors of the wigwams . . . slaughtering the enemy in their beds" as Native women screamed and children cried. White Texans violently subdued Native Americans for a half-century, the bloodshed not ebbing until after the Anglo victory against the Comanche and Kiowa in 1874–75. As they stole Native American land and killed the state's indigenous population, whites morally reassured themselves by claiming that their victims were not fully human. Mirabeau Lamar, president of the Texas Republic from 1838 to 1841, cynically drew on exaggerated claims of Indian menace as he condemned the "wild cannibals of the woods" who attacked the vulnerable on the frontier "with the ferocity of tigers and hyenas." Lamar suggested that Anglos and indigenous people were biologically incompatible and, "The white man and the red man cannot dwell in harmony together. Nature forbids it. They are separated by the strongest possible antipathies, by colour, by habits, by modes of thinking, and indeed by all the causes which engender hatred, and render strife the inevitable consequence of juxtaposition." Such dehumanizing language incited mass murder and forced removal of Native Americans during the time from Lamar's presidency into the early 1870s.[47] For some Anglos in the coming decades, it seemed perhaps a compassionate transition to move from battlefield genocide to nonconsensual sterilization.

"Savage Warfare": Violence and The Fear of Racial Pollution

As Anglos in Texas created a continuous, racialized culture of war in the antebellum period, they battled not just indigenous people but also the Mexicans in their midst. They increasingly ridiculed Mexicans as hopelessly lazy, superstitious, lacking in creative thinking or a capacity for democratic government, unhygienic, and a source of cultural and biological pollution.[48]

To Anglos who valued racial purity, Mexicans and Tejanos represented a disastrous blend of "inferior" races. Texas Anglos widely believed Mexicans were more closely related to African Americans and Native Americans than whites and perhaps lesser than both.[49] Just as eugenicists would obsess over the dangers posed by interracial reproduction, Texas Anglos in the first half of the nineteenth century associated Mexicans with racial contamination. An 1834 white Texan letter writer to the *New Orleans Bee* newspaper expressed revulsion about Mexicans, who he characterized as "degraded and vile, the unfortunate race of Spaniard, Indian, and African . . . so blended that the worst characteristics of each predominate." Even before eugenicists like Grant, many Anglos believed that race-mixing produced degeneracy.[50]

Yet, anti-Mexican racism centered on the same paradox as later eugenicist fears. Somehow Mexicans were at the same time weak, unproductive, unintelligent, and incompetent but still threatened the very survival of an allegedly superior, stronger, smarter white civilization. The Texas Revolution offered Anglo Texans a host of racial fables available for the state's eugenicists to exploit in the future. Anglo stories about the Texas Revolution depicted Mexican soldiers as ruthless rapists and killers who shot the unarmed without qualms.[51] Based on these myths, increasing Mexican immigration led some Texas Anglos to conclude that racial violence represented self-defense.

To justify their war crimes, white Texans accused Native Americans and Mexican Americans of the very cruelties they committed against the racial enemies they vanquished. Richard Slotkin, an historian of racial ideology on the imaginary and ever-fluid American frontier, argued that whites concocted a myth in which the people of color they conquered waged "savage war" to halt the spread of civilization. Whites projected their own sins on the victims of their violence, reversing facts in such a way that, for instance, "made the Indians scapegoats for the morally troubling side of American expansion." Slotkin observed that this ex post facto reversal of blame provided psychological balm. "In its most typical formulations, the myth of 'savage war' blames Native Americans as instigators of a war of extermination," Slotkin wrote. "Savage wars" could only result in total victory because, as Slotkin described the mindset, "the ineluctable political and social differences—rooted in some combination of 'blood' and culture—made coexistence between primitive natives and civilized Europeans [or their descendants] impossible on any basis other than subjugation."[52]

Later, the state's eugenicists would rationalize their medical abuse by drawing on distorted memories of indigenous and Mexican oppression of whites, asking the broader public to imagine the horrors of a world in the clutches of such people.[53] The purifying knife would spare future generations of whites unchecked rapine and slaughter at the hands of "lessers," the movement reassured uneasy Anglos.

The Problem of "Lesser" Whites

As Larson argued, southern eugenicists focused on the problem of white purity. Racial contamination certainly became an obsession of Texas's ruling racial caste in the years before the eugenics movement appeared. Soon after Anglo Texans achieved independence from Mexico in 1836, the Texas upper and middle class disdained what came to be known as "white trash."[54] They seethed with contempt for whites at the economic bottom, particularly for their cross-racial fraternizing. In Texas and across the South, wealthy enslavers complained about "this exasperating pest of poor whites." To the more affluent, "low unprincipled" working-class whites reeked of racial impurity as they fraternized with enslaved African Americans at dances in the port at Galveston and other nascent urban centers.[55]

Antebellum southern elites perceived the poor white as being of a different color than their more economically advantaged peers, a sign of their racial deficiency. They wrote of poor whites having skin the shade of "yellow parchment" or having a "yellow mud complexion." Some of these descriptions might be due to the poor nutrition and maladies like hookworm that can cause pallor, but as historian Keri Leigh Merritt wrote, "Regardless of the causes . . . by categorizing poor whites as *not* white, slaveholders could classify the poor as racially inferior."[56]

The political restiveness of the white poor and working class certainly stirred elite apprehension about their biological quality. As in the rest of the nation, Texas eugenics arose amid decades of political tumult, economic transformation, and challenges to the white male monopoly on power. Texas joined the Confederacy's war against the United States and became a racial killing field during Reconstruction. It suffered repeated downturns in the agricultural economy from the 1870s to the 1890s, which inspired the rise of Populism and other forms of agrarian radicalism, movements ultimately suppressed. The turn of the century saw major strikes in some Texas cities, alarming the powerful, who instigated widespread violence against labor unions. The lynchings of African American, Mexican, and Mexican American victims divided the working class along racial lines. To impose coherence and order on a swirl of anarchy, the upper class across a wide ideological spectrum, from political reactionaries to Progressives, supported eugenics in Texas just as they did in the rest of the country in the years from the turn of the century to the 1930s. Reshaping human biology, elites hoped, would bring calm and stability to the political order, and thwart revolution.[57]

Around the United States, eugenicist sentiment also rose as the population climbed and urbanization increased.[58] Texas experienced both

phenomena from 1900 to 1940. In those four decades, the Texas population jumped 110 percent, the second biggest increase among the eleven
former Confederate states. Only Florida, which had a much smaller population over those forty years, experienced a larger increase (259 percent).
By 1940, a higher percentage of Texas's population lived in metropolitan
areas than in any other state in the old Confederacy except, once again,
Florida. The percentage of Texans living in metropolitan areas more than
doubled in a twenty-year period (from 14.6 percent in 1920 to 30.6 percent
in 1940). Although the number of foreign-born immigrants was small
compared to other centers of immigration like the US Northeast or the
West Coast, the number of foreign-born Texans climbed noticeably, from
5.9 percent in 1900 to 7.8 percent in 1920. Mexican immigration particularly captured the attention of eugenicists. Although that population frequently crossed the border back and forth, at least 100,000 Mexicans
entered the state between 1910 and 1920, the decade of the Mexican Revolution, and probably far more.[59] Demographic changes in Texas from 1900
to 1940 favored a eugenicist backlash, but even with this factor in its favor,
the movement often hit a brick wall.

Resistance to Eugenics in the Lone Star State

In spite of all the factors that should have favored the growth of eugenics in
Texas, the movement still encountered a unique combination of obstacles.
Eugenicists faced the opposition of cotton growers and other employers
who wanted a steady stream of Mexican workers to enter the state regardless of the eugenic danger some academics claimed they represented. Business leaders, particularly in South Texas, may have been racists but as a
group they still mostly desired to exploit abundant and underpaid immigrant field hands as a means of lowering business costs.[60]

Texas eugenicists also had to contend with the suspicion of science and
higher education beyond vocational training that was prominent among
the state's political leadership. Politicians undercut funding for, and
undermined the prestige of, the state's few colleges and universities, institutions vital for the prominence of eugenicist thinking in other states. As
Ty Cashion put it in his book, *Lone Star Mind: Reimagining Texas History*,
"Texans have earned a reputation for many things, and as a hard-and-fast

but admittedly self-declared rule, they come in only one size: big. Unfortunately, being known as big thinkers has somehow eluded them."[61]

Eugenicists enjoyed honor, and held the greatest influence, where higher education received the greatest support. Charles William Eliot, president of Harvard University from 1869 to 1909, trumpeted the blessings of eugenics in a 1912 address in San Francisco, declaring, "Each nation should keep its stock pure. There should be no blending of the races." His leadership at Harvard immediately gave him international prestige and an audience. The First International Eugenics Congress, which met in London that same year, would honor him with its vice presidency. Yale economist Irving Fisher won respect for the movement on the national stage, and Stanford University's first president, David Starr Jordan, who sounded the alarm at what he saw as the prodigious reproduction of Mexican immigrants, gained plaudits as he became one of the country's most prominent advocates of both eugenics and tight immigration quotas.[62] Outside Texas, eugenicists received copious funding and high profiles with which to gain a wide audience. The contrast with the treatment of eugenics advocates in Texas could not be more glaring.

The Texas legislature starved public education of funds, from kindergarten to graduate school. The state government trimmed school calendars so poor and working-class children of all colors could be exploited as agricultural laborers. Meanwhile, elected officials such as Governor Jim "Pa" Ferguson (in office 1915–17) and his wife, Miriam "Ma" Ferguson (who served two gubernatorial terms, 1925–27 and 1933–35) obsessively attacked the University of Texas. They accused the school of being a nest of dangerous radical elitists mocking the rural values. Resentment against higher education hampered recruitment and retention of prestigious professors such as the ones who provided leadership in the eugenics movement in other states. Attacks on colleges and universities, therefore, provided the unintentional benefit of shielding the poor and politically powerless in Texas from a horrifying, widely shared elite agenda that prevailed elsewhere.[63]

Texas Progressives also focused obsessively on Prohibition to the near exclusion of other causes such as selective breeding.[64] Finally, in the first two decades of the twentieth century, fundamentalists politicized, transforming the state from a previously wide-open theological frontier into the proverbial buckle of "the Bible Belt" and, in the process, thwarted the implementation of eugenics policies.[65] Energized by the war on demon rum, the early twentieth-century religious right rejected Darwinism, questioned modern science, and (outside of Prohibition) adamantly opposed the Progressive agenda. That included calls for selective breeding, which they saw as the ominous overreach of big government and heathen interference in the sacred realm of the family.[66]

Yet, in spite of these obstacles, on numerous occasions, sterilization bills almost passed the state legislature. The heads of Texas colleges and universities hailed eugenics as a revolutionary scientific breakthrough that would ensure the species a brighter future. Historians even at religious institutions such as Baylor University in Waco and journalists at Southern Baptist newspapers praised eugenicist books and the subject became part of the standard science curriculum across the state.[67] An alternative path in which Texas joined the rest of the nation's sterilization frenzy always remained within the realm of the possible. The difference between the fate of eugenics in Texas and much of the rest of the world deserves close study. Yet, as noted above, until now there has been no comprehensive history of the eugenics movement in Texas.

The Purifying Knife will join company with other detailed local studies of eugenics such as Victoria F. Nourse's *In Reckless Hands: Skinner v. Oklahoma and the Near Triumph of American Eugenics* (2008); David Smith's *The Eugenic Assault on America: Scenes in Red, White, and Black* (1993). a work that focuses on Virginia; Nancy Gallagher's *Breeding Better Vermonters: The Eugenic Project in the Green Mountain State* (1997); Alexandra Minna Stern's examination of the movement in California, *Eugenic Nation: Faults and Frontiers of Better Breeding in Modern America* (2005); as well as Larson's brilliant, groundbreaking regional study, *Sex, Race, and Science: Eugenics in the Deep South* (1995). Larson depicts the heart of the Old Confederacy as being not an originator of eugenic thought but an enforcer of eugenics policies conceived of in other regions. As will be shown later, this was not entirely true in Texas.

Analyzing eugenics poses some challenges for modern writers. The eugenics movement in Texas was, with the exception of Muller, dominated by white supremacists who habitually used dehumanizing terms to describe not only Native Americans, African Americans, Tejanos, Jewish people, Asian immigrants, and other oppressed groups, but also those with disabilities. Dated and offensive language filled much eugenicist writing and public speeches. The authors have tried to limit the use of eugenicist terminology but also want to avoid whitewashing the language and thought of those who advocated the coerced sterilization and mass detention of millions of Americans. Through confronting this pernicious worldview by exposing its ugliness, in words and deeds, the authors hope to counter the recent attempt by some to rehabilitate the eugenicist project. Typically, offensive terms will be avoided but occasionally the authors have tried let the eugenicists speak for themselves in order to accurately capture an odious worldview that caused suffering across the state.

The history of Texas eugenics encompassed startling twists and turns, eccentric characters, warped idealism, malignant prejudices, surprising defeats, and a disturbing, though subtle, durability into the twenty-first century. Texas eugenicists never achieved what Lewis Meriwether Dabney dreamed of—a dictatorship of the "superior man . . . the torch bearer of the race."[68] They did, however, intensify the xenophobia, religious intolerance, state-sanctioned violence, hard-heartedness toward the poor, and support of mass incarceration that define much of the state's politics in the twenty-first century. The chronicle of an often-frustrated but still influential movement follows.

CHAPTER ONE

A Brief Prehistory of Texas Eugenics

1853–1874

O N M AY 15, 1859, Gideon Lincecum posed a startling question to his New York friend, Dr. R. P. Hallock. Lincecum, a minimally trained physician, had become a much-ridiculed political activist over the previous half-decade. His inquiry related to his new high-profile role in Texas policy debates. In a letter to Hallock, Lincecum asked: "Did you ever see a eunuch? I have been familiarly acquainted with five of them. One of them I made myself. He was a degraded drunken sot—in *delirium tremens* at the time and I did it in a kind of youthful frolic. It cured him, however, and made an honest man of him and he often thanked me for it . . . He became quite industrious, religious, and studious."[1]

Lincecum authored this note to his friend after repeated frustrated attempts to persuade the Texas legislature to pass a radical law. Fifty-four years before Indiana enacted the United States' first compulsory sterilization law in 1907, the Lincecum proposal would have allowed state authorities to order castration—the application of what the doctor called "the knife of purification"—of criminals and others deemed unfit, to prevent the transmission of deficient biological characteristics to their progeny. He hoped his proposed legislation would, over generations, eliminate crime and a host of other problems plaguing his adopted home state. At the time of the letter, Lincecum had lobbied for his "Memorial" since 1853, the year his idea first came up for discussion in the state capitol in Austin. Lincecum wrote the law when uncertainty over whether "defectives," particularly poor whites, would undermine white supremacy in Texas. Lincecum believed he had proven the effectiveness of this method to eliminate asocial behavior with his improvised experiment on his alcohol-dependent patient.[2]

At the time Lincecum moved to Texas, medical practice had entered a period of chaos across the United States. Doctors shed ancient paradigms such as the humoral theory, the belief that an imbalance of four essential bodily fluids produces disease and techniques such as bleeding could restore a person's health. Physicians pondered a flurry of often half-baked theories about the human mind and body, such as phrenology. Texans attended lectures by phrenologists who claimed they could decipher patients' intelligence and character by interpreting the size and shape of the bumps on their skulls.[3] On the other end of the spectrum of scientific rigor, Darwin's theory of evolution had even reached distant outposts like Texas, inspiring sometimes angry debate and wild speculation about humanity's origins and its possible futures. In this intellectually fertile atmosphere, doctors contemplated radical ideas, like state-imposed selective human breeding, as a pathway to eliminate disease and disability. In spite of its reputation as always and relentlessly resistant to new thought, Texans showed themselves receptive to novel concepts, including sometimes tragic ones.

Lincecum's proto-eugenical proposals went nowhere politically and met mockery. Yet, his ability to persuade members of the state legislature to at least give his plan for coerced sterilization a hearing, even one marked by derision, provides evidence that Texas, a contested racial borderlands riven with class conflict, offered fertile ground for eugenical ideas decades before the movement became a force in national politics. Lincecum was not without supporters. Texans began arguing the merits of fully developed eugenics theory in the 1880s, but by then core eugenical concepts had a prehistory of decades.

The "Pioneer Emasculator"

An enslaver who owned a plantation he dubbed Mount Olympus in Long Point, Texas, some eighty-five miles east of Austin in Washington County, Lincecum made Texas his home in 1848 after a career as a physician in his native Georgia.[4] Lincecum certainly did not appear to have the background to become "the earliest American advocate of sexual surgery to

control or eliminate social ills," as Mark Largent, a scholar of science policy, described him. Born April 22, 1793, in Warren County, Georgia, to a
cotton-growing father who "knew nothing of books" and a mother Lincecum described as "entirely illiterate," he received five months of education
provided by a "drunken teacher" in a crudely constructed and poorly sup-
plied temporary school in the Georgia backwoods. There, he "sat in a sea
of burning shame" because of his ignorance, he later wrote.[5]

A turning point in his life came as he made friends with a local physician, Dr. Henry Branham, who not only began Lincecum's medical training but also introduced him to Erasmus Darwin's *Zoonamia, or the Laws
of Organic Life* (published 1794–96). Darwin's grandson, Charles, would
rock the world in the 1850s with publication of his book *On the Origin of
Species.*[6] Erasmus Darwin asked readers to "imagine that all warm-
blooded animals have arisen from one living filament." Lincecum believed
the older Darwin's work heralded a new age, an era in which "the sun of
science had arisen already and before its effulgent rays, the witches, ghosts,
angry gods, and the frightful ghosts of antiquity would soon have to fly to
the mountains or somewhere else for protection." The young man excitedly
wrote a letter to his new idol and to his delight received "a very polite,
friendly, and most interesting reply . . . full of philosophical good sense, and
useful information . . . exactly such a paper as my blank intellect needed . . .
It changed my crude notions in almost everything."[7] *Zoonamia* created in
Lincecum's mind "a perpetual discontent with the imperfection of man and
a more profound appreciation of nature," his biographer Lois Wood Burkhalter said.[8]

Lincecum would later carry on a similar brief correspondence with
Charles Darwin. Lincecum read *On the Origin of Species* one year after its
publication in late 1859. As impressed with the younger Darwin' s work as
he had been with that of his grandfather, Lincecum found a new hero.
"Professor Charles Darwin . . . at the moment . . . occupies the highest
plane of intellectual advancement," Lincecum enthused. As he had earlier
with Erasmus Darwin, Lincecum exchanged letters with the evolutionary
theorist and in one missive elaborated his theory that harvester ants possessed a surprisingly high level of intelligence, practiced agriculture, and
enslaved black ants to do the field work. Charles Darwin apparently later
read Lincecum's theories about harvester ant society to the Linnean

Society of London. The Civil War, however, abruptly shut down this trans-atlantic scientific dialogue.[9]

Already a religious skeptic, Lincecum gathered from Erasmus and Charles Darwin that species, supposedly static from the beginning of time according to prevailing Christian doctrine, could under the right conditions and over enough time morph into markedly different life forms, better suited for new conditions.[10] The thought occurred to the Georgia transplant that perhaps scientists could consciously remake humankind for the better and with greater speed and efficiency than random forces of nature.

Lincecum never attended medical school, "a situation not uncommon in the profession in those days," Burkhalter noted. Ironically, a man who later campaigned to give physicians the right to castrate those they found defective in mind and body also became a persistent critic of the aggressive style of medical care in his era. In his time, "allopathic" physicians typically practiced "heroic" medicine, treatments that at times more closely resembled torture, such as bleeding and the aggressive use of purgatives and other harsh medicines.[11]

Lincecum became skeptical of mainstream medicine during a cholera epidemic sometime after 1815. The purgative "cures" he administered not only failed to provide relief but probably made his patients sicker. In one case, he witnessed with horror the death of a toddler under his care: "I lost a two-year-old child under circumstances which left no grounds to doubt that death was occasioned by allopathic remedies," he wrote in the 1830s. "And whilst I was gazing on the twitching muscles of the dying child[,] I made a solemn vow that I would never administer another dose of the poisons of the system." For a time, he considered abandoning medicine. "I was greatly discouraged," Lincecum admitted. "This, and the hundreds that were dying all around me in the hands of other physicians, convinced me that our remedies were impotent. I felt tired of killing people and concluded to quit the man-killing practice and try to procure a living by some other method."[12]

After moving to Texas, Lincecum intermittently treated patients, turning to homeopathy, a school of thought which operated on the principle that "like cures like" (that small enough portions of a substance thought to cause a particular disease would strengthen the body's resistance to it).[13] But in an ironic twist, Lincecum's advocacy of castration as a cure for aberrant behavior exceeded the most aggressive allopathic techniques.

Lincecum lobbied for Texas to adopt medicinal castration as a policy in an era of American medicine in which doctors achieved national fame, and acclaim, after subjecting marginal and disenfranchised patients to involuntary and often excruciating medical experimentation. A contemporary of Lincecum's in antebellum Alabama, Marion Sims, became famous (and later infamous) as the "father of American gynecology" in part on the strength of his experiments, performed without the benefit of anesthesia, on enslaved women as he developed a new surgical technique to repair vaginal tears experienced during childbirth.[14]

A tireless letter-writer, in the 1850s Lincecum papered the state with correspondence to other doctors, as well as to scientists, lawyers, newspaper editors, admirers and detractors alike. These missives detailed schemes for selective breeding that went beyond castration of the unfit. He urged the state to ensure that the most gifted bore the largest families, a long-term project that could not yield tangible results for scores of generations but that he believed would at some point usher in utopia. "Gideon dreamed of a perfect world inhabited by a physically superb race of men and women, morally and intellectually perfect, who selectively reproduced for even higher attainment," as Burkhalter wrote.[15]

Lincecum saw selective breeding laws as a pressing matter. Like later eugenicists, he believed that those he saw as biologically inferior naturally succumbed to their sexual impulses, making them disastrously fertile. Lincecum concluded that the sex drive led not just to nervous tics like shifting in a chair or "gnawing on the finger nails" but, more importantly, to every destructive, anti-social behavior, including something he considered an aberration, homosexuality. "*All* murders, robberies, thefts, suicides, the downfall of all nations [and] cities from long before the fire and brimstone affair of Sodom and Gomorrah . . . are the ordinary signs and manifestations of unappeased, restless, insatiable amativeness." In calling for a coerced sterilization law, Lincecum knew he was asking the state legislature to begin what would be a long crusade. "[He] arrived at the conclusion that sexual behavior was the stimulus for the evils of the world," Burkhalter wrote. "He did not expect to make much headway in a program which could not be effective for thousands of years but he felt that the criminal class of Texas would make a good starting place."[16]

"Calculated to Excite Ridicule and Opposition": The First Sterilization Bills

From 1853 to 1856, Lincecum sent copies of his "Memorial," as he called his proposed law, to 676 legislators, newspaper editors, doctors, and other Texas notables.[17] In his advocacy for the new law, he employed one of the oldest of racist tropes, the supposed threat that a Black man might rape white women. He wrote of an enslaved African American whom he described as "vicious" and "drunken." This man, Lincecum wrote, habitually raped African American women to the point that the owners of neighboring plantations "threatened to shoot [him]." The local white community reached its limit when the enslaved man impregnated a white girl with a mental disability. Lincecum wrote:

> At that act of unparalleled depravity, the people were highly excited, and . . . three gentlemen who understood the cause of the negro's depravity, as well as the remedy, went into the field where he was at work and castrated him. Two years later, I heard his mistress say that she would not take a thousand dollars for her share of the negro's services . . . when he came in at night of his own accord, he never slept, until every young and tender thing about the place—lamb, pig, or young chicken—all received his protecting care.[18]

The doctor, dubbed a "pioneer emasculator" by a later biographer, saw castration as a means of curing what he considered the innate animal nature of criminals. He bristled at critics who charged that such surgical violence violated human rights. Lincecum argued castration provided a humane alternative to the methods of execution and other physical penalties imposed on criminals in his day. In any case, punishing a criminal was acting too late. The focus should be on crime prevention. Eliminating the existence of the criminal class in future generations would make various forms of corporal punishment then in use, such whipping and branding, obsolete. If his proposal required some bloodshed, it was a cure for future mayhem, an act of self-defense like "sawing off the horns from the brow of the draco [dragon] . . . [or] the crushing of an ant egg." He urged the legislature to imagine a world without gallows because murder ceased to exist. "The only available remedy is the knife," he wrote. "Its power to deter and to save the wicked is indisputably efficient . . . [A]s to the 'inhu-manity,' and 'cruelty' of the proposed changes in our penal code, when compared with the rope, penitentiary, and the branding iron, it is an objection that will never be brought forward by intelligent men."[19]

A more utopian future, one with less crime and insanity as well as fewer individuals depending on charity, would be realized if Texas would only adopt his surgical solutions to social problems, Lincecum wrote in the 1870s to his friend W. Richardson. "Pass the memorial into a law and let it be faithfully carried into execution, and one single generation under its influence, will empty all the penitentiaries, prisons and lunatic asylums in the state," Lincecum said.[20]

Similar to later eugenicists, Lincecum also believed that humans could be mated scientifically like cattle and sheep and a golden race far superior to present-day humanity could be created in several generations through selective breeding and aggressive sterilization of the "unfit." As he wrote, "Like begets like. The laws of hereditary transmission cannot be over-ruled. When the horse and the mare both trot, the colt seldom paces, as the saying goes . . . To have good honest citizens, fair acting, truthful men and women, they must be bred right. To breed them right, we must have good breeders."[21]

Lincecum did not care if planned mating occurred inside or outside of marriage. He wanted to change laws so only the healthy and strong could marry. He even proposed that couples not married to each other should be encouraged to "copulate only for the purpose of procreation." His plan, he believed, would inevitably spawn a master race. He pre-dicted that if the unfit were rendered surgically sterile and the fit encour-aged to reproduce, "five generations will not pass until men will be found who are tall, straight, and beautiful." In one letter, he imagined a world "10,000 or 15,000" years ahead in which "the best-bred men and women would proliferate and create a type of being [with] . . . intelligence far superior to the race of *genus homo,* that they will amuse and enrich themselves by boxing us up and exhibiting us in their menageries. Then we, like the inferior types of animality now view us, will look upon them as gods."[22]

Lincecum hoped not only that his extreme measures would be adopted in Texas, but also that his memorial would serve as model legislation for the world. He promoted sterilization not just within Texas but across the country, sending appeals for such legislation to friends, judges, and newspaper and journal editors in Georgia, New York, Ohio, and Tennessee. To his frustration, he could not even advance his proposed law in Austin. He reacted with fury when his proposal met with ridicule, indifference, or fierce opposition. He complained in an 1859 letter that only two newspapers in Texas, the *Colorado Democrat* and the *Ranger,* published his "Memorial" in full, and most others referred to it only briefly "for the fun of the thing than any other consideration."[23]

As the proposal met with increasing disdain, particularly from the Texas press, the doctor railed at newspapers for standing in the way of progress. He bitterly joked that society might be best served if the surgical knife were used to castrate journalists. "[T]he press must have the benefit of the purifying instrument itself before they can be moved to the advocacy of righteousness," he wrote in an 1859 note to a friend. Politicians also drew his contempt. During the Civil War, he said of the state's political leadership that the human species might benefit if the knife of purification were applied to "such filthy, unreliable beings."[24]

Benjamin E. Tarver and John Sayles, who represented Lincecum's Washington County, introduced the "Lincecum Law" in the Texas House on November 16, 1853, but the proposal provoked snickers. "They did it in a manner better calculated to excite ridicule and opposition than a philosophical consideration of the matter," Lincecum said. Without the efforts of Harris County representative Dr. Ashbel Smith, he complained, "nothing would have been done [with the proposal] further than a few sarcastic remarks accompanied by a great deal of half-drunk, goggle-eyed laughter."[25]

Lincecum found scattered support from "a few outspoken women, doctors, scientists and some lawmakers," notably F. H. Merriman, a former state representative from Galveston. Upon receiving a copy of the Lincecum castration proposal in 1856, Merriman pledged his support. "I believe your doctrine is a sound one, and has nothing in it that is terrible except to evil doers, and that it is well calculated to extinguish bad blood more effectively than the assumption of the doubtful right of taking the life of a fellow being," Merriman wrote.[26] The one-time lawmaker, however, warned his friend that the idea was likely to inspire opposition from soft-hearted individuals who saw the plan as "one calculated to abridge what they conceive to be a natural right."[27]

Word of the nation's first proposed forced sterilization bill spread
through the South. It also provoked controversy outside Texas. Later a
friend in Tennessee, Josiah Higgerson, described the range of reactions to
Lincecum's "Memorial" in the Volunteer State. In his letter, Lincecum's
supporter expressed a contempt for democracy typical of later eugenics
advocates. "The subject matter of your memorial caused a sensation here
for a time," Higgerson wrote. "There were various opinions about it. Some
were violently opposed to it, others in favor of it. One old gentleman said
he had been in the notion to go to Texas, but that he would turn his idea
towards hell before he would go to any country whose legislature would
even entertain such a memorial . . . In such a government as we have it will
always be impossible to get a majority in favor of it. Majorities are always
opposed to curtail their right to do wrong . . . This law could be carried out
by an autocrat but he would never do it for the reason that he has a use in
his subjects for the very elements of character that would be destroyed by
it."[28] The Texas legislature rejected the "Lincecum Law" in 1853 and 1856,
both times with copious mockery. The legislation in the later session provoked a "smart amount of angry discussion" before lawmakers referred it
to the "stock and stock raising committee." There, it died an ignoble
death.[29]

After the 1856 failure, the Texas legislature never again discussed the
Lincecum Memorial. Despite his frustrations, Lincecum would not be
the only Texan to sterilize non-consenting subjects in the nineteenth
century. "During and after the Civil War, the purifying knife was frequently and illegally applied, and some Texans regretted the legislature
had not given more consideration to the proposed Lincecum Law," Burkhalter wrote. In an October 25, 1864, letter, Lincecum noted with great
interest a case in Belton in which a jury sentenced an enslaved man to be
castrated as a punishment for rape. "The operation being performed, I
understand [it] turned out to be a complete success and that the negro is
now well and returned to his duties as a slave." When authorities arrested
another African American for attempted rape in Brenham, Lincecum
wrote to the presiding judge, urging him to apply a "Belton verdict" arguing that, "If a man has a vicious bull that is hooking and gutting his stock
about his lots he knows very well how to tame him and make a docile steer
out of him besides stopping the increase of that breed of cattle. Man is an
animal." The Brenham suspect received a "not guilty" verdict, exceedingly

rare for an African American defendant, and did not get castrated. "Oh well," Lincecum wrote wistfully. "It was only an *attempted* rape."[30]

Lincecum's Final Years

Lincecum could not tolerate the political environment in Texas as Reconstruction began. Always a believer in Black inferiority, he was dismayed by African American emancipation. He felt even greater rage at the extension of citizenship rights and equal protection under the law, as well as voting rights, to African Americans after ratification of the Fourteenth and Fifteenth Amendments to the United States Constitution. Bitter at what he called "our Yankee masters," Lincecum decided to boycott northern scientists and would no longer share research, written observations, or specimens with them. "I am too highly disgusted with everybody north of the Mason and Dixon line to associate satisfactory with them on the high plain [*sic*] of science," he wrote in his diary on August 29, 1867. In a follow-up note on September 5 he said, "I have conscientious scruples as to the propriety of sending my collection [of insect species] to the Northern institutions . . . The radicals are oppressing us here with disenfranchisement and heavy taxation. They have robbed us of our property [the enslaved] and now threaten us with confiscation of our lands."[31] This self-imposed intellectual exile obliterated any chance he had to spread proto-eugenical ideas north. For all his regrettable prescience, Lincecum represented a symptom of early Texas anxieties over human degeneracy, but he also provided a fascinating yet ephemeral glimpse into the future rather than a major influence on what soon became a world-shaping science.[32]

The Lincecum law never again saw the light of day. Edmund J. Davis, a wartime Union supporter and Republican who would serve as Texas's governor from 1870 to 1873, was slightly acquainted with Lincecum before the Civil War. The two stood on opposite sides on most of the important political issues of the era. Yet, Davis expressed regrets that Lincecum's initiative failed. Davis later wrote a friend, "The doctor was nearer right in his theory than people were willing to give him credit for . . . I have no doubt that if all the world could be submitted to that process for some generations[,] we would have a better class of people."[33]

Lincecum's big ideas, selective mating and forced sterilization to improve the human breed, would survive his death in 1874. Francis Galton would coin the term "eugenics" nine years after Lincecum's demise. A genuine eugenics movement would rise in Texas during the last two decades of the nineteenth century.

African American enfranchisement, the spread of railroads, the growth of towns, the transformation of towns into cities, the beginning of a new wave of foreign immigration into the state, and the rise of labor radicalism and strikes all fed new anxieties among the wealthy in the coming years. The Texas bourgeoisie fretted over the stability of white supremacy, the future of capitalism, and the possible threat posed by those elites defined as "lesser" whites. Dr. Ferdinand Eugene Daniel, the state's most important medical journalist, became an advocate for eugenics on the national stage and, even if he was never aware of Lincecum, his arguments and proposals echoed that of his increasingly obscure predecessor. Daniel would support forced sterilization as a means of preventing crime, insanity, and mental disability as well as limiting sexual behaviors, such as homosexuality and masturbation, that he feared threatened the future of humanity.

Lincecum never achieved major fame. Daniel would, however, and his medical publications provided a forum in for doctors to debate not just eugenics but whether so-called new immigrants from eastern and southern Europe posed a danger to the future of Texas, how to deal with what was seen as an explosion in the population of the mentally ill and disabled, and whether the state (in order to ensure the quality of white bloodlines) should modify its policies prohibiting abortion. Like Lincecum, Daniel plunged into Texas politics. Similar to his predecessor, however, he found Austin to be hostile territory.

CHAPTER TWO

Regulating Reproduction in Texas

1883–1914

I N HIS 1899 MEMOIR, *Recollections of a Rebel Surgeon*, F. E. Daniel included some unsolicited wisdom for newly minted graduates of what he called Texas Medical College. That institution had closed in Galveston in 1891, so Daniel probably meant the University of Texas Medical Branch, which was still operating in the same city. Born in Emporia, Virginia, in 1839, Daniel was sixty when his autobiography was published. He wrote that hubris was typical of young doctors. Beginning physicians, he said, usually believe they possess a limitless ability to cure the literal ills of the world. "[I]n our young days we are very conceited, and think we know a great deal of medicine," he wrote, "It takes an average lifetime to find out that we don't know anything worth mentioning . . . Somehow, one's head seems to leak medical knowledge, as the bones harden, and the sutures close up. Just the reverse of what we expect,—but it is a fact I think most doctors my age will admit it,—the older we get, the less we know."[1]

Such humility is remarkable, given that Daniel shared Gideon Lincecum's obsession with the purifying knife as a shortcut to elevating the human condition. Daniel never suffered any pangs of doubt about mandatory sterilization as the cure for whatever ailed society, or about biology as the answer to such mysteries as why humans vary in sexuality, and why some individuals become criminals, others end up in asylums, while others achieve greatness.

When he lived in Fort Worth, Daniel started editing and publishing one of the state's first medical journals, which began in 1883 under the name the *Texas Courier-Record of Medicine*. After relocating to Austin, he redubbed the periodical *Daniel's Texas Medical Journal*, later shortened to the *Texas Medical Journal*. Dull scientific treatises did not fill its pages. Violet Baird, who traced the history of Texas medical publications, described Daniel's writing persona as that of "the typical Southern gentleman—quick to defend his rights and his prejudices, colorful and peppery in editorials, ready and eager to fight for 'organized medicine' and other medical causes."[2]

Daniel and Dixie Progressivism

Daniel embodied the values of the southern Progressive movement that became a powerful force in Texas politics in the early twentieth century. The causes he touted in the pages of the *Texas Medical Journal* included opposition to alternative medical approaches such as homeopathy and osteopathy, rejection of African American membership in the state medical association, as well as support for Jim Crow laws and Black disenfranchisement. He also endorsed licensing women as doctors, immigration restrictions, and sterilization laws to eliminate disabilities.[3]

Progressives sought to save capitalism from itself. If guided by the wisdom of well-educated experts, adherents believed, the government could solve a wide range of vexing social ills ranging from congested streets to alcoholism, from crime to poverty, and from environmental degradation to what eugenicists called "degeneracy." In so doing, the Progressives thought, they could quell dangerous discontent, and turn a sick, underfed workforce into a robust machine of industrial and agricultural production.

The Progressive impulse, however, was weaker in the South compared to other regions. Southern Progressives remembered that a powerful central government in the past abolished slavery and gave African Americans citizenship and the right to vote.[4] Some southern Progressives, like their peers in other regions, fought against child labor laws. Daniel, quoting Abraham Lincoln, described child labor as "grinding our seed corn" and saw it as dysgenic, a phenomenon that could kill potentially fit children. Southern Progressives, including those in Texas, fought for woman suffrage and legislation protecting women from abusive conditions in the industrial workplace. However, as historian of the Progressive Era Alan Dawley has argued, southern Progressive leaders were more affluent, well-educated, and powerful than their peers in other regions. They were happy to promote projects that aided big business, such as road building and improving schools for the purpose of creating a better-trained workforce.[5] On the other hand, southern Progressives in particular sought social order, an impulse that at times bent toward authoritarianism.

While one branch of Progressivism evolved into modern-day liberalism, the quest for conformity and the desire to impose a uniform Americanism on a polyglot population led other Progressives by the 1920s to admire fascists like Benito Mussolini.[6] Southern Progressives leaned toward the latter camp. In Texas, Progressives believed they could cure political corruption and the repeated election of ill-qualified, self-serving demagogues by barring the purportedly ignorant and unintelligent voters from casting ballots. Genuine democracy brought the chaos southern Progressives disdained. Political power had to be left in the hands of the "better sort."

Daniel notwithstanding, eugenics policies never rose to the top of Texas Progressive priorities, but sometimes the Progressives supported other policies that achieved eugenic ends, such as eliminating the political threat posed by poor and working-class whites. Statewide, Texas Progressives achieved two significant goals: passage of woman suffrage and Prohibition, causes with largely overlapping constituencies. Southern white suffragists often believed that giving women the ballot would not only empower them, but also would increase the number of white voters and strengthen a racial dictatorship.[7]

But Texas Progressives recorded a meager list of triumphs regarding the quality of life for the poor and working class. "While some child labor legislation was enacted, its enforcement was haphazard in the absence of sufficient money and trained personnel," Texas historian Lewis Gould wrote. A minimum-wage law for women and children that passed in 1919 was wiped off the books in only two years, and the state legislature met other recommendations for workplace reforms by the Texas Conference of Social Welfare with stony silence. The Texas Progressive movement would focus on Prohibition and suffrage to the exclusion of almost everything else, including a hearty campaign for a mandatory sterilization law.[8]

Such an extreme measure, Daniel believed, had become a moral necessity. "[T]he elimination of the preventable and the cure of the curable elements of race decay—is the mission of rational medicine, to which all 'exceptional men,' the enlightened, should address themselves," he said.

"Duty requires it; true philanthropy dictates it; policy suggests it, and it is demanded by every consideration of humanity and race integrity. Will Congress heed the warning?"[9]

The Technology of Sterilization

Daniel served as secretary of the Texas Medical Association and officially helmed his journal until his death in 1914. With his prominence, he attempted to redirect the focus of Texas Progressives. He achieved a standing surprising for a doctor based in a state still regarded by many as an underdeveloped frontier. Daniel printed 2,000 copies of his journal per month and its subscribers included John B. Hamilton, US surgeon general from 1879 to 1891. The *Journal* enjoyed an especially impressive readership considering that in Daniel's era membership in the Texas Medical Association peaked at around 500.[10]

In his publication, Daniel called for wielding the scalpel on an ever-expanding list of the "diseased" threatening the species. Gay men, the sexually promiscuous, those with mental illness, those with disabilities, the criminal, and even masturbators all sat side-by-side in the waiting room of his imagination, destined (he hoped) for sterilizations that would cure them of what he saw as aberrant behavior. Even as Daniel got older and, according to his own calculations, knew less, he became increasingly confident advocating permanent, maiming surgery for an ever-wider swath of humanity.

As Daniel editorialized and spoke on behalf of the just-developing international eugenics movement, the technology of sterilization refined and expanded. Some doctors still "castrated" patients, the term they used for removing the testes and scrotum of men and the ovaries of women to leave those "unfit" patients infertile. Such dramatic methods continued until the 1930s and were often used to both "cure" and punish some of society's most despised, including pedophiles, rapists, and gay men. Doctors later designed more targeted approaches such as the vasectomy (first available in the late nineteenth century) and the "spermectomy," in which doctors severed the vas deferens and its attached network of veins and nerves in order to prevent ejaculation. After the turn of the century, hysterectomies became the preferred means of ending the reproductive capacities of women eugenicists viewed as "defective."[11]

Even if Daniel said doctors "don't know anything worth mentioning," he entertained no doubts that he knew how to reshape the species for the better. Daniel enjoyed a respect and audience Gideon Lincecum never achieved. The prime of his influence stretched from the 1880s until the second decade of the twentieth century. In this era, Texans felt increasing anxiety about immigrants arriving from eastern and southern Europe and Mexico, many of whom were Catholics and Jews. The media portrayed these immigrants as carriers of diseases and as criminals tending toward anarchism, socialism, and communism. Amid these demographic changes, Protestants felt their previously unassailable hegemony slipping away. If immigration remained unchecked, white supremacists warned that the newcomers would swamp the "biologically fit."

At the same time, eugenicists and less scientifically oriented urban elites feared the potential political power of these newcomers. Immigrants came to be associated with the far left. Calls for immigration limitation and political disenfranchisement went hand-in-hand with a rise in anti-Semitism and denunciation of southern and eastern Europeans as biological "degenerates." To limit the influence of immigrants and African Americans, as well as politically unreliable poor whites, the wealthy white men who controlled the Democratic Party hardened their grip on power through the passage of poll taxes in Texas in 1902–03. The poll tax and other voter suppression schemes enacted in the early twentieth century disenfranchised nearly 70 percent of Texas voters. However, that was not enough for the state's growing eugenicist movement. To them, the fate of civilization would not be secured at the polls. The quest for permanent elite political dominance must extend from the ballot box to the operating room.[12]

Lincecum had been essentially a lone wolf. Daniel, however, enjoyed ever-expanding support. He lived to see the Texas legislature in 1907 and 1913 consider the first mandatory sterilization bills since the "Lincecum Memorial" failed twice in the 1850s. The legislature voted down both measures.[13] Nevertheless, to date no such bill in Texas history had advanced so far. In Daniel's time, a genuine eugenics movement in Texas began, the language of its increasing number of advocates became more vociferous, and its anti-immigration campaign accelerated and won some victories. Yet, the battle for selective breeding still faltered.

Finding Danger Everywhere

The most notable Texas eugenicists like Daniel shared an iconoclasm sometimes spilling over into misanthropy. They expressed their myriad objections to conventional wisdom with a sarcasm that undoubtedly undermined their effectiveness as heralds for a new and shocking crusade. While living in Mississippi in 1860–61 when the Civil War broke out, Daniel disdained the irrational exuberance that seized the white men of the state as they first marched to their military recruitment offices.

"I cast my maiden vote against secession," he later recalled. "I was opposed to secession not because I thought the South was not justified, under the circumstances, but because I did not believe there was a possibility of the South's being permitted to 'go in peace.' The love of the Union was strong [in the free states] and the opposition to slavery . . . had attained the aspects of a religious crusade."[14]

Unlike others who later bragged of their service, he claimed no special heroism for enlisting in the Confederate army. Enacted on April 16, 1862, the Conscription Act made all white men between the ages of eighteen and thirty-five subject to compulsory military service. "[E]verybody had to go into the army," Daniel remembered. He got out of combat as quickly as possible. When the Confederate government offered a release from battlefront service for soldiers wanting to study medicine, Daniel jumped at the chance. "I returned home and immediately went to New Orleans and took another course of lectures and got my diploma and got out just before [United States General] Ben Butler captured the city," he said. "I was given a commission by the Secretary of War as surgeon." By the age of twenty-three, Daniel was a "full surgeon" holding the rank of major.[15]

By the time of his memoir's publication, he scorned his fellow southerners, who obscured the causes of the Civil War. The Civil War was fought about slavery, plain and simple, insisted the doctor. "[C]all it by whatever name we will, put the pretext for secession on 'principle,' State Rights, or what not; refine it as we will, slavery was the real issue of the war . . . had the South gained independence, slavery would, in all human probability, have still been an 'institution' in the country," Daniel wrote.[16]

Although he claimed that before the war he favored gradual abolition, the way emancipation played out had been a biological disaster, he said. Daniel attributed the "social degeneracy" of the late nineteenth and early twentieth centuries primarily to freed African Americans and immigrants. "As in the individual, there are in the race elements of decay, which, like the worm in the bud, sap the strength and cause death . . . sooner or later," Daniel said in an address to the Seventh District Medical Society in Austin in 1907. Attributing the fall of the Roman Empire to its "benevolent assimilation" of "barbarians," Daniel proclaimed. "The United States government made the initial mistake in permitting the importation of black cannibals as slaves—from whom have descended ten millions of the most undesirable citizens; and our people have mixed with them until . . . fully half of them have an admixture of white blood; and although intermarriage with them is prohibited in most states, miscegenation is going on, with all its evils upon our race attendant upon hybridization—the admixture with inferior blood."[17]

Even for his day, Daniel stood out for his racism. He opposed admission of African American doctors to the American Medical Association and proposed an amendment to the Texas State Medical Association (TSMA) constitution imposing an explicit color line on that group's membership. His publication casually referred to African Americans by a racial slur. He wanted the group's constitution reworded to permit entry only to "all the reputable, white physicians of the state." A TSMA committee rejected the "Daniel Amendment" because of its redundancy. Organization bylaws, if not the constitution, already prohibited Black members.[18]

Daniel casually dehumanized poor whites. He called one impoverished white man he encountered the "apotheosis of laziness. He was too lazy to stop eating when once under good headway (provided the grub didn't give out). He rarely ever got to the field till knocking-off time for dinner at noon on one excuse and another." The man's poverty, Daniel implied, derived from inborn sloth, not a system dependent on mass want.[19]

American immigration policy, an exasperated Daniel declared, only multiplied the number of those he adjudged as a biological threat to the country. In his 1907 speech to Texas doctors, he decried the quality of immigrants coming to the United States and their impact on the vigor of the white race. After importing Africans, he said, "The United States government made the further mistake of welcoming to its shores and absorbing countless hordes of individuals of inferior races—the scouring and outcasts . . . paupers, syphilitics, consumptives, criminals, anarchists," Daniel said. "The American people have already lost most of their race characteristics by interbreeding with these, until we are rapidly approaching, if we have not become, a race of mongrels . . . The tendency here is to race suicide."[20]

Daniel moaned to his medical audience that because of the American embrace of democracy, no Caesar or Napoleon wielded the absolute power needed to halt social and political decline. It might be too late, he warned, to save the nation through the mass deportation of immigrants and the total segregation of African Americans, which he argued might be the only way to avoid "race war." Daniel rattled off the evils wrought by interracial sexual reproduction and wide-open immigration: increasing rates of alcoholism, the spread of tuberculosis and sexually transmitted diseases, and the overflow of those with mental illness in asylums already stretched beyond capacity. Daniel claimed he could see a physical decline in American men since his youth. Because of interracial reproduction and "interbreeding with the refuse of Europe," Daniel claimed, "the [white] race has dwindled physically . . . the men are smaller and feebler. A strong, broad-shouldered, manly man is the exception." American men had become "small, narrow-chested, slim-legged little shrimps, and they are to be the fathers of the next generation . . . Their inheritance will be neurasthenia [a tendency toward panic also called "hysteria" at the time], unstable constitution[s], maybe the curse of alcoholism or of alcohol insanity."[21]

Daniel's reliance on subjective and anecdotal evidence in this speech reveals one of the major flaws of the eugenic method. Immigrants arriving from poverty-stricken parts of eastern and southern Europe tended to be smaller and suffer frailer health upon arrival in the United States compared to their American-born neighbors because of a lifetime of poverty. However, they fared better physically with improved nutrition, and their children grew stronger and taller. Although about 11.3 million eastern and southern Europeans arrived in the United States between 1890 and 1910, average American heights and weights increased steadily from the 1890s through the 1950s.[22]

To Daniel, biology was destiny and all efforts to help the poor and those with disability, however well-meaning, posed a threat to humanity. He urged compassion for "the race" rather than the individual. "All our humanitarian work, pity for the defectives, fosters the survival of the unfit by the perpetual propagation of the defectives which, left to the operation of natural law, would be eliminated," Daniel claimed. Extending a helping hand to the unfortunate only allowed those looked on as "dysgenic" to propagate without constraint and become a burden on society.[23]

An Imagined Epidemic

Four factors weighed heavily in the rise of eugenics in Texas from 1880–1914. First, Anglos panicked about immigrants and their reputed biological worth. Second, Texans increasingly associated immigrants such as the Chinese and eastern European Jews with the spread of epidemics. Third, xenophobes linked a supposed increase in mental illness in the state to the expanding presence of eastern and southern Europeans. Fourth, immigrants suffered blame as well for labor radicalism and the spread of socialism. The press played a major part in the eugenic movement's growth, sounding the alarm about an immigrant "invasion." In 1893, during the height of a depression that gripped the nation until 1896 and caused high unemployment, the *Galveston Daily News* proclaimed,

> It is a well-known fact that for a number of years a very undesirable class of immigrants has . . . landed at the principal American ports from European countries . . . [T]he prevention of immigration from Russia, Hungary, Austria and Italy is greatly to be desired because it would not only shut down the possible carriers of infection but at the same time exclude immigrants of the least desirable and the worst classes—immigrants whose habits are repulsive, whose ignorance is peculiarly dense, who are incapable of comprehending of government, and whose characteristics may be studied at the anarchists' meetings on the east side of this city."[24]

In 1908, Dr. William Brumby, the chief health officer in Texas, accused immigrants of not only stealing jobs from Americans but bringing to Texas trachoma, a bacterial eye infection that can lead to blindness. The *Brownsville Herald* characterized immigrants as dangerous disease vectors and condemned "some persons more anxious to obtain laborers than [to look after] the welfare of the country." The *Herald*, however, lamented that the desire to stop the spread of trachoma meant the state would restrict "free admission" of Mexicans from across the border since "Mexicans when healthy are considered a desirable class of immigrants." Throughout the eugenics era, Texas business leaders sometimes curbed their racism and xenophobia to encourage the migration of more easily exploited, low-wage immigrant labor. In this case, the *Herald* believed the spread of trachoma overrode all other concerns. In spite of these worries, in the years just before World War I, Galveston became known as the "Ellis Island of the West" and a popular entry point for eastern European Jews fleeing Russian anti-Semitism. This provoked a backlash. As the number of Jews shut out of Galveston because of "poor physiques" skyrocketed, the Jewish Immigrants' Information Bureau exposed a local US Immigration Bureau medical examiner, identified as "Dr. Corput," as an anti-Semite who vowed to keep as many Jews out of the country as possible. Even after protests resulted in Corput's replacement, immigration officials made flimsy excuses to deny entry to Jews seeking refuge.[25]

Journalists depicted immigrants as mentally unstable. "In the country at large, there is an excess of foreign-born insane," the *Fort Worth Record and Register* told its readers in 1901. "In all the Western states, the proportion of the foreign-born insane to native insane is very large." Mentally ill immigrants cost taxpayers dearly, the newspaper said, with the state footing the cost for food, clothes, medical care, and infrastructure for hospitals and asylums, a bill that amounted to $3,000 (about $105,000 today) per inmate over a ten-year period.[26]

Meanwhile, Texas maintained shabby, overcrowded mental health institutions. In 1856, the legislature authorized the establishment of the state's first mental health facility, the Texas State Lunatic Asylum, in Austin. That facility opened in 1861, followed by the North Texas Lunatic Asylum in Terrell in 1883, and the Southwestern Lunatic Asylum in San Antonio in 1894. Texas mental facilities housed not only those suffering from mental illness, but also epileptics, violent criminals, and sufferers of dementia. These institutions became warehouses for those deemed incapable of caring for themselves or who ostensibly posed danger to others. In the early years of the Austin asylum, doctors deployed ancient and abusive "treatments" and methods of controlling those suffering from psychosis, such as plunging the heads of patients into cold-water baths, locking them in small boxes, handcuffing them, or confining them in restraint chairs. In 1871, Superintendent T. F. Weiselberg banned these practices and instead confined violent patients in padded rooms.

In spite of the best efforts of some nurses and doctors, violence and filth marked life inside asylum doors.[27]

Conditions at those facilities became a running scandal. In the late 1870s, "Dr. Turner," an Australian expert on such institutions, reported that "corridors were disgustingly filthy, walls were cracked, ceilings were falling down, and furnishings were in fragments." In 1881 alone, about 10 percent of the residents died, in part because overcrowding contributed to the spread of dangerous diseases.[28]

Dr. M. L. Graves, the superintendent of the Southwestern Insane Asylum, suggested that Texas could not keep up with a growing number of those suffering from mental health disorders. By the 1880s, when the state operated facilities only in Austin and Terrell, he argued in a lecture to the University of Texas Medical Department in Galveston on March 24, 1905, "[i]t soon developed that these two institutions were incapable of accommodating the ever[-]augmenting army of the insane." Even with the addition of a new asylum in San Antonio, overcrowding at state mental institutions could force the state to release the "criminally insane" who, upon freedom, would wreak mayhem on a defenseless public, Graves claimed. "It is my conviction that all insane criminals and criminal insane who pled insanity as a defense for such major crimes as homicide, rape, etc. . . . should be committed . . . to an insane hospital for not less than five years."[29]

Mental illness, Dr. Graves said, was hereditary, and those carrying these traits needed to be stopped from mating. Graves became one of the growing number of Texas physicians joining the eugenics cause. He expressed dismay at how easy it was for Texas couples to marry, no matter how much "bad fruit" had sprung from their family tree. He told his colleagues, "We spend much time in breeding our livestock; pedigrees are sought and keenly scrutinized, and enormous sums of money are paid for pure breeds in animals. But what of our children? Those unfit by reason of mental, physical, and moral degeneracy are still permitted to marry without restraint or restriction, never a care to stem the awful tide of heredity." While admitting the cost would be enormous, Graves urged the state to fund mass, sex-segregated detention of the supposedly "unfit," claiming, "it is an expenditure for the improvement of the race in body, mind, and in morals, and no one will question its wisdom or necessity."[30]

A book by an amateur scientist from England who settled in New York in the 1860s and 1870s intensified a growing American obsession with those with mental illness and disability, a panic that reached Texas. Richard Dugdale began to interview prisoners in a quest to uncover the cause of crime. When he discovered that six prisoners in one facility came from the same family, which he gave the fictional name "Jukes," he conducted a genealogical investigation of their family tree and claimed that he found five generations of paupers and criminals. He presented a paper on the family of miscreants to the American Social Science Association in 1877 and that year published a best-selling study of the clan titled *The Jukes*. The work convinced a many Americans that bad blood caused poverty, criminality, and other undesirable traits.[31] Daniel believed that only direct intervention in nature would ensure the extinction of criminals. Shutting down wide-open immigration provided one easy path toward this goal. Sterilization provided another.

Immigration and Xenophobia in Daniel's Texas

In the Gilded Age, Texan xenophobia rose far in excess of the actual numbers of the foreign-born arriving in the state. Immigrants mostly settled in towns and cities. Czechs, eastern European Jews, Germans, and Italians came to Texas in smaller numbers than to the Northeast or Midwest, but they formed communities large enough to constitute identifiable ethnic enclaves in Houston and alarm their neighbors. During the first four decades of the twentieth century the state's urban population grew rapidly. The number of urban residents leaped from 17 percent of the population in 1900 to 41 percent by 1930.[32] The ethnic diversity of the state's growing cities did not escape notice.

In the eugenicist mind, the immigrant trickle seemed like a flood. According to a 1906 US Census report, Texas remained overwhelmingly a land of white "Anglo-Saxon" Protestants whom eugenicists defined as true Americans. The report revealed that slightly less than 75 percent of Texans[33] identified as Protestants. About 25 percent of Texans—Mexican, Czech, southern German, and other "ethnic" whites—adhered to the Catholic faith. Texas represented the second most Catholic state in the old Confederacy after Louisiana. Due to Mexican immigration, particularly because of the numbers fleeing to the state to escape violence after the 1910 revolution, Catholicism dramatically grew from 150,000 members of the church in 1880 to 750,000 in in 1930.[34] Daniel and his growing number of allies saw these immigrants as Trojan horses whose presence would bring white civilization tumbling down.

Between 1907 and 1914, about 10,000 eastern European Jews settled in Galveston on the Texas coast as part of the "Galveston Plan" supported by New York investor Jacob Schiff. Schiff hoped that the United States would provide a happier, more prosperous life for Russian Jews, but worried about an anti-Semitic backlash as the number of Jewish residents greatly increased in northeastern metropolises like New York and Philadelphia. To prevent American gentiles from perceiving a Jewish "invasion," Schiff advocated dispersal of immigrants across the Midwest and West, including Texas.[35] Hollace Ava Weiner, a chronicler of the Jewish past in Texas, argues that Texas exhibited only "a modest degree of anti-Semitism, although in general there seems to be more ignorance and curiosity about Judaism than prejudice." Nevertheless, Beaumont rabbi Samuel Rosinger sadly remembered that when his son Leonard attended his first day of classes for the 1914–15 school year, classmates ridiculed him with anti-Semitic slurs. Rosinger observed that Christian Texans, taught in their churches that Jews murdered the son of God, were quick to fall back on deicidal myths when Jewish people offended them. "Let a Christian and a Jewish child have a falling out, the first epithet the Christian child will throw at his Jewish antagonist is, 'You are a Christ-killer,'" he said. Jewish people would never emerge as the primary outsider group in the imaginations of most Anglo gentiles in Texas and would never endure the level of persecution suffered by African Americans, Mexicans, and Mexican Americans. But they would still loom large in the warnings of Texas eugenicists like John Box and E. E. Davis, who depicted them as a disloyal racial fifth column that sought to undermine white supremacy in a plot to gain political and economic control of the nation.[36]

A humor magazine founded in Austin in 1881 by Alexander E. Sweet and John Armory Knox, *Texas Siftings*, eventually reached a readership of 150,000 when it relocated to New York. Cartoonists filled *Texas Siftings* with drawings of Jews as hook-nosed villains with "gross lips, and crude, ostentatious manners" who spoke with exaggerated accents. The magazine featured a character named Mose Schaumburg, a fictional, stereotypically greedy Jewish merchant. Schaumburg routinely cheated his customers, overcharging them, and made exaggerated claims about the quality of the shoddy wares he peddled.[37]

Texas Siftings depicted other immigrants as drunken, Marxist bomb-throwers, such as in a poem about a German immigrant based on Johann Most, an anarchist executed after the 1886 Haymarket Square bombing in Chicago. As one verse describes the character:

> He came to America's shore
> With a new patent bomb-shell or ball
> With a thirst for destruction and gore
> And a liver distended with gall[38]

Even the smallest immigrant communities alarmed white Texans. Between 1890 and 1920, the entire Asian-born population of Texas grew from 713 to only 1,260. The first Chinese immigrants arrived in Dallas in the early 1870s after a strike against the Houston and Texas Central Railroad, which had exploited Asian workers. One historian estimates that the entire Chinese American population in Dallas County reached only thirty-three as of the 1886 census year, with fourteen Chinese-owned laundries operating in the city at that time.[39]

White Dallasites charged that the owners of Chinese laundries hurt white competitors. "The white laundries of Dallas are complaining that the patronage of many of the people who can afford to patronize institutions giving work to white labor is given to . . . inferior Chinese laundries of this city," the *Dallas Daily Times Herald* warned in 1894. The *Times Herald* told its readers that contact with the Chinese could result in someone "contracting some vile disease." The Eureka Steam Laundry ran an ad in the *Texas State Gazetteer* with an illustration depicting a white man with a clenched fist chasing a Chinese man wearing a queue and carrying a bag of money above the slogan, "The Chinese Must Go!" The *Dallas Morning News*, meanwhile, regularly portrayed the Chinese in the city as "criminal." A petition sent to the Dallas City Council and published by the *Morning News* on July 18, 1886 included the "Chinese Must Go!" slogan and accused such immigrants of bringing prostitution to the city. Calling for Dallas to remove "pesthouses, commonly called bagnios [brothels]" from the city's First Ward, the petitioners complained that because of the sex trade in their neighborhood, "[o]ur wives and daughters dare not appear in the streets or at our doors without risks of the grossest insults." The signers of the petition demanded an end to such "degrading contamination."[40]

"Non-infanto Mania": A Panic About Race Suicide in Texas

In the minds of eugenicists like Daniel, the increasing number of immigrants made the fertility of biologically fit white women in Texas essential to the survival of the white race. Daniel felt that if it served society's interests, doctors could perform life-altering surgery without patients' consent. Bodily autonomy never fully existed for African Americans in the United States and it badly eroded in the 1800s for whites as well. By the late nineteenth century, for instance, the male medical establishment had already stripped white women of their right to decide whether or not to have children.

Based on common law, the British colonies in North America prior to the Declaration of Independence allowed termination of pregnancy up to the quickening, when a woman can feel fetal movement. This served as the first clear sign of impregnation. This moment varies widely for women, but it generally happens during the fourth or fifth month. American society widely accepted abortion before the quickening and after in order to preserve a woman's life. Even the Catholic Church adhered to the quickening standard until after the American Civil War. The public generally accepted it when American women attempted to end suspected pregnancies by a variety of means such as hot baths, abortifacient herbs such as pennyroyal or savin juniper, riding a horse bareback, or consuming a blend of iron and quinine.[41]

Abortion became so commonplace in the United States by the 1840s that midwives promoted such services in euphemistic though transparent terms, in advertisements carried by widely read newspapers such as the *New York Sun* and the *Boston Daily Times*.[42] A dramatic shift happened after the 1847 founding of the American Medical Association (AMA). Members of the all-male group called "Regulars" sought to impose standards on the profession and to eliminate competition from rivals who rejected allopathy. That category included midwives, who provided most abortions nationwide. Nationally, doctors like Harvard-educated Horatio Storer became successful crusaders against what they called "*non-infanto mania*," the trend of affluent white women having fewer children. Medical journals began to dismiss midwives and male doctors who provided abortion services as dangerous, ill-informed "quacks." Regulars still neglected adequate sanitary practices in their examinations and during surgeries, thus causing many of their patients to die of sepsis. Nevertheless, the AMA persuaded major press outlets such as the *New York Times* to sensationally cover cases in which women died during abortions performed by midwives. By 1880, the hair-raising accounts of women's deaths at abortionists' hands created momentum for the enactment of laws banning and criminalizing abortion in every state except Kentucky, where state courts already had rendered such procedures illegal.[43]

Whether or not they called themselves eugenicists, the doctors who successfully banned abortions across the nation shared eugenical concerns. The "wrong" women, they believed, were having babies. At the same time, women whom the racist medical establishment hoped would be fertile too often terminated their pregnancies. "Anglo-Saxon" Protestant birthrates plummeted while eastern and southern European Catholics and Jews in the United States begat large broods. Storer and future United States president Theodore Roosevelt issued eugenics-based warnings about the nation's demographic trends.[44]

Texas passed its first anti-abortion law in 1856, a carryover from its days as a Spanish colony ruled by a Catholic monarchy. By the late nineteenth century and early twentieth century, the state criminally prosecuted those who performed abortions or made the attempt. Illegal abortions were often performed not in the proverbial "back alley" by poorly trained amateurs, but by physicians who provided the service for a variety of reasons including sympathy for married women who could not afford to have more children or single women terrified of poverty and the destruction of their reputation and future marriageability. Because abortion represented an illegal, underground activity unless the procedure was "therapeutic," many physicians lacked adequate training and made fatal mistakes. Authorities arrested Dr. S. M. Jenkins of Waco on November 1, 1899, on charges of performing an abortion and murder after one of his patients, Mary "Madie" Wheat, died in the city hospital on October 8. When Jenkins brought Wheat there, he claimed she had dysentery. After her death, an examination by the city physician revealed a bowel perforation. Authorities charged Jenkins with having performed an abortion at the home of a "Mrs. Smith" ten days before he checked Wheat into the hospital. Jenkins testified that the fetus had died and that he performed the abortion in order to save Wheat's life. "The defense seemed to be well satisfied with their showing so far and public opinion had changed considerably in favor of the defendant," a reporter for the *Houston Post* wrote, when the trial came to a shocking end. The deceased's brother, Hugh Wheat, fatally shot Jenkins just below the ribs while court was in session. John Halligan, Jenkins's brother-in-law, fired at the killer as he fled the courtroom but missed.[45]

In June 1892, a state court of appeals reversed the conviction of a man in Jack County who had attempted to "produce an abortion by administering cotton root tea" to a pregnant woman. The court reversed the verdict because the jury had not been instructed by the trial judge to consider whether "the tea was sufficiently strong to produce abortion."[46] These cases validate an observation by an historian of American abortion policy, Leslie Reagan: criminal prosecutions of those charged with violating abortion laws frequently failed. The general public, and even some doctors and judges, broadly sympathized with women who for a variety of reasons felt the need to end a pregnancy. "The anti-abortion views written into statutes nationwide not only did not reflect reality, but were hostile to the attitudes and behavior of many Americans," Reagan wrote.[47]

Daniel published articles that bemoaned well-off women obtaining abortions while at the same time supporting exceptions to the state abortion ban. The eugenic dream of racial "purity" influenced *Daniel's Texas Medical Journal*'s position on abortion. Texas allowed therapeutic abortions meant to protect the life of the mother. In the late 1800s, doctors often performed abortions and did not face prosecution in cases where women suffered *hyperemesis gravidarum* or severe, pregnancy-induced vomiting, then deemed a life-threatening condition. Daniel's journal republished a sympathetic account of such a case that first appeared in the *St. Louis Courier of Medicine*. A "Dr. Scott" described treating a patient suffering from constant vomiting. Scott clearly pitied the woman, an acquaintance since childhood. A young bride, she had just returned from her honeymoon pregnant. Over a period of a day and night, as Scott supervised, a peer, "Dr. Moses," gave the woman "belladonna suppositories" and used scraping tools to induce a miscarriage. "From the very time that the fetus came away her nausea left her," Dr. Scott wrote. "I was satisfied that this was the only thing which would be of any good," he said. "This was the third [such] case . . . within eighteen months . . . and when I produced an abortion[,] the patients were saved."[48]

Daniel became fascinated with the use of electricity in medicine. He wrote approvingly of how it could be used to end ectopic pregnancies, cases in which fertilized eggs attach to the fallopian tubes or elsewhere outside the uterus. Ectopic pregnancies can kill or leave a woman infertile, outcomes undesirable for eugenicists caring for "fit" white patients. Apparently believing that doctors could ethically perform abortions to save the life of a woman, Daniel shared with his readers details from an *International Journal of Surgery and Antiseptics* article on how to use electricity in such cases. The article advised doctors to attach a negative electrode to an insulated stem inserted in the vagina and "guided to the point where the enlargement is most distinctly felt." The article instructed doctors to release an interrupted galvanic current of a strength "between fifteen and twenty milometres."[49]

In Daniel's journal, doctors also debated the ethics of providing abortion services to women who might not be able to find a fit partner later in life if they carried to term an unwanted pregnancy. The October 1887 issue described a debate held by the Terrell Medical Society. Dr. Webb (first names weren't provided in the story) delivered a paper on "whether or not it was criminal to induce an abortion, otherwise than to save the life of the mother?" Dr. Nelson suggested that perhaps abortion services should be provided "if an intelligent and chaste young woman should be deceived by her lover [who without] any interference would be forever disgraced and lead the life of the abandoned, whereas to interfere she could, or might, be restored to her family and society, becoming both an ornament and a useful member of the same." Nelson made clear he did not want such an exemption from abortion bans abused, but wondered if an exception could be "applied to special cases."[50]

Dr. Webb characterized such a change in the law as "a hazardous experiment," but two other doctors defended Dr. Nelson's position. Dr. Anthony said "that in such cases as really demanded protection from a life of shame and misery, the physician would not only be justified, but lauded in his virtuous endeavors, to snatch, as it were, a brand from the burning." Dr. Smiley argued that "to induce an abortion to protect a woman's virtue or character, which had been betrayed, if a crime, was less a crime than to send the woman headlong to ruin."[51]

On one level, this debate could be read as reflective of the compassion some medical men felt toward women trapped in the sexual double standard. Gilded Age men got away with sexual license outside of marriage and could walk away from their children and the women who bore them with much less risk of social sanction. Women bearing children out of wedlock, however, would be seen as morally deficient and "fallen" and not as desirable mates by potential "fit" partners. But by underscoring that they only supported exceptions to abortion bans for supposedly intelligent women of character, the doctors revealed a eugenical concern as well. A woman supposedly desirable from a biological standpoint who suffered a lapse in judgment and delivered a child outside of marriage would likely never have a relationship with a man of similar biological "worth," some eugenicists reasoned. Better to abort one child conceived out of wedlock, they were arguing, and allow woman from respectable backgrounds to have a large family with a suitable mate in the future. Meanwhile, Dr. W. C. Fisher, in an 1888 paper delivered at the Galveston County Medical Clinic, complained that some of the most "fit" women aborted children even if married and in comfortable circumstances, "[T]he blood of the unborn infant has decreased in value. We do not meet these abortions alone in women of low moral standing, or in girls, the victims of misplaced confidence who will resort to every means to hide their shame, but often in women whose standing is high, and whose moral characters are considered above reproach, and their only reason is because the demands of society are such that it is *distasteful* and *unfashionable* to have more than one or two children."[52]

Fisher angrily denounced the medical "perpetrators of such heinous crimes," which he described as "low old women, or doctoresses who are willing to produce abortions, or physicians who prefer to make a living by murdering the unborn infant, to following their legitimate calling."[53]

Fisher's anger in 1888 over upper-class white women choosing to limit the size of their families anticipated a moral panic that gripped the nation in the first decade of the twentieth century over race suicide, a phrase coined by sociologist Edward A. Ross to describe the declining birth rate of "old stock" Americans and the accelerating reproduction by African Americans and immigrant families. President Theodore Roosevelt attacked the "selfishness" of biologically superior couples he claimed thought "only for ease" while shirking "the most elemental duties of manhood and womanhood." Roosevelt called for "patriotic," racially fit couples to bear at least four children. "If all our nice friends . . . have only one child, or no child at all, while all the Finnegans, Hooligans, Antonios, Mandelbaums, and Rabinskis have eight, or nine, or ten—it's simply a question of the multiplication table," Roosevelt said. The future of American civilization depended on reproductive math.[54]

The Sanitary Utopia

Daniel would be a thinker of underappreciated, if malign, influence. By the late 1880s eugenics won wide acceptance in the medical community. Daniel would play a key role at this critical moment. As eugenics historian Mark A. Largent observed, Daniel was the "first American professional to bring together the critical elements of the arguments in favor of compulsory sterilization," including claims that so-called defectives were growing in alarming numbers, the supposed link between certain sexual acts and "biological and mental inferiority," and "the potential of sexual surgeries to treat existing problems and to eliminate the source of these problems from future generations."[55]

Daniel's increasing calls for castration came in response to the social and economic convulsions in Texas and the rest of the country in the Gilded Age and early twentieth century. After the beginning of the "market revolution," in the 1830s and 1840s, American thinkers worried that the misdirected sexual energy undermined worker discipline and depleted the masculine vigor needed to propagate the master race in sufficient numbers. Masturbation and homosexuality, doctors and race theorists argued, left weakened minds and bodies vulnerable to disease, reduced white reproduction, and might actually harm the white "germ seed." As a result, a "masturbation panic" spread first in Great Britain and then to the American medical community.[56] A parallel "gay panic" spread as well.

The nineteenth century saw the creation of a "homosexual" identity. Previously, often murderous anti-gay sentiment had marked European and then American culture for much of the Christian era. Ecclesiastical and legal authorities persecuted people for sexual acts deemed sinful. The idea that a person's identity could be based primarily on their sexual behavior and romantic attractions, however, derived from a new nineteenth-century science, psychiatry. Doctors applied a variety of names to gay men and women, including "invert" (referring, in part, to the notion that men attracted to men were inwardly women and that women attracted to other women were men within). The medical community coined the term "homosexual" in this period.[57] Scientists in Europe and the United States pathologized this new identity, and Daniel jumped on that bandwagon.

Cultural movers and shakers posed unregulated sexuality as an enemy to the white race and capitalist production. The market economy of the 1840s displaced old notions of masculinity as defined by self-sufficiency. As industrialism spread, increasingly men worked for other men who dictated their working hours, closely monitored their output, judged the quality of their labor, parceled out their financial rewards, determined the length of workdays, and judged the status of their employment, thus triggering masculine insecurities. Some, like health faddist Sylvester Graham (1794–1851), a Presbyterian minister from New England, saw the mind as a closed system with a finite amount of power that had to be shepherded carefully. Any form of excess sexuality might deplete life-giving energy, especially outside of marriage.[58] Masturbation and homosexuality represented threats to the health of men, he insisted, leading to physical weakness, "effeminacy," insanity, suicide or premature death by natural causes.[59]

The medical war against masturbation outlived Graham, who died in 1851. Authorities warned young men that masturbation caused maladies ranging from pimples to spinal tuberculosis, from epilepsy to what came to be known as "masturbatory insanity." A perceived epidemic of the latter ailment supposedly caused asylums to overflow, and was second only to alcohol as a danger to mental health. Doctors saw masturbation as a gateway addiction, leading to alcoholism and opium abuse, scourges endangering the white war of reproduction against other races.[60]

Eager to preserve the health of their children, American parents spied on their offspring and used a variety of techniques to protect their young ones from self-harm, including making them wear gloves at nighttime, tying their hands to headboards when they went to bed, or even attaching toothed rings around boys' genitals that would cause pain in the event of an erection.[61] Doctors offered circumcision as a means of preventing masturbation but also proposed a more radical solution to this concocted problem.[62]

In the minds of most of Daniel's generation of doctors, the masturbator, as well as gay men and woman, had deteriorated and had flipped the reverse switch on human evolution. As humanity advanced, race scientists said, human thoughts centered more on elevated ideas and less on sexual urges. Masturbators and homosexuals, succumbing to primitive impulses, revealed themselves as "atavisms," prone to committing a host of crimes, the medical community proclaimed.

Early in its history, Texas used its police authority to attempt to stamp out homosexuality, grouping it with bestiality in an 1860 law specifying that if "any person shall commit with mankind or beast the abominable and detestable crime against nature, he shall be deemed guilty of sodomy, and . . . shall be subject to confinement" for five to fifteen years. However, Daniel thought society had acted too late by the time it punished a person for sex crimes.[63] In one much-discussed paper, Daniel wove together several prevailing intellectual threads about criminality, sexuality, insanity and mental disability, fears about an approaching collapse of the American mental health care system, and the need for a dramatic new approach to curb the supposed epidemic of "lunacy" haunting the state.

Daniel delivered his paper, "Should Insane Criminals, Or Sexual Perverts, Be Allowed to Procreate?" before important audiences, first at the Joint Session of the World's Columbian Auxiliary Congress in New York on August 16, 1893, and then before the American Medico-Legal Society on October 11 of the same year. The speech, printed in Daniel's own publication, as well the *Medico-Legal Journal*, the *Psychological Bulletin*, and reported in the popular press, reached a wide national audience. Daniel warned of a threat to worldwide white supremacy posed by homosexuals. Daniel insisted that all behavioral traits in humans remained static from birth on. "No fact is better established than that drunkenness, insanity, and criminal traits of character, as well as syphilis and scrofula, may descend from parent to child," he wrote. Society, however, was doing nothing effective to halt the spread of these diseases and "defects."

With the exception of improved hygiene in lunatic asylums, and more enlightened and rational treatment, nothing or nearly nothing is being done in the way of rational prophylaxis against a long list of maladies that destroy both body and mind. In no State are such restrictions placed upon the privilege of marrying as are calculated to arrest the propagation of consumption, syphilis, insanity, drunkenness, and criminal propensity; nor is any method resorted to,

calculated to counteract, or lessen, the degrading effects of hereditary transmission of these vices.[64]

Daniel portrayed non-heterosexual behavior as a plague devastating the
country. He did not use the term "invert" or "homosexual" but referred to
gays indirectly with his use of the word "pervert," and he argued that African Americans tended toward all forms of "illicit sex," a trait they shared
with the "lower classes" of all races because, he asserted, they had not fully
evolved.[65] Daniel argued that masturbators and gay men and women posed
a threat to humanity in the here and now not only because they allegedly
committed crimes like rape, but also because, due to what he claimed was
their lack of sexual discipline, they likely would bear many descendants.[66]
Regardless of what constituted cause and what was effect, that is whether
mental illness caused masturbation or vice versa, the twin maladies endangered the nation.

Institutional confinement would fail as a means of preventing such
"defectives" from destroying the human race, he said. The obviously defective, and those carrying incipient traits that had not manifested, lurked
everywhere and exceeded in number the capacity of society to prevent
their reproduction. "The wealth of all the Czars would not be adequate to
provide asylum and medical treatment for the progeny of these people in
fifty years from now," he predicted.[67] Viewing "sex criminals" such as child
rapists as insane, Daniel did not hold them fully responsible for their deeds.
Like Lincecum, he opposed the death penalty. Instead of executing those
arrested for such crimes, Daniel called for "a removal of the causes that
lead to [the crimes], and reform, rather than the extermination of the
vicious."[68]

Rejecting "hanging, electrocution, or burning at the stake" as a solution to sex offenses, Daniel called for the abolition of the death penalty
and then offered his favorite answer to social chaos. "In lieu [of execu-
tions] thereof . . . and as a measure calculated to fulfill all the ends and
aims of criminal jurisprudence, castration is proposed," he said.[69] Daniel
then begged society to imitate nature. "The lower animals limit reproduction and eliminate the weaker by battles between the males for the possession of the female," he told his peers. "[A]nd certain of the rodents, the
squirrel I am told, castrate the young males. But with civilized man the
procreative function, and the right to exercise it *ad libitum* [at liberty]

seems something sacred . . . Is it not a remarkable civilization that will break a criminal's neck, but will respect his testicles?"[70]

Daniel then made an extraordinary claim indicating the influence the fledgling eugenics movement had already gained in Texas. He told his audience that he had spoken to Governor James Hogg (in office from 1891 to 1895) about his idea of using castration "as a therapeutic measure." After noting that Hogg had served as state attorney general and "is distinguished for his great legal ability," Daniel said, "[h]e assured me that there is not a doubt of the legal right on the part of a superintendent of an insane asylum to castrate a patient for mental trouble . . . He would have the same right to castrate a patient as he would have to bleed him in the arm, or to amputate a limb, or to do any other operation."[71]

Daniel concluded his 1893 speech fantasizing about the golden future that could be molded for humanity through widespread castration. Lincecum had dreamed of a time up to 15,000 years in the future when the remainder of Homo sapiens might be kept in zoos where they would look up to the super-race created through selective breeding. Daniel saw a shorter path to a better age through the surgeon's blade. "While we cannot hope ever to institute a sanitary Utopia in our day and generation, it would seem within the legitimate scope and sphere of Preventative Medicine, aided by the enactment and enforcement of suitable laws, to eliminate much that is defective in human genesis . . . I predict that in twenty years the beneficial results of castrations for crimes committed in obedience to a perverted and (diseased) sexual impulse will be established and appreciated."[72]

In his journal, Daniel applauded when Dr. Hoyt Pilcher, the superintendent of the Asylum for Idiots and Feebleminded Youths in Winfield, Kansas, in 1894 publicly acknowledged that he had sterilized, without legal authority, forty-four mostly teenaged boys and fourteen girls of a similar age because he deemed them compulsive masturbators and feared their behavior would aggravate their mental disabilities.[73] In spite of his frustrations in getting legislation passed, Daniel exalted that his ideas won acceptance by some in his home state. As the Pilcher controversy raged in Kansas, Daniel praised a new superintendent of the State Lunatic Asylum in Austin, W. S. White, as a "strong advocate of castration as a therapeutic measure." White advocated legalizing such operations "at the physician's discretion."[74]

After the turn of the century, race scientists, the medical community, educators, authors and journalists across the United States launched a propaganda effort to create Daniel's sanitary utopia. Despite the advances the eugenics movement made in Texas under Daniel's leadership and his growing stature, the movement faltered in the Lone Star State. Deep-seated suspicions about the moral values at Texas colleges and universities hampered the ability of the intelligentsia to shape public opinion for good or ill. Even upon the establishment of what eventually became Texas A&M University and the University of Texas, state leaders saw higher education as a luxury to be enjoyed only by the rich.

"Kid-Glove Silk-Stocking Aristocrats": Class Conflict and Higher Education in Texas

The ideas Daniel promoted withered in an environment of skepticism towards intellectuals. Eugenical ideas spread in a climate in which intellectuals were broadly respected. Leaders of the Lone Star State had different priorities. Texas politicians financially bent educational priorities to fit the needs of big planters and industrialists, who wanted a plentiful, divided, and poorly paid workforce they hoped would remain ignorant of their rights. Burnishing insincere populist credentials, officeholders castigated colleges and universities as frivolous financial burdens on the common folk and mocked professors as effete snobs who held the masses in contempt. These accusations claimed eugenics as collateral damage.

Elsewhere in the country, where colleges and universities enjoyed rich endowments, eugenicists made waves and attained high status. One, A. Lawrence Lowell, won appointment as president of Harvard in 1909. In that office, he imposed quotas on the number of Jewish students who would be admitted each year, banned the minuscule number of African American students at the university from taking residence in Harvard Yard, and called for a sharp reduction in immigration. He insisted that only racial homogeneity in the United States would guarantee that American democracy could survive. A Harvard economist, Frank W. Taussig, author of the 1911 book *Principles of Economics*, one of the most widely adopted textbooks in the country, referred to the poor and criminal classes as "parasites" and wrote, "The human race could be immensely improved in quality, and its capacity for happy living immensely increased, if those of poor physical and mental endowment were prevented from multiplying." One of the earliest American geneticists, William Ernest Castle, joined the long roster of influential Harvard eugenicists, authoring works on biology such as *Heredity and Eugenics* assigned across the country, including at North Texas Agricultural College in Arlington. Outside of Texas, eugenicists became some of the most famous faculty at private colleges and (as will be discussed latter) public institutions like the University of California system. From that privileged perch, they influenced policy on topics ranging from immigration to care for those with mentally disabilities. Meanwhile, Texas academics, whether or not they embraced eugenics, largely toiled in obscurity and frequently became the objects of disdain.[75]

After the Republican-led Texas legislature made an unprecedented commitment to education during Reconstruction, the effort to teach the masses took a body blow when the unrepentant antebellum Texas planter class regained total political control in 1876. Only elite children, they believed, had need of extensive book learning. So-called Redeemer Democrats repealed Republican reforms such as compulsory school attendance and limited public schooling to children between the ages of eight and fourteen. The 1876 school law created poorly funded and unregulated "community schools." Badly trained teachers, with little more education than their students, staffed temporary classrooms, with the depth and breadth of the curriculum varying widely from place to place. A vast education gap opened between rural and city schools. On average, by 1900, school years in cities lasted 162 days compared to a 98-day calendar for rural school systems. Rural schools also received parsimonious funding, with $8 spent annually per student in city schools compared to $5 per child in rural schools ($294 per student compared to $183 today, adjusted for inflation).[76]

Suspicion of colleges and universities predated the Civil War. In 1860, Sam Houston, president of the Texas Republic from 1836–38 and from 1841–44 and governor from 1859–61, dismissed a state university as ". . . a matter alone for the future." Instead, he said, state revenues would be better spent on "the protection of the frontier."[77] Officeholders who wished to be seen as a voice of the average person castigated proposals to invest in higher education as an attempt to drain money from common schools in order to lavishly fund a luxury that would be enjoyed only by the children of the rich.

During legislative debates over the establishment of a university in Texas in the 1850s, some in the legislature castigated the proposed institution as a "rich man's school," or an "undemocratic" place where "the children of the rich may be educated and those of the poor neglected." Colleges and universities, one lawmaker said, inevitably became "hot-beds of unmorality [sic], profligacy, and licentiousness" that had "a tendency to create aristocracy and class legislation among the people." State Senator David M. Whaley agreed. "Lawyers and doctors!" he exclaimed." It is not right that the people should be taxed for the education of such professional men, whose services are so extravagantly paid for." During debates over funding higher education in the 1870s, the *Comanche Chief* newspaper charged that a state university would "amount to nothing more than a house of refuge for a few kid glove, silk-stocking aristocrats and a corps of well-paid teachers while the masses will have to be content with free schools for four or five months of the year."[78]

The Texas Agricultural and Mechanical College near Bryan, authorized by Reconstruction-era Republicans, did not open until the fall of 1876, when it had one hundred and six students and six faculty members. The origins of the college, destined to become Texas A&M University (or A&M), as a land grant college placed the school in a curricular straitjacket. The legislature intended the school to provide knowledge of modern agricultural techniques for the upcoming generation of farmers. A&M was seen as a seat of practical knowledge, while the esoteric arts of philosophy, literature, history, mastery of dead classical languages, and theoretical science were best left to pricey private schools. Oran M. Roberts, a reactionary Democrat elected governor in 1879, declared that A&M's top mission should be to teach students how "to produce two ears of wheat and corn and two bales of cotton by the same labor and capital that have been heretofore producing but one." A&M students didn't need literature and science, Roberts proclaimed, because fancy city folk interested in such abstractions "are seldom found to spend their lives between the plow handles or in the workshops." A shortage of textbooks on agriculture and engineering persuaded the school's first faculty to teach a traditional liberal arts program. For not fulfilling the school's intended mission, the

Board of Directors (the administrative body of the college) fired A&M's first president and every professor.[79]

The following year, Governor Roberts proclaimed his support for building "a university of the first class," by which he meant the University of Texas (UT) in Austin. From its 1883 founding and over the next seven decades, UT would be the center of law, science, and the liberal arts, while A&M remained a backward, forgotten little sibling. Already in the 1880s, politicians in Austin spoke of closing A&M and converting it into a mental health institution.[80] As would later happen with the University of Texas, A&M acquired a bad reputation as a den of iniquity where faculty "drank liquor and played cards" and students burned outhouses and frequented brothels. A former state senator wrote that he would sooner give his son "a pony, six[-]shooter, bottle of whiskey and deck of cards . . . as to send him to the A&M C[ollege]."[81] The Carnegie Foundation for the Advancement of Teaching inspected the school in 1908, snidely commenting that "It is a display of great leniency to term the Agricultural and Mechanical College of Texas an institution of higher education at all."[82]

Supporters of higher education faced a similar hard struggle in establishing the University of Texas. Roberts, governor from 1879–83, enthusiastically supported this cause, noting that the best common-school students in Texas went out of state to get degrees. The University of Texas, with academic and law departments, opened its doors with twelve faculty members September 15, 1883, the same year Francis Galton coined the term "eugenics." Its faculty included Presbyterian minister Robert Dabney, recently a professor at Union Theological Seminary in Virginia who once served as Confederate general Thomas "Stonewall" Jackson's chaplain. Dabney, appointed Professor of Moral and Mental Philosophy, argued that abolition of slavery had been the work of Satan and that citizens' rights should be doled out based on their inherent abilities. He adamantly rejected providing schools for African Americans, but also opposed the idea of universal education for whites, believing that the "little education [common schools] might succeed in giving [poor whites] will prove dangerous," encouraging them to seek social and political equality. Dabney's son Lewis would later become a spokesman for the eugenics cause in Dallas.[83]

As with A&M, the flagship University of Texas started its existence as a ramshackle, less- than-half-hearted enterprise. The concept of academic freedom did not exist at the University of Texas for decades. The legislature granted the board of regents, appointed by hyper-conservative Texas governors, the power to "fire anyone they decided to fire" and "the power to regulate the courses of instruction, and prescribe" the books and authorities used.[84]

The original faculty toiled in primitive conditions unappealing to top scholars in the rest of the country. Occasionally, the echo of fired bullets from gunfights playing out in the surrounding capital city could be heard. The reputation of the faculty matched the humbleness of their surroundings.[85] Politicians tightly scrutinized professors to ensure they clung to political orthodoxy and did not poison students with the heretical concepts of modern science, such as the theory of evolution. Faculty had to adapt their "teaching, research, and style of speaking and writing to 'the independent state of Texas,'" as Alvin Johnson, an economics professor at UT from 1907–09, observed. Already in 1893, a decade after the founding of the university, a state legislative committee was investigating "unfriendly criticism" of the institution by the public. Constituents were upset that a faculty member received a pension as a Civil War veteran of the United States Army. The committee reported that "[s]ome of the professors, it seems, are from Northern States" with one "perhaps a Republican in politics." David Franklin Houston, a political scientist and later president of UT from 1905 to 1908, fended off accusations of radicalism from eight members of the legislature. He had authored a book on the South Carolina nullification crisis of the 1830s deemed by members of the state house to be insufficiently pro-southern. Politicians charged that some professors held "our traditions and our institutions in contempt, and circulate and teach heresies in place of the system of political economy that is cherished by the people." In a resolution, the legislators asked for insufficiently pro-establishment professors to be fired. Houston was forced by legislators to renounce his own work.[86]

A gifted economist, Johnson, who had taught at Columbia University in New York and held a professorship at the University of Nebraska for one year before landing an appointment at the University of Texas in 1907, had been warned about the highly politicized and ideologically driven atmosphere at UT. "Some of Johnson's academic colleagues had warned him that by going to Texas he was giving up academic liberty," a journalist and chronicler of the University of Texas, Ronnie Dugger, wrote. Johnson saw the institution treated as "just a football of politics and every ignoramus was privileged to give it a kick." Dugger quotes Johnson as saying that in the earliest years of the university, "the only way a geologist could squeeze evolution into the six thousand years 'since the Creation according to Moses' was to argue that God, being omnipotent, could make and kill off the dinosaurs and lay stratified rock six miles deep in a twinkling." No one in the legislature was inclined to listen to UT faculty on any matter, particularly something as controversial as mandatory sterilization. "The resources of the University of Texas were untapped and there was no relationship between school and state to match [other states where the Progressive movement thrived]," as historian Lewis Gould wrote.[87]

Vivisection and *The Strange Case of Dr. Bruno*

In 1906, the Iowa legislature debated an ultimately unsuccessful bill allowing euthanasia for "patients in incurable cases where there is intense suffering and also in the lives of hopelessly idiotic or deformed children" if three physicians gave consent. [88] Although Daniel never endorsed euthanasia for the unfit, a position later advocated by pioneering Oregon physician Ella K. Dearborn in the pages of the *Fort Worth Telegram* about the same time, he did have some provocative ideas about how to make scientific use of condemned prisoners.[89]

An opponent of the death penalty, Daniel apparently accepted that capital punishment would thrive in the foreseeable future, but regretted that hangings and electrocutions damaged organs holding irreplaceable scientific data. The same year Iowa politicians debated its euthanasia law saw the publication of a science fiction novel by Daniel, *The Strange Case of Dr. Bruno*. Told in a common Victorian fashion through a series of fictitious letters, diaries, and newspaper stories, the tale advances through a series of over-the-top, Shakespearean-style mistaken identities. Dr. Bruno is incorrectly informed that the woman he has eloped with, Katie Kardelle, is his long-separated sister. Traumatized, Bruno wanders in a state of amnesia, only slowly recovering his identity after he is placed in an asylum. Meanwhile, Katie disappears, her fate unknown. Heartbroken, Bruno subjects himself to an experimental drug derived from the venom of a "mud wasp" or dirt dauber," which the insect uses to paralyze its prey."[90]

The drug dramatically lowers his body temperature, slows his heartbeat and respiration almost to the stopping point, and leaves him with no need for food and water. Bruno provides detailed instructions to a fellow physician about how to properly look after him in his altered state. While Bruno drifts in suspended animation, his friends discover that not only was his wife, Katie, not his sister, but that that she became pregnant during their brief marriage. Katie found refuge with Ursuline nuns who, after Katie dies, raise his daughter, who is now a grown woman who looks almost exactly like her mother. Bruno awakens from his deep sleep and upon seeing his daughter and thinking his wife has returned from the great beyond, dies almost instantly from shock.[91]

Daniel's convoluted and melodramatic tale would be completely forgettable if the author had not acquired a national audience. F. E. Daniel clearly speaks through Dr. Bruno. To Bruno, like his creator, the advancement of scientific knowledges justifies almost any action. How much kinder, Bruno argues, is it to prevent criminals from being born then to allow them to experience lives that end in an electric chair or at the end of the hangman's rope. "[I]n an age before antibiotics and insulin, before Western medicine's therapeutic capacities began to emerge, preventing the birth of individuals encumbered with genetic ailments seemed the only humane and prudent cure to many [in the medical profession]," Largent said.[92] Nevertheless, in his novel and in an interview following its publication, Daniel made a proposal designed to shock the sensibilities of the early twentieth century.

In *The Strange Case of Dr. Bruno*, Bruno asks his friend, an oculist named Clancey Courtenay, for his opinion of the death penalty. Courtenay supports executions. Bruno objects, saying it does not deter crime, might actually encourage violence, and "destroys a producer" whose surviving family members might become a burden on the state.[93] Nevertheless, Bruno concedes the death penalty enjoys popular support, so he proposes a gruesome way to make these spectacles of death a net gain for society. Anticipating the death-by-lethal-injection execution protocol that became Texas law in 1977 and was first carried out in 1982, Bruno not only advocates a new means of capital punishment but a terrifying new purpose for the death penalty: "[W]hy not put [the condemned] to death speedily and without pain? Instead of the horrible spectacle of hanging him by the neck with a rope, or killing him by means of the no less revolting electrocution, a bungling and costly process, why not use a hypodermic syringe, charged with a dram of hydrocyanic acid, which will stop the heart instantly and cause instant and painless death? Or better, *why not make use of him*?"[94]

Bruno then suggests that perhaps the best means of making the death penalty a benefit to society would be to use the living bodies of the condemned for scientific research. Courtney's face betrays shock so Bruno tries to reassure him of his reasonableness. "Remember that so long as the victim is alive[,] he would be in a state of complete anesthesia . . . So where is the harm? What is there revolting, or inhuman, or cruel or horrible in it, more than there is in the brutal methods employed in all countries for putting out the life of a criminal?" Certainly, Bruno says, dissecting a live condemned prisoner while the person is unconscious, is better than making one suffer in the electric chair.[95]

The author advocated such a policy in an interview printed in the December 1906 edition of the *Texas Medical Journal*. Daniel did not lobby for vivisection of prisoners like he did other dramatic and controversial proposals, but he supported the proposal made by his literary creation. Confirming that the ideas of Dr. Bruno were his own, Daniel said, "Why not turn [a condemned prisoner] over to a regularly appointed State's physician to have him inoculated for the benefit and enlightenment of the human race? Inject into him various disease germs, watch their progress, and when through with him, inject about ten drops of prussic acid into the veins of his arms and he will die a painless death."[96] Ideas like Daniel's would be put into practice in Nazi death camps little more than three decades later.

A Utopia Thwarted

Because of the work of pioneer eugenicists like Daniel, coerced eugenic castration began in other states as early as the 1880s. As incarceration in sex-segregated facilities of those with mental illness and disability climbed, the campaign to tighten marriage laws to maintain supposed white racial purity accelerated. In 1877, Texas reinstituted a ban on miscegenation that had been repealed during Reconstruction, while similar prohibitions became law in Alabama, Arkansas, Indiana, and Louisiana between 1871 and 1907. Connecticut passed a first-in-the-nation law in 1895 outlawing the marriage of those considered defectives, with violators subject to prison sentences. This opened the floodgates for similar legislation. By 1913, twenty-four states, Washington, DC, and Puerto Rico had ever-tighter laws on the books prohibiting epileptics, those with mental illness, and those diagnosed as having mental disabilities from joining hands at the altar.[97]

The movement for compulsory castration advanced as well. In 1899, a physician at a reformatory in Jeffersonville, Indiana, Dr. Henry Clay Sharp, performed a new surgical procedure, a vasectomy, on a nineteen-year-old, "dull and unable to make progress in school," who complained he suffered from a compulsion to masturbate. After the operation, Sharp claimed the patient thanked him for improved concentration. Sharp made sterilization of youths his unauthorized specialty and from 1899 to 1907 he reportedly carried out a total of 176 vasectomies. Sharp began publicizing his operations and lobbied the Indiana governor for a compulsory sterilization law as a way of "preventing procreation in the defective or degenerate classes." A respected physician, Sharp was able to persuade the Indiana legislature to pass a sterilization bill, allowing the state to impose such procedures on "confirmed criminals, idiots, rapists, and imbeciles." On March 9, 1907, it became the first such law in the United States. Within three years, Washington, California, and Connecticut passed similar laws. By the time of Daniel's death in 1914, twelve states allowed state-ordered sterilizations, including the most populous (New York), the eighth-most (Michigan), and the eleventh-most (New Jersey).[98] But not Texas.

Governor James Hogg told Daniel he supported sterilization but never followed through by proposing or supporting legislation. In 1907, the same year Indiana passed its law, Daniel fought hard for a Texas bill making castration the punishment for rape, assault while attempting rape, and incest, writing a March 20 letter to state representative C. K. Walter in which he cited the then-late Hogg's opinion that "the surgeon of any institution has the right to do this operation." Blaming rape in particular on African American men, he insisted that "[t]he crime is on the increase in spite of most drastic measures, and if we would avert a race war of extermination, *something should be done.*" The bill passed the state house, with only two representatives voting against the measure, but died in the senate because it was not approved before the legislative deadline. This represented the third time a sterilization bill expired in Austin.[99]

Daniel gamely carried on. The Texas Medical Association named him the chair of the Section on State Medicine and Public Hygiene and he presented a paper, "Sterilization of the Male Insane," in which he predicted, absent a sterilization law, that the number of those with mental illness in Texas would, by 1930, require the state to maintain ten mental health hospitals and that the care of the inmates would consume much of the Texas budget. The growing number of eugenicists in Texas led to the founding of the Texas State Society of Social Hygiene led by Dr. Theodore Young Hull, the medical director of the Lutheran Sanatorium in San Antonio. Based in the Alamo city, the society named Daniel its first vice president, while a University of Texas education professor, A. Caswell Ellis, served as second vice president. A 1912 statement by the group published in the *Texas Medical Journal* declared, "we are on the threshold of deliberately planning characters of health, probity, courage, and honor, or weed[ing] out characters of weakness, dishonesty, cruelty, immorality, etc." Texans never crossed that threshold, and the hygiene society seems to have made little impact on policies ratified under the capitol dome.[100] Daniel would not live to see a sterilization law passed in his home state.[101]

As Daniel got older and sicker, his wife, Josephine, took command of the *Texas Medical Journal*, and she explicitly rejected her husband's ever-more extreme beliefs. In 1912, the journal added a "Women's Department" written by and compiled by her. It focused on issues central to the Progressive political agenda, like the need for pure food laws and women's suffrage, plus her own particular interests like promoting sex education in public schools. She explicitly dismissed the idea that behaviors, good or ill, are inherited. "The people of the twentieth century can no longer stand quietly by and acquiesce in the exploded world-old theory that we can't help our shortcomings and failures because we inherited them," she wrote in the *Texas Medical Journal* in 1912. "We may have inherited a disposition towards evil, just as we may have inherited a predisposition to consumption. We know now that we don't inherit consumption, and we also know that no man inherits a bad habit from an ancestor."[102]

Daniel not only could not convert his wife to his extreme biological determinism, he could not persuade the legislature of the need for mass sterilization. In 1913 the Texas senate rejected another eugenics bill. For Lincecum, it must have been a bitter defeat. As he wrote, "That government should—possessing the power and means to do so—prevent an increase in the criminal element is a proposition which requires neither argument nor defense; that it should permit—nay, deliberately propagate and encourage an increase of criminals out of all proportions to population, is monstrous." In his mind, the state of Texas had made such a monstrous choice by the time he died on May 14, 1914.[103]

Yet, all the elements that fueled the birth and rise of a genuine eugenics movement in Texas remained in place. If anything, the dread over immigrants and radical politics, the worry about the decadence in growing Texas cities, and the warning that the population of the mentally ill was spiraling out of control only intensified after Daniel's death. In spite of the failure of a sterilization bill in Texas in 1913, such laws continued to pass across the country and took deep root in states like California and in nations around the world. A eugenicist soon gained appointment as head of the Gainesville School for Girls, a major component of the state's juvenile justice system. The eugenics movement won backing from a particularly unexpected source within the state, a Catholic cleric in San Antonio who supported sterilization of criminals in spite of the long-standing opposition of the church to any birth control measures. Yet, Texas cotton growers would soon seek poorly paid Mexican labor as a major source of labor, running afoul of the eugenics agenda and creating a powerful new constituency that wanted no part of Daniel's sanitary utopia. To Daniel and his allies, a dreamed-of scientific golden age through surgical sterilization disappeared over the horizon.

CHAPTER THREE

Eugenics, Disability, and Anti-Democratic Discourse in Texas

1890–1925

THE STATE SCHOLASTIC CENSUS, a yearly enumeration of students in Texas, where they attended school, and other data regarding education, rarely made compelling reading. However, one word in the 1916 census stuck in the mind of Dr. E. F. Bramlette, the superintendent of the Texas School for the Blind.

The author of the report, Superintendent of Public Instruction Dr. W. F. Dougherty, classified students with blindness as "defectives." Bramlette immediately knew the potentially terrible consequences of that label. "Defective" was a charged word. Across the United States, those bearing that label faced sterilization and confinement. Bramlette sent an urgent letter to Dougherty, pointing out the inclusion of such children in the section, "Report on Defectives." He wrote: "Your census reports have reference to educational matters, intellectual matters, and the term 'defective' applied to the blind child thereon must mean that the child is intellectually defective, whereas a blind child is just as capable of the highest intellectual and moral development as the seeing child . . . A blind child is no more defective than a one-armed or wooden-legged man."[1]

Bramlette then raised a key question about the entire eugenic effort. If human imperfection was universal, why were only some individuals pathologized to the point that others desired their extinction? "If a blind person is defective," he pointed out, "so is the man defective who has to wear glasses; for everyone in this sense of the word is defective, no one being perfect physically or in all his physical senses."[2]

The superintendent found himself battling the supposedly dispassionate scientific language pervading the early twentieth century. As historian

Martin Pernick wrote, "'Defective' was the commonly used medical term for a person with any serious disability, primarily but not necessarily a birth defect. . . . These professedly neutral labels were often adopted to distance objective medical science from the pejorative value judgments associated with older words like 'freak.'" Such professed neutrality, however, may have compromised the empathy of the general public to those coping with blindness, deafness, and other traits in a world often hostile to disability. "[T]he use of objective-sounding terminology also attempted to exclude from medicine the benevolent sentimental overtones of such previous euphemisms as 'afflicted misfortunates,'" as Pernick observed. In fact, such terminology did not erase the value judgments about those with disability deeply embedded in American culture during the eugenics era. As historian of disability Sarah Rose has noted, morally sanctioned behaviors like alcoholism and prostitution were not attributed solely to the influence of immoral, shiftless, and even criminal parents. Eugenicists assumed that a dysfunctional homelife could harm the "germ plasm" and create children with physical disabilities. Doctors and the general public, therefore, often linked supposed immorality with physical "defect." Bramlette knew that such labels could cause the children with blindness he cared for a type of social death.[3]

Bramlette asked Dougherty to consider people who had achieved greatness in spite of blindness, such as the seventeenth-century English poet John Milton or Thomas Gore (1870–1949), then serving as a US senator from Oklahoma. "Who would dare classify Milton . . . Senator Gore . . . and hosts of others among the epileptic, the imbecile, insane, etc.?" he asked. Bramlette sought a hierarchy of disability. Those with intellectual challenges were biologically hopeless, he argued, and perhaps should be bred out of the species, but certainly the merely blind and the deaf deserved higher status.[4]

Bramlette's worst fears proved prescient. Just five years after he sent his letter to Dougherty, the Eugenics Record Office in New York and the American Medical Association Section on Ophthalmology drafted "model legislation" that would allow any taxpayer who objected to the marriage of a couple in which at least one partner suffered a "visual defect" to legally intervene. Under such a law, the marriage could be forbidden upon the certification of one ophthalmologist and one eugenics expert. The model statute, written in broad enough terms that it could have also ensnared the nearsighted, the farsighted, and those with astigmatisms, never passed, but similar proposals continued for decades.[5]

Lucien Howe (1848–1928), a researcher at Harvard Medical School, proposed that those with blindness should be given the option of living sexually segregated from the sighted community or being sterilized. Meanwhile, restrictions on marriage became a priority for Texas eugenicists from 1914 to the 1930s. In that time, Texans learned about eugenics in their schools and read about it in their newspapers, saw movies about eugenics in their theaters, attended lectures about the subject at their clubs, and heard their preachers deliver sermons about the blessings of sterilization. Discussions about selective breeding became commonplace at the YMCA, at fairgrounds, and in newspapers. Increasingly, Texans called for the institutionalization of those categorized as inferior. For eugenicists all such evangelizing failed. The state not only did not pass a sterilization law, but in 1923 gave a thumbs-down to a bill that sought to impose eugenic prerequisites on prospective marriage partners. Texas still did not join the ever-lengthening list of states regulating the right to reproduce.

An Emerging National Obsession

Just before and after US entry into World War I, eugenicists sought to catalog the number and variety of American "defectives" and document their behavior and shortcomings. In 1909 Mary Harriman, the wealthy mother of a future governor of New York, William Averell Harriman, richly endowed what came to be known as the Eugenics Record Office (ERO), headquartered at Cold Spring Harbor on Long Island. John D. Rockefeller and the Carnegie Foundation also provided substantial funding for the ERO in subsequent years. Charles Davenport became director, warning about the urgent need to close the American gate to eastern and southern European immigrants he described as "darker in pigmentation, smaller in stature, more mercurial, more given to crimes of larceny, kidnapping, assault, murder, rape, and sex-immorality."[6]

Harry Hamilton Laughlin became the ERO superintendent. Under him, the ERO became a clearinghouse of eugenical data, with field workers fanning across the country, examining public documents and newspaper accounts and conducting interviews in order to compile a massive file-card database recording family histories. Eventually they reached the Gainesville State School for Girls in northeast central Texas to record the family backgrounds of the young women detained by the state's juvenile justice system. The field investigators administered a variety of highly flawed intelligence tests that correlated familiarity with American culture with mental acuity and made anthropometrical measurements of their subjects' cranial capacities. Field workers looked for test subjects in prisons, asylums, and hospitals and evaluated the biological worth of immigrants arriving at the Ellis Island processing center. The gathering of family histories, intelligence test scores, and physical measurements of individuals unfolded between 1910 and 1926. By 1928, an internal committee of scientists concluded that the million index cards and forms filled out by field workers lacked scientific worth. With the helter-skelter mountain of data at hand, Laughlin drafted model compulsory sterilization laws he hoped would be adopted by every state in the union. Laughlin disseminated pro-eugenics propaganda nationwide through the *Eugenical News*, distributed to about 1,000 supporters across the country starting in 1916. The ERO tirelessly lobbied for states to implement strict limitations on who could marry, and to carry out mass government screenings to find those tarred with the "defective" label, to imprison them in institutions where they would be divided by sex, force birth control on those eugenicists considered as lacking worth, and (most notably) carry out a vigorous program of surgical sterilizations to wipe out undesired bloodlines.[7]

Laughlin claimed that "defectives" accounted for 10 percent of the American population, but he said even that could be an underestimate. However, another and perhaps greater threat loomed, he warned. "There are many others of equally unworthy personality and hereditary qualities who have . . . never been committed to institutions," he said, parents who "may themselves be normal, but who may produce defective offspring."[8] If states enacted and thoroughly enforced ERO's suggested legislation, he predicted, the United States might eliminate most of the so-called defective population within fifteen to thirty years. Unfortunately, he said, as of 1914 laws were too weak and narrow. Just the year before, Texas eugenicists had seen the failure of their most recent effort to pass sterilization legislation. [9]

Cook's Report

A dehumanizing term, the word "defective" stigmatized children and their families, implying economic and biological failure. Regardless of its harm, this damaging language began to be hurled at an ever-lengthening list of Texans. In 1910, Dr. W. G. Cook shocked Fort Worth parents when he claimed that one out of ten children in the city's public schools, more than 1,000 in all, showed "physical defects or disease." The Fort Worth school district became a pioneer in the state, the first to appoint a medical supervisor, handing Cook the job the same year he issued his report. Cook's health inspection of the students started on March 24 and ended June 10. The *Fort Worth Record* reacted to Cook's report as evidence of declining eugenic health in the general population, but what he actually recorded was widespread want in one of the state's fastest-growing cities. Six children "with defective eyesight," the newspaper said, "have been compelled by their parents to study lessons while wearing their grand-mother's glasses." Other students suffered from poor dental health, had "defective ears," anemia, or tuberculosis, while "[o]ne of the most pitiable discoveries was that some of the school children of the city are compelled to go to school without their breakfast on account of the poverty of parents." The report could have prompted a campaign for clean neighborhoods, decent wages, and quality health care for all. Instead, it and similar press stories inspired lamentations about, to use the language of that era's eugenicists, the "degeneration" of the American population.[10]

Texas eugenicists insisted the state faced a biological crisis but they disagreed on the solution. Between 1914 and 1925 they diverged into two camps. One favored confinement and sexual segregation of the "unfit." That group advanced some of its goals. The other still clung to Gideon Lincecum's purifying knife as the instrument of salvation. The latter group found only frustration.

More Legislative Futility

In 1913, the Texas legislature considered a bill introduced by Representative Daniel F. Parker from Calvert, a town of fewer than 2,600 people in the middle of cotton country in south-central Texas. Parker's bill provided for the creation of a two-person medical commission with the power to order "the sterilization of certain classes of citizens and degenerates," including the "insane" and "criminally insane," male and female, "thereby preventing the reproduction of their species." The bill generated "a more intense general interest . . . than has been shown in many other measures before the Legislature," the *Marshall Messenger* reported on March 11, 1913. The *Messenger* said that a majority in the state house opposed the measure when first introduced. But after lawmakers narrowed the list of potential sterilization targets to exclude a broad category of convicted criminals, and following rousing speeches by Parker and William Lewis Hill of Huntsville in favor of the bill, momentum shifted toward passage. Only William Benjamin Goodner, a doctor from Dublin in Central Texas, spoke in opposition. The bill then advanced to the state senate, where an amended version provided for sterilization of "lunatics, epileptics, and syphilitics."[11]

A senate committee reported on the legislation favorably, but the bill died when it reached the full chamber. Several senators believed that the proposal was immoral and represented a governmental overreach even as they derided the hubris of scientists. Wright Morrow of Hillsboro, the senate president pro tempore, deemed the law "contrary to the spirit of the constitution in that it gives to a commission of two specialists the power intended by the organic law to be exercised by a jury of one's peers." Senator Ed Westbrook of Sherman worried about the growing power doctors held over public policy. He "argued that the medical community has already usurped more public functions than are good for the general welfare," the *Houston Post* reported. Clinton Nugent of Conroe pointed out that the condition of a mentally disturbed person might improve but too late to reverse a permanent physical mutilation. "[T]he bill seeks to take away an inalienable right from the individual," the *Post* wrote, paraphrasing Nugent's argument. "[T]he operation might often be performed on persons who would later regain their normal selves." Homer Brelsford of Eastland zeroed in on the arrogance of the eugenics enterprise. Brelsford pointed out that the medical wisdom and knowledge of the present day quickly fades into quaint obsolescence. "The scientist of today is the tyro [novice] of tomorrow," he said, arguing that doctors in the future might be able to cure intended targets of the sterilization bill. Brelsford and his allies prevailed. The state senate rejected the bill, fourteen votes to eleven. The change of just two votes might have inaugurated a campaign of forced sterilization in Texas such as the one that scarred and mutilated tens of thousands of Americans in other states across the country in the coming decades.[12]

In its May 3, 1913, issue, the *Lancet-Clinic* medical journal expressed dismay at the move by the Texas senate. Ignoring the substantial arguments made against the bill, the Cincinnati-based publication ridiculed politicians for being uninformed rubes oblivious to cutting-edge science. "We ought not to expect too much from our legislatures as at present constituted, but it would seem to be a reasonable proposition that they allow themselves to be guided by expert opinion in technical matters," the *Lancet-Clinic* complained. The medical journal made light of a state senator who described coerced vasectomies as "cruel and unusual punishment" and therefore "unconstitutional." The *Clinic-Lancet* then endorsed an editorial in the *Texas Medical Journal* underscoring "the necessity of some effort to arrest this deluge of idiots, imbeciles, lunatics, epileptics and hereditary and confirmed criminals."[13]

Continued Barriers to Texas Eugenics in the Early Twentieth Century

Brelsford and like-minded state senators were not alone. The eugenics movement in Texas and other former Confederate states faced a considerable political obstacle. "The institution of eugenics in the South created a particular problem for conservatives, in part because of its progressive nature," as literary scholar Betsy Nies suggests. "Progressives emphasized the authority of the state over the family." Eugenicists proposed shifting care of children with disabilities from extended family networks to state institutions, which Nies said southerners perceived as "an intrusion of northern mores . . . Southerners had a history of keeping the mentally and physically challenged at home." Although the sponsor of the bill, Parker, came from a rural house district, senators from farming regions also formed the most outspoken opposition to the 1913 sterilization bill. They might support policies that made life harder for the poor, but such senators won votes posing as voices for the downtrodden hewers of wood and tillers of soil. That image proved hard to reconcile with the eugenicists' blunt appraisal that "poor whites were as degenerate as Blacks." The Jim Crow regime rested on an artificial white racial solidarity across class lines posed against an imagined threat of "Black rule." Eugenicists, however, fragmented white identity into the fit and the unfit, the truly white and lesser, not-quite whites. The planter elite and their voices in the Texas legislature demonized urban sophisticates, their supposed decadence, and their "godless" ideas like evolution and adjacent concepts such as eugenics in order to forge a phony agrarian solidarity. Rural districts, chronically overrepresented in the state legislature in the twentieth century, held the power to stymie much of the urban Progressive agenda.[14]

The 1913 bill also failed by a razor's margin because eugenicists suffered (like the Progressive movement as a whole) from the "comparatively small size of the region's urban middle class and the feebleness of its professional organizations and educational institutions," as Larson wrote of the Deep South. "Elsewhere in the country, for example, progressives relied heavily on the scientific and social-scientific expertise provided by leading universities. This approach proved less effective in the Deep South."[15]

No matter how widely their ideas were discussed and even accepted, Texas eugenicists could not shake their image as strangers in a strange land. After F. E. Daniel died, the most notable advocates of the eugenics movement in Texas were often outsiders, such as Julian Huxley from England or Hermann Joseph Muller from New York. "[S]outhern eugenicists were cast in the role of missionaries preaching a foreign gospel in hostile territory because even eugenicists who hailed from the South typically stood apart both as members of the region's small professional class or its beleaguered Progressive minority and as zealots of a new, scientific doctrine that had originally developed elsewhere and that still flourished outside the region," Larson said. Rural backlash against arrogant urbanites formed a substantial barrier to the movement's success.[16]

Left Behind: The Spread of Eugenics Outside of Texas

Six more states implemented sterilization laws between Daniel's death in 1914 and 1920: Nebraska (1915), New Hampshire, South Dakota, and Oregon (all in 1917), and North Carolina and Alabama (both in 1919). The latter two stood as the first states to pass sterilization laws in the old Confederacy. By 1920, eighteen of the forty-eight states included such statutes in their law books.[17] Eugenics mostly staggered in the vast American Southwest. New Mexico joined Texas in never passing a sterilization law. Eventually thirty-two states legalized sterilization; in per capita sterilizations,

Arizona ranked twenty-ninth. California proved an exception, becoming a national eugenics leader. It ranked first in the number of coerced sterilizations performed (at least 20,108) and third in per capita operations (one sterilization out of every 526 residents) through 1980. About one-third of the known victims subjected to coerced sterilizations in the entire nation underwent operations at the hands of California doctors.[18]

As in all the states along the southern border with Mexico, California Anglos grew up with a sense of their racial destiny as conquerors of what they claimed were "lesser" peoples, a posture that became known in the nineteenth century as "Manifest Destiny." As was the case with Arizona, New Mexico, Texas, and the rest of the West, many Californians saw themselves as part of a new civilization, "a refuge from the problems of the Gilded Age, a place free of urban slums, machine politics," as a historian of the region, Jason E. Pierce, said. Westerners generally shared a sense of the exceptionalism so famously associated with Texans. "Those who made it to the West, whether native-born or foreign, represented the best of the best, the bravest, the fittest, most energetic examples of humanity," Pierce wrote.[19]

Unable to resolve the relationship between heredity and environment, some eugenicists pointed to the challenging, supposedly unsettled environment in what was once known as the "Great American Desert" as a crucible that forged racial greatness. Charles Davenport certainly saw that as true of the Anglo conquest of the Southwest, insisting that migrations have "a profound eugenic significance. The most active, ambitious, and courageous blood migrates. It migrated to America and has made her what she has become; in America another selection took place in the western migration, and what this blood—this *crème de la crème*—did in the West all the world knows."[20]

A historian of California eugenics, Alexandra Stern, points out unique features of California history that explain the vast differences in the history of the movement there and in other southwestern states. Agriculture formed a major part of the economy in both Texas and California, but the latter state took a significant lead in the science of crop production. Among intellectuals, "hereditarianism . . . ran exceptionally deep." Horticulturalists like Luther Burbank and Joseph P. Widney applied sophisticated methods of selective breeding to dramatically enhance crop production, providing a model for scientifically planned human reproduction. While a vicious attack on higher education unfolded in Texas, in California, "[b]y the 1910s, a dynamic network of scientists, reformers, and professionals were consolidating and launching eugenics projects and endeavoring to make hereditarianism integral to the state's priorities and practices."[21]

If Texas disdained the intellectuals at its universities and colleges, California celebrated them, including eugenicists. "California eugenicists were players on the national scene from the outset," Stern points out. Burbank, a prominent American botanist from Santa Rosa, and David Starr Jordan, the founding president of Stanford University, both became leaders of the pioneering American eugenics organization, the American Breeders' Association, established by Davenport in 1906. By the 1920s, California could boast several active, influential pro-eugenics civic organizations, such as the California Division of the American Eugenics Society. "[U]nlike other Western states . . . California possessed a dense and multilayered matrix of educational organizations, civic groups, business associations, medical societies, and philanthropies that subscribed to eugenic philosophies," Stern wrote.[22] Numerous Californians became national leaders of the eugenics movement: Jordan, Lewis Terman (who led the campaign to get intelligence tests administered to students across the United States), and Paul Popenoe. The latter, an expert in plant heredity, became one of the most significant popularizers of eugenics in his position as a columnist for the *Ladies' Home Journal*.[23] California eugenicists achieved the Texas movement's wildest dreams in an atmosphere that cultivated their talents and loudly trumpeted their ideas.

Captive Audiences: Eugenics in the American Classroom

Eugenics joined reading, writing, and arithmetic in school curricula across the nation. Pro-eugenics textbooks became standard course material in public school and college biology courses. In 1914 George William Hunter authored *A Civic Biology: Presented in Problems*, a text that accused unfit families in the United States of "spreading disease, immorality, and crime to all parts of the country."[24] Between 1914 and the 1940s, Texas followed the national trend and incorporated eugenics into public school lessons.

The Dallas school board first adopted a pro-eugenics textbook, *New Biology* by W. M. Smallwood, Ida L. Reveley, and Guy A. Bailey, on March 1,

1926, and stuck with it for more than a decade. "There are two ways of bringing about human progress," the authors stated in the 1924 edition. "The first is by improving the environment, the second consists of seeking a better inheritance with which to begin life. This is called eugenics."[25] The authors lengthened the section on eugenics from two to four pages from the 1924 to the 1934 edition. In the latter version, students were taught that only certain members of the human family had contributed significantly to human progress. "Men living in the temperate regions have contributed most to our modern civilization," the authors insisted in the conclusion of their section on human biology, a supposition that portrayed whites as the nearly exclusive authors of progress.[26]

As a cautionary tale, *New Biology* told the then-famous and widely believed saga of a tragic American family, the Kallikaks. A psychologist and preeminent eugenicist, Henry H. Goddard, spun a terrifying tale about an extended family he supposedly discovered while treating a woman, Emma Wolverton, at the New Jersey Home for the Education and Care of Feeble-Minded Children. Goddard, an acclaimed expert on intelligence, gave the clan a fictitious name, Kallikak, a blend of the Greek word for "beauty" (*kallos*) and bad (*kakos*). Goddard reported he had traced Wolverton's ancestry to a successful aristocrat from the time of the American Revolution who had an affair with a "feeble-minded tavern wench" whom he abandoned after impregnating. The gentleman, however, later married a "worthy Quakeress" and raised a second family. The descendants of the first woman produced a long line of alcohol-dependent criminals and those Goddard disdained as sexual deviants, while the latter produced a family composed "wholly of upstanding citizens." Goddard's influential 1912 illustrated book *The Kallikaks: A Study in the Heredity of Feeblemindedness* involved sloppy research methods, including imprecise tracing of the two Kallikak family lines.[27] In addition to sharing the cautionary tale of the Kallikaks, *New Biology* taught Dallas students that not just intellect, but traits like honesty and a work ethic were inborn. "[General] ability and a tendency to industry and thrift are qualities that can be inherited," the authors said. "The men and women who possess such mental traits carry on the business of the country and pay taxes, not only to support the government, but also to care for the idle, the shiftless, and the criminal."[28] Those thought to be born to shiftlessness thus represented an unfair burden on the eugenically healthy. Such lessons spanned the curriculum, appearing in not just biology classes, but also in history, geography, and literature courses.

A Fundamentally Selfish Disposition: Eugenics in Higher Education

By the second decade of the twentieth century, top universities and colleges offered eugenics classes, with courses on the subject taught at Harvard, Northwestern, Princeton, Stanford, Yale, the University of California at Berkeley, and the University of Chicago. By 1897, the University of Texas had appointed its first eugenicist to the faculty, Alexander Caswell Ellis (1871–1948). Ellis started as an adjunct professor of pedagogy in 1897, but he moved up, serving as a professor of education philosophy from 1908 to 1926. A native of North Carolina who received his doctorate from Clark University in Worcester, Massachusetts, Ellis devoted much of his thought to the presence of good and evil in humans and how that shaped the way individuals learn. Ellis taught his students that modern humans were deeply shaped by their animal past and that the primitive instincts necessary to survival in distant yesterdays had to be suppressed in children today in order for the advance of civilization to continue.[29]

"Characteristics that in one stage of human development were necessary and good, may from the changes in a later and higher stage of development be then bad." Ellis wrote in his dissertation, "Suggestions for a Philosophy of Education." "[I]f there be any truth in the doctrines of heredity and in the evolutionary theory of the fierce and selfish struggle for existence in past ages of development, then man has inherited a disposition that is . . . fundamentally selfish . . . These facts can hardly be denied."[30] Ellis saw the mission of twentieth-century "advanced" civilizations as taming the beast within each person and preventing those lacking such advanced traits from ruining all that preceding generations had painstakingly built.

Humans were evolving upward, he said, but such progress could not be taken for granted. The threat that humanity might revert to a more primitive state loomed large in the eugenicist imagination. Ellis believed that professors and public school teachers had an obligation to tamp down the baser instincts of their students."[T]he educator, knowing the history of the race and the laws of heredity must ever watch the outcrop of those hereditary tendencies that belong to an age gone by and point to a reversion, or to a regression, from the present high scale of being," Ellis wrote.[31]

UT political science professor Lindley M. Keasbey (1867–1946) also advocated eugenics. A graduate of Columbia Law School and the School of Political Science, Keasbey imbibed socialist politics during his postdoctoral studies in Berlin and Strasbourg.[32] Keasbey became popular among students and the sponsor of the Economic and Political Science Association at the school while achieving influence beyond his discipline. He delivered a paper, "Competition," at the 1907 American Sociological Association in which he compared natural selection (not only between species but within species) to economic competition among modern humans. He argued that just as biological inequality could be eliminated through selective breeding, economic inequality could be eliminated through the provision of free land to the rural poor.[33] Poverty, physical disabilities, and intellectual impairment could all be overcome through science, he contended.

Keasbey's life also provided one of many examples of how the state's disregard for academic freedom and its fierce skepticism of intellectuals thwarted advocates of selective breeding. In 1908, the *Bulletin of the University of Texas* published a Keasbey paper on biology and competition. The same year, a former student accused the professor of indoctrinating his students with socialism, a charge made in a letter to Governor Thomas M. Campbell and passed on to UT president David F. Houston and the UT board of regents. Keasbey denied the accusation, but in spite of students who jumped to his defense and called him their favorite professor, the university removed him from his political science professorship and appointed him the chair of a just-established Institutional History Department. A scholar might reasonably fear that commenting on any public controversies, including whether the state should impose sterilization on certain citizens, could prove dangerous to one's career and might prefer, instead, to avoid any political advocacy.[34]

Eugenics in Texas Popular Culture

If Lincecum and Daniel mostly shared their ideas with their educated peers, Ellis saw the world as his classroom. He tirelessly and happily delivered his message regarding eugenics, and his general educational philosophy, wherever he could find an audience. From 1926 to 1941, Ellis taught at Cleveland College in Ohio, an adult education program affiliated with

Western Reserve University. In 1940, the year before Ellis returned to the University of Texas, *Skyline*, a Cleveland College publication, paid glowing tribute to his devotion to sharing his hotly contested worldview with the masses. "He talked about it to waitresses in the restaurants and to companions during intermission at the symphony," the article noted. "He expounded from any platform offered him and over the air. He wrote articles for newspapers and magazines. He purchased space in the daily papers."[35]

In his speeches, Ellis tried to make all, regardless of his estimation of their worth, stakeholders in the eugenic enterprise. The gifted, Ellis argued, created jobs through their innovation and their profit-expanding efficiency. Quoting a T. W. Carson, Ellis called for the selective breeding of biologically "superior" workers. "The limiting factor in the expansion of industry is seldom the lack of unskilled workers; it is invariably the lack of high-grade men," Ellis quoted Carson in another scribbled note he wrote while preparing a speech. "To reverse this limiting factor, therefore requires that men of the highest grade should be multiplied, if that is possible. If that can be done, it will make more jobs for men in the lower grades."[36]

The audience for eugenical ideas reached an exponentially growing audience in Texas, even casting its shadow over entertainment. An infamous eugenicist who euthanized a baby with life-threatening disabilities played a character based on himself in a silent film shown across Texas in 1917. *The Black Stork* screened at the Crystal Theater in Dallas and other venues. It gained wide press coverage and played for weeks in Fort Worth and elsewhere in the state. *The Black Stork* contended that euthanasia of infants in some circumstances becomes a moral necessity. The film was based on the "Bollinger Baby" case in Chicago. On November 12, 1915, Dr. Harry Haiselden decided that a baby born to Anna Bollinger, who apparently lacked part of his neck and was diagnosed by Haiselden as suffering severe mental disabilities, should not receive surgeries needed for survival. Haiselden directed that the newborn be placed in a bare room, exposed and left without care. The district attorney in Cook County declined to bring murder charges against Haiselden, who became a public advocate for euthanasia as a legitimate option for doctors confronting patients with serious physical vulnerabilities. After briefly achieving celebrity, Haiselden fell from public view, and in April 1919 he immigrated to Cuba, where he faced accusations that he performed medical experiments on nonconsenting patients. He died of a cerebral hemorrhage in June 1919.[37]

Haiselden agreed to portray Dr. Horace L. Dickey, a pro-eugenics physician, in the movie *The Black Stork*, later distributed as *Are You Fit to Marry?* In the film, a man hides from his fiancée his family story, based on the already well-worn Kallikak fable. His bride gives birth to a baby with disabilities. One doctor offers to perform life-saving surgery on the infant while another, played by Haiselden, volunteers to perform euthanasia. The mother has a vison of her child growing up, cruelly shunned by his peers, unable to find love, and murdering the doctor who saved his life but condemned him to misery. After being released from prison, he lives in poverty and fathers a large family of children missing limbs and battling other physical challenges. Awakening from this nightmare, the mother asks for her baby to be put to sleep.[38]

The film screened at the Texas Theater in Austin October 25–26, 1917, and it convinced a journalist in the capital city of its central thesis, that marriage and childbearing by the "unfit" should be prevented by any means necessary. "There can be no doubt of the interest the picture will arouse, both because of the theme and because of the wide publicity the doctor and the story [of Haiselden] . . . have received," the journalist wrote. "And the production will doubtless satisfy the audiences it attracts since it argues the case well and fulfills its purpose."[39]

Newspaper advertisements promoting the movie featured Dr. Haiselden's name prominently. An advertisement in the *Fort Worth Record* advised audiences to "Come to the matinee if it is possible, and avoid the night rush." The October release apparently drew large enough audiences that it still played in Fort Worth as of November 4. Ads for the film warned Laredo audiences that "Every man, every woman, must fear the danger of 'THE BLACK STORK.'"[40]

Better Babies and Fitter Families in Texas

To further spread warnings of impending racial doom, eugenics supporters staged better baby and fitter family contests across the country. Often sponsored by groups like the American Eugenics Society, such contests often featured display boards that "revealed with flashing lights that every fifteen seconds a hundred dollars of your money went for the care of persons with bad heredity, that every forty-eight seconds a mentally deficient person was born in the United States, and that only every seven and a half minutes did the United States enjoy the birth of 'a high-grade person.'"[41]

Texans flocked to such exhibits. The Texas Congress of Mothers often sponsored these events even as the University of Texas's Home, Child, and Welfare Division provided assistance in staging them. Audiences of thousands attended better baby contests in Austin, Fort Worth, Houston, Longview, Marshall, Mineral Wells, San Antonio, and other locations. At a 1914 better baby contest at the State Fair of Texas in Dallas, parents willingly subjected 500 babies to a battery of tests, including skull measurements, conducted by doctors. According to one reporter, examiners documented "the most minute defect physically or mentally as to even consider the finger dimensions and maturity of hair and the like" at the Pure Food and Better Babies Exposition in Dallas in May 1914. Even as the owners of "cattle, chickens and pigs" earned blue ribbons elsewhere on the fairgrounds, parents could win $15 for having the "best" child, any class, and $5 for the best twins and triplets.[42] The white, blond offspring of elite families who prevailed at the better baby contests at the Texas state fair met eugenicists' ideal Nordic profile. Ellis spoke at the 1914 better baby contest at Fair Park in Dallas. As was his style, he opened by flattering the crowd, insisting that, "Texas babies are better babies than the babies of any other state," before he "lightly touched on eugenics."[43]

Such contests continued into the 1930s. Mary T. Watts of the National Eugenics Society, described by the *Dallas Morning News* as the founder of the "better babies" movement, arrived in the city to launch a "Fitter Families" contest during the state fair in October 1924 to "interest people in racial betterment and stronger and more virile families." Faculty from the Southern Methodist University psychology department administered a battery of "physical and psychological tests." A Texas A&M College geneticist made presentations on "inheritability and family trait features."[44] Dr. H. L. Gosline, the Dallas Child Guidance Center's director and psychiatrist-in-chief, told a *Morning News* reporter that "[h]uman characteristics are inherited in exactly the same manner and proportion as they are in guinea pigs . . . With this in mind, it is the aim of the fitter families contests to create interest in better quality children."[45]

The Ableist Gaze

Intentionally or not, the better baby and fitter family contestants provided a sharp contrast to those fair exhibitors demeaned "human oddities," often men and women of color, presented for entertainment at the Texas state fair's so-called freak shows. Fairs and circuses across the state displayed these people, including those with disabilities or representatives of allegedly "primitive cultures," like zoo animals. White supremacist ideas saturated such amusements. The shows served to make their white middle-class and working-class audiences revel in a shared certainty about their superiority to the people humiliated on stage and to fear their propagation.

From the early 1890s through the first decade of the twentieth century, African American conjoined twins Millie and Christine, alternately identified as "Millie Christine," drew crowds at the segregated state fair. The women had four arms and four legs but shared a torso and amazed audiences as one twin spoke French and the other German. The twins musically accompanied each other, singing in alto and soprano simultaneously, and danced to polka music.[46] These exhibits encouraged white spectators to suspect that those of African descent carried not just bad blood but remained stuck in an earlier stage of evolution. The 1907 Texas state fair featured a "freak captured in the hinterland of South Africa" with "a face in every detail similar to a monkey" and "feet and hands . . . long and monkey-like."[47]

From the earliest days of the state fair, Black and Brown people were depicted as "savages" and intentionally displayed like gorillas and chimpanzees in inauthentic dioramas. In some cases, such exhibits featured performances by African Americans garbed as the show's white producers imagined the peoples of Africa and the South Pacific dressed. In 1894, a replica of a Dahomey settlement drew visitors to the fair midway. "You can form some sort of idea of how they live in 'darkest Africa,' if you visit the Dahomey Village in the rear of the race course grand stand," a Texas newspaper promised. Spectators could watch Africans performing on "quaint and peculiar musical instruments" as they played "war songs . . . not so entrancing to the cultivated ear as a Strauss waltz." Among the inhabitants of the temporary Dahomean village was "the only cannibal child born in the United States," given the name of "Texas." Readers were told that the tribe deferred to local laws and did not nourish the youngster with human fluids but on chicken blood. The 1905 fair starred thirty-two supposed members of the Bontoc Igorrote (Igorot) nation from the far northern part of the Philippines. At the fair, they dwelled in a duplication of a native village dubious in accuracy, and stood scantily clad. The Igorrotes practiced throwing spears and supposedly dined on dogs for their evening meal in front of fascinated and horrified white audiences. The *Dallas Morning News* left readers with the impression that Igorrotes were immune to new ideas. "It is said that the Igorrotes have made no progress in civilization since their arrival in America, the education advantages of the great land failing to wholly influence them, and that they will appear at the State Fair in their original savage state, dog-eating custom and all."[48] The Igorrotes' scripted primitiveness, according to local newspapers, extended to homicidal behavior. "In the party will be three or four famous chiefs, each with a record as a head hunter," the *Dallas Morning News* promised when the "tribe" was scheduled to return to the city in 1907.[49]

Ticket buyers received clear warnings that unregulated human reproduction led to disability and that darker people in particular tended toward biological "defect." The Sells-Floto Circus toured Texas in the early twentieth century, including shows in Dallas. Late in the second decade of the twentieth century, a Texas railroad worker named Pasqual Pinon, billed as the "two-headed Mexican," joined the troupe. He claimed to be a refugee from Mexico's 1910–20 violent revolution. He appeared to have a second, smaller face with a nose and immobile eyes and a mouth growing out of his forehead. Carnival barkers told audiences that his second head at one point could speak but that the face eventually lost the ability to move. One writer contends that Pinon was a phony whose second face was a large tumor outfitted with prosthetics. Others claimed that a makeup artist created a fake head Pinon attached to his scalp.[50]

A thirty-five-year-old "Australian Wild Girl" exhibited in 1894 weighed only thirty-five pounds and had a "head smaller than any ordinary baby's." A "Professor Fowler" pronounced her "the missing link in Darwin's theory between man and brute creation."[51] Using callous, dehumanizing language, the State Fair of Texas and similar extravaganzas routinely presented non-whites as "misshapen," small-brained, "wild," impulsive, impervious to progress, and as headhunters and cannibals. Fairgoers were presented two alternative futures: a world filled with the

alleged human near-perfection at the better baby and fitter families contests, and one populated by the supposed human "horrors" on the midway.

"Saved Through Child-Bearing": Black Eugenics in Texas

White eugenicists routinely degraded African Americans, ranking them
the lowest when comparing the intellects of racial groups. African American elites, however, turned out to be surprisingly ambivalent about eugenics. Black leaders themselves worried about the survival of their community
and considered steps to forestall extinction. Concerned, on the one hand,
that their numbers would drop through Black immigration to perceived
safe harbors such as Liberia, at the same time they acknowledged the attri-
tion within their community caused by white violence (such as in the
repeated public spectacle of lynching), mass imprisonment, and poverty.
Fisk University professor Eugene Harris bemoaned that too many Black
women bore only two or three children, "considerably less that it ought to
be," while too many engaged in the "crime of mothers" by having abortions.
Some Black thought leaders worried that homosexuality and masturbation
within their community diverted sexual energy from the imperative to
reproduce. A growing number of African Americans formulated their own
version of eugenics, believing that the survival of their community depended
on not just the quantity of Black babies, but the quality. Community leaders
educated Black parents about the need for healthy food and exercise for
developing children, and the importance of carefully screened romantic
partners as a means of upgrading the Black race.[52]

In a 1903 essay, W. E. B. Du Bois, one of the preeminent intellectual
forces of the twentieth century, articulated his vision of how African
Americans would rise from a past shaped by slavery, poverty, and white
racial violence. In his essay "The Talented Tenth," Du Bois embraced a
decidedly elitist vision of racial uplift. Du Bois did not foresee the Black
freedom struggle triumphing at the behest of the masses.[53] In his "Talented Tenth" essay, he declared, "The Negro race, like all races, is going to
be saved by its exceptional men. The problem of education, then, among
Negroes must first of all deal with the Talented Tenth; it is the problem of
developing the Best of this race that they may guide the Mass away from
the contamination and death of the Worst, in their own and other races."[54]

Du Bois also saw the Talented Tenth as a bulwark against the "submerged tenth," which he demonized as "criminals, prostitutes, and loafers."[55] Du Bois rejected the idea of white supremacy, but believed that society would be best served by increased reproduction on the part of the biologically and intellectually gifted of all races and reduced fertility among the eugenically degenerate to be found in all colors. Du Bois also believed that part of the African American race had been polluted by white rapists who had produced, with their African American victims, mixed-race children who biologically carried the criminal tendencies of their fathers. The NAACP's national field secretary, William P. Pickens, launched a campaign in the mid-1920s encouraging local NAACP chapters to hold baby contests that would serve three major purposes. First, entry fees for the contests would fund a political effort to end lynching in the United States. Second, proceeds from the contests would be spent to promote healthier care of babies in the Black community. Third, the baby contests would encourage the Talented Tenth to raise larger families.[56]

The Dallas Express, an African American newspaper, regularly mocked Nordicism—the idea popular among eugenicists that Nordics (those descended from northern Europeans) were superior not only to African Americans and other people of color but also to other Europeans.[57] It furthermore ridiculed the white panic over "race mixing." In a 1925 story, The *Express* derided the Virginia registrar of vital statistics, Dr. W. A. Plecker, who predicted that because of "miscegenation," in the year 2000 or 3000 "all of the inhabitants of America will be brown skinned." Plecker called for strict laws against interracial marriage across the country to preserve the white race. The *Express* pointed out that Nordic rapists of Black women, during slavery and afterward, had produced most of the United States' large mixed-race population. "[T]he freakish complexions and lightened skins of 'Negroes' . . . have resulted from the age long helplessness of the Negro woman and the attraction which they have seemingly held for the males of other bloods," the *Express* writer said. "It is not the fault of the Negro that the 'best blood' of America flows through the veins of so many of those who are now . . . classed [as Black.] . . . Let the laws protect Black women as well as others and there will be fewer mulattoes."[58]

The *Dallas Express* delighted in turning the racial hierarchy created by eugenicists upside down, sometimes suggesting there was scientific evidence of Black superiority. An April 18, 1925, story pointed out that African American test subjects during World War I withstood exposure to the poison gas "tetra-nitroaniline after NORDIC blonds and Jewish chemists had keeled over at a laboratory at Bound Brook, N.J." As the story noted, "the lightest skinned keeled over in a week, and were resuscitated with difficulty. It was found that the dark-skinned Negroes withstood the fumes and enabled the chemists to complete the experiment."[59]

The *Express* believed the story punched holes in contemporary racial theories. "[S]urely leading chemical experts of the country should feel much better now since they have gotten off their chests something about the 'superiority' of Negroes," the newspaper said.[60] The newspaper also delighted in using the language of eugenicists against them, employing the categories of mental disability coined by Henry H. Goddard to describe white criminals. "White Moron Admits Assault on Little Negro Girl," screamed a banner headline in the October 3, 1925 issue. (In the IQ scale developed in 1910 by psychologist Goddard, a eugenicist, so-called morons were those subjects with an IQ between 51–70 on the Stanford-Binet scale, "imbeciles" with an IQ between 26–50, and "idiots" an IQ score of 25 or below.)[61]

Meanwhile, the *Dallas Express* shared deep anxiety over Black fertility. African Americans shrank sharply as a percentage of the state population, from 20.4 percent of the total in 1900 to 15.9 percent in 1920, probably because of white and Mexican migration into the state in those two decades.[62] African Americans feared even greater political marginalization as their relative numbers declined.[63] Doctors' advertisements on improving fertility appeared frequently. One ad offered a free book by a "Dr. Burroughs, a graduate physician who has spent forty years treating women for diseases peculiar to their sex and in his book explains why so many married women have been denied the blessing of children—why they are broken down physically in early life." Another advertisement offered information on the fertility treatment "Steritone." The manufacturer insisted, "Every woman who wants to live a normal happy home life with little ones around her should consider it her first duty to find out what Steritone is."[64]

Even before the NAACP promoted similar events, the *Dallas Express* started holding "Better Baby" contests "[i]n the interest of better bred and cared for Negro babies in Dallas." In a contest the newspaper sponsored at the Pythian Temple from July 1–3, 1920, "a special corps of physicians and trained nurses will examine, weigh, and give instructions to mothers on the care and feeding of their babies," the *Express* promised. Mothers of "the healthiest, best developed babies" won prizes.[65]

Eugenics in Black Texas Literature

Some African American intellectuals in Texas, however, were concerned about which African Americans bore children, believing, as did Du Bois in the early twentieth century, that "among human races and groups, as among vegetables, quality and not mere quantity counts."[66] Eugenical ideas and anxieties about the worth of and dangers posed by the underclass appear in the writing of early twentieth-century author Sutton R. Griggs.

A novelist, author, political polemicist, and preacher born on June-teenth 1872 in Chatfield, Texas, and educated at Bishop College in Marshall, Griggs founded the American Baptist Theological Seminary in Nashville, Tennessee, and served as the school's first president from 1925 to 1926. Griggs began his political life as an advocate of Black separatism, articulated in his 1899 novel *Imperium in Imperio: A Study of the Negro Race*. In the novel, a secret African American society seeks to create an independent Black republic within the boundaries of the current United States. Griggs gradually transformed into a Booker T. Washington-style accommodationist who accepted segregation as a means to convince whites to accept and support Black economic progress. Though he spent little time in Texas during his prolific writing career, his ideas reflected attitudes held by some African American elites in the state during the early twentieth century.[67]

Independent, thoughtful, and creative, Griggs still suffered at the hands of what the historian Carter G. Woodson once famously characterized in 1933 as the "miseducation of the Negro" in the late nineteenth and early twentieth centuries. As Woodson noted, African American students suffered not only because of the segregated, underfunded, overcrowded, and poorly equipped Jim Crow schools, but also toxic ideas within the curricula offered Black students of the era. As Woodson pointed out, "the philosophy and ethics resulting from our education system have justified slavery, peonage, segregation, and lynching. The oppressor has the right to exploit, to handicap. Negroes daily educated in the tenets of such a religion of the strong have accepted the status of the weak as divinely ordained, and during the last three generations of their nominal freedom, they have done little to change it." While Woodson seriously underestimates the resistance African Americans offered to white supremacy, it is undeniable that they, like their lighter-skinned peers, were taught that only white people created technology and worthwhile culture and that Black people were at best apprentices at the feet of their smarter, more creative white superiors.[68]

Such attitudes appear in Griggs's works, such as when he referred to one of his grandfathers, born in Africa, as a "savage."[69] The Black separatism Griggs endorsed in his novel was, by definition, partly a eugenicist enterprise, providing not only an escape from white economic and political exploitation, but also sexual boundaries that would shield African American women from sexual pollution by the white criminal element.[70]

White racists heavily populated Griggs's novels and one of the most ominous is a mad scientist, a white eugenicist named Dr. Zackland who, in *Imperium in Imperio*, spies a brilliant African American, Belton Piedmont, at a train station. Zackland decides that he must study the body of Piedmont—"a fine specimen of physical manhood" with "limbs . . . well formed and proportioned and . . . as strong as oak." Zackland decides to dissect his prey, hoping to present parts of Belton to his medical colleagues during a lecture. Belton survives a lynching attempt and Zackland, unaware that his victim is still alive, seizes his body. Belton awakens on the dissection table and overpowers Zackland, fatally stabbing him and making an escape.[71]

Griggs's readers must approach his books with caution. He presents African Americans' ideological spectrum in the form of dialogues and it is not always clear which ideas expressed by his debating characters most closely resemble his own.[72] Yet, in spite of his gruesome depiction of white racial science, Griggs obviously accepts many premises of eugenicism. If he rejects white supremacy, he still views many of the poor as dysgenic and fears that Black women raped by the white underclass will produce inferior children. Some of his characters repeatedly worry about whether their blood has been permanently contaminated by sexual assaults upon their ancestors, and urge African Americans to take all means necessary to avoid race mixing. Griggs's novels featured some characters who advocated various schemes of selective breeding and some who called for interracial mating as a means of eliminating prejudice. Other Griggs characters, such as Letitia Gilbreath, a character in his last novel, *Pointing the Way*, encourage all African Americans to bear children with lighter-skinned Blacks in the hope of whitening the race. Gilbreath hopes this will reduce prejudice. Griggs did not accept such ideas, but that does not mean he was not deeply concerned about both the Black and white unfit.[73]

Griggs specifically rejected crossing the color line sexually. He advocated selective breeding for ability, believing that the path to a better future lay in the "better element" of the white population and "worthy" Negroes bearing larger families than the violent, lazy, immoral, and unintelligent of both races.[74] He also seems to have supported the idea of restricting voting to the "fit" of both races. His 1908 novel *Pointing the Way* depicts a white politician, Seth Molair, the mayor of the fictional town of Belrose, accepting that voting restrictions aimed at African Americans should be dropped because it is a racial insult to set a higher standard for Blacks than for whites. "Unqualified" whites, including many in the lower class, should also be disenfranchised, Molair suggests. The novel argues that the way forward to a better tomorrow is for quality whites and Blacks to make common cause against the unruly "lower" sorts. As critic Kenneth Warren suggests, Griggs seems to be arguing for an "interracial alliance of the better classes by making dead certain that there will be no challenge from below."[75]

Every Nation Dies of a Rotten Heart: Texas Religion and Eugenics

Religious life in the state remained in flux in the late nineteenth and early twentieth centuries. Controversies over institutional governance roiled denominations, and even conservative Protestants divided over the accelerating drive for a Prohibition amendment because of the concern some had about eroding the wall between church and state. Protestants split over eugenics for decades as well, and clerics stood on both sides of the intensifying divide regarding the new, faddish science. The papacy had opposed birth control for centuries, but only definitively opposed abortion in all cases in the nineteenth century. The Vatican remained uncertain about eugenics, but the Texas movement received support from one startling source, Catholic theologian Theodorus Laboure, an oblate of Mary Immaculate and professor at the Diocesan Seminary in San

Antonio. Laboure argued that in extreme cases, preventing the manifestly dangerous from having children represented a moral necessity, with the safety of society taking precedence over all other theological concerns.[76]

Laboure wrote, despite the long-standing ban by the Roman Catholic Church on contraception and on inflicting "grave" bodily mutilation, that performing sterilizations on criminals and the "sexually depraved" did not violate church law. "A grave mutilation may be lawfully effected by the public authority if it is a means morally necessary to the preservation of Society," Laboure argued in a printed debate on the ethics of state-imposed vasectomies that appeared in a 1911 edition of the *Ecclesiastical Review*. Laboure, who was ordained in 1906, insisted that legally imposed vasectomies could be morally justified in cases when a man "who does not want to submit his will to reasons of the moral order, who does not want to abstain from the act of generation, and who, on this account, is a peril to Society."[77]

Laboure had many critics within the Catholic Church, some of whom cited the church's moral doctrine that "it is never lawful to do evil in order that good may result therefrom."[78] Catholic doctrine condemning various voluntary forms of contraception date back to the third and fourth centuries. Catholics in the early twentieth century, however, did not always see the moral issues of contraception and eugenics as synonymous. Eugenical sterilization, Catholic defenders argued, aimed at preventing social evils such as rape and the spawning of future criminals. Ambivalence on the issue stemmed in part from the defensiveness of some Catholics in the late nineteenth and early twentieth century toward charges that the church was anti-science and also from an awareness of the increased economic stress experienced by large families in the industrial era.[79] Texas Catholics would eventually play a major role in the eugenics debate, but not as advocates. Once the Vatican clarified its opposition to coerced sterilization in 1930, the Catholic Church in Texas mounted a persistent Depression-era campaign against proposed sterilization laws.

Ever-splintering and fractious Protestants certainly did not speak with a united voice on eugenics. Southern Baptists, the state's largest religious denomination and about to become the politically dominant one, focused narrowly on Prohibition as they neared victory in banning alcohol. Eugenics did not emerge as a major topic in the *Baptist Standard*, a newspaper long published in Dallas. The *Standard* judged eugenics to be a less pressing issue than drinking, dancing, gambling, and other signs of modern moral decay. In 1923, however, the *Standard* positively reviewed a eugenicist book, *If America Fail: Our National Mission and Our Possible Future* by Samuel Zane Batten, a Baptist minister from New Jersey. In *If America Fail*, Batten repeatedly cites Charles Davenport and predicts an inevitable clash of races on American soil.[80]

Largely secular, and sometimes assertively atheist, the eugenics movement nevertheless recognized the power of religion in early twentieth-century America. The American Eugenics Society (AES) devised an audacious plan for outreach to people of faith. The AES Committee on Cooperation with Clergymen (CCC) launched its sermon contest in 1926, with preachers, rabbis, priests, and divinity students all eligible to compete. Prizes ranged from $100 (about $1,680 now, adjusted for inflation) for third place to $500 (about $8,400 today) for first place. The only condition required that entrants had to deliver a sermon on the topic, "Religion and Eugenics: Does the Church Have Any Responsibility for Improving the Human Stock?" The committee distributed *A Eugenics Catechism* to clergymen from coast to coast, seeking to prove that eugenics science upheld biblical principles. The publication included a questions and answers section with the following entries:

Q: Does eugenics contradict the Bible?
A: *The Bible is one of the finest eugenics books. The connection of most of the great men mentioned therein with great families is carefully recorded . . .*
Q: What is the most precious thing in the world?
A: *The human germ plasm.*

Clergy, overwhelmingly Protestant but a few rabbis as well, submitted about two hundred sermons to the CCC the contest's first year.[81]

A. F. Cunningham, a Presbyterian minister who at times lived in Austin and Temple in Central Texas, submitted an entry.[82] He delivered a sermon titled "Eugenics or the Young Man Foursquare" at commencement ceremonies at Burnet High School in Central Texas on May 11, 1926. Cunningham campaigned for eugenics tirelessly, delivering versions of his talk in fifteen other Texas towns and three in Oklahoma. "Foursquare" referred to the physical, mental, moral, and spiritual health of any good

American. Cunningham urged his young audience to consider the good of the race and the nation when they chose romantic partners. He reminded them of the dangers women faced when they gave birth. "[E]very time the woman goes down into the valley of the shadow of death in order that a man-child might be born into the world, she has a right to demand of the father of that child, a child that is free from disease, deformity, and degeneracy," Cunningham said. "[A]nd the child has a right to be well-born, to demand from both mother and father a clean, healthy body with which to enter the world."[83]

Future parents, Cunningham told high school students, had a moral obligation to learn all they could about eugenic principles. As he wrote: "If we are to eliminate our insane asylums; if we are to reduce the institutions for the feeble-minded; if we are to eradicate illiteracy from our land and country; if we are to produce a race of high thinkers and intellectual peers who will solve the problems of the day and of life, we must not only have institutions of learning, but also have new standards and values of education, and new legislation that will prevent the reproduction of imbeciles."[84]

The sermon did not earn Cunningham a prize in the AES contest, and over the years judges generally felt cold about the entries. One judge, Dallas Short, complained, "The lack of originality both in matter and manner is rather appalling." The AES effort to recruit pastors as part of a eugenics army faltered. When financial contributions to the AES dwindled during the Depression, so too did financial support for the sermon contest. "By 1938, the AES still had not paid the prize money to the winners of the 1930 sermon contest," Christine Rosen, an historian of the relationship between eugenics and American religion, wrote.[85]

"Where Girls Go Right": Eugenics and the Gainesville School for Girls

On the surface, eugenics appeared to be a movement of, by, and for men, but women played a significant role in advancing the cause. Across the country, many early twentieth-century feminists (most famously Margaret Sanger) supported sterilization laws along with suffrage and access to birth control.[86] Carrie Weaver Smith (1885–1942) became one of the few women eugenicists to gain a position of power and influence in Texas and achieved national acclaim along the way.

Smith, born in Fayetteville, Georgia, came from the kind of distinguished lineage eugenicists hoped to make common in the world. Smith's grandfather taught classics at Emory University, her father earned stature as a Methodist minister, and her mother taught music. Orphaned and raised by more distant relatives, at age ten she decided to chase a rarely realized dream for young women, becoming a doctor. With a brilliant mind but unfocused intellectual interests, Smith took longer to realize her ambitions than she initially hoped. Fascinated by both medicine and in missionary work, she attended La Grange Female College in Georgia and then Scarritt Bible and Training School in Kansas City, Missouri, which had a nursing program, but she did not finish her medical training. She took up studying Hebrew rather than taking the math and science courses needed to become a physician. Although she wanted to preach the gospel in China, her rebelliousness got in the way of her career plans, and not for the last time. She earned a degree from Women's Medical College in Philadelphia in 1910, and interned at Worcester Memorial Hospital in Massachusetts, but "because of her so-called unorthodox beliefs concerning the church, she was rejected for work in the missionary field," according to an early biographer. Smith first gained the attention of the wider world when the Dallas-based Virginia K. Johnson Home and Training School hired her as a doctor tending the young residents. The Johnson Home aimed to rehabilitate wayward young women between the ages of twelve and twenty-five "to whom all doors are closed, frequently the doors of their own homes . . . saving them from utter despair and a greater sin and deeper degradation."[87]

The center, located in Dallas's Oak Cliff neighborhood, gave in-residence training and counseling for up to two hundred women, often unwed and pregnant, and taught its residents office skills, homemaking, and religious instruction. Smith decided that the limited intellectual stimulation and the penal atmosphere of the Johnson Home would not provide real redemption. Smith rethought the approach of such institutions, calling for juveniles gone astray to be given more access to the larger world and greater exposure to the arts and other intellectual stimulation. She also wanted to eliminate corporal punishment for girl "delinquents." Her ideas on the origins of criminality received national attention, with the Social Hygiene Association of New York asking her to put together an exhibit about juvenile crime for the 1915 Panama-Pacific International Exposition in San Francisco.[88]

Because of Smith's growing national reputation, Texas in 1916 appointed her the first director of the newly established Gainesville School for Girls in far northeast Texas. She saw her new job as an opportunity to not only promote more humane treatment of juvenile offenders, but also to advance eugenics policies. Smith's rehabilitation methods stood in sharp contrast to prevailing norms at Texas state schools. Before construction of the Gainesville school had been completed, Smith prepared by inspecting the Dallas County Industrial Girls Home. She discovered that the girls there suffered from hookworm due to the tainted meat fed them and that attendants disciplined the children with chains and whips.[89]

Other Texas facilities for girl delinquents offered even more nightmarish scenes. In 1911, the Texas Board of Prison Commissioners established Goree Prison Farm, an unprofitable 1,000-acre state-owned planation near Huntsville. There, young imprisoned African American and white women tended corn, cotton, sugarcane, and other crops in the blazing sun. Black girls faced frequent beatings and rape by guards. Smith inspected the site in 1916, the same year she was appointed in Gainesville. There she visited with a "fifteen year old child who, at eleven years of age, had received a sentence of forty years." Smith observed that, "The negro women were sleeping in a dormitory where beds were one foot apart, [and] an open unscreened toilet was in this dormitory." In the dining room, she saw pulleys suspended from the ceiling. Guards handcuffed inmates who misbehaved from the "torture instrument." Smith asked a guard, "Do you allow the women to keep their feet on the floor?" He said, "That depends on how mean they've been," a reply she recalled, "burned into my brain."[90]

The Gainesville School for Girls sat on 160 rural acres sixty-seven miles north of Dallas. It subjected new arrivals to close physical examinations. Half of the teenagers suffered from venereal disease. Once Smith took over, she ran a program that one social work publication, *The Survey*, described as "where girls go right." The school housed a tough crowd—youths Smith described as "the children of squatters" who came from "shotgun houses" and "covered wagons," distinguished by "moral and physical filth." Often raped by male relatives, the girls grew up in households marked by substance abuse. One girl told Smith she was used to "having half a pint of whiskey and two packages of Camels [cigarettes] a day." Many never had a room to themselves until the courts dispatched them to Gainesville, where they encountered comfortable, stylish furniture and a Victrola phonograph that played classical and religious music.[91]

Smith banned corporal punishment. The Gainesville girls received a local charter from the Girl Scouts of America, and members quickly earned more than three hundred merit badges. The Gainesville girls played sports like basketball and tennis. To instill discipline, Smith made the inmates wear uniforms and kept them to a schedule. Girls learned stenography, bookkeeping, and other stereotypically "feminine" skills, but also went on numerous field trips, such as to local movie houses, groceries, and department stores. Smith established a museum on the grounds where inmates could leave flowers they encountered on walks. If other state schools emphasized criminal correction, Smith's school "began with the assumption that its charges were children and adolescents who could be rehabilitated," as the historian William S. Bush noted.[92]

Progressives across the country applauded Smith's efforts. "Dr Carrie Weaver Smith of the Texas State School at Gainesville has probably gone farther than anyone else in stressing the school side of the [rehabilitation] program," wrote acclaimed sociologists William I. Thomas and Dorothy Swaine Thomas. "Nothing is allowed to interfere with education . . . [T]he girls engage in a scientifically balanced diet of study, work, and play."[93] Texas legislators would later decide that these reforms cost too much money. Smith spent more on her young charges than other state school directors. She also provided her girls sex education. Through educating her inmates about birth control, she certainly hoped to protect her girls from unwanted pregnancies but also hoped to keep more supposedly innate criminals from entering the world. Smith's spending and her insistence on combating sexual ignorance provoked the ire of the state legislature, which fired her in 1925.

Like many eugenicists, Smith held contradictory beliefs regarding the role of nature versus nurture in shaping individual destinies. As she pursued rehabilitation, she also spoke and wrote like a strict biological determinist. In her presentation "The Unadjusted Girl," delivered at the National Conference of Social Work in Chicago in 1920, Weaver noted that the girls at her institution often arrived poorly nourished, uneducated, abused, and damaged by years of poverty. She decried unregulated capitalism's role in allowing children to grow up in substandard housing. But even though she conceded the many ways in which a deprived environment could hinder development, she still blamed criminality to a large degree on biology. "Eugenically, the delinquent girl is a terrible misfit, and reflects the folly and criminal negligence of the state in regard to marriage regulations," Smith said. "Idiots, epileptics, syphilitics, tuberculars, marry ad libitum. We dare not interfere with their personal liberty, we much prefer to take care of their offspring in the penitentiaries, asylums, schools for the feebleminded, and finally thrust some of them into oblivion by the hangman's noose or the electric chair." Paradoxically, even though she sought to improve the outlook for the girls in her school, she also hinted that such efforts came too late for many of her inmates. "For a child to be normal, born in the environment, and with the heredity I have indicated is impossible, is inconceivable," she said. Even if reformatories could be made gentler, more compassionate respites from a cruel life, to Smith selective breeding offered the only definitive answer to the problem of inherent biological failures.[94]

Smith profusely thanked one of the chief leaders of the eugenics movement in the United States, Charles Davenport, and his Eugenics Record Office for providing the Gainesville school a "eugenics field worker." Cornelia Augenstein of Kent, Ohio, was assigned to Gainesville in 1919, the first such worker ever dispatched to Texas by the ERO. Eugenics field workers investigated the family backgrounds of delinquents and others suspected of being dysgenic, subjected them to intelligence tests, created psychological profiles of them, and then sorted and sent the data to ERO headquarters in Cold Spring Harbor.[95]

Smith believed she needed the help. She entertained no doubts that the Native Americans in her charge ranked among the "unfit" and were born criminals. "At the Texas Training School for Girls, our greatest problems are the girls who have one eighth and one sixteenth American Indian blood," she said. "These girls show the racial facial types and marked physical strength, are mentally exceptionally bright, and have varied interests. They are inclined to be physically unclean, frequently objecting to the routine of daily bathing. Morally, they are indiscriminating and sensual to a morbid degree, seeking indulgence with either sex. They are ego-centric, selfish, resentful of authority, but generally [have] ... considerable personal magnetism. It seems to me that these individuals might be a subject for special research and that the results might indicate the necessity of regulating marriage with Indians."[96]

Smith received wide support from early twentieth-century Texas feminists. She regularly corresponded with Elizabeth L. Fitzsimmons Ring (1857–1941), whose lobbying for prison reform led to the formation of the Texas Committee on Prisons and Prison Labor (TCPPL). Some feminists also saw the prison reform campaign as an opportunity to conduct eugenics research. Alexander Ellis participated in the TCPPL, which formed a subcommittee to determine which mental tests and educational measurements should be conducted on imprisoned youths. The prison committee conducted "anthropometric measures" and psychiatric examinations of prisoners in order to clearly link bad biology and criminality.[97]

Smith, however, faced repeated challenges to her tenure from the state legislature, which tried to pull funding for the institution over issues ranging from how much tax revenue the school spent per inmate to her refusal to build a fence around the campus to prevent the resident girls from running away. Smith worried that the fence would limit her girls' ability to explore the grounds around the school and create the prison-like atmosphere she was trying to avoid. The state relented on the fence, but Smith's time presiding over the school was running out. In spite of widespread support from feminist groups in the state such as the Dallas Women's Political League, Smith's promotion of sex education, her ban on corporal punishment, and her supposedly lenient treatment of hardened criminals clearly alienated many state legislators. By July 1925, Smith's run as the Gainesville school superintendent had ended. "There is dissatisfaction over the conduct of the school and I for one believe that the cost per girl placed there is too high," R. B. Walthall, a member of the state control board, said before the board voted unanimously to dismiss her. The dismissal did not silence Smith, who continued to protest class biases in the state's juvenile justice system. "When a poor girl gets into a scandal or is charged with a minor crime, she goes to court," Smith said in a Chicago speech on December 14, 1925, five months after Texas sacked her. "When a wealthy girl gets into a similar difficulty[,] she is bundled off to finishing school until the scandal blows over."[98]

Smith left Texas and eventually administered the National Training School for Girls in the nation's capital beginning in 1936.[99] Smith's unconventional approach to juvenile corrections, however, again got her in trouble. When a fight broke out between white and Black girls at the National

School, the Washington, DC, Board of Commissioners dismissed her for being "too lenient." Smith never again worked in juvenile justice. She opened a bookstore. In an autobiography she provided the *Washington Evening Star* toward the end of her life, she ruefully described herself as a "Physician and thoroughly discredited social worker in the field of juvenile delinquency. Dubbed an impractical dreamer and theorist. Unable to get any job in my field, so—am running a book shop." She died in Washington, on May 22, 1942, of a heart ailment, her passing apparently receiving no journalistic attention in Texas, where she once stirred such controversy.[100]

"Colonization in Reverse": Madison Grant's Long Shadow in Texas

By the time of World War I, not just the affluent, but a broad swath of the growing middle class embraced eugenics, and with it a hostility toward broad-based democracy that let the "wrong people" vote. A Columbia University-educated attorney with no scholarly expertise in biology or evolution who nevertheless became a self-trained naturalist, Madison Grant, played a critical role in making eugenics "common sense" for much of the American public after the 1916 publication of his book *The Passing of the Great Race, or the Racial Basis of European History.* Grant became one the most widely known eugenics advocates in the United States, playing a central role in convincing Congress to enact draconian immigration restrictions in 1921 and 1924 as well as garnering most of the credit for nineteen states passing sterilization laws after the release of *Passing of the Great Race.*[101]

Not surprisingly, this nationally prominent figure influenced the well-read in Texas. Grant made a major impact on two Texas supporters of eugenics in particular: Lewis Meriwether Dabney and, more importantly, Dallas dentist Hiram Wesley Evans. Evans rose to become the national leader of Ku Klux Klan when it reached its peak of power in the 1920s. In his book, Grant divided humans into three categories of descending biological worth: "Caucasians" (a popular term of the time derived from an erroneous assumption of where "white" people originated, the Caucasus mountains between the Black and Caspian seas); the "Mongoloids" (Asians); and "Negroids." He further subdivided Caucasians into three subspecies, on a scale from Nordic (Northern European) supermen, to the biologically middling central and eastern European Alpines, down to the racially contaminated and backward Mediterraneans of southern Europe.[102]

Grant argued that race mixing, not just between whites and Blacks, but between Nordics and "inferior" European subgroups (as well as Jews) threatened Nordic dominance in the United States. The sexual crossing of racial types, he said, always resulted in offspring who reverted "to primitive type." Race mixing, wide-open immigration and moves toward universal suffrage brought the United States, by the time of World War I, to the edge of collapse. Grant believed that the expansion of voting rights only led to chaos: "colonization in reverse" in which backward people replaced superior ones. With universal suffrage, Grant said, "[p]ower passes to inferior hands ... the transfer of power from the higher to the lower races, from the intellectual to the plebeian classes predominantly of Alpine and Mediterranean extraction." Such steps toward universal franchise could only produce electoral triumphs for dangerous mediocrities.[103]

Eugenics and the War on Democracy in Texas

There was no greater acolyte of Grant in Texas than Lewis Meriwether Dabney.[104] The son of University of Texas philosophy professor and Confederate apologist Robert Dabney, Lewis studied English and philosophy, as well as Greek, Latin, and French at UT, which offered him a professorship in English literature that he turned down. Meriwether did not inherit his father's piety. Even though he often referred to God and Christianity, he dismissed the "Christian cult, brotherhood of man, altruism, etc." in his writings. Dabney opened his Dallas law practice in 1888 and quickly moved in the city's most influential circles.[105] In the years before the United States' entry into World War I, Lewis Dabney urged the nation to shut the door to immigration of those from eastern and southern Europe and to eliminate the right to vote from all but the most intelligent and talented white men.

"To my mind the best proof of evolution is that ninety-five per cent of the human race are so ape-like in animal stupidity and in being attracted to glittering baubles," Dabney said in a letter written sometime between 1913 and 1915 to his brother-in-law E. Y. Chapin. He mocked the demands for voting rights by women and other disenfranchised groups. "If [expanded rights] are shiny, seem new and alluring, [women and the underclass] . . . will continue to grab them no matter how many apes before them have scorched their fingers. Man's essential animalism is also demonstrated by the fact that he is lazy, greedy, and lascivious, won't work if he can pilfer, has no foresight, and precisely like any ape believes that which he desires to believe. In some respects man, in his evolution, has not reached the stage of self protective [*sic*] development of a gopher or a squirrel."[106]

Having such "poor" human material to work with, Dabney argued, nations such as the United States (and by extension states like Texas) faced disaster by extending the franchise. "The trouble about a democracy is that things are settled by voting and ninety-five percent of the voters, not having the sense of an ant or squirrel in the summer, but having the vote, will ravage the stores of those who have laid up a few nuts when they could," he wrote. "Like any other maddened baboon[,] they will tear the whole fabric of civilization to pieces," he insisted.[107]

Dabney practiced law when immigration into Texas intensified during the violence of the Mexican Revolution that began in 1910 and as land-owners increasingly demanded easily exploited immigrant labor.[108] Mexi-can immigration in particular seemed ominous to Dabney. He ridiculed those who thought that the imperialistic American military interventions in Mexico in 1913 and 1916 were an opportunity to civilize a country Dab-ney dismissed as primitive. He was particularly outraged by the pre-dawn raid on Columbus, New Mexico, led by followers of Mexican revolution-ary leader Francisco "Pancho" Villa on March 9, 1916, which prompted a retaliatory US Army invasion led by General John "Blackjack" Pershing. In Dabney's words, "I take not the slightest interest in educating throat-cutting Mexicans . . . I cannot understand the theory that seems to possess all the American people who do not live near the border, *viz.*, that the Mex-ican people will become eventually sweetly mild and reasonable if we continue to let them rob Americans and thus follow the practice of the Zoo with the boa constrictors; that is, keep on feeding them skinned rabbits until their bloodthirsty appetite is satiated and they become mild, loving, and reasonable."[109]

He perceived Mexicans as invading the state, not just in the farmlands of South Texas, but his home base of Dallas. Between 1910 and 1920, the percentage of Dallas residents who had parents born overseas increased by

51 percent, with a large percentage coming from eastern and southern European and Latin American backgrounds. At the beginning of the century, under 16 percent of immigrants living in Dallas came from eastern and southern Europe, Mexico, Central America and South American, or Asia. By 1920, more than 54 percent of immigrants in Dallas came from these parts of the world, with the largest single group migrating from Mexico.[110]

Dabney made no effort to hide his disgust with this growing diversity. "[M]ongrelized Asiatics, Greeks, Levantines, Southern Italians, and sweepings of the Balkans, of Poland and of Russia" filled the urban landscape, Dabney complained in a speech, "Is Civilization Returning to Barbarism?" delivered to the Dallas Critic Club, an organization of local movers and shakers, on December 4, 1922.[111] To friends, Dabney expressed particular horror at what he saw as the dysgenic consequences of World War I. "[S]talwart, clean-cut" Anglo-Saxon men died by the millions in Europe, Dabney wrote, to "preserve liberty and happiness for the swarms of maggots of the human kind I see wriggling in the vile heaps we call our cities. Are our sons to give their lives to preserve the happiness . . . of these mongrel wretches, none of whom are going to sacrifice anything?"[112] To Dabney, eugenics was proven science and he wanted Texas to adopt eugenics laws. ". . . [I]ntelligence and genius . . . are a matter largely of family and men of genius drawn from a few families," he said.[113]

Animated by intense anti-Semitism, Dabney called for immigration control partly to keep Jews, who he accused of being strongly prone to political radicalism, from swaying gullible minds, particularly at the state's colleges and universities. Though he was the child of a college professor, Dabney believed it was time to curb free speech in higher education as a means of preventing revolution. "[F]ar too many men are tolerated in our colleges who are busy poisoning the rising generation with doctrines all right for Russian Jews but not to be tolerated by any free Anglo-Saxon soul," Dabney said in a November 23, 1917, letter to a relative. "However, the only reason they are more dangerous than others is that they enjoy the peculiar privilege of braying their nonsense into the tender ears of the young and moulding their minds while plastic. They should be rooted out of every college, and particularly out of state-controlled colleges."[114]

Dabney heavily borrowed language from not just Madison Grant but also celebrity eugenicist Lothrop Stoddard and his 1922 book, *The Revolt Against Civilization and the Menace of the Underman.* Dabney wanted the United States to be a biological aristocracy ruled by "superior man . . . the torch bearer of the race." Dabney's "superior man," of necessity, needed the management skills of "mediocre man," Dabney's term for those of average ability. Mediocre man, in turn, he said, "accepts the work of genius, and performs the interminable and complex tasks necessary to construction and preservation of what the superior man devises." Mediocre man would be lulled into compliance with the political dictates of their betters, he predicted, because of the creature comforts the later fashioned.[115] Mediocre man would unite with superior man because both faced a common danger: possible revolt by "under man, the congenital savage, incapable of civilization, hating it, and desirous of reverting to the primitive, under the unchangeable biological law of his being."[116]

By curing diseases, improving food production and distribution, and by advancing human comfort and safety, however, superior man had ensured the survival and rapid reproduction of what Dabney saw as a menacing biological underclass that, as it increased in numbers, demanded political rights and a redistribution of wealth. "As society has advanced from the primitive to the semi-civilized . . . its functioning has been biologically adverse to the best strains and favorable to the worst," Dabney said.[117]

The "underman," as Dabney called them, used democracy to seize the wealth created by superior man, he claimed "Democratic institutions have placed upon the upperman increasing burdens," he said. "The voice of democracy is ever to tax and harass the most capable . . . The superior man exerts himself and secures a profit; it is taxed, he works harder, and it is surtaxed . . . To prevent his children from sinking in the social scale, he has few, and as his burdens increase, his family diminishes. Democracy, therefore, is dysgenic, tending to restrict the reproduction of the best strains, and to promote large families among the unfit. The race is gradually milked of its best blood at the top, while it reproduces the worst at the bottom."[118]

In spite of the many gifts provided him by his "betters," Dabney argued, the appetites of the "underman" could not be satisfied. Ever-jealous, the underman lusted for power. "[L]ike the Red communists, [he] believes that if society could be rid of all its superior elements, of all restraints of religion, ties of family, rights of property . . . a peaceful Arcadia of easy living would be attained," Dabney wrote. "[T]he undermen become preponderant either by birth or immigration, the social structure cracks and gives way, [and] the underman rises and smashes that civilization which he can never restore, often practically extirpating those of superior mentality."[119]

Dabney told a Dallas audience in 1922 that the rise of the "underman" could be prevented only by teaching "superior men and women" that they had a moral duty to increase the size of their families; by discouraging birth control in "the upper and better classes" while promoting contraception among the lower classes; through banning marriage among or sterilizing "criminals, lunatics, idiots, defectives and degenerates"; and by ending "promiscuous immigration" into the United States by the "dregs of Europe and Asia." He colorfully added, "The United States is a nation, not a sewer."[120] Dabney died July 11, 1923, shortly after his speeches to the Dallas Critic Club.[121] Partly through the efforts of a University of Texas professor, his dreams of harsh immigration restriction would become reality the following year.

The second Ku Klux Klan dominated Texas politics in the first half of the 1920s and its leaders also embraced Grant's vision of impending racial apocalypse. With about 200,000 members statewide by its peak year in 1922, the reborn KKK essentially controlled cities like Dallas. The terrorist group's growth in Texas stemmed in large part from the energetic organizing of a dentist, Hiram Wesley Evans (1881–1966), who first headed Dallas Ku Klux Klan No. 66, but he eventually became the "Imperial Wizard," or national leader, of the Klan from 1922 to 1939.[122] Evans's thoughts on race echoed that of Grant closely and the Klan leader declared that "the races and stocks of men are as distinct as breeds of animals." Only pure "Nordics," he said, were bred to participate in ancient Athenian-style democracy. Teaching "inferior" immigrants unwilling or even incapable of respecting American institutions to be good citizens was as pointless, Evans said, as training "a bulldog to herd sheep." Quoting Grant, Evans warned that, "The dangerous foreign races will in time drive us out of our own land by the mere force of breeding."

Racial Panic and Texas's Eugenic Culture

Evans praised Grant's *The Passing of the Great Race.* "Modern research [such as in Grant's writing] is finding scientific evidence" supporting the Klan's racial ideology, he wrote.[123] As elsewhere, the second Klan came crashing down in Texas in the mid-1920s, partly because it became a victim of its successes. Two of its top legislative priorities, immigration restriction and Prohibition, were popular enough by 1924 that they became national law. The ban on alcohol and the dramatic drop in immigration after passage of the 1924 National Origins Act rendered the Klan largely redundant.[124]

The eugenics movement in Texas outlived the second Klan. Eugenics theories, once only bantered about in medical journals and academic conferences, won acceptance in high school, college, and university classrooms, and in widely read newspapers and at club meetings. Eugenicists gained supporters in the state legislature even if they remained a minority. Meanwhile, even a governor of Texas, Pat Neff (who served from 1921 to 1925), sounded a eugenical warning that the state could soon be swamped by Dabney's "undermen." In a speech in the Texas Panhandle in April 1922, Neff warned that the state faced a crisis as there were "over 6,000 insane in the institutions of Texas . . . We are just breeding lunatics in Texas and it must be stopped."[125]

In spite of the growing acceptance of eugenics and Neff's use of his bully pulpit to promote the cause, his plea fell on deaf ears in terms of legislation. At the very time the eugenics movement in Texas reached its peak, a combination of forces (including relentless attacks on the supposed subversive influence of higher education, paltry state spending on research, and the economic interests of landowners seeking to exploit the labor of Mexican immigrants) handed the movement its final legislative defeats. Eugenics shaped Texas culture, but not its policies. If Texas was breeding "lunatics," as Neff claimed, eugenicists would remain powerless to stop it.

Edgar Odell Lovett, the first president of what was then called the Rice Institute in Houston, described eugenics as a foundational science that would "add cubits to the stature of the race." He hired two acclaimed biologists, Julian Huxley and Hermann Joseph Muller, in an attempt to make Rice an epicenter of eugenics research. Photo courtesy of Rice University Archives general photo files, Woodson Research Center, Fondren Library, Rice University.

Dr. Edgar Lovett, second from the right, poses with faculty members and students at Rice's first commencement ceremony in 1916. Photo courtesy of Rice University Archives general photo files, Commencement, 1916, Woodson Research Center, Fondren Library, Rice University.

Edgar Lovett decorated the campus's main building with bas-reliefs of the men he believed had most significantly shaped modern society, including not only St. Paul, Michelangelo, Thomas Jefferson, and Charles Darwin, but also the so-called "father of eugenics," Francis Galton. The Galton relief is pictured here. The building featuring this sculpture is now known as Lovett Hall. Photo courtesy of Judy Botson.

Renowned English biologist Julian Huxley (left) relaxing with Hermann Joseph Muller (center) and Muller's longtime friend Edgar Altenberg (right) during a visit to the Marine Biological Laboratory in Woods Hole, Massachusetts, in 1917. Huxley served as a mentor to Muller and recruited him to research and teach at what is now Rice University. Both Huxley and Muller advocated eugenics as a path to human improvement. They also became controversial figures within the eugenics movement and spent troubled careers in Texas. Photo courtesy of Rice University Archives general photo files.

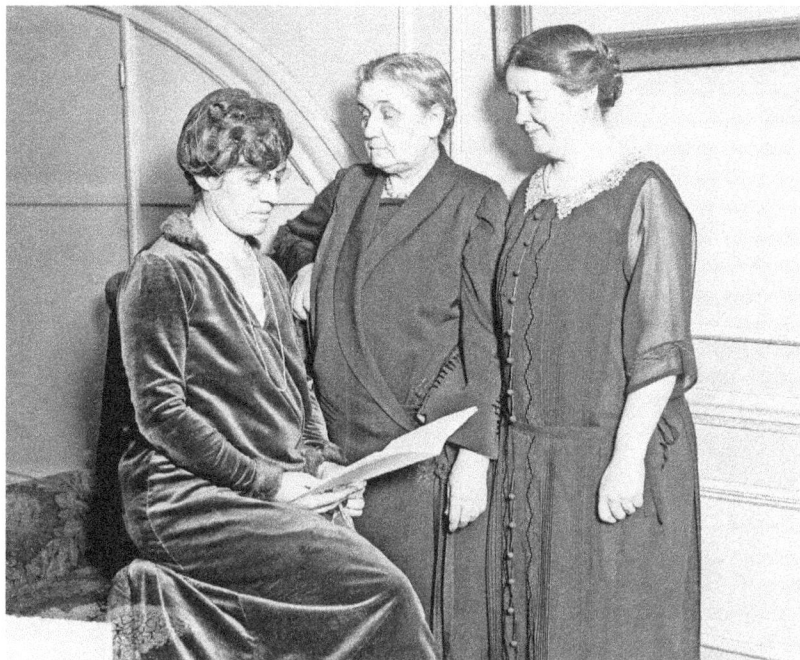

Carrie Weaver Smith (right), stands next to fellow Progressive Era reformers Jane Addams (center) and Mrs. William Lewis at a 1925 gathering in Chicago. In 1916, Smith gained renown as the first director of the Gainesville School for Girls. A eugenicist who believed that indigenous women in particular were biologically prone to crime, Smith also argued that factors such as sexual abuse, poor nutrition, and a lack of education led girls to a life of delinquency. Photo courtesy of the *Chicago Sun-Times/Chicago Daily News* collection, Chicago History Museum DN-0079697.

The family of O. B. Rollins, an assistant Bexar County farm agent, and his wife, a Girl Scout director identified in a press report only as "Mrs. Rollins," won not only the 1925 fitter family contest held at the Texas State Fair in Dallas but a similar contest at the Texas Cotton Palace in Waco in 1927, according to the March 28, 1928, *Dallas Morning News*. In the Waco contest, "[t]hey were adjudged 'fittest' after examination, both physical and mental, by experts and analysis of their genealogy back through generations," the *Morning News* reported. Photo used by permission of the American Philosophical Society, AES, Am3,575.06,86.

In the eugenics era, so-called freak shows were often held alongside fitter family and better baby contests and often featured non-white performers with disabilities. Audiences were warned that the supposedly unfit reproduced more rapidly than the gifted. A Texas railway worker, Pasqual Pinon, billed as the "two-headed Mexican," frequently toured as part of the Sells-Floto Circus freak show that crisscrossed the state in the early twentieth century. His second head was likely prosthetic or a benign tumor enhanced with makeup. Photo courtesy of the Ronald G. Becker Collection of Charles Eisenmann Photographs, Special Collections Research Center, Syracuse University Libraries.

A University of Texas psychologist, Clarence Stone Yoakum (pictured here),
along with a fellow eugenicist, Robert Yerkes, designed intelligence
tests administered to 1.75 million US Army recruits during World War I. Yerkes
and Yoakum instigated a national panic over the threat supposedly posed by the
low IQs shared by immigrants from eastern and southern Europe to the nation's
biological future when they published the results of their research, *Army Mental
Tests*, in 1920. Photo courtesy of Bentley Historical Library, University of
Michigan, Faculty and Staff Portraits, ca. 1860–1960.

University of Texas psychologist Clarence Stone Yoakum called for the mass detention of the mentally ill and disabled at institutions such as the Texas State Hospital. Yoakum and fellow eugenicist Carrie Weaver Smith wanted to make such state facilities more beautiful and humane. Here, an unidentified woman enjoys the garden at the Texas State Hospital in Austin. Photo courtesy of the Austin History Center, Austin Public Library PICA-14480.

Attorney and eugenics advocate Lewis Meriwether Dabney's grave. In 1922, Dabney warned the Dallas Critics Club that the United States was on the verge of reverting to barbarism because the country had been overwhelmed by immigrants he called "maggots of the human kind." He called for immigration restrictions. He died and was buried at Dallas's Grove Hill Memorial Park in 1923, the same year the Texas legislature killed a bill favored by the eugenics movement restricting who could marry. Photo courtesy of Susanne York.

Motivated in part by anti-Semitism, Congressman John Calvin Box from Crockett, Texas, played a major role in securing passage of the 1924 Johnson-Reed Act, which set harsh limits on the number of immigrants allowed into the United States each year from eastern and southern Europe. In spite of the support of his fellow eugenicist, Dean E. E. Davis of the North Texas Agricultural College and others, he failed to convince the Congress to set a quota for Mexican immigrants as well. Photo courtesy of the Harris & Ewing Collection, Library of Congress, Prints and Photographs Division, Washington, DC.

Hermann Joseph Muller, far right, uses a magnifying glass to examine a specimen in his famous "Fly Room" at the University of Texas. By the mid-1920s, Muller had studied the effect of x-rays on the genetics of flies and was aided in his research by zoologists Theophilus Shickel Painter (seated on the far left) and Wilson Stone (standing in the back), as well as research assistant Clarence Paul Stone (facing the camera). Muller won a Nobel Prize for this research. An antiracist outlier in the eugenics movement, Muller's awareness of the harmful impact of radiation led him to become an antinuclear activist in his later years. Photo courtesy of the Lilly Library, Indiana University, Blooming-ton, Indiana, and with the kind permission of Helen Juliette Muller.

E. E. Davis served as dean of North Texas Agricultural College in Arlington from 1925 to 1946. He sent a copy of the eugenicist bestseller *The Rising Tide of Color Against White World-Supremacy* to Texas congressman John Box to encourage the politician to impose immigration quotas on Mexico. Davis wrote a novel called *The White Scourge*, in which he characterized both Mexicans and poor whites as "human silt" biologically threatening the United States. Here, Davis contemplates a bust of himself. Photo courtesy of the *Fort Worth Star-Telegram* Collection at the Special Collections Division of the University of Texas at Arlington Libraries.

CHAPTER FOUR

Eugenics, the IQ Panic, and Immigration

1915–1940

EDGAR ODELL LOVETT literally chiseled eugenics into the landscape of Rice Institute, a private college established in Houston two years before the First World War unleashed havoc in Europe. From the beginning, the Rice board of trustees sought to win the institute, later renamed Rice University, a reputation as a hub of top-tier research. They picked Lovett, a highly regarded Princeton astronomer and mathematician, as the school's first president because of his sterling achievements. He hesitated at first to take the appointment because of the risk posed by leaving a renowned school for a yet-unopened academy in a state not known for educational excellence. However, he found it hard to turn down a chance to shape a university in his own image. Rice Institute first opened its doors to seventy-seven students in 1912. In his inaugural address on October 12 of that year, Lovett described eugenics as the "newest" of the foundational "applied sciences," although it was "really in idea no younger than Plato." Once applied, Lovett believed eugenics would "add cubits to the stature of the race." In his speech, Lovett then listed past "saints and seers" he believed had most advanced civilization. Rice's first building (now named Lovett Hall) would feature colonnades with reliefs of those visionaries, including St. Paul, Michelangelo, Thomas Jefferson, Charles Darwin, and the "father of eugenics," Francis Galton.[1]

Rice's existence rested on the state's history of white supremacy and the belief in a hierarchy of human races. Its founder, Massachusetts-born William Marsh Rice, immigrated to Houston in 1837, enslaved at least fifteen African Americans, and derived part of his eventually massive wealth from their blood, sweat, and unpaid forced labor. In 1891, he endowed the Rice Institute for the Advancement of Literature, Science, and Art. For more than two decades, the college existed only on paper. The endowment specified that the institute was meant for the education of white students only. After Rice's lawyer and valet murdered him in 1900 in a scheme to steal his estate, control of the $5 million fortune built on bondage passed to the trustees of the still-unbuilt school.[2]

Those trustees hired Lovett on the recommendation of several luminaries, such as fellow Princeton professor and future US president Woodrow Wilson. Upon his appointment as Rice president, Lovett traveled the world in search of esteemed scholars who would lend the school instant stature. His global shopping spree for brilliance yielded promising results. In 1912, Oxford graduate and already internationally famous zoologist Julian Huxley, one of the most renowned advocates for eugenics in the world, won appointment as one of the dozen original faculty members. Lovett believed eugenics would change the course of human evolution, but if he hoped Rice would play a key role in the advance of that science, he would be deeply disappointed. Huxley's time at Rice, from 1912 to 1916, proved tumultuous, sporadic, and ultimately ineffectual. Huxley delayed settling in Houston permanently because of previously planned laboratory research in Germany. His engagement to a former student still living in England, Kathleen Fordham, fell apart one year into his appointment. He felt deeply depressed and suffered frequent emotional breakdowns. Huxley's support for eugenics and stature made no measurable impact on Texas public opinion, and, to the contrary, seems to have on at least one occasion antagonized a member of the state's religious community at a time when Protestant fundamentalism achieved political hegemony in the state.[3]

Democracy, God, and Man at Rice

In 1916, S. M. Provence wrote an angry letter to the *Houston Chronicle* after attending a one-hour lecture by Julian Huxley at Rice on "Biology and Religion." According to Provence, Huxley said that human progress would unfold only "providing that men will give up whatever religion they have and accept the Darwinian theory of evolution." Provence believed the Darwinism embraced by Huxley presaged a savage future in which "the weak are without friends, a triumph that would make might the standard of right, reduce love to the passion of the brute, paralyze altruism, destroy at once 'faith, hope, and charity,' demand the apotheosis of the 'superman' and throw the whole superstructure of civilization into the melting pot to come out (if it should ever come out) without form or substance."[4] Huxley's public promotion of Darwinism probably did the state's eugenics movement no favors. His talk came less than a decade before bills calling for limits on how the theory of evolution could be taught in Texas classrooms came up for debate in the state legislature.[5]

Nevertheless, Huxley still persuaded the Rice Institute to add another eugenicist, future Nobel Prize laureate Hermann Joseph Muller, to its faculty. Yet, in spite of President Lovett's enthusiasm for the cause, the college would no more advance the science of selective human breeding than eugenics would add cubits to humanity's stature. Recurring bouts of debilitating sadness and anxiety haunted Huxley, who would be in and out of nursing homes throughout his life. Speaking of his time at Rice, biographer Alison Bashford wrote, "It was a messy and short-lived appointment." He left Texas in 1916 to serve in the British Army Service Corps during World War I, signaling a permanent end to his punctuated, ephemeral career as a full-time academic in the state.[6]

He returned to the Lone Star State only to deliver guest lectures, occasions on which he advocated hot-button, emotionally charged political positions. In a 1924 visit to Texas, for instance, he advocated repeal of the Comstock Act, which in 1873 banned the distribution of birth control information and contraceptive devices in the United States mail. Always painfully out of step with most Texans, he delivered his Houston lecture at a time when two crude pseudo-Populists, James "Pa" Ferguson and Miriam "Ma" Ferguson, had grasped political power partly by attacking ivory tower academic elites they accused of disdaining the masses. Likely oblivious to the political moment, Huxley bluntly called for authoritarian rule by intellectuals combined with a socialist redistribution of wealth.[7] His words seemed uniquely designed to antagonize the Texas ruling class even as he condescended to the average voter. Huxley told his Houston audience:

> I think it would be well if we asked ourselves whether our present brand of democracy is calculated to give us the best organs of social control and differentiation. The advantage of democracy is the raising of the condition of the mass of the people to a good average. The curse is the tendency to pull down what is above the average to the level of the average's mediocrity. A democracy of material opportunity freely

surrendering itself to the guidance of an aristocracy of thought—that seems to me to sum up pretty closely the biological ideal for society.[8]

Huxley's mostly forgotten walk-on part in Texas history encapsulates several difficulties faced by the eugenics movement in Texas. As noted earlier, the South produced few eugenicists equal in prestige or influence to their peers in California, in the Ivy League, or overseas. Instead, as Larson noted, they were primarily uncomfortable outsiders like Huxley, "preaching a foreign gospel."[9]

Racial Panic and Violence in Texas

Not in tune with their neighbors culturally, politically, or religiously, even acclaimed researchers who saw themselves as reform activists, like Huxley and his friend Muller, struggled to overcome their outsider status and mobilize the public behind science-based policies in Texas. Yet, the state between 1915 and 1940 continued to offer a potentially rich environment for eugenicists to shape law and state policy. The merits of selective breeding had been heavily promoted in popular culture. Local journalists approvingly quoted eugenicists, and students learned about the new science in public schools. Meanwhile, Texas's status as a racial crossroads magnified the fear of foreigners that served as the sine non qua of the American eugenics movement. A combination of xenophobia and a dread of Blackness in the white community produced explosive results.

The historian Edward L. Ayers noted that two overlapping southern subregions saw exponential increases in lynchings in the late nineteenth century: the Gulf Coast states stretching from Florida to Texas and the cotton uplands of Arkansas, Louisiana, and Mississippi, an area that also included the eastern reaches of the Lone Star State. A rapid growth in the African American population from 1880 to 1900 tied these regions together, with the Black population in Texas growing by 71 percent in that time frame. Panic over Mexican immigration and anti-Tejano violence peaked in the years of the 1910–20 Mexican Revolution, even as lynchings of African Americans across the state stained the soil red. According to the Lynching in Texas database created by Jeffrey Littlejohn of Sam Houston State University, 207 documented lynchings of Black and Brown Texans unfolded from 1910 to 1920, inclusive, including 99 in 1915, a peak year for anti-Mexican and Mexican American murder.[10] Meanwhile, the slaughter of Mexicans and Mexican Americans became so commonplace between 1915 and 1920 that a San Antonio paper reported "the finding of dead bodies of Mexicans . . . has reached a point where it creates little or no interest." Not all racially motivated murders from the time period may have been accounted for. Mexican and Mexican American casualties might have eventually resulted in "the killings of hundreds, possibly thousands, and the flight of so many more." The death toll of Mexicans and Mexican Americans at the hands of Anglos in that period possibly reached as many as 5,000.[11]

As this racial mayhem spread and Black and Brown casualties piled up, the political menace supposedly posed by poor whites occupied the minds of the well-off. To some, the tragedy of lynching stemmed not from the horror it inflicted on communities of color or the suffering of those tortured to death. Instead, they worried whether it activated the allegedly primitive instincts of the lower income white mob. "I maintain that the negro rapist should not for a moment be considered," L. B. De Pontes wrote to the *Houston Post*. "Will his death at the stake more surely prevent the recurrence of like crimes? If it will, then let him be burnt, and let the burning be accompanied by any additional terrors that will operate in the same direction. If, on the contrary, burning will not have this effect, then it should not be practiced; not because of the cruelty to the negro; for by his crime he has forfeited all title to consideration, but because it unquestionably has a tendency to brutalize the participants."[12]

Even as African Americans declined as a percentage of the total population, they grew in raw numbers. This led many whites to violently lash out even as the mainstream press instigated a dread of Black and Brown men routinely depicted as innately inclined toward rape and murder.[13] Meanwhile, some like De Pontes worried that the white masses, enraged by the supposed threat of their racial rivals, would slip from elite control and unleash a war on civilization.

Texas eugenicists had long warned of such a nightmare scenario and from 1915 to 1940 they offered a set of solutions to keep the unpredictable masses in check and maintain the orderly rule of the "Superior Man": strict limits on who could enter the state, restrictions on who could marry, mass detention of those with mental disabilities to prevent them from reproducing, and a program of prolific coerced sterilizations. The poisoned racial climate seemed the right time for eugenicists to achieve their extreme policy objectives. The Texas movement offered what they presented as objective evidence of their theories. They published intelligence tests they claimed proved the state's population was caught in a spiral of biological deterioration and blamed immigration as the major culprit in this declension. The situation would only get worse unless harsh measures received legal sanction.

Yet, at the same time, the colleges and universities that formed the home base for Texas eugenicists came under sustained attack by the state's politicians, including from both Fergusons during their governorships. Small-government conservatives effectively pushed back against measures to restrict marriage and to spend more money on sex-segregated facilities for the mentally ill and mentally disabled. Wealthy growers, seeking low-wage immigrant labor, furthermore blocked eugenic efforts to tighten immigration laws to reduce entry into the country by Mexicans. The resistance by these combined forces proved insurmountable.

Direct eugenics proposals, or those inspired by eugenical concerns, came before the Texas legislature repeatedly between 1915 and 1940, including a proposed 1923 marriage restriction law and 1935 and 1937 sterilization laws. All went down in flames. By 1940, explicit calls for eugenics became rare in the state. Davis, the college dean in Arlington, became a lonely and ignored voice for what had become a southern lost cause. Daniel's dream of a "sanitary utopia" in Texas would never be realized.

Eugenics, Class Politics, and Education in Texas

By 1915, California eugenicists enjoyed pull and acclaim. That state invested heavily in its schools and its scientists. Like Lovett at Rice two decades later, David Starr Jordan in 1891 received an offer to become the first president of a just-established and richly endowed institution of higher education, Stanford University. An ichthyologist, Jordan won fame far beyond the Stanford campus, cofounding the Sierra Club with John Muir. Jordan "abundantly believed that some species needed to be protected and preserved while others should be eliminated or excluded," historian Alexandra Stern writes. "He applied this logic to plants, animals, and people alike." While Texas eugenicists struggled to get funding and worried about keeping their jobs, Jordan and his allies persuaded his state to adopt highly controversial and often brutal policies that inspired little organized opposition. Along with his eugenicist Stanford colleague Lewis

Terman, Jordan transformed the state's public schools and its treatment of the mentally disabled, an often-baleful impact that would soon be replicated coast to coast. "From his base in northern California, Jordan became one of the most prominent Progressives and eugenicists in the early twentieth century and played a pivotal role in the formation of the [Eugenics Record Office] in 1910," Stern observed.[14]

Terman, who taught psychology at Stanford, played perhaps the most significant role in developing the field of psychometrics, the effort to measure human intelligence as precisely as the body can be measured in pounds and feet. As will be discussed later, his work led to the creation of what came to be known as the Stanford-Binet IQ test, an instrument used to supposedly prove a correlation between race and intelligence and the mental inferiority of African Americans, Mexicans, and Mexican Americans, as well as the immigrants arriving daily in the United States from southern and eastern Europe. As a result of Terman's work, the California Bureau of Juvenile Research subjected young immigrants, particularly Mexicans, to the National Intelligence Test, which was largely derived from its Stanford-Binet predecessor. In the 1920s, the Los Angeles school district tested eighty thousand children at 219 elementary schools across the system. Educators concluded that students born in Mexico had a mean IQ of 69.4 (at the borderline of mental deficiency), while Mexican American students earned a low normal mean score of 74.6. California school systems exploited the results, "channeling . . . [Mexican] schoolchildren into vocation tracks and the manual trades." Once their families crossed the US border, young Mexicans entered a white-dominated land whose leadership was determined to confine them to low-wage labor, the only roles influential California eugenicists believed suitable for the migrant community. "[T]hose newcomers and their children, if attending school, encountered a segregated universe that had been intensified by scientific racism and intelligence testing," Stern argues.[15]

On the West Coast, not just educators, but doctors, psychologists, legislators, and an ample army of Progressive activists rallied to the eugenics cause, creating "professional networks of sterilization crusaders," the high status of advocates "imbuing their mission with the aura of officialdom and the stamp of governmental legitimacy." Unlike in Texas, in California eugenical policies gained credibility when embraced by scholars, and ideas incubated in academia were transformed into action in the real world. California enacted one of the harshest sterilization laws in the nation. Until the

1909 law was amended after World War II, California did not allow the institutionalized to challenge sterilization orders and did not notify parents or guardians of impending surgeries unless a case involved an underage "idiot." As Stern notes, the California law "never faced any serious legal challenge." By 1921, twelve years after the state had passed its sterilization measure, 2,248 of those labeled "unfit" had gone under the knife, a number representing 80 percent of all sterilized in the entire country by that point. The general population broadly accepted this idea hatched in the ivory tower. Politicians and academics, meanwhile, heaped praise on Jordan, acclaimed as a "great man," a "prophet of freedom," "one of the most versatile men," and "one of the most fertile and inspiring geniuses of his day."[16]

As Jordan and his allies won plaudits, Lovett, Huxley, Muller, and other Texas eugenicists struggled to find a voice and an audience, and the state's political leadership came not to praise such scientists but to bury their reputations. James and later Miriam Ferguson skillfully tapped into popular rage against elites that still simmered in the state after the fall of the Populist movement in the 1890s.

The Fergusons and Eugenics

Ironically, not even ostensible voices of the forgotten and downtrodden like the Fergusons remained untouched by eugenical ideas. The couple's newspaper, the *Ferguson Forum*, sometimes featured coverage of eugenics. The *Forum* ran a story headlined "Many School Children Held to Be Defective by Bureau of Hygiene" on June 11, 1925, during Ma Ferguson's first term as governor. A 1933 article, "Hospitals for Insane Crowded," echoed a major eugenicist panic during her second term even as the publication covered better baby contests.[17]

The *Forum* published an explicit endorsement of eugenics with a May 28, 1919, opinion piece written by Katie Daffan, at one point first vice president of the Texas State Teachers Association. Daffan (1874–1951), who belonged the Texas State Historical Association, the United Daughters of the Confederacy, and the Daughters of the Texas Revolution, embodied the type of energetic clubwoman who advocated for the eugenics movement across the South. As Larson documented, "in every Southern state, 'women's clubs' vied with medical associations, in providing the most ready audiences for eugenicists . . . Eugenicists recognized southern clubwomen's political influence and potential interest in scientific childrearing, and cultivated the support of these women." Daffan certainly was an influential believer in the eugenic creed. "Blood, the source of life is eloquent, convincing, it proves every point, and finally settles everything," Daffan wrote in an essay published by the *Forum*, "Blood, the Tell-Tale." Daffan argued that ancestry predestined each individual's life course:

> [Blood] gives good manners, proper appearance, and dignity, or the absence of each of these in each individual . . . Some of us possess good, reliable blood, some of us do not, some of us are 'just mongrels,' and though we do not realize it ourselves, everyone else usually does . . . Blood speaks no less in animals than in human beings, for, some animals are richly 'blooded,' that is they possess a record of birth . . . We buy horses, mules, and cattle, placing a value thereon according to what we are able to prove of their records. We might gain somewhat if we dealt with men and women only after demanding their "records."[18]

Eugenics, by its nature an aristocratically inclined project, viewed those at the economic bottom not as the exploited but as biological failures. Yet, the economically dispossessed formed an important part of Ferguson's constituency. To reassure the *Forum* readership, Daffan, a child of affluence, insisted that many so-called blue bloods were often overrated and had gained unearned reputation because of their attenuated connections to acclaimed figures. Neither James nor Miriam Ferguson ever campaigned on eugenics or proposed legislation allowing forced sterilizations or restricting marriage for the biologically "unfit." Eugenics remained tucked away in their worldview. But the surprising appearance of eugenical ideas in a propaganda sheet that ostensibly hailed the struggles of the poor and working class provides evidence of how deeply the movement had influenced the state's politics and culture, even if support seems to have remained confined to the more educated and affluent.

Eugenics advocacy likely would not have won "Farmer Jim" Ferguson any votes. But he did know that his rural backers resented how the state shortchanged their children's education. During his governorship, he focused on the supposedly extravagant expenses lavished on the University of Texas. Its students believed to be the heirs of riches, the university allegedly drained money from the little red schoolhouses on the state's prairies. Elsewhere, the academic credentials of eugenicists like Jordan, Terman, and Madison Grant gave them credence and a ready-made audience. In Texas, however, to hold a professorship was to invite suspicions of snobbery and (worse yet) anti-Americanism. Ferguson eagerly exploited this sentiment. Eugenicists in the state became incidental victims in James Ferguson's ongoing war with its flagship institution of higher learning.

"It Costs Too Much": Ferguson's Fight with the University of Texas

Ferguson knew that the Progressives and Prohibitionists who dominated the UT faculty opposed his gubernatorial candidacy. While running for governor in 1915, he characterized UT as a money pit that starved rural schools of resources. His first serious clash with UT came over his attempt to appoint Reverend A. F. Cunningham as state librarian. As noted in the previous chapter, Cunningham would later submit an entry in the American Eugenics Society's sermon contest. He had no qualifications to serve as the state librarian. His nomination was pure political patronage. Cunningham endorsed Ferguson during the latter's gubernatorial bid. The Texas State Library and Historical Commission oversaw the state librarian's office. Eugene Barker, a UT historian, served as an ex officio commission member. He sent a letter to Cunningham asking him to reject the post. This infuriated Ferguson, who saw Barker as undermining his authority. Not wanting to serve without the commission's unanimous support, Cunningham withdrew his name from consideration.[19]

An outsider in Austin politics, Ferguson entered into a protracted battle over who would serve as president of the University of Texas with the UT Board of Regents, which was filled with traditional elites like Will Hogg, son of former governor Jim Hogg.[20] When the regents appointed the president of the Austin Presbyterian Theological Seminary, Robert E. Vinson, over Ferguson's objections, the governor presented Vinson a list of seven faculty members he wanted fired immediately. The list included the school's most outspoken eugenicist, A. Caswell Ellis. Ferguson's targeting of Ellis had nothing to do with the latter's advocacy of selective breeding, but stemmed from the professor's support of Prohibition (Ellis believed drinking was dysgenic) and woman suffrage. The governor opposed both.[21] When reelected, Ferguson stacked the UT Board of Regents with allies who promptly fired Ellis and five other professors.[22]

Not done with his vendetta, on June 17, 1917, Ferguson vetoed the entire appropriation for the university in the coming two years. In a message to both houses of the state legislature, Ferguson presented the UT faculty as enemies of struggling workers and farmers. "When higher education becomes either autocratic or aristocratic in its ways . . . [and] begins to arrogate to itself an unwarranted superiority over the great masses of the people who make higher education possible, then I am against higher education and I consider it 'book learnin' gone to seed.'" He said that fraternity members lived in "stately mansions." Ferguson claimed that the state had appropriated $350 for each university student while spending only $7 or $8 each for "the boys in the country schools." The universities overpaid the big-name professors who worked only fifteen hours a week, he said, only taking into account their time in the classroom. With the United States at war with Germany, Ferguson questioned the UT faculty's patriotism. "I have found far more disloyalty in the state university at Austin than among the Germans [in Central Texas] or the people of any other nationality."[23]

The budget veto prompted a swift response. The legislature, already investigating Ferguson's corrupt finances, went into special session and, on August 25, 1917, they removed Ferguson from office, banning him from ever holding any elected post again. However, the panic Ferguson helped instigate about disloyalty and even treason during World War I claimed at least one casualty among Texas eugenicists. The university reinstated Ellis. The sole UT professor fired for political reasons during Ferguson's crusade against the school would be a supporter of the disgraced governor's proposals on the issue of farm tenancy. Eugenicist Lindley Keasbey is believed to have written some speeches for Ferguson. A scholar concerned with persistent economic want in the state who had been removed from his position in the political science department because of his socialist ideology, Keasbey went a bridge too far when he opposed American involvement in World War I. His association with Ferguson only added baggage. Keasbey became a pawn in the struggle over control of higher education. At Vinson's urging, the regents fired him.[24]

Even someone as prominent as David Starr Jordan might have struggled to thrive in such an environment. Professors like historian Charles Ramsdell (1877–1942) celebrated the departure of Ferguson from the governor's mansion.[25] However, the wounds Ferguson inflicted on the university festered for years, making Texas a less appealing place for scholars to make their careers, including eugenicists. Out of office, the former governor would not relent in his attacks on the Austin school. In 1918, the year after Pa was driven from office, editorial cartoons attacking "political professors" filled the *Ferguson Forum*. Six years later, the newspaper presented investment in public schools or universities as alternatives rather than complementary efforts. "The teacher who teaches forty children is rendering a greater service to the world than the high brow [*sic*] university professor who teaches only eight or ten in the useless knowledge of Greek and Latin and Trigonometry," an editorial said. "And besides, it costs too much."[26]

UT historian Eugene Barker (1874–1956) believed that the university's meager resources harmed teaching quality at the school and made it unattractive to the best scholars in any field. Referring to the lack of faculty salary increases in 1921, Barker said, "This, of course, removes every incentive from the younger men and will make it impossible for us to get new men for instructorships and subordinate places who can go elsewhere." Barker sent his worries directly to UT president Vinson, stating, "The University cannot hope to compete with other universities," considering its paltry wages and lack of research funds.[27]

The triumph of fundamentalism in Texas politics further eroded academic freedom. In 1923 regents approved, with only one dissent, a policy that declared, "that no infidel, atheist, or agnostic be employed in any capacity in the University of Texas, and . . . no person who does not believe in God, as the Supreme Being and the ruler of the Universe shall be employed." Potential faculty around the world no doubt received the message that higher education at UT had become thoroughly politicized and security of employment could not be counted on, an uninviting atmosphere for anyone who might use their academic position to promote an idea as contentious as eugenics.[28] No Texas school would become the equivalent of Stanford University in advancing eugenics policies.

An Examination is Better Than a Coffin: The 1923 Texas Marriage Bill

California eugenicists not only won plaudits but turned hospitals for the mentally ill and disabled into sterilization factories even as that state's schools sorted students into the "fit" and the "unfit," a selection process that condemned some children to no future other than backbreaking labor. On the other hand, Texas eugenicists fought to merely keep their jobs. At the same time, eugenicists' beleaguered political allies struggled to get laws out of state legislative committees.

In 1915, the Texas legislature briefly considered the merits of legislation referred to in other parts of the country as an "ugly law." The bill would have forced "cripples and the blind, etc., to keep out of the state." One observer said of the disabled frequently seen in towns and cities, "It was claimed they are a lot of boozefighters, gamblers, and impudent toughs; that the women are harlots and the men bawd-masters." Susan M. Schweik, an historian of disability in the United States, argues that eugenicists played a major role in passing such ordinances across the country. Such laws prohibited anyone "diseased, maimed, mutilated, or in any way deformed so as to be an unsightly or disgusting object . . . to be allowed in or on the streets, highways, thoroughfares, or public places" as a Chicago ordinance put it. Those with disabilities, to the eugenicists supporting such laws, were not only unpleasant to look at, but a peril to public safety, with their outward appearances reflecting moral and character "defects" as well.[29] "Ugly bill" advocates believed that if they did not yet have the power to carve up the bodies of the disabled to ensure their eventual disappearance, they could keep them out of sight, out of mind, and off the streets until the state authorized more drastic measures. However, the Texas ugly law permanently stalled.[30]

The state's eugenicists continued their efforts to prevent the disabled from being born in the first place. Women in the gallery of the Texas state house cheered on the afternoon of March 2, 1923, after Representative Edith Wilmans of Dallas delivered a fiery defense of a eugenics bill she submitted at the beginning of the session. The legislation, House Bill 85, would have required all couples applying for a marriage license in Texas to undergo a medical examination and receive "a certificate from a reputable physician" confirming the couple's physical fitness. "Fitness" in part meant that a potential married couple had avoided contracting what was then termed venereal disease, but the bill's mandate was broad enough to give doctors the power to halt nuptials based on a variety of physical and mental traits. Such laws had become a national trend. By 1914, thirty states had enacted new marriage laws with eugenic intent, beginning with Connecticut in 1896. Such laws gave the government the power to annul the marriages of "idiots and of the insane" and barring licenses to the those with mental disabilities or "afflicted with venereal disease."[31]

Wilmans (1882–1966) broke barriers in 1922 when she handily defeated John E. Davis of Mesquite, a ten-year veteran of the Texas house, in the Democratic primary, winning 54 percent of the vote. This ensured her place as the first woman to serve under the capitol dome in Austin. Wilmans filed several bills in her one term. Besides her "eugenic or health bill," she submitted legislation establishing a domestic court in Dallas that would, in part, allow women greater access to divorce proceedings, a compulsory education bill for children under the age of sixteen, and another providing state support for children of fathers imprisoned or confined to asylums. A member of two anti-communist groups formed in Texas during the Red Scare of 1919–20, the Minute Women and the Paul Revere Club, Wilmans could not secure the support of the anti-Klan Dallas County Citizens League after she declined to state clearly her opposition to the terrorist group. Her sympathies, or at least acceptance of the Klan, became clear when she enthusiastically supported the Klan candidate for the US Senate, Earle B. Mayfield, as a "great Prohibitionist who will bring credit on Texas" at the 1922 state Democratic Party Convention, to repeated ovations.[32]

Wilmans argued that sexually transmitted diseases, if passed on to the child, could cause premature death or leave offspring "invalids for life." She was supported by Dr. J. A. Dowd, a physician representing Bowie County, but the opposition focused on the cost and the humiliation involved in mandating such tests. Representative Jesse Lee Jennings of Canadian, Texas, admitted that the bill might curb syphilis and gonorrhea, but said requiring such intrusive medical screenings "cast a reflection on the morals of many young men and women who are pure and physically fit as those of any other state." Quizzed about the fairness of the financial burden the medical examinations entailed, Wilmans said the cost was well worth it to any decent couple. "[T]here was applause . . . when Mrs. Wilmans replied . . . it would be far better for a couple contemplating marriage to spend $15 for such examinations than $15 later for a coffin for a child born insufficiently nourished," the *Dallas Morning News* reported.[33]

Wilmans and her allies defeated an amendment by Charles Rice of Houston County. Rice wanted only men to undergo examinations and to limit the medical examinations to tests used for detecting venereal disease. Wilmans argued such a change would probably render the bill unconstitutional and that the "things which the bill seeks to guard against" were not just sexually transmitted diseases and were not "limited to one sex."[34] Wilmans's efforts never came to fruition. The legislature ultimately killed the bill on a second reading by a vote of sixty to fifty-one. (In the Texas legislature, bills go through three separate "readings," with majorities required to approve the legislation in both chambers of the legislature on the second and third reading before the bill can be forwarded to the governor for signature or a veto).[35]

It was the seventh legislative defeat for eugenics advocates in sixty-nine years, and in the coming decade two more statehouse failures awaited. The backlash against the experts so revered by the Progressive movement that erupted under Ferguson had not ebbed, and the Protestant ministers who now wielded such political influence in Texas no doubt resented the intrusion of the state into what they saw as their domain: who could come to the marriage altar. Wilmans's bill also was the first "democratic" eugenics measure. It did not exclusively target those already presumed to be unfit, such as those with blindness or mobility impairments. All—rich and poor, Black, white, and Brown, strong or weak, male or female—would have to submit to the judgment of a doctor regarding their physical worth. The ruling class did not appear eager to have their fitness subjected to the judgment of doctors. The comments of male legislators also suggest that forcing white women, particularly the better-off financially, to answer humiliating questions about their sexual cleanliness, and the prospect of them perhaps being publicly deemed as unworthy of a trip to the altar, represented an unacceptable and embarrassing enlargement of state authority.[36]

Such failures proved commonplace elsewhere in the former Confederacy. "The failure of state legislatures in the Deep South to enact eugenic marriage statutes at a time when such laws passed in most other states suggest that southern lawmakers (and, by inference, the southern public) never fully accepted eugenics," Larson wrote. That pattern certainly held for Texas as well, where proposals for marital examinations were resented as raising questions about loving couples' morality, intellect, and whiteness. As previously noted, Larson suggested that "comprehensive eugenics schemes" in the South included four major elements: sterilization laws, marriage restrictions, mass detention of the unfit, and shutting down immigration into the United States by certain racialized groups. Thwarted at restricting marriage to the presumed "most" evolved and legalizing state-ordered sterilizations, some Texas eugenicists by the second decade of the twentieth century pivoted to those last two approaches: greatly expanding the capacity of mental institutions, and choking off the flow of immigrants accused of "inferiority" from overseas. This approach to maintaining the purity of the white race would be justified by use of one of the newest and seemingly objective instruments offered by race science: the intelligence test.[37]

The IQ Panic In Texas

From the start of the Great War in Europe in 1914 to the mid-1920s, Texas eugenicists terrified the public, warning the country that it had been swarmed by the "unfit," both those born in the United States and immigrants. Teachers offered eugenics as objective fact to students from the earliest grades to doctoral programs. Regardless of how this messaging translated into legislation, increasingly, Texas mothers and fathers, Black and white, not only anxiously counted fingers and toes upon the delivery of their babies but, as their children grew, they worriedly contemplated the length and breadth of their young ones' skulls. Parents sought affirmation from fairground judges as to the physical and mental worthiness of their offspring. Experts promoted anxiety about dating, warning the white public that their romantic lives no longer centered on the quest for personal happiness. Upon their choices in the bedroom rested the fate of civilization. Biological "defect" lay hidden everywhere. Sinister family secrets about ancestors who made unwise choices in their sex lives decades earlier could resurface with the birth of any allegedly deficient child. Uneasy rested the head of the racially superior Anglo-Saxon, squeezed between what were commonly called "the colored races" pouring into the country from without and the often poor and eugenically suspect whites promiscuously spawning within.

Yet, an enormous gap yawned between the widespread sense of menace and action to thwart it. Poor whites of western European descent fought fiercely to assert their worth although scientists charged them with inferiority. "New immigrants" sought whiteness. Although aspirations to belong to the state's racial aristocracy remained the pathway to a better life, the masses did not forget their status in the Texas economic hierarchy. Widespread strikes in the late nineteenth century, the rise of Populism, and the efflorescence of Fergusonism all stemmed from a consciousness, some-times misdirected, of exploitation and neglect by the ruling class and an awareness of the contempt in which they were held.

Much of the public readily believed charges that the University of Texas represented Babylon on the Colorado River, a swamp of sexual de-cadence and privilege where spoiled young people fiddled away time pur-suing "useless subjects" as they waited to inherit fortunes and gain political power. Resentment specifically against what were incorrectly perceived as wealthy professors, and for urbanites in general, served as a proxy for the class struggle in the rural districts. Ma and Pa Ferguson happily nourished themselves with this toxic energy. Eugenicists faced a Texas audience primed to be skeptical precisely because they had been crowned experts.

Even much of the scientific world remained skeptical of eugenicists' more sweeping conclusions. French psychologist Alfred Binet (1857–1911) questioned how eugenicists categorized grades of intellect and racial worth. Interested in predicting how students would fare in school, in the late nineteenth century Binet measured skulls, as had eugenicists around the world. Eugenicists believed that the back of skulls would measure noticeably larger in smarter persons than in those less intelligent. In fact, Binet wrote, the differences in skull measurements between successful and failing students were, in his words, "extremely small." Binet realized that his knowledge of individual students' classroom performances dis-torted "unconsciously and in good faith" the precision with which he measured skulls, and warped his findings. He found that differences in skull sizes remained insignificant even when he used his measurements to record the "cephalic index" of those labeled "idiots," a group soon to be subjected to medical violence in the United States. As Harvard evolution-ary biologist Stephen Jay Gould wrote, "Craniometry, the jewel of nineteenth-century objectivity, was not destined for continued cele-bration." Binet would provide a new tool to measure the power of minds, but one soon dangerously misused despite his original intent.[38]

In 1904, the French government hired Binet to design tests for students struggling with certain proficiencies, such as counting, reading compre-hension, and so on, with the goal of developing programs to mitigate those shortcomings. What Binet developed by 1905 came to be known as the intelligence quotient, or IQ, test. Students taking the original Binet tests were asked to demonstrate they had mastered skills associated with certain ages. They started with the most basic tasks and advanced to the most difficult until they could no longer correctly respond to prompts. The last task successfully completed indicated the student's "mental age." Aware of the difficulty of attempting to measure something as vaguely defined and complex as intelligence, Binet admitted that scores on his tests represented "only an average of many performances, not an entity unto itself . . . Intelligence . . . is not a single, scalable thing like height." Binet foresaw how his test could be misused. "[H]e worried that his practical [diagnostic] device . . . could be perverted and used as an indelible label, rather than a guide for identifying children who needed help," Gould wrote. He insisted that his test did not measure inborn intellectual capacity. Scores could improve with remedial education. He expressed his disgust with a common French motto of the era, "Stupidity is for a long time" and urged French educators to not let the first impression students make in the classroom bias their expectations of a child's future.[39]

Binet's concerns turned out to be prophetic. Americans modified Binet's instrument, soon to be known as the "Stanford-Binet" test, and subverted its intended use. American eugenicists employed the test not to identify treatable education gaps but as a measure of unalterable deficiencies. American eugenicists would interpret IQ scores as a result of heredity rather than a product of a person's environment or state-of-mind at a given moment. Soon, they assigned mental ages to entire "races." They assumed the existence of general intelligence rather than exploring the possibility of "multiple intelligences," the concept that individuals vary widely in skill levels based on specific mental tasks, such as math or language. They also did not consider that the Binet test was not designed to measure more abstract abilities such as creativity.[40]

A trio of American eugenicists, H. H. Goddard, L. M. Terman, and R. M. Yerkes, ignored these limitations, redefined the Binet scores as a measure of an individual's permanent mental capacity, and promoted a widescale campaign of IQ testing in the United States. Yerkes convinced the United States government to administer tests to 1.75 million US Army recruits during World War I.[41] In that effort, Yerkes received critical help from a University of Texas professor, Clarence Stone Yoakum. In the 1920s, Yerkes and Yoakum would release the result of the army IQ tests. The two assigned mental ages to entire segments of the population such as African Americans and Polish, Italian, Russian, and Jewish immigrants. Their conclusions terrified the public, convincing them that continued high levels of immigration into the United States would reduce the nation to mental unfitness.

Yoakum's research validated for much of the public the wisdom of a long-held eugenicist goal: passage of draconian immigration laws to keep most Italians, Jews, and others newcomers portrayed by American race scientists as inferior out of the United States. Like his eugenicist peers across the South, Yoakum believed that mental disability could not be reversed, primarily derived from heredity, and that the "feebleminded" lacked sexual restraint and bore many children. Thus, he held that without sterilization laws in place, only "eugenic segregation could alleviate the problem and stem the tide of idiocy." Richard I. Manning, the pro-eugenics governor of South Carolina from 1915 to 1919, insisted that "the feeble-minded must be kept from propagating themselves" but insisted that sterilization "has not been welcome by public opinion to any very considerable extent" in his state.[42]

Yoakum doubted not only the likelihood of a sterilization law passing in Texas, but also questioned its practicality. The UT psychologist believed that a legion of eugenicists wielding Lincecum's purifying knife might not be able to keep up with the mythical fecundity of those with mental disabilities. As Larson noted, southern eugenicists thought that mass confinement of the intellectually inferior would be an easier sell than sterilization. Doctors supporting such a program believed "southern legislators could approve of establishing such facilities without necessarily endorsing eugenics." The pro-eugenics medical community in the South could more easily promote mental institutions as humanitarian enterprises where inmates could learn to grow their own food, make their own clothes, and build their own shelters. Their labor would make the effort self-funding. Yoakum made a similar case to the Texas legislature on eugenic grounds and achieved a limited success that evaded his peers.[43]

Texas, however, differed from the rest of the South in one important way. As Larson argued, opposition to immigration was one of the planks of the eugenics program, but the issue held far greater salience in Texas than in most of the former Confederacy. As immigration laws tightened in the United States in the 1920s, southern members of Congress mostly issued predictable xenophobic warnings about American civilization falling and the American breed declining at the hands of outsiders, but such denunciations could at most be seen as perfunctory nods to popular prejudice. During the debate on the 1924 Immigration Act, "[c]ertainly, members from the Deep South made their fair share of racist speeches and arguments in favor of the legislation, but none of them . . . displayed the slightest interest in biological or eugenic justifications for the measure," Larson said. "Because so few immigrants, and so few persons of southern or eastern European descent, lived in the Deep South, nativist politicians from the region could more easily present such foreigners as abstract threats to the established order than as sources of eugenic contamination." [44] That last observation, however, was most certainly not true of Texas.

As already shown, eastern and southern European communities already had made their presence felt in rapidly growing cities like Dallas, Galveston, and Houston, but one US representative, John Calvin Box from Crockett in deep East Texas, saw particular menace from one set of newcomers who had already been besieged by violence from Anglos in the state: Mexicans who formed a key part of the labor force in both agriculture and industry. Controversies over immigration roiled Texas. In the period from World War I to the 1930s, Yoakum and Ellis sounded the alarm that an epidemic of mental defect threatened the future of the state. Much of the "idiocy" epidemic, they claimed, came from south of the Rio Grande. Both would join Box in urging an almost complete end to Mexican immigration. Box would play a significant role in passage of the 1924 Johnson-Reed Act largely shutting down immigration from eastern and southern Europe, but the law included what he saw as a dangerous loophole. The 1924 law did not apply to Mexicans.

Texas eugenicists by then crossed swords with an economically powerful group. Planters desired a steady supply of workers from across the border. Growers certainly believed that their immigrant workers lacked intelligence and character, but insisted that their labor force would not be capable of challenging the political status quo in a white-dominated country. The United States Congress declined to impose immigration quotas on Mexicans at the behest of the politically connected and wealthy. In this particular case, greed outweighed racism.

John Box and the Mexican Border

In the 1920s, John Calvin Box from Crockett in deep East Texas became one of the latest and most prominent eugenicist prophets of doom. With an impressive resume that included stints as a Methodist minister, original trustee of Southern Methodist University in Dallas, county judge, and mayor, Box first won election to the United States House of Representatives in 1918. He served there until 1931, obsessing over the supposed biological and political dangers posed to the United States by Mexican immigrants. The one-time cleric authored a guest column published by the Michigan-based *Dearborn Independent* on Christmas Day 1920. The *Independent* that year gained infamy for spreading anti-Semitic conspiracy theories. Box saw the publication owned by automobile magnate Henry Ford as the best platform for sounding his warning that white Americans faced oblivion. Box (1871–1941) chose to not refer to Christian Gospel accounts of Christ's birth in his holiday missive. Instead, his words sounded more like the grim warnings of impending mayhem found in the Book of Revelation: "If America is lost, the world will grow visibly darker, even to the people of foreign lands, and all that is worth living for will have been lost for us, whether we came recently or our fathers came long ago . . . America's civilization is facing the threat of the ages—the onrush of alien hosts."[45]

Bought by Ford in 1919, the *Dearborn Independent* gained worldwide attention beginning on May 22, 1920. with the first installment of an essay series titled "The International Jew: The World's Foremost Problem." Ford later reprinted these articles as four bestselling booklets. The series drew from a 1903 forgery disseminated by supporters of Czar Nicholas II called *The Protocols of the Elders of Zion*. Supposedly the minutes of a meeting held by the most powerful Jewish leaders in the world in 1897, the *Protocols* portrayed this imaginary cabal discussing how they would gain control of the world's finances and politics, sow war, and instigate revolutions in order to bring Christianity to its knees. The *Protocols* themselves were plagiarized from an 1860s French novel satirizing the reign of Napoleon III and his grandiose ambitions.[46]

Building on dehumanizing stereotypes, "The International Jew" series accused Jewish people of spreading anti-Christian ideas like Marxism, of triggering the 1918 communist revolution in Russia, and poisoning gentile youth with alcohol and sexually charged jazz music and movies. Jews instigated World War I in order to provoke the Christian kingdoms of Europe to maul each other, the *Independent* charged, so they could then profit from the resulting arms sales.[47]

Ford's anti-Semitism seems to have been influenced by several major figures in the eugenics movement, such as Stoddard, Jordan, Burbank, and Charles Elliott of Harvard. Ford insisted patriotism inspired his publication of "The International Jew" and lamented signs of American racial decay. "[O]ur imagination may picture the United States of fifty or a hundred years hence as a land inhabited only by Slavs, Negroes, and Jews," one installment of "The International Jew" declared.[48] Box shared this dread.

Box saw wide-open immigration laws as part of a sinister Jewish conspiracy to make the United States vulnerable to its enemies by flooding it with foreigners of suspect biology. World War I instigated a xenophobic frenzy. Congress in 1917 passed the most sweeping restrictions on immigration up to that point in American history. In a series of laws beginning with the 1882 Chinese Exclusion Act, Congress had banned almost all prospective immigrants from southern or eastern Asia, those with tuberculosis or epilepsy, or the mentally ill. The new law added members of radical political organizations. For the first time, American immigration law required newcomers to be able to read between thirty and forty words in their native language, a provision that exempted children under sixteen and women accompanied by a literate husband or adult-aged son. However, to Box's disappointment, the bill provided an exemption from the literacy test requirement: those fleeing religious and political oppression.[49]

Box mocked what he deemed misplaced compassion. "When half-hearted reluctance to admit newcomers has been manifested," Box claimed, "the undesirable has had but to murmur in some form 'persecuted' or 'oppressed' and the utterance has proved an unfailing password."[50] According to Box, two groups tried to manipulate well-meaning Americans into allowing them US entry. Writing nineteen years before the start of the Holocaust, Box wrote: "Happily, religious persecution has passed from the world, although Jews and Armenians, two of the races which furnish the greatest menace in present American immigration, are fond of ascribing their unpopularity to religious grounds rather than to industrial oppression in which they themselves have been the oppressors."[51]

When Box authored this jeremiad, Turkish leaders were committing genocide against Armenians, a campaign of extermination between 1915 and 1922 that eventually claimed 1.5 million victims. Also, between 1881 and 1906, waves of persecution by the Czarist government in Russia, and then during the 1918–20 Russian Civil War, resulted in the torching of villages, seizure of property, and assault and murder of hundreds of thousands of Jewish people across the empire. Box dismissed these tragedies as lies designed to extort undeserved mercy from white Christians and gain entry into the United States.[52]

In his 1920 *Dearborn Independent* essay, Box bitterly denounced what he saw as a cynical loophole in the new statute. "Each immigrant must read 30 words or more, selected by the immigration authorities," Box said. "But instead of reading them in English he is expressly permitted to choose any language, *including Hebrew or Yiddish*. Never in any legislation has bolder class legislation been perpetrated than this express sanction of one foreign race's tongue." The only reason for this provision, Box insisted, was "Jewish influences on Congress." The 1917 law had been fatally undermined, he mourned, and "the immigration gates remained as wide open as ever."[53]

Xenophobia, Lone Star-Style

Box did not represent a fringe in the Democratic Party. Always a central part of the eugenics agenda, immigration restriction in and of itself became a far more popular idea in Texas than proposals to restrict marriage or to allow court-sanctioned sterilizations. Fierce anti-immigrant sentiment shaped Texas schools, which in the 1920s imposed English-only lessons in Texas classrooms.[54] White women's clubs in the state increasingly called for eugenics legislation, blocking Mexicans from entering the United States, and repealing early twentieth-century Texas voting laws that allowed noncitizens to vote if they notified authorities that they intended to become naturalized, what was called "first papers."[55]

In spite of this rampant fear of outsiders, from 1914 to 1924 Texas eugenicists still found their ambitions thwarted. The eugenics movement in Texas scored its only major legislative triumph at the state level with an expansion of mental facilities. Those confined in the state's expanding network of facilities for the mentally ill and disabled lived hellish lives.

The ruling class had little interest in quality care for those they saw as a drain on society. They prioritized getting those they called "mental defectives" off the streets, where they could make trouble, and into presumably safe, sexually segregated incarceration. Yoakum, like most eugenicists, saw himself as a humanitarian. He called for improved conditions in what he labeled "colonies" for those with mental illness. Regardless, the state legislature demurred at spending more than the minimum to care for the helpless.

Warehousing the Unfit

The same year that Texas's pioneer eugenicist, F. E. Daniel, died, Yoakum, the head of the Department of Philosophy and Psychology at the University of Texas from 1908 to 1919, echoed the old surgeon and medical journalist's oft-repeated forecast: Without dramatic action, the number of those with mentally disabilities in the state would expand to the point of endangering the social order.[56] In *Care of the Feeble-Minded and Insane in Texas*, published in 1914 at the behest of the Committee on Mental Hygiene of the State Conference of Charities and Corrections, Yoakum warned that "the defective and the insane"—groups he described as "most frequently found among the poorer classes"—constituted a financial burden for taxpayers. He noted that Texas's three insane asylums cost taxpayers $700,000 a year (almost $21 million in 2023 dollars). Half the state's incarcerated population, he estimated, were "feebleminded" and incapable of "of managing themselves or their affairs with ordinary prudence." Yoakum claimed that such professedly crime-prone inmates cost another $10 million (about $296 million in 2023, adjusted for inflation) in law enforcement costs.[57] He reported that working Texans supported between 5,000 and 10,000 children and adults with mental disabilities. The number, he said, had increased by more than 20 percent in the previous decade.[58]

"The feeble-minded are increasing at a faster rate than the general population," he warned.[59] That rising tide, he said, represented both a biological and budgetary crisis. Yoakum insisted that, "Defective strains are of no value; they cost every man, woman and child on an average of $3.00 per year in direct state taxes [about $89 in 2023] and [in] indirect sums that are and always will be unknown."[60] Yoakum doubted the practicality of surgical sterilization as a means to dam the coming deluge and was

skeptical of other eugenic-inspired legislative initiatives. "Restrictive marriage laws and customs are important, but fail to reach the irresponsible
and degenerate until too late," he wrote. "The 'socially inadequate' are so
named just because they are without the influence of law and order. Eugenic
education, better environment, and systems of matings purporting to
remove 'defective' traits do not affect the impure blood and inheritable
factors with safety necessary to eliminate defects."[61]

Yoakum argued that separating the mentally unfit from the rest of
society and placing them in sex-segregated facilities would eventually
result in the extinction of what he called "defective strains." He advocated the position adopted in 1911 by the eugenicist American Breeders
Association that "*segregation* [as opposed to sterilization]" provided "the
most feasible, most easily put into force, and least subversive of constitutional prerogative" means of culling a population he found undesirable
from the population.[62] Yoakum wanted the state government to invest in
creating more and much bigger facilities for those with mental disabilities, institutions that would provide decent housing, clothing, and a
level of job training appropriate to the inmate's abilities and needs. Yoakum hoped that once that population had been bred out of the human
species, investment in incarceration would pay for itself. As Larson
noted, southern eugenicists promoted detention as a humane and more
popular alternative to sterilization. At the time of Yoakum's report, however, committing the insane and the mentally disabled in Texas lay in the
hands of county commissioners who often threw those with mental illness and developmental disabilities into local jails in conditions that horrified the UT professor.

"In [the Bell County] jail. . . . a negro woman . . . had been in the jail a
year," the report read. "She was kept in the basement and refused to wear
any clothing or to even keep a blanket in the cell. When seen she was lying
on her back on the cement pavement in semi-darkness . . . [In] Bexar
County . . . sanitary conditions are very poor. . . . as many as fifteen have
been kept in [a] . . . 'monkey cage' for weeks. It is approximately 21×24 feet
in size . . . One of these was so dark that the back wall could not be seen
and contained nothing but the naked insane patient—no bedding, chair,
no matting of any sort was to be seen."[63]

In 1913, Yoakum supported a bill introduced in the Texas house that
would have created a farm colony. Governor Oscar Colquitt vetoed

funding for the project. Yoakum, however, would eventually experience more legislative success than his eugenicist predecessors. The legislature passed a law creating the State Colony for the Feebleminded just outside of Austin in 1915. Opened in 1917, the colony, renamed the Austin State School in 1925, predictably left the inhabitants in overcrowded dormitories and in the care of undertrained staff. Inmates butchered meat, provided farm labor, and manufactured brooms and mattresses. Assuming the promiscuity of the inmates, John Bradfield, superintendent from the colony's opening until 1936, enforced separation of men and women, thus preventing pregnancy among detained women.[64]

Meanwhile, support for such facilities in other southern states like Alabama and Georgia grew. "The story was much the same throughout the region," Larson reported. "The concept of sexually segregating . . . [those with mental disabilities] to prevent them from reproducing had begun gaining adherents among southern mental health officials and physicians early in the century." However, the theoretical biological and fiscal payoff for building such costly facilities lay far in the future, and southern state governments continued to be among the stingiest in the land even in the face of the evolutionary catastrophe many feared loomed in the future. "The statutes [creating facilities for the mentally disabled] contained inadequate appropriations to meet local needs or to match elsewhere in the country. According to mental health hygiene surveys, there were in the Deep South far more people who should not breed than could fit in the new institutions."[65] This was the case in Texas. In spite of his initial success, Yoakum could not inspire the Texas legislature to spend enough to meet what he considered a mounting crisis. No mass construction of mental health colonies followed. Yoakum, however, shifted focus to another supposed source of degeneracy that served mostly as an abstract threat in the rest of the South: immigrants.

Immigration Quota and the Mexican Exclusion

When the United States entered World War I, eugenicists saw a golden opportunity to prove a major thesis. Previously, the movement had largely relied on subjective descriptions of immigrants' culture and behavior, supplemented by measurements of skulls, to prove their inferiority. Some in the scientific community already questioned evaluations of skull sizes and shapes as a means to document inadequate intelligence. The IQ tests developed by Binet in Europe and modified by eugenicists at Stanford University, however, provided the illusion of objectivity and precision. Yoakum teamed up with Harvard psychologist Yerkes to subject army recruits heading to combat in Europe during the First World War to intelligence testing. About 1.75 million individuals, sorted by race and national origin, underwent such examinations. With unchecked confirmation bias, Yerkes and Yoakum analyzed the mountain of data and subsequently informed a shocked public that so-called new immigrants running amuck in the United States had the minds of children. As a result, the nation itself was in mental decline.

Charles Davenport, the director of the Eugenics Record Office, taught Yerkes when the latter was an undergraduate at Harvard earning a psychology degree. By 1915, Yerkes chafed at the widespread perception of psychology as a "soft," impressionistic science lacking empirical data. The Stanford-Binet IQ test, he believed, would provide psychology the credibility it lacked in academia. "Yerkes and most of his contemporaries equated rigor and science with numbers and quantification," Gould said.[66] When the United States declared war on Germany on April 4, 1917, Yerkes, then president of the American Psychological Association, grabbed a chance to legitimize psychology and its latest toy. Commissioned as a colonel, Yerkes convinced the army to test soldiers as they were processed into the service. Yerkes, Yoakum, Terman, and other specialists in the emerging field of psychometrics designed three tests—the so-called Alpha test for literate recruits, the Beta test using pictures for illiterate recruits and those who failed the Alpha test, and a third based on the standard Stanford-Binet IQ tests. The tests rested on deep cultural biases. Many of the recruits tested were recent immigrants still mastering English. Administrators asked subjects questions specific to American history and culture such as, "[George] Washington is to [John] Adams as first is to . . ." or "Christy Mathewson is famous as a: writer, artist, baseball player, comedian." In short, the written test had less to do with intellectual ability than with mastery of culturally specific trivia.[67] Recruits took tests in crowded rooms. They sometimes sat on the floor and often could not hear instructions that, for many, were given in a barely understood second language.[68]

When published under the authorization of the United States War Department, the results shocked the American public and inspired calls for strict immigration laws. Yerkes, Yoakum, and the rest of the team had supposedly discovered that the average American had a "mental age" of thirteen, near the level of so-called morons. (As noted earlier, in 1910 psychologist Henry H. Goddard developed an IQ scale that divided the population of those suffering from mental disabilities into the categories of "morons," "imbeciles," and "idiots," terminology now rejected as offensive by those in the psychiatric and psychological professions.) According to the army tests, 37 percent of whites ranked as "morons" and 89 percent of African Americans did.[69]

Yerkes's team sorted the test results by ethnicity and declared that army recruits of eastern and southern European heritage scored lower on the IQ tests than those of northern and western European origins. According to the army IQ tests, Russian immigrant recruits had a mental age of 11.34, Italians, 11.01, and Poles 10.74. African Americans scored last among all racial groups, with a supposed mental age of 10.41. The report did not highlight that African Americans in northern states scored higher than southern whites. The study clearly revealed that higher test scores correlated to the quality of schooling available. Northern schools were better funded and hired better-trained teachers than southern schools. Yoakum and Yerkes published their book, *Army Mental Tests*, in 1920. They ostensibly proved the need to stop immigration from eastern and southern Europe. It is unclear if the test results had any impact on members of Congress as they debated immigration restrictions, but it undoubtedly influenced public opinion. The subsequent Emergency Quota Act of 1921 gained the support of strange bedfellows, such as labor unions dreading job competition, the Ku Klux Klan, and leading eugenicist groups like the Immigration Restriction League. The 1921 law imposed the first-ever immigration quotas on specific nationalities. Congress limited immigration from each nation to 3 percent of the total number of persons of that nationality living in the United States in 1910. An immediate and profound impact followed. In the year before Congress passed the Quota Act, authorities admitted 805,228 newcomers into the United States. In 1921, that number dropped to 309,556 and then cratered to a mere 40,319 in 1922. The new quotas particularly targeted potential eastern and southern European immigrants. Because of the new system, Greek immigration, for instance, dropped form 28,503 a year before the law to only 1,998 the year after the law.[70]

The new rules were harsh, but not enough for eugenicists like Texas congressman John Box and his allies. Roy L. Garis, a Vanderbilt University economist, successfully lobbied Congress to establish new quotas based on the numbers of immigrants of a particular nationality present in the United States in 1890 rather than 1910. The year 1890 fell before the biggest wave of immigration from eastern and southern Europe. Such a tweak, Garis argued, would greatly tilt immigration quotas in favor of "Nordics." The army IQ tests led many Texans to support the further immigration restrictions Garris proposed. Responding to the tests, one editorialist for *The Granbury News* warned in 1922 that "We have been adding low mentality to our mental outfit with a vengeance for forty years now, and the inferiority is reflected in our politics, our writing, our morale." In 1924, Congress passed the Johnson-Reed or Immigration Restriction Act, which incorporated the Garis guidelines. The Johnson-Reed Act reduced the total yearly immigration quota from 355,000 under the 1921 law to 165,000 after 1924. The number of "new immigrants" from eastern and southern Europe allowed each year plummeted to a negligible 20,477.[71]

The US House passed the Johnson-Reed Act with 308 votes in favor to 62 against, and it prevailed in the Senate on a 69 to 9 vote. The *Saturday Evening Post* credited passage to John Box and a short roster of his colleagues, "devoted and patriotic men without much regard for party lines." Box and other House members like him ensured enactment of new legal barriers "designed to raise the quality of our immigration and to forestall the day when we shall have a completely mongrelized American," gushed the *Post*. Box enjoyed a national audience throughout the 1920s, his congressional efforts receiving approving coverage by, among other publications, the *Eugenical News.* That newspaper quoted him as warning in 1927 that "[e]very Chinaman or 'mixed breed' born to these seasonal laborers [in agriculture] under the flag of the United States is, by the provisions of the Constitution, a citizen entitled to go from one part of the nation to another freely and to remain, and have his children remain, forever."[72] Box believed increasing numbers of these children, which the anti-immigration right wing in the twenty-first century would label "anchor babies," would erode American identity. Even if he played a major role in the passage of Johnson-Reed Act, Box was not entirely pleased with the results. He believed that Mexicans had invaded his home state and threatened its future. He regretted that the quota system had not been imposed on the Western Hemisphere. Had the Johnson-Reed law set such limits, it would have capped Mexican immigration at 2,900 individuals per year.

In spite of Box's best efforts, Mexico and Central and South America eluded the tight restrictions imposed on eastern and southern Europe.[73]

Congress's implementation of quotas turned out to be a mixed blessing for the eugenics movement. With the sharp decline in immigration after 1924, one of the movement's major goals had been achieved. The sense of urgency for eugenics measures evaporated. Twenty-one states implemented sterilization laws by 1924. Four more—Idaho, Maine, Minnesota, and Utah—followed suit the following year as the statute's impact was just beginning to be felt. Only seven passed sterilization bills after 1925, and sixteen never did.[74] Sterilizations would go on for decades but a national eugenics mania ebbed. To Box, however, little had changed in his home state. The number of Mexicans in Texas still increased every day, and Box saw this as a biological disaster.

"Racial Differences in General Intelligence": The Abuse of IQ Tests in Texas

The exclusion of Mexico and Central and South America from national quotas presented a menace to the nation, Box insisted. "For the most part Mexicans are Indians, and very seldom become naturalized," he declared in 1928. "They know very little of sanitation, are very low mentally, and are generally unhealthy." He continued his crusade to extend immigration quotas to the Western Hemisphere until he left the Congress in 1931. "The fight over that question [immigration] will go on as long as America is less crowded, less hungry, more peaceable, and better in every way than the crowded, miserable countries of the old world east and west, and Mexico south," he said. "Vigilant measures to prevent their coming will have to be continued. The moment our bars go down they will rush in from everywhere."[75]

Alexander Caswell Ellis agreed that open borders endangered Anglo-Saxons. He survived Jim Ferguson's attempts to fire him and resumed his duties at the University of Texas education department in 1917, preaching the eugenics gospel there until 1926, when Cleveland College in Ohio, an adult education facility, named him director. Ellis held steadfast to the belief that intellectuals like him could alter the human mind, anatomy, and destiny. His papers include an undated typed quote from the investor Charles Schwab. "There are those who are devoting their scientific attention to the problems of Human Engineering and their solution of these problems is carrying us forward to greater things."[76] Like Yoakum, Ellis promoted the IQ test as a means to detect and enumerate the level of biological defect in the general population.

With the support of Ellis, the Texas Mental Health Agency (TMHA) examined the intellects of Texas school children. Ellis saw the effort as a means of documenting eugenic "degeneration" in the state. In the same year Congress passed the Johnson-Reed Act, 1924, the TMHA released the *Psychiatric Study of Public School Children in Eleven Counties, Children in State and County Institutions for Delinquents and Dependents, Inmates of Eleven County Poor Farms [and] Inmates of Eighteen County Jails*. The TMHA believed it had documented high levels of low intelligence among that state's young. Ellis and his staff offered racial inheritance as the be-all and end-all explanation for variations in IQ scores.[77]

The TMHA examined 3,208 Texas school children, including 122 African Americans, 421 "Mexicans" and 2,665 "others." The report vaguely defined those in this indeterminate category as "white." Echoing the dubious results and the insulting language of the army IQ tests, the authors of the Texas report stated that just short of a quarter of Texas school children fit the definition of mental "defectives" or as suffering from "borderline mental defect" or tending "toward the feeble-minded." Supposedly 8.3 percent of Texas students suffered from "gross personality defect."[78]

According to the IQ tests, in Texas not a single African American child could be considered intellectually "superior." (Only 2.4 percent of white children reached that rank.) The agency reported that 1.9 percent of Tejanos and 0.9 percent of Tejanas achieved the highest intellectual classification. Meanwhile, according to the report, low intelligence among African Americans, Mexicans, and Mexican Americans reached epidemic levels. Test analysts ranked a remarkable 34.4 percent of African American school-age children and 23.4 percent of Mexican and Mexican American children as suffering from low intelligence. White children fared much better, but even in that group, 5.7 percent of those tested as "defective," a worrying number, particularly given the eugenicist panic that those of low intelligence reproduced at higher rates than the "normal" and "above normal."[79]

As with the army IQ tests, the Texas exams rewarded mastery of trivia. The test asked students who wrote the poem "Hiawatha." The multiple-choice exam offered James Fenimore Cooper, Henry Wadsworth Longfellow, Edgar Allan Poe, and John Greenleaf Whittier as possible answers. Those who answered Longfellow got credit for a correct response.[80] When the Texas Mental Hygiene Society published its report in 1924, it called for improved mental health care and rehabilitation in the state, but did not seem to consider that the poor scores on the IQ tests actually gauged the inadequacy of Texas schools. As a result of paltry funding of education, Texas schools rated poorly compared to other states. One 1920 survey placed Texas schools thirty-ninth of the forty-eight states in terms of quality.[81] Yet, many Texas scholars and political leaders believed the problem was not misguided spending priorities, but the infusion in the state of new immigrants. Mexicans, eugenicists warned, would do more than steal jobs, lower wages, and spread disease. Mexican women in particular represented a source of "contagion" that would undermine white civilization.

"The Catholic Organization is Behind It": John Box and Mexican Immigration

The state legislature unsuccessfully attempted to enact a Texas version of the 1921 and 1924 federal immigration laws. In 1923, the Texas house contemplated a concurrent resolution introduced by Dallas representative Lewis Carpenter that would have granted states an unprecedented role in setting immigration limits, a power constitutionally reserved for the federal government.[82] If approved, Carpenter's plan would have permitted every governor and state legislature to determine "the kind and character and number of immigrants which any given State is willing and ready to receive for any given year or period of years." States could then request a quota based upon its particular labor needs. Had this plan become law, American immigration quotas would have become a patchwork, varying from state to state, ebbing and flowing based on the economic priorities of any particular year. To ensure that migrants did not attempt to stay in Texas illegally, Carpenter said that states should hold them in custody until they either were naturalized or returned to their homelands. Born of frustration over Congress's refusal to stem the growth of the Mexican population in Texas, Carpenter's decentralized immigration quota system would serve the labor needs of big business while maintaining "the preservation of a homogeneous race" in Texas and beyond. The house leadership forwarded Concurrent Resolution Fifteen to the Committee on Federal Relations. The committee, however, rejected such a radical expansion of state authority at the expense of the federal government.[83] The blowback from business interests proved too fierce.

For years, cotton growers worried that immigration restrictions, regardless of the eugenical consequences, might make it harder to hire even cheaper labor than was provided by poor whites and African Americans. After passage of the nativist 1917 Immigration Act, Texas planters and growers successfully lobbied Secretary of Labor William B. Wilson to allow the temporary entry of "otherwise inadmissible aliens" to offset labor shortages created by the American entry into World War I. Eugenicists led a chorus of protest against the quota waivers, leading Wilson to rescind his exemptions of Mexican workers after the war. Once again, the big planters and growers insisted they needed Mexican workers, who, they argued, were uniquely suited physically to pick crops. The exemptions were extended until 1920. By the time the US Congress passed the Quota Act in 1921, Mexican farm labor had become even more important, and again the rich landowners got all the poorly paid migrant field hands they wanted. Many Anglos, on the other hand, worried about the alleged genetic inferiority of Mexicans as well as their possible radical politics. It made no sense to Box to keep Italians, Greeks, and Jews out but let Mexicans and others from the hemispheric south in.[84]

Anglo farmers of modest means made up most of the population in Box's homebase of Cherokee County. Chronic overproduction of cotton and the exploitation of cheaply compensated migrant labor from Mexico made it harder for small landowners across East and Central Texas to break even. Industrial workers bitterly complained that the presence of immigrants drove down wages. As one historian, Marshall Roderick, put it, "Box formed his policy proposals in this milieu of small farmers, racist sentiment, and Anglo violence."[85]

In 1925, Box introduced House Resolution 6741, which would have extended the Johnson-Reed quota formula to Mexicans. As the historian Mark Reisler observed, the landed class viewed Mexican workers as "docile, indolent, and backward," and therefore easy to manipulate and control. Anglo workers and nativists worried that these same supposedly shared traits posed a threat to American labor organizing and made foreign workers prone to insidious control by outside powers such as the Vatican. As a result, Mexican immigrants became a convenient punching bag for those angry with the economic inequities in Texas life.[86]

As the scholar of race relations Neil Foley put it, "Mexicans were accused of every conceivable social ill, of carrying diseases, lowering wages, accepting charity, displacing Anglo workers, molesting white women, and even stealing Irish American melodies and making them their own." Mexicans drained the resources of whites, some charged. As Dr. W. M. Branch wrote to Box in an April 22, 1927, letter, "Waco is a white man's town, but how long, oh how long will their boasted white supremacy last in the face of a deluge of ignorant illiterates . . . who will choke the wheels of justice, overrun the public schools, pay little or no taxes . . . and reduce the moral standing?" To eugenicists, the bigger worry was that somehow the same Mexicans they accused of being lazy and submissive would, with sufficient numbers, overthrow the existing American economic political order. If the flow of immigrants from south of the Rio Grande continued unabated, one member of the Texas delegation to the US House, Eugene Black, claimed, "Radicalism and discontent would Samson-like . . . pull down the pillars of our whole economic structure on our heads."[87]

Arthur E. Knolle of San Antonio predicted that the overthrow of the Anglo-Saxon in Texas would probably come without a gunshot being fired but by gradual racial pollution. Urging Box to read Lothrop Stoddard's *The Rising Tide of Color,* Knolle prophesied that:

[T]he Mexican will finally conquer the American, not by force of arms, but by the slow and sure process of infiltration . . . It has happened again and again, during the world's history, that a strong, virile race gradually disappears when enveloped by a numerous, weak, servile population. The young Mexican girls are undeniably pretty and charming. While their morals are rather lax before marriage, once married they are usually very faithful to their spouses. Their fecundity is amazing. Mixed marriages and alliances without the sanction of the church and state have become rather common in Southwest Texas for many years. It is very rare that a Mexican woman will do anything to prevent conception, this being strictly forbidden by the Catholic Church.[88]

After calling for a complete ban on Mexican immigration and mass deportation of all noncitizens from the state, Knolle insisted that the greed of the business community and the cowardice of politicians not wanting to anger commercial interests would prevent either from happening. He repeated his earlier prediction of almost universal hybridization. "I anticipate no violence, bloodshed, nor race riots. The Mexican is pliant and docile to the last degree. He will have his revenge by slowly enveloping the white overlord, giving him his daughter in marriage, gradually undermining his habits and prejudice—until after the lapse of slow centuries the 'Gringo' strain will have been bred out and the characteristics of the inferior race will predominate as has happened many times before in the history of the various branches of the Nordic race." E. E. Davis also applauded Box for his immigration proposals and furthermore encouraged him to read Stoddard's *The Rising Tide of Color.* The college dean said that Stoddard laid out the best case for "restricting the lower races of humanity from free admittance to the United States."[89]

Some of Box's correspondents saw an international conspiracy behind the growing Mexican menace. Some complained of "foreign priests" taking up residence and others called for the exclusion from Texas of "degenerates, idiots, criminals, common laborers, paupers, prostitutes, revolutionists, political agitators, and paple nuncies [sic]." (Apostolic nuncios are diplomats from Vatican City.) Mexican immigration was part of a Vatican plot to seize Texas from whites, one man charged. In an April 9, 1928, letter to Box, W. C. McDonald of Corpus Christi complained that a "white laborer can not [sic] get work in this city and others are affected. The paying teller at my bank is a Mexican. All the stores have Mexican clerks. One Mexican owns 3 Chain Grocery Stores as good as any in the City [sic]. Filling stations are run by them and they are running the town. Young men of our race and religion are leaving or starving. The catholic [sic] organization is behind it all."[90]

In spite of the widely held belief in Mexican inferiority and the conviction of many Texans that "new immigrants" had irreparably tainted Anglo-Saxon blood, Box's efforts to impose Johnson-Reed limitations on immigration from south of the border failed. The bottom line of wealthy cotton cultivators represented an objective reality that the unproven science of eugenics could not overcome. "In the end, the needs of southwestern industry and agribusiness prevented labor interests, patriotic organizations, and eugenicist groups from imposing immigration restriction on Mexico," as Foley observed. "The expansion of industry and agriculture in the Southwest depended on Mexican labor and therefore outweighed nativist considerations that Mexicans would radicalize and mongrelize the Southwest."[91]

Texas capitalists assumed that white workers would reject the low wages the rich wanted to pay and the hard physical labor associated with Black and Brown servitude. "Who is going to do the rough work on the Texas ranches?" the *Austin American* wondered as it contemplated a Mexican quota. "Who is going to pick the cotton crop of Texas? Who is going to fell the trees and grub the stumps? Who is going to do the rough work on the railroads? American boys? Not on your life."[92]

C. L. Willis of Beaumont, owner of 1,740 acres of cotton land, spoke for many in a January 23, 1924, letter to Box when he expressed alarm about a labor shortage. "[I]n East Texas, there are hundreds of thousands of cut-over pine lands lying idle for lack of development, that should be bringing in some revenues," he told Box. "You and I both know that the average Texan or American man who has been brought up in the past 25 to 40 years is not inclined to buckle down to farm work; in fact as soon as they get large enough they leave the farm as quickly as possible, and unless we bring a desirable class of immigration to build up our farming sections of our state, we are not going to progress as we should, in fact we will retrograde." Meanwhile, major lobbying groups like the Dallas-based Cotton States Protective League complained about "the continuously increasing exodus of our Mexican labor to the North and East."[93]

A member of the Texas delegation to the United States House, John Nance Garner, who would eventually become Franklin Roosevelt's first vice president, turned the stereotypes of Mexicans on their heads, arguing that their supposed docility and their lack of intelligence would make it easy to tightly control them and squeeze every possible penny out of their labor. The representative from Uvalde County declared that Mexicans in Texas "do not cause any trouble, unless they stay there and become Americanized." In spite of eugenicist claims that Mexicans could retake Texas without firing a shot, growers mocked the idea that such immigrants could topple Anglo-Saxon dominance. "Have you ever heard, in the history of the United States or in the history of the human race of the white race being overrun by a class of people of the mentality of the Mexicans?"

one cotton grower said.[94] To the wealthy landowners exploiting migrant labor, the threat of paying higher wages proved far more frightening than any dysgenic nightmare that Box and his allies could conjure.

In spite of Box's repeated efforts, he could not persuade the United States Congress to impose Mexican immigration quotas. The low cost of Mexican labor and the spending by Mexican workers provided too important a stimulus to the South Texas economy to consider eugenicist appeals. The idea of immigration limits, in any case, became redundant by the time that Box lost his bid for reelection, in the July 29, 1930, Democratic primary, to the future instigator of the second American Red Scare, Martin Dies.[95]

During the 1929–39 global economic meltdown, perhaps more than 250,000 Mexicans fled Texas because of vanished jobs, reduced wages, or forced expulsions. The exodus unfolded mostly from farming regions in the state, but the biggest urban centers such as Dallas, El Paso, Houston, and San Antonio saw a dramatic drop in the Mexican population as well. Racial violence, subsidies provided by the Agricultural Adjustment Administration (which slashed the cotton acreage cultivated in Texas by hundreds of thousands), and deportations of Mexicans and American citizens of Mexican background by federal law enforcement, the Texas Rangers, and local law agencies began in the lower Rio Grande Valley in 1928 and continued throughout the 1930s. In some small rural towns, the Mexican community almost vanished. Box made immigration quotas the central theme of his 1930 reelection bid, but the twin effects of "voluntary" repatriation and deportations rendered the central objective of his political life superfluous. His successful opponent, Dies, neutralized immigration as an issue with his own rabid xenophobia. Dies eventually introduced a bill that would have deported "communist immigrants." For a time the panic about a Mexican "invasion" receded, only to come roaring back in the 1950s.[96]

Eugenics in the Shadows: Hermann Joseph Muller's Painful Sojourn

By the 1920s and 1930s, Edgar Lovett's dream of making the Rice Institute a hub of eugenics research had fallen apart. Lovett's first star hire, Julian Huxley, had returned to England and alienated his peers in the global movement with his increased focus on how the physical and social

environment shaped bodies and minds. Huxley even admitted that eugenics had failed to prove its most important suppositions, and began to
question race as a valid biological concept.[97] Another of Lovett's promising early hires, one-time Huxley acolyte Hermann Joseph Muller (1890–
1967) had moved on to Columbia by 1918. After two years there, he received
an appointment as a zoology professor at the University of Texas, where
he worked from 1920 to 1936. Like Huxley, Muller's immense abilities did
nothing to advance the eugenics cause in Texas and, similar to his mentor,
his personality and his politics alienated more than they persuaded.[98]

Muller achieved worldwide stature at the University of Texas. However,
he found himself in the uncomfortable position of being a communist
public figure in an archconservative state. An opponent of both capitalism
and segregation, he struggled to keep his politics hidden from his university administration. In spite of his immense talents, because of the oppres-
sive political environment in Texas, he tried to keep secret his passion for
both socialism and eugenics.

A native New Yorker whose ancestors fled Germany for the United
States during the anti-monarchist revolutions that spread across Europe
in 1848, Muller grew up in a leftist home, eventually attending Columbia
University in New York City. He obtained a doctorate from Columbia's
zoology department while teaching biology at the Rice Institute. A lifelong friend, Edgar Altenburg, later observed that while a Columbia student, Muller "traded in the three R's for the three S's—science, sex, and
socialism."[99]

Working with Huxley, he would teach as an instructor in the still-new
biology department at Rice from 1916 to 1918. While at Rice, he not only
finished his doctorate, but also coauthored a groundbreaking work on
genetics, *The Mechanism of Mendelian Heredity* (1915). He furthermore
began his experiments proving that radiation from X-rays produced
mutations in fruit flies, research that would eventually win Muller a Nobel
Prize in the physiology or medicine category in 1946.[100]

By 1921, Muller's interests extended beyond fruit flies. He turned his
keen mind to the mysteries of human inheritance when he closely examined the lives of identical twin girls who had been separated shortly after
birth and raised separately in Wyoming. One girl, however, had enjoyed
a mere four years of formal schooling and later attended a business
school for nine months of vocational training before becoming a

business owner. The other earned a high school diploma, attended some university classes, and became a teacher. The twins' divergent destinies led Muller to abandon the strict biological determinism dominating the eugenics movement. Muller concluded "that both heredity and environment play very important roles in determining mental traits."[101]

Through twin studies and his own laboratory work, Muller became convinced that "the positive biological improvement of mankind" could be achieved through a combination of guided breeding and a radical redistribution of wealth that eliminated poverty, malnutrition, and other ills engendered by capitalism. Human engineering could be successful only if "the social reconstruction occurs first." In 1925, while at the University of Texas, Muller authored *Out of the Night: A Biologist's View of the Future*. Yet, he hid the manuscript for fear it would jeopardize his academic career in Austin. Initially an admirer of Soviet leader Joseph Stalin, Muller praised the "great and solid actualities of collective achievement which are increasingly evident in that one section of the world—the Soviet Union."[102]

The biologist hoped that the USSR, with its stated commitment to class consciousness and human equality, would use eugenics to eliminate disabilities like genetically related paralysis, blindness, and mental limitations that blocked so many in their quest for economic survival. With its top-down authority structure and central planning, Muller believed the Soviet system was the best designed to implement the "real biological upbuilding of humanity."[103] In a move that proved deadly to his career in Texas, Muller anonymously wrote many of the articles for and edited a radical underground newspaper, the *Spark* (named after a newspaper Vladimir Lenin, the founder of the Soviet state, edited while in exile in Switzerland). Muller's students distributed the *Spark* at the UT campus and, through a network of friends, at Rice.[104]

Achieving international fame for his work in the burgeoning field of genetics, beginning in 1933, Muller went on extended leaves in Germany and then the Soviet Union, but his political activism caught up with him.[105] He was scheduled for a return to Austin in the 1936–37 school year. Instead, in 1936 University of Texas president Harry Yandell Benedict sent Muller a letter accusing the scientist of violating his contract. In 1932, police had arrested an accused communist activist in San Antonio and found in his possession a letter from Muller indicating the professor's heavy involvement with the *Spark*. Benedict claimed Muller's secret relationship with the publication violated university policies. Benedict demanded Muller report to Austin for a hearing on his future with the school. Muller retorted that he would wage a public fight against the charges. Such a legal battle would likely bring uncomfortable attention to the university. Benedict blinked and decided not to fire Muller. Instead, Muller agreed to resign on April 17, 1936, and returned to a tumultuous career in the Soviet Union that would end with him fleeing to Spain to avoid possible liquidation in a Stalinist purge.[106]

Open eugenicists remained in Texas academia, but their public profile dwindled to the vanishing point. Texas public schools and higher education remained poorly funded. The continued diminishment chilled the recruitment of scholars, especially those who wanted to plunge into treacherous political waters to advance hotly contested policies like forced sterilization. In California, eugenicists served as key players in mobilizing political support for the eugenical program of sterilization, detection of biological "failure" through standardized testing, mass detention of those with intellectual challenges, and closing entry to immigrants racists labeled as inferior. Texas politicians backing eugenics received no such support. In the 1930s, as the Texas legislature debated once again how best to regulate human reproduction to better the species, the academy fell silent.

Mexican Eugenics and the Tejano Press

The 1930s saw the last sterilization laws passed in the United States, in Oklahoma, Vermont, South Carolina, and Georgia. Virginia and Georgia made liberal use of the purifying knife, ranking eleventh and fourteenth in per capita sterilizations among the thirty-two states adopting such laws.[107] Texas remained part of a dwindling minority of states with no sterilization laws. While Texas eugenicists fumed at their legislative frustration, they witnessed eugenics prospering just south of the state's international border. In Mexico, intellectuals deployed eugenics as a means of valorizing the 1910 revolution. Mexican intellectuals "felt the political need to answer European racial mythologies with mythologies of their own." Unlike their peers in much of the rest of the world, Mexican eugenicists, at least officially, celebrated what Anglos called "race mixing." The Mexican population consisted of individuals of indigenous, African, and European descent. Nationalism surged after the overthrow of longtime dictator Porfirio Díaz in 1910. Revolutionary thinkers like Manuel Gamio chafed at the economic colonialism that Mexico had suffered at the hands of the United States and the major European powers under Díaz. He asserted his nation's cultural and biological greatness. Gamio and fellow radicals like José Vasconcelos acknowledged Mexico's mixed racial heritage, its *mestizaje*, and argued this was a national strength, not a weakness. That was the official national ideology, at least. In reality, Mexican society continued to economically and politically reward whiteness, or *blanqueamiento*, harshly condemning the contemporary Native population to poverty and political marginalization.[108]

Gamio's influence and scientific acclaim won admiration from the editors at *La Prensa de San Antonio*. In an October 4, 1920, edition, the Spanish-language newspaper in Texas crowed about "the honorable distinction" given the anthropologist when Gamio was named vice president of the Second International Eugenics Conference, which would be held in New York the following year. "The appointment of Mr. Gamio has made a marvelous impression in intellectual and scientific circles in Mexico, where he enjoys a well-earned reputation." The appointment, the San Antonio newspaper argued, earned credibility and honor not just for Gamio, but for "all of Mexico's intellectual community as well."[109]

Most of the world's eugenicists, including those in the United States, based their theories on Mendelism, the idea that biological traits passed from generation to generation through what were eventually labeled genes. Mexican eugenicists embraced a Lamarckian view of evolution. Named after Jean-Baptiste Lamarck, an early nineteenth-century French naturalist, Lamarckians emphasized environmental factors in heredity and postulated that physical changes over an organism's lifetime can be transmitted to offspring. With this framework in mind, Mexican eugenicists sought to change the social environment in their country in the hope of upgrading *la raza cosmica* (the "cosmic race").[110]

Not just in Mexico but across Latin America the notion of Europeans and their descendants embodying the pinnacle of human evolution and the peak of civilization literally blew up on the battlefields of World War I. Europeans slew each other without restraint, behaving with the savagery that they had always claimed defined Black and Brown people. Latin American eugenicists believed they could provide a counternarrative to classic white supremacism. The global south was not a primitive backwater but offered a saner model for the planet.[111]

By the 1920s, as they perceived their state as darkening, Anglo eugenicists in Texas like John Box and E. E. Davis sounded like doomsday preachers when they speculated about the state's racial future. In Mexico, however, one scientist dedicated to the cause, Alonso L. Herrera, predicted in 1921 that through selective breeding, a super race would "populate the earth with a new and perfect humanity." Eugenicists in Mexico and the rest of Latin America also largely shunned sterilization laws. As historian of Latin American eugenics Nancy Leys Stepan notes, the movement in Mexico and the rest of Latin America focused on "matrimonial eugenics," in short "impeding the acquisition of degenerate characters that were transmittable by heredity . . . [through] controlling the marriages between the defective and the degenerate." Only one Mexican state, Veracruz, was able to implement a sterilization law, partly because of intense anti-clericalism there that hampered the influence of the Catholic Church, which by the 1930s definitely weighed in against eugenics. Open political mobilization for sterilization, however, lost steam as in the United States. Sterilizations unfolded in Mexico independent of statutory authorization, with medical authorities overwhelmingly targeting poor and indigenous women.[112]

The Spanish-language press in Texas echoed the views of Mexican eugenicists, emphasizing both the importance of a healthy environment in improving the race while still hailing selective breeding as a long-proven technique for human improvement. Translating a *Los Angeles Times* story in 1916, the *El Paso Times* quoted an English explorer, J. H. Balmer, who claimed that the Zulu people of Africa had "solved the eugenics problem" through euthanasia. "When a child is born, and it seems inferior to the Zulu norm, it gets a gentle 'tap' on the head; after that there is a burial. The Zulu people do not allow imperfect children to live, and if one of them happens to become older, they are made to disappear at the first opportunity. This is the reason that the Zulu people are superior to other races."[113]

Tejano journalists seemed to share the optimism of many race scientists in Mexico and South America that eugenics could be advanced through education of the best and the brightest rather than coercion. The editors of the *El Paso Times* kept their readers abreast of the newest developments in human engineering, covering events like the 1915 Race Betterment Conference at Battle Creek, Michigan, and a better baby contest the same year in Los Angeles. Descriptions were made of perfect potential mates. The *Times* quoted Dr. A. J. Read, a speaker at the Battle Creek gathering, as claiming that, "The ideal woman of the eugenic age will be taller than the average woman today. She will be plump and well-rounded, but not fat. Her complexion will be ruddy or brown not pale, because pale skin is a badge of disease rather than health." The tone of the coverage of eugenics in the Mexican American press in Texas was generally optimistic, suggesting that a future, more scientific society would birth a better, healthier human species and that individuals could help sculpt a better breed through informed romantic choices rather than awaiting government coercion.[114]

The contrast with the political environment among Anglos in Texas could not be starker. Mexican eugenicists waxed euphoric about human potential. The cataclysmic clash of empires unfolding across the Atlantic from 1914 to 1918, however, reddened the European soil and darkened the mood of white eugenicists in the United States. At the race betterment conference in Michigan, David Starr Jordan glumly told his audience, "The European conflict is draining Europe of its best blood, and will leave its . . . imprint on the lives and progress of several future generations."[115]

Anglo Texas eugenicists no longer rhapsodized about futuristic supermen who would one day look upon present humans as mere ants. Instead, they tried desperately to prevent their state from falling off what they feared would be the biological cliff. The Texas legislature would take up proposed sterilization bills two more times during the Great Depression. Neither effort would succeed. Meanwhile, although forced sterilizations continued for decades, eugenics began to attract influential critics across the country and collectively these doubts led to a slowdown in eugenics legislation. Genetics grew rapidly as a science and as early as the 1920s some in that field, such as Johns Hopkins University zoologist Herbert Jennings, charged eugenics leaders like Harry Laughlin with grossly oversimplifying human heredity. Jennings, as historian of surgical sterilization Philip R. Reilly wrote, rejected sterilization of those with mental disabilities "because he believed that the insignificant improvement it would provide the gene pool was outweighed by the dangerous political precedent that it constituted." Social scientists like Harvard's Lester Ward strongly argued that the "swarming, spawning millions, the bottom layers of society . . . are by their nature the peers of the boasted 'aristocracy of brains.'" The struggling fell to the economic bottom due less to biological deficiency than a lack of inherited privilege. Franz Boas, the Columbia University professor who came to be known as the "father of American anthropology," began shredding the sloppy scientific methods employed by sterilization advocates such as Laughlin. Such academic skepticism likely reached few in Texas, but a more important element for the first time forcefully weighed in against eugenics: the Catholic Church.[116]

Earlier in the twentieth century, Theo Laboure, the San Antonio priest, urged the sterilization of dangerous criminals but in the end, he wound up an outlier among the Catholic clergy. As seen, Protestants in Texas fell on both sides of the eugenics debate. In general, across the South, religion played a less-than-decisive role in the controversy. "At least in the Deep South, values founded on traditional religion and concerns for individual rights served more as a protection against the excesses of eugenics than did any internal regulatory mechanism within medicine or science," Larson wrote. "[However,] religion acted more as a brake than as a barrier to eugenics in the Deep South."[117]

As with immigration, the role of religion in arguments over selective human breeding played out differently in Texas than in the Deep South. In the 1930s, the Catholic Church grew rapidly in the Lone Star State, and when the Vatican finally issued a definitive condemnation of eugenics in 1930, the faithful played a powerful activist role in the defeat of sterilization proposals they labeled arrogant and totalitarian. The lack of respect for academic eugenicists, combined with planter self-interest, conservative skepticism about growing government power (especially amid the building of Franklin Roosevelt's New Deal), and the growing belief among some Texans that eugenics represented nothing less than grave sin, left Texas outside the American mainstream. This situation caused one of John Box's most enthusiastic fans, E. E. Davis, to despair that the state was doomed to be dominated by the rural poor he described with disgust as "the white scourge."

CHAPTER FIVE

Texas Eugenics From 1931 On

POLITICIANS LONG AGO learned that terrorizing voters about out-of-control crime provides a reliable path to electoral success. Typically, the formula calls for linking an unpopular, outnumbered group with urban chaos, and calling for more and better-armed police to round up the miscreants, who should then be dealt harsh sentences. When he unsuccessfully ran for the US Congress from the tiny town of Littlefield northwest of Lubbock in the Texas Panhandle in 1931, Arthur Duggan sounded like a typical "tough on crime" candidate.

With the Depression approaching its nadir and newspapers spilling oceans of ink on bank robbers like Charles Arthur "Pretty Boyd" Floyd and mafiosi like Al Capone, Duggan decried a lawless nation collapsing into anarchy and perhaps bloody revolution. "Crime is now, in this fair land of ours, one of the best organized businesses of the day," Duggan said in his printed campaign platform. "It is run by master minds. It is commercialized, works to the Nth degree of efficiency, and is spreading from the large cities to the smaller towns and rural communities... Unless crime is checked we have the alternative of facing bolshevism, anarchy, or something like the French Revolution." When it came to solutions to crime, however, Duggan (1876–1935) veered from the conventional script. His campaign literature offered alternative solutions. "Our jails, penitentiaries, electric chairs and gallows are not reforming the offenders," Duggan's election platform said. "They are getting bolder every day... What is to be done about it? Mr. Duggan's solution is: 'Stop making criminals.' Our present method of 'reformation' is not only a failure, but it is working on the symptoms instead of the disease. Let's begin at the other end, stop making criminals, and in a few years, the problems will be solved."[1]

Born in Hays County in Central Texas, Duggan was a well-educated man, receiving a bachelor's degree from Texas A&M College in 1895 and then a law degree from the University of Texas in 1898. He worked as an attorney in Galveston before moving west and become a social and political giant in Littlefield. Earning riches in the real estate market, he eventually served as president of the school board and became president of the town's first bank before being selected as president of the local chamber of commerce. He advocated tirelessly for more state investment in Texas Technological College (now Texas Tech University), which opened in Lubbock in 1925. When he ran for Congress, he believed that improved schools would halt the American crime wave. "Take the children when they are young. When their minds are plastic . . . train them to be patriotic, law abiding, self respecting [sic], clean, honest and unselfish citizens. Teach them that Alcohol is a poison to be avoided and let alone . . . It will never be solved in any other way. Law enforcement is necessary, but the making of real citizens of our children, so they will never need law enforcement, is the only solution of this crime problem."[2]

Duggan's 1931 platform also called for training future teachers to educate their pupils on the basics of good citizenship.[3] As the Depression dragged on, however, he grew considerably gloomier. Improvement in education would not be sufficient. In notes for an undated speech, Duggan wrote that he believed the state, and the country, were being dragged into a financial pit by a growing army of idlers. "Out of 100 average men 25 years of age, forty years later—one will be rich," he calculated. "Four will be well[-]to[-]do. Five will be supporting themselves by work. 36 will be dead. 54 will be dependent upon friends, relations, and charity."[4] The productive center of the Texas economy could not hold with such numbers. The shirkers would have to be surgically excised if the state were not to sink into a morass of poverty. Serving in the Texas senate from 1933 until his death in 1935, Duggan became the last Texas legislator to make passage of a eugenics law a centerpiece of his political career.

Duggan chaired the Senate Education Committee and from that perch introduced legislation that would have given the state the power to authorize the sterilization of inmates at prisons, mental hospitals, and institutions for those with disabilities. Sterilization in such cases, Dugan insisted, would be "a protection rather than a punishment." Surgeries might allow the targeted individual to return to "normal life...who would otherwise be confined in institutions for years." The state had no other options, he said. Duggan pointed out that the population at charitable institutions increased by 33 percent the previous year. Housing and feeding prisoners and wards of the state, Duggan calculated, cost Texas taxpayers $5,994,732 (or almost $131 million, adjusted for inflation, in 2023). "Cost in money is trivial compared with the crime, heartache and horror that find origin in these defectives," Duggan argued to his fellow legislators. "Anything sanctioned by common sense and good morals, which can prevent this accumulation of human misery and degeneracy should be done."[5]

Once Duggan won a Texas senate seat, mental health professionals begged him to get a sterilization law enacted by the state legislature. In 1934, Claude Teer, the chair of the Texas Board of Control, established by the legislature in 1919 to oversee expenditures for charitable and educational institutions, pleaded with Duggan to file a sterilization bill. "The conditions in this State and Nation are alarming with reference to insane and feebleminded people," Teer wrote in a November 5, 1934, letter. "The only hope that we could see to check this horrible condition is through sterilization. I am not prepared to say that sterilization would eliminate entirely our present bad conditions, but I feel that it would improve the same. It seems to me that it is nothing less than criminal to allow children to come into the world when we know that they are going to be imbeciles, idiots, or insane. Their very existence is a mental and physical curse to themselves and a great sorrow to their families and friends."[6]

The *Dallas Morning News* heartily supported Duggan's legislation and ran a patronizing editorial about its critics. "Sterilization makes its way slowly, yet a misguided sense of humanity opposes it," said a January 18, 1935, editorial endorsing the law. "It is far kinder to prevent the birth of persons doomed to become public charges or to drift early to crime or institutional care than to permit their introduction into the world."[7] The newspaper predicted that Duggan's bill, and a rival sterilization bill proposed that session by Senator Pat Jefferson of San Antonio, would face intense opposition. Alonzo Wasson of the *Morning News* characterized the bill's opponents as being in part motivated by constitutional concerns regarding the right of states to force sterilizations on criminals and those suffering from mental illness. The journalist believed those concerns had been "largely dissolved" because of the 1927 United States Supreme Court's *Buck v. Bell* decision that upheld a Virginia sterilization law. Other opponents of the Duggan bill, Wasson said, believed the legislation violated their religious beliefs. "The arguments left to those opposed to sterilization," Wasson wrote, "are not much more than comes from sentimentalism and certain religious concepts which antedate even the notion that insanity and other mental ills were penalties visited upon the wicked by a wrathful Providence."[8]

Duggan's 1935 law would have allowed prison and state institution superintendents to identify inmates they believed would parent children "with serious physical or mental deficiencies" upon release. The patient ordered to be sterilized or their guardians would have the right to appeal to a new State Board of Eugenics. Those inmates would then, upon approval of doctors, be subjected to a "vasectomy for males, a salpingectomy (removal of one or both fallopian tubes) for females or some similar operation that will not unsex the patient." Objections were raised because the bill only targeted the "insane, imbeciles, the feebleminded and epileptics" confined in state institutions but gained support when the provisions were expanded to cover "persons twice convicted of felony" and "sufferers of specified disease." "I'll admit the Bible says to multiply," said Representative J. C. Duvall of Fort Worth, "but not to multiply the insane faster than the others." However, during a hearing on the bill, Representative J. Franklin Spears (a San Antonio lawyer with a large Catholic constituency), drew on his experience in criminal trials and got Dr. C. H. Standifer from the Austin State Hospital to admit that physicians sometimes disagree regarding a diagnosis of insanity. "We are delving into something we have no business to touch," Spears said. Spears and Clarence Farmer went further, calling the proposal "vicious."[9]

Mobilizing Catholics

Public opposition intensified to both the Duggan and Jefferson sterilization bills, as Wasson predicted, and indeed religious belief played a major part. The Catholic Church had finally weighed in definitively against eugenics in 1930 with Pope Pius X's *Casti Connubii* encyclical. The pope condemned those who put "eugenics before aims of a higher order, and by public authority wish to prevent from marrying all those whom, even though naturally fit for marriage, they consider . . . [might] bring forth defective offspring . . . [T]he family is more sacred than the State . . . Public magistrates have no direct power over the bodies of their subjects; therefore, where no crime has taken place and there is no cause present for grave punishment, they can never directly harm, or tamper with the integrity of the body, either for the reasons of eugenics or for any other reason." [10]

Pius's words echoed across Texas. In a May 24, 1935 story, the Spanish-language newspaper *El Heraldo de Brownsville* covered Pope Pius XI's condemnation of eugenics and sterilization, as well as what he called the "paganism" of Nazi Germany. The pontiff, *El Heraldo* reported, said his opposition to forced sterilization stemmed from the Catholic Church's "love of humanity." By 1930, the state's population of 5.8 million included about 750,000 Catholics, about 13 percent of the total. They served as a powerful and now mobilized voting bloc. The most determined protests against Duggan's legislation came from the *Southern Messenger*, the official Roman Catholic newspaper in Texas. which proclaimed in a January 3, 1935, front page headline, "Texas Should Not Resort to the Practice of Sterilization," and from the Catholic service organization the Knights of Columbus.[11]

Across the state, Knights of Columbus chapters flooded the offices of legislators and Governor James Allred with anti-sterilization resolutions that described the sterilization bills as "in conflict not only with the moral law and the fundamental, natural, and religious rights of the people, but with the basic American principles of the State and Federal Governments of these United States." The Texas debate over the law received national attention. Susan V. Gill of Jacksonville, Illinois, saw Duggan's proposal as part of a communist plot. "Reds highly favor laws for compulsory sterilization," she warned Allred in a March 15, 1935, letter. "They will see to it that we lose some good loyal citizens to it. Even the least dangerous of them believe with their leader that it would not matter if three fourths of the population of our country be sterilized if the other fourth would become communists."[12]

Meanwhile, at the Eugenics Record Office in New York, Harry Laughlin worried that Duggan's legislation might not go far enough. In a March 1,

1935, letter to Allred, Laughlin asked, "Does the present legislation apply only to the sterilization of defectives confined within the institutions or does it apply to defectives in the population at large?" Allred's secretary, C. R. Miller, replied that no final version of the legislation had reached the governor's desk, so no details on the proposed targets of sterilization could be provided.[13]

A subcommittee approved Duggan's bill by a narrow eight-to-seven margin. House Bill 107 passed the lower chamber. However, on February 14, 1935, state Senator Olan Rogers Van Zandt (1890–1985), who had been blinded in two different childhood accidents (one involving a slingshot and the other when a stick injured his eye while he was cattle driving) killed the senate version on a point of order.[14] Duggan failed but wanted to continue the same battle in the next regular session in 1937. Such dreams vanished on September 6, 1935, when the senator died of heart failure.[15]

Upon Duggan's death, efforts to implement a Texas eugenics law two years later fell to members of the state house. Four representatives—Conde Hoskins of Gonzales in Central Texas, Minet Davis of Kirbyville in southeast Texas, C. L. Stocks of Gainesville in north-central Texas, and John Dollins of Waco—backed a new sterilization measure in the lower chamber in the 1937 regular session.[16] House Bill 555 received an eight-to-four favorable report from the Public Health Committee, after provisions allowing the forced sterilization of habitual criminals and "degenerates" were deleted, leaving "incurable insane people" as the only potential target.[17] Once again, there were critics. One *Dallas Morning News* reader worried that the sterilization bill, if passed, would become a slippery slope leading to euthanizing the elderly. Mrs. Cecil Smith of Sherman in North Texas compared the bill to President Franklin Roosevelt's so-called court-packing scheme, which allowed the chief executive to select an additional Supreme Court justice for every sitting justice more than seventy years old, euthanasia policies in Nazi Germany, and King Herod's massacre of newborns in the Christian Gospels. In a worried letter, Smith said, "If today, seventy years be the Supreme Court limit, tomorrow it may be the life limit. What with euthanasia for the suffering, sterilization for the unfit, and King Herod for the unborn and for the senile . . . it behooves us elderly to walk warily." Smith need not have worried. The legislation never came to the full house for a vote.[18]

Ten bills proposing coerced sterilization, limiting who could marry, keeping those with disability out of public view, or providing for warehousing of those with mentally illness or disability had been debated by the Texas legislature since 1853. The Texas house or senate had rejected nine of these initiatives. After the 1937 sterilization bill's failure, the Texas Board of Control felt exasperation, telling the press that "it knew of no other method [other than imposed sterilization] for the prevention of the several types of insanity, imbecility, and idiocy definitely known to be hereditary." The last attempt to pass a sterilization law in Texas barely got covered by the press, which wistfully noted that Georgia lawmakers had recently accomplished something their peers in Austin could not. The Georgia law, the last to be passed in the United States, allowed for the sterilization of inmates in state institutions deemed likely to "procreate a child or children who would have a tendency to serious physical, mental, or nervous disease or deficiency," the *Wichita Falls Times* reported.[19]

The Georgia bill had "rumbled around the state for two decades," as Larson put it, before it became law. As in Texas, women's groups played a major role in campaigning for the Georgia legislation. Many women active in the Junior League in Augusta became eugenics supporters as a result of their exposure to widespread disease, hunger, and disability among the infants from impoverished families brought to clinics and a milk station operated by the group. Efforts to legalize sterilization, however, hit a brick wall in the person of Georgia's far-right governor,. Eugene Talmadge, who reflexively vetoed any legislation he deemed Progressive, including eugenics measures. In 1935, the Georgia legislature passed the proposal but Talmadge vetoed it as well as 162 others, including bills that would have provided students free textbooks and pensions for the elderly. Talmadge's successor, E. D. Rivers, however, was not so allergic to government activism and, when it came to his desk, he signed a new version of the sterilization statute in 1937.[20]

Texas eugenicists looked on in envy. The *Wichita Falls Times*, in a reprint of a *San Angelo Standard* editorial, mourned that Texas women could not, as the writer saw it, protect themselves the same way as their peers in the Southeast. "A West Texas woman, mother of several children, herself almost went insane from dread when she learned that her offspring, whom she loved and adored as any mother could, were threatened with hereditary insanity," the journalist wrote. "The secret had been kept from the family for years." The father had been institutionalized and two of the children followed in his unfortunate footsteps. The remaining children spent their lives dreading they too might end up in asylums. The state had left every family vulnerable to "degeneracy," the *Times* claimed.[21]

C. W. Post and the Escape from Illusions

By 1940, E. E. Davis (1881–1950) had long hoped to make F. E. Daniel's sanitary utopia a reality. He now feared that Texas might one day become a state-sized asylum. Davis had already participated in one failed attempt to create a little piece of heaven on earth. A descendant of Daniel Boone born in Williamsburg, Missouri, Davis received a bachelor's degree in literature from John Tarleton College (now Tarleton State University) in Stephenville in 1906, teaching there for a brief time. He moved through a variety of jobs, including stints at a Big Spring lumberyard and an appointment as principal of a tiny public school in rural Erath County community of Lingleville, about 101 miles southwest of the Dallas–Fort Worth area. He won the admiration of the breakfast cereal magnate Charles William Post, who tasked him with laying out the eponymous Panhandle town of Post. The Michigan entrepreneur created the town to serve as a model community that would keep an unpredictable working class under tight control.[22]

Davis's time working for Post shaped the future college dean's career choices. Born in Illinois, Post in 1874 married Ella Leticia Merriwether from Battle Creek, Michigan, the city that would become the center of his business empire. Troubled all his life with debilitating depression and stomach pains, he invented foods he hoped would heal the body, including Post Toasties Cereal and Postum, the latter originally conceived as a healthier alternative to coffee. He attempted to create his first utopian community in 1888 on two hundred acres in east Fort Worth, including what is now known as the Riverside neighborhood. That venture fizzled financially. Emotionally broken, in 1891 he went back to Michigan and sought a restoration of his mental health at the famous Battle Creek Sanitarium, originally established by the prophecy-oriented Seventh-day Adventist denomination in 1876. There, a man destined like Post to become a giant in the breakfast cereal industry, Dr. John Harvey Kellogg, served as medical director. (In 1906, Kellogg co-founded the eugenicist Race Betterment Society with Charles Davenport.)[23]

Post found life in the sanitarium too restrictive, and soon left. He never specifically endorsed eugenics, but he held eugenicist-adjacent ideas. Post cited eugenics leader Herbert Spencer as a major influence. He too hoped he could guide evolution and produce a better breed of Homo sapiens. Post saw a future in which humans would shed their skin and live as fully realized spiritual essences. He promoted eugenicist fears of an imminent working-class rebellion against the ruling clique. Post believed that the body, which he called the "mud doll," represented an illusion, as did disease. The way to health and full potential was to "turn from the world of illusion to the world of eternal realities." Fully developed humans would shed their mud doll bodies and become imbued with the "Universal Divine Mind," a type of evolution Post called "enfoldment."[24]

Post once again looked at Texas, with its racially divided workforce and its record of crushing strikes, as the best location for his second attempt to create an ideal community. In 1907, he established Post City on the edge of the Llano Estacado. He hoped that the colony, built in a location that received only twenty-two inches of rainfall annually, would grow rich from cotton farming. The Panhandle, he hoped, sat far enough away to keep the workers there shielded from the spell of the foreign "jaw smiths" and anarchists Post believed stirred discontent among the working class in Michigan. Post, Texas, never became a hotbed of cotton farming. Between 1911 and 1913, Post tried to alter the environment, attempting rainmaking by setting off explosives near the town, to no detectable effect. He lost interest in his namesake town and, during an excruciating attack of appendicitis, died by suicide in 1914.[25]

Davis and Post held similar ideas about the malign influence of foreigners. Davis, however, quickly tired of his position as Post's urban planner. He later wrote that it "thoroughly turned me against the idea of wasting a perfectly good life on the ignoble pursuit of vulgar dollar chasing." Davis earned a master's degree from the University of Texas in 1913 and served on the staff as a "rural research specialist."[26] This job hardened his attitude about the pernicious effects of cotton production in Texas and the resulting migration into the state of African American, Mexican, and Mexican American cotton-pickers, and what he saw as the "inferior" whites who tended the crop.

The Last Eugenic Warrior

In 1923, Davis left his post as a rural researcher and returned to the education field for the first time since he served as a Lingleville principal, organizing the education department at Stephen F. Austin State Teachers College in Nacogdoches. In 1925, he began his twenty-one-year tenure as the dean (the equivalent of president) of North Texas Agricultural College (NTAC), a two-year institution affiliated with the Texas A&M system. (NTAC became the University of Texas at Arlington, or UTA, in 1967.) When Davis arrived, "N-Tac" as it was known by students, suffered from paltry state funding. Located in Arlington, between Dallas and Fort Worth, the school had a small enrollment and did not meet Davis's standards. He found the buildings "run down and poorly kept" and judged the faculty to be "both incompetent and incapable of working harmoniously with their co-laborers."[27]

According to Gerald Saxon, a historian of UTA, Davis decided to "'purge' the student body of those he saw as undesirables and 'rehabilitate' the faculty with 'virile,' competent young people of high attainment and proper educational perspective." Davis sought to rid both the faculty and the student body of "dead-beats," expelling 102 of the 456 students in 1925–26 and firing twenty-three out of forty faculty members by the 1927–28 term. He later complained that the state wasted a quarter of its higher education budget "on inferior students."[28]

Under Davis, a culture of casual, mocking racism thrived. In 1934, he approved the constitution of a student organization, the Kampus Klub Kadets, which announced it aimed to "promote a better feeling of fellowship among the residents of [the] dormitory." In the early 1920s, the Ku Klux Klan dominated politics in the city of Dallas, just twenty-one miles east, and in Fort Worth, which bordered Arlington. It strains credibility to think the group's initials, KKK, represented anything but an ugly racist joke given official sanction by the dean.[29]

Davis carried his deep white supremacism from his time as a rural researcher to his new job. Heading an agricultural college in Texas, Davis reflected long and hard on the impact of the state's massive cotton industry. Tending to the cotton crop required little to no intelligence, he believed. The industry, he concluded, attracted workers of lower intelligence to the state like "iron filings to a magnet." The Central Texas cotton fields filled with "lowly blacks, peonized Mexicans, and moronic whites" who produced degenerate children representing America's "worthless human silt."[30]

Mexicans and Mexican Americans became a particular target of his ire. The cotton industry, he said, was "Latinizing" the state. Landowners recruited prodigious Brown labor because the Mexican was "specially fitted for the burdensome task of bending his back to picking the cotton, and the burdensome tasks of grubbing the fields." Bringing in Mexican workers, Davis complained, large landowners destroyed the livelihoods of small, independent white farmers. He compared Mexican and Mexican American field hands to ravenous insect pests. "The Mexicans did not hit the interior cotton lands with the impact of a hurricane, but seeped in silently and undermined the rural social structure like termites out of the sills of a wooden house," he wrote.[31]

Davis complained to George Witte, secretary to the mayor of San Antonio, on March 26, 1941, that, "[c]otton can be grown with slave intelligence. Very little skill is required for the production of cotton . . . I regret that most of the sociologists teaching classes in the colleges in the South have not yet recognized very clearly the fact that cotton, illiteracy, poverty, and humanity of a low biological type have a bond of inescapable affinity tying them inescapably together."[32]

In an essay, "King Cotton," Davis charged that Mexicans not only "poisoned" Anglo blood through sexual contact, but also damaged education in the state. "The American children and the clean, high-minded Mexican children do not like to go to school with the dirty 'greaser' type of Mexican child," Davis wrote. "The better thing is to put the 'dirty' ones into separate schools till they learn to 'clean up' and become eligible to better society." White schools in Texas had been overrun by the "biologically impoverished tribes of marginal humanity" who had turned quality campuses "into crumbling monuments of vanishing white communities."[33]

"I Think It is a Very Good Book": E. E. Davis and *The White Scourge*

Davis won respect from his peers, such as H. L. Pritchett, associate professor of sociology at Southern Methodist University, who in 1935 invited the NTAC dean to join the Texas Mental Hygiene Society. Davis declined, noting that he had ended his involvement in the "State Teachers

Association and all things of that sort. I have even withdrawn from the Baptist Church." Davis wanted to devote himself to a more immediate task. "Last year I prepared the manuscript for a novel which I think is a very good book, though I have not yet been able to make satisfactory arrangements for a publisher." Davis had penned *The White Scourge*, which he hoped would persuade elites to transform the economy of Texas and preserve what was left of what he perceived as its treasure in Anglo-Saxon blood.[34]

Davis's quest to find a publisher would take five years, and his friends in academia predicted it might ignite a firestorm. The year after finishing his opus, Davis sent a portion of the manuscript to his friend, University of Oklahoma (OU) president W. B. Bizzell. He told the OU administrator that his time as a rural researcher inspired the work, a time when he was disgusted "by the squalid humanity [working in the cotton fields]." The university president was impressed with the work. "I think you will have no trouble getting it published if the material you submitted is typical of the literary quality of the entire manuscript," Bizzell wrote in response. "I am inclined to believe that the book will bring harsh criticism as well as praise for you are dealing with a delicate subject and one that touches the conflicting interests of many people."[35]

Hades on Earth: A Dystopia Has Come Upon Us

Cotton, as the title of his novel suggested, was a white scourge but so, Davis said, was the population it drew to the state. As he claimed in the introduction, "The southern cotton fields have a greater affinity for illiteracy and thriftlessness than the corn fields and wheat fields of the great Middle West. It doesn't require as much intelligence to raise cotton in Texas as it does to raise corn and feed livestock in Iowa." In one passage from *The White Scourge*, the narrator gazes at the smart and hardworking, biologically fit white farmers of Texas, "generally sober and peaceful, but like Nietzschean supermen, hard as nails and intrepidly fearless," unknowingly sealing their doom as they seek the potential but unreliable financial rewards of cotton production: "These earnest farmers thought they were planting cotton seed. But they were doing much more than that. They were burying their very children's hopes. They were tampering with the most treacherous plant God ever gave to man. It would pollute the soil with contagion and disease, undermine the homes they were seeking to establish, and fix the curse of pauper labor forever on their backs."[36]

Poor whites, readers would learn, constituted "a deadly root rot fungus more infectious than leprosy." Davis sets the novel in Cross Timbers, "a point eighty miles west of where the city of Fort Worth .. stands." A thriving community develops, led by Isaac Hobson who on the first page declares "I hate cotton." Cotton, Hobson says, led to *Uncle Tom's Cabin*, "negro slaves," and "the misguided Yankee who caused the [Civil] War." He feared the growing reliance on cotton farming would lead to Cross Timbers's societal collapse. Hobson seeks to enlighten the town by recruiting a preacher for the local church who would "hear society's plaintive call for practical community builders and social engineers,"[37] perhaps the type of community Post failed to build in West Texas. Hobson eventually finds one of those social engineers, an eloquent, passionate white preacher named Tom Leonard.

Leonard quickly warns that greed has caused racial "degeneration" to unfold in Cross Timbers. He urges his congregants to do nothing to help the poor and miserable in his community. Well-intentioned but misguided generosity, he believes, will prolong their suffering and jeopardize the survival of the human race as a whole. In one scene Leonard noted, "I heard David Starr Jordan say in a public address one time that nothing contributes so much to the world's volume of human misery and its perpetuation as modern charity in the way it's conducted." Meanwhile, Leonard tells his congregation that the presence of Mexican labor would only increase demands for handouts and produce generations of dependents. "Look at the great army of unwashed Mexicans now crossing the Rio Grande in peace, with sandals on their feet, rags on their backs, and vermin in their hair. Into our cotton fields, they are spreading like a corrosive blight ten thousand times more dangerous than Santa Anna's invading hosts of 1836! Too much of Mexico's least desirable human blood is seeping into the very veins of our social body."[38]

Davis presents the dysgenic white, however, as the chief blight destroying rural Texas. Milton Lagrone serves as *The White Scourge*'s primary villain. Lagrone's "only conception of success was to go into the world and gather dollars. He let the dollar glamor blind his eyes to better things and gathered dollars just for the paltry dollar's sake." Lagrone, described as the weasel-eyed "Shylock of Clear Creek," buys up old houses and builds new ones, intending these flimsy hovels to provide shelter for the army of reputedly inferior whites he wants to work in his fields. Warren Hunter provided illustrations for *White Scourge*. In one sketch for a chapter titled "Vampires," Hunter depicts Lagrone as a giant, bat-winged man wearing a Hassidic-style black hat, grasping a poor man and woman in rural dress with his clawed hands. Davis never specifically identifies Lagrone as Jewish, but the money-grubbing nemesis, referred to as a member of an "ornery tenant tribe," is clearly coded as one. The association of Jewish people with vampires dates to at least the twelfth century, stemming from the "Blood Libel" myth that Jews kill Christian children during Passover and use their blood while making matzoh for their rites. Shylock is the Jewish villain of William Shakespeare's play *The Merchant of Venice* who demands a pound of flesh as collateral for a loan. Performances of *The Merchant of Venice* had provoked anti-Semitic rage in American audiences since the 1850s. Like John Box, Davis implies that Jewish people bore guilt for promoting interracial sex in the United States and exploiting poor whites.[39]

Lagrone forces the "human silt" living on his vast estate to dwell in "shoddy tenant houses . . . more like cow sheds and pig stys [sic] than places for human abode . . . The negro slaves in the Mississippi delta were housed better than the tenants on Milton Lagrone's farm . . . The negro slave had the advantage of being property and had to be cared for, but the only real property of concern to Milton Lagrone was the bale of cotton." The dilapidated housing for the tenants comes to be known as "Hades." Davis wrote some of his cruelest passages when describing the tenant farmers represented by the Silas Green family, "insensitive little morons" too unintelligent to know how bad off they were. "The destitute Greens, mentally and physically undernourished, biologically inferior, and wholly untouched by the warmth of social sunshine and cultural joys" struck the main characters as unpleasant eyesores needing eradication from the landscape.[40] Tom Leonard condemns the Greens for taking free flour and meat from bureaucrats and then supposedly undermining the American work ethic with their expectation of welfare. Leonard laments: "[T]hey poison the government as bad as they taint their children's blood. Their attitude towards the government that's a helpin' an' protectin' them's as rotten as old Green's festerin', syphilitic body. On election day here they come, the whole kit an' bilin' of 'em . . . with ballots in their hand an' chips on their shoulders."[41]

Leonard warns that the Greens represent both a biological time bomb and a political danger. If they continued to breed in prodigious numbers and their discontent intensified, the preacher predicted, they would be gullible enough to fall prey to communists or anarchists. "Some day, mangy folk, like the scum of 'Hades,' will challenge the peace of our land," the preacher said. One character, Isaac Hobson, laments that Lagrone cannot be executed for bringing such people into the state. Later, Leonard begins to consider genocide as the only viable solution to the problem of poor whites as he listens to "a great biologist" speak at Yale, proclaiming the blessings of the "[b]lack plague and the ravages of small pox that in the thirteenth and fourteenth centuries . . . cleaned out the dirty dens and mean streets where sorry people dwelt, removed the moron; and killed off the unfit like flies fed on cobalt." Unfortunately, because of scientists like the French microbiologist Louis Pasteur, Leonard realized, such a purifying plague seemed less likely in the future.[42]

In *The White Scourge*, a racial apocalypse had already arrived. Texas had become hell on earth. A sterilization bill aimed at "imbeciles, morons, inebriates, the viciously diseased, and habitual criminals" is debated in the state legislature toward the novel's end, but the characters seemed resigned to failure. "Of course it will fail," a group of professors watching the debate comment. "But look at its educational value—how it will put people to talking and thinking—what striking headlines it will make for the state dailies." But the professors' optimism comes off as halfhearted. The bill falls short after one state representative predicts that if it passed, "doctors would sterilize everyone but themselves." Davis's novel does not end with redemption, but with the state Latinizing and whites sinking in poverty. Every inch in the vast state to the "very blue horizon was cotton! cotton! cotton!"[43] *The White Scourge* got a positive review in the 1941 edition of *Journal of American History*.[44] However, Davis's prose made no discernible impact on policy. Texas remained an exception in a nation that sterilized tens of thousands.

After Davis's time as dean, NTAC went through several name changes. In 1967, it became the University of Texas at Arlington. For decades, UTA's administrative headquarters bore the name Davis Hall. In 2018, the authors of this book wrote a column for the student newspaper, the *Shorthorn*, detailing Davis's history of racism. In response, the Student Congress passed a resolution in April 2020 recommending a name change. The

University of Texas System Board of Regents unanimously voted to approve the move. "The task force's research of archives and other published documents revealed that Dr. Davis publicly advocated for the sterilization of the disabled, segregation based on race and social status and the adoption of eugenics," UTA interim president Teik C. Lim said in a statement. "The task force understandably determined that these ideas do not represent the values of UTA today and are not reflective of our richly diverse community." In any case, before students campaigned to remove Davis's name, his doleful legacy had vanished almost entirely from public memory.[45]

"Not a Punishment but a Protection": Eugenics and Texas's Neighbors

In spite of a past defined by racial violence, in the Deep South the medical mayhem represented by involuntary sterilization never became as commonplace as in the Northeast, the Upper South, Midwest, and the Pacific coast. African Americans suffered castrations and other forms of brutalization at the hands of frenzied white mobs more often than they were sterilized by surgeons. As medical historian Mark Largent observed, "Of the six founding members of the Confederate States of America—Alabama, Mississippi, South Carolina, North Carolina, Florida, and Georgia, only North Carolina and Georgia had high per capita numbers of sterilization." Largent offers two explanations not entirely applicable to Texas. "[F]irst, sterilization laws in most states were adopted as part of the broader progressive movement," he argued, a movement that faced more resistance in that region than elsewhere. "The second reason compulsory sterilizations were not widely performed in the American South lay in the lower number of institutions in most of the states. Few southern states invested the significant amounts of money necessary to establish mental health facilities during the first half of the twentieth century. Lacking these institutions, compulsory sterilizations were not performed even when the laws were adopted."[46]

As previously observed, the Progressive movement was more vibrant in Texas than in the Deep South, but it was narrowly focused on matters like Prohibition and reform of urban governments. Progressives dealt with prolonged frustrations in passing a suffrage law and experienced meager results on issues like child labor, which cost the ruling class money.

Meanwhile, Texas eugenicists constantly complained about the inadequate number and poor funding of mental facilities. Texas, of course, had not passed a eugenics law by the time sterilizations began to decline across the United States. At the same time, eugenics made barely a dent in most of the states surrounding Texas. Like the Lone Star State, Arkansas, Louisiana, and New Mexico never launched a sterilization program. Oklahoma, by contrast, provided a stage for vibrant Progressive and labor movements, and even Socialists there made waves. That state adopted eugenics legislation, yet it ranked only twenty-second among the thirty-two states with such statutes in per capita sterilizations.[47]

Oklahoma governor William "Alfalfa Bill" Murray, a populist who pledged to stand by the "farmer without seeds to plant," signed a sterilization law in 1931 with the intention of reducing the future costs of detention.[48] The Oklahoma law focused on habitual criminals and was revised in 1933 and 1935 in order to decrease from three to two the number of felony convictions necessary before surgery could be ordered. Only certain felony convictions counted. Regardless, 525 sterilizations took place in Oklahoma from 1933 to 1942. This prodigious wave stopped when the United States Supreme Court unanimously overturned the 1935 law in the 1942 *Skinner v. Oklahoma* case. The state of Oklahoma had violated the Constitution's Fourteenth Amendment requirement of equal protection under the law because it drew distinctions between felons. As Justice William O. Douglas put it, under the legislation, "Embezzlers are forever free. Those who steal or take in other ways are not." [49]

The *Skinner* decision, however, did not end all sterilization, but considerably slowed down the rate of such procedures across the country. Between 1931 and the *Skinner* decision in 1942, Oklahoma carried out about forty-four sterilizations per year. By the time of *Skinner*, doctors had already performed 83 percent of the total of 626 legally authorized sterilizations in the state's history. Oklahoma carried out its last operation in 1960. Largent estimates that 63,841 legally authorized coerced sterilizations took place in the United States between 1907 and 1980. If that number is accurate, just short of 60 percent of those procedures occurred before the 1942 *Skinner* ruling. The end of Texas legislative debates on the merits of sterilization fit with these national trends. After the 1940s, eugenicists adopting a "democratic eugenics" discourse shifted to calls for what supporters insisted were purely voluntary sterilization. The number of these, often happening after patients were misled by doctors with eugenic aims, would far exceed state-mandated procedures.[50]

Searching for Respectability Post-Holocaust

Growing awareness of the brutalities committed by the ultra-eugenicists in Nazi Germany did not kill the movement in the United States. Sterilizations continued through the 1970s and beyond. However, ruthless assaults on Jews, such as Kristallnacht, and the horrific tales told by Jewish refugees made the close collaboration between American eugenicists and the murderous scientists associated with the Hitler regime a public-relations problem even before World War II.

In January 1939 the Carnegie Foundation, which had supported eugenics research (including by Nazis), informed the Eugenics Record Office it could not count on future funding. Unable to find a new financial backer, the ERO closed shop.[51] After the liberation of Nazi death camps, a growing number of geneticists, anthropologists, and other scientists began to poke substantial holes in the eugenics thesis.[52] Frederick Osborn, the nephew of leading eugenicist Henry Fairfield Osborn, suggested that biology alone did not shape a person but the environment also influenced a person's development. The younger Osborn now advocated only voluntary sterilization for individuals whose family had a history of disabilities. He also promoted voluntary birth control. Even though he still supported involuntary sterilization for those he called "feebleminded," *Time* magazine called this repackaging of old ideas "eugenics for democracy."[53]

However, since *Buck v. Bell* has never been overturned and remains the law of the land, sterilizations continued for decades. California remained a leader in forced sterilizations after World War II. Largent estimates that 2,709 such operations took place in the state between 1945, the year World War II ended, and 1980, an average of about seventy-four a year. That number likely is an undercount, as American eugenics entered a more shadowy, under-the-radar phase after the surrender of the Axis powers.

Defusing the "Population Bomb": Eugenicist Euphemisms

As the term "eugenics" became disreputable, not only did calls for new sterilization laws vanish, but neo-eugenicists in California tried to shift the focus, avoiding directly calling for sterilizing people of color, but pushing for population control on the grounds that the rapidly increasing population endangered the environment. *The Population Bomb*, published by the Sierra Club and authored by Stanford biologist Paul Ehrlich, popularized the phrase "population explosion" and became one of the surprise bestsellers of 1968. It frightened readers with its Malthusian depiction of a future in which humans could not produce enough food to feed the exponential increase in the species. Famine, riots, and deadly pollution could only escalate with the population. Ehrlich focused his efforts on places with dark-skinned populations like Africa, India, and China. He made the fanciful suggestion of infusing local water supplies with "sterilants." His book led to the formation of Zero Population Growth (ZPG) at Stanford, an organization that reached a membership of 33,000 shortly after its 1968 founding. ZPG and similar groups in California and beyond "relied on decades-old stereotypes of Mexicans and Mexican Americans as diseased hyperbreeders and demonized Spanish speakers and undocumented immigrants," Stern writes.[54]

Under the rationale that welfare recipients had already cost the taxpayers too much money and the public should not subsidize further childbearing, social welfare workers in the neo-eugenics era pressured poor women, particularly if they were Black or Brown and had borne large families, to consent to surgery. An Oakland doctor told the husband of one African American patient who had just delivered that she should get her tubes tied because "with the pill, she'll get a blood clot to her brain; with the IUD, a pregnancy in her tubes." Through intimidation and deceit, scholar Gregory Michael Dorr said, the period between 1968 and 1973 marked "a sterilization explosion," a time when two million men and women underwent "voluntary" procedures.[55]

Native American women living on reservations and African American women at public health facilities across the South were deceived into agreeing to hysterectomies and tubal ligations from the 1960s into the 1980s. In the late twentieth and twenty-first centuries, many conservative lawmakers proposed requiring women to receive Norplant, a long-term contraceptive implant, as a requirement for receiving welfare benefits.[56] After 2000, eugenics practices and beliefs began a comeback nationwide. The popular press frequently promoted the concept of biological determinism with the press informing readers that scientists had reportedly discovered the "alcoholism gene," the "gay gene," the "conservative" and "liberal gene," and even a "God gene," which supposedly led an individual toward religious belief.[57] At the same time, government officials, if not explicitly pushing for selective breeding, continued to implement policies reminiscent of the eugenics era. In White County in Tennessee in 2017, a judge started offering reductions in prison sentences to inmates who accepted sterilization procedures (vasectomies for men and Nexplanon contraceptive implants effective up to four years for women). The right-wing Project Prevention, under the slogan "Don't Let a Pregnancy Ruin Your Drug Habit," handed out payments as little as $300 to induce drug addicts to agree to sterilization.[58]

By the late twentieth century, states that enacted sterilization legislation half-heartedly reckoned with their eugenics past. In 2003, California governor Gray Davis apologized for his state's horrific program of forced sterilizations, legal in the state from 1909 until 1979. Disproportionately, the poor of color and the disabled underwent these operations without consent. Davis referred to this period of medical terrorism as "a sad and regrettable chapter . . . one that must never be repeated." Nevertheless, the Center for Investigative Reporting revealed that as recently as 2010, prisoners in the state had been sterilized without proper assent. California approved legislation to compensate eugenics victims in 2021.[59]

In 2014, North Carolina began paying compensation to some victims of that state's forced sterilization program, but it excluded many whose surgery had not been approved by the state's Eugenics Board.[60] In 2015, the Virginia General Assembly agreed to a program of reparations as well, setting aside $25,000 for each victim of its eugenics law, which had been repealed in 1979.[61] In 2016, President Barack Obama signed legislation that exempted from taxation all compensation payments made to eugenics victims.[62] Still, only a tiny percentage of Americans brutalized by these programs have received compensation, apologies, or even official acknowledgment of their suffering.

Eugenicists in Texas harmed more by words than deeds. Even though forced castrations took place in Texas, because the state never passed a eugenics law there has been no frank discussion of the damage the movement inflicted through its legitimization of xenophobia, racism, anti-Semitism, and homophobia, viewpoints that at times have fueled terrorist violence.

Eugenics in Texas After E. E. Davis

In 1948, three years after the end of World War II and the Holocaust, new employees of the Austin State Hospital (ASH) received a training outline noting that twenty-five states still had sterilization laws on the books. Even though sterilizations had taken place at the ASH without clear legal authorization, and would in the future, the outline claimed that Texas could benefit from such statutory authority. It approvingly quoted Supreme Court associate justice Oliver Wendell Holmes's opinion in the 1927 *Buck v. Bell* decision that upheld the constitutionality of Virginia's sterilization law. "Three generations of imbeciles are enough," Holmes declared, a brutal sentiment the ASH endorsed.

Eugenics continued to be part of the common sense of the Tejano public well into the 1950s, but a type of eugenics that had moved well past biological determinism and placed a heavy emphasis on environment. Tejano newspapers continued to give eugenical advice about how the pick the most fit partner as well as how to create a nurturing home life in which any inborn gifts held by a child could be actualized. In the August 21, 1958, issue of San Antonio's *La Prensa*, readers could order booklets with titles like *Love, Convenience, and Eugenics*, which an advertisement said would cover "conjugal and moral obligations" shared by couples, and *Eugenics and Sex Harmony*, "an encyclopedia on marriage, prophylaxes, ailments, and organic disorders."[63] Consistent with Mexican eugenics, Tejano journalists told their audiences to not just consider a spouse's biology when considering whether to have children. One August 27, 1955, article in *El Puerto de Brownsville* said a positive home life was an important aspect of "eugenesia" (eugenics). The author urged men to remember that mothers, "the only vessel where the child is formed, has more responsibilities than the father himself because . . . she is giving it life from her life, as well as giving the child her ideas . . . her thoughts as an inheritance." Domestic discord, the journalist suggested, could spoil whatever genetic gifts the child might have inherited. "The tiny newborn . . . becomes a vessel that fills up little by little with the sensations it receives . . . if the father argues with the mother to the point of blasphemy and humiliation . . . if the mother, drunk with desperation, feels her poorly contained rage against her husband boiling in her chest, there is a witness who feels the scenes he has seen or heard being etched into his brain, who in turn will become a young one eager to fight, to humiliate, to hate." To have fit children, the newspaper urged, the parents must provide not just a quality family tree but an environment in which the child would not develop a mind filled with "banalities, with trivialities, and miasmic ideas that lead only to perversity, to crime and to perdition."[64]

Meanwhile, the kind of wistful, explicit calls for sterilization such as those made by the Austin State Hospital staff, the labeling of the mentally ill or disabled as a biological danger, or the specific denunciation of immigrants as dysgenic dangers ceased to be part of mainstream discourse among Anglo Texans after the 1940s even if ableism, racism, and xenophobia remained commonplace. In the Anglo world, particularly as de jure segregation crumbled in the state in the later decades of twentieth century Texas, among mainstream scientists and physicians' eugenical ideas retreated to the shadows.[65]

Resistance and the Politics of Reproduction in Texas

Eugenics in Texas, as elsewhere, was defined by a belief in immutable biological differences between human races in terms of intelligence, physical strength, endurance, and character. Texas eugenicists shared a certainty that Europeans and their descendants were divided into a number of races, with those descended from northern Europe ranking as superior to central and eastern Europeans as well as southern Europeans. Sexual mixing of such European groups posed a danger to the future of the human race. Similarly, they held that mixing of any European group with Africans, Asians, and others resulted inevitably in biological "degeneracy." Finally, they assumed that the natural process of evolution could not be trusted to ensure human survival. Only the rigorous political regulation of who would and would not be allowed to live in and reproduce in Texas could steer the state from biological decline.

Texas eugenicists pursued several means of winning the public over to their agenda. They sought to educate those designated as fit about their moral obligation to bear children and to incentivize them to be fertile. They hoped to imprison those with mental illness and the intellectually limited. They battled for legal sanction to unsheathe the purifying knife on the "unfit" and campaigned to shut out of the state racial groups they smeared as inferior.

Clearly, the eugenics message reached a mass audience in Texas. In some cases, proposed sterilization legislation failed by narrow margins. But the movement scored virtually no legislative triumphs. In terms of education, eugenicists successfully delivered their message to millions of students, fairgoers, lecturer and movie audiences, although public polling data does not exist to suggest how many Texans were converted to the eugenics cause by this relentless campaigning.

Full-time academics, however, earned too little funding and respect and were too distracted by attacks on higher education to make a politically significant impact in the Texas capitol. In terms of regulating reproduction, the movement achieved decidedly limited results. Throughout the twentieth century, the state expanded the number of asylums and "colonies" in order to prevent sexual contact among the intellectually disabled. However, it was never enough to satisfy eugenicists like Yoakum who not only wanted mass detention but humane treatment of the inmates as well. Well into the twenty-first century, those suffering from mental illness often became homeless and the only "care" they received came in the form of neglectful confinement in local county jail cells where they remained vulnerable to sexual assault and unwanted pregnancies.[66]

Efforts to curb or even eliminate Mexican immigration to Texas in the eugenics era flopped. The agricultural industry and factory owners wanted Mexican workers in order to exploit them economically, and such elites proved too powerful to ignore. The Great Depression, with its "voluntary" and explicitly forced repatriation of Mexicans, in any case rendered the effort moot by the time Duggan's law was debated. Finally, in terms of the state of Texas asserting control over sexual reproduction, Catholic opposition to Duggan's sterilization proposals proved insurmountable.

Abortion, Eugenics, and Limiting Government Power

As previously explained, eugenical concerns played a major role in the politics of abortion in Texas and across the United States. Major national political figures such as anti-abortion crusader Horatio Storer and President Theodore Roosevelt warned that the United States was committing "race suicide" because, they argued, the wrong women limited the size of their families through contraception and abortions. F. E. Daniel clearly saw abortion as a potential hazard to the future health of the American "race." Yet, some of his medical peers worried at the same time that the state's sweeping ban on abortion might deny eugenically desirable women who got pregnant outside of marriage a chance to later produce racially superior children with biologically fit husbands.

Evidence suggests that throughout the twentieth century, Texans massively resisted the state's abortion restrictions.[67] White residents almost universally accepted the state's ban on interracial marriage that, except for a brief period during Reconstruction, stood from 1837 until the United States Supreme Court's 1966 *Loving vs. Virginia* decision, which overturned such anti-miscegenation laws. (The Texas legislature repealed the state's anti-miscegenation law in 1967 in response to that decision).[68] Texans seemed considerably less friendly to the idea of granting the government a role in white family planning. Numerous Texas doctors performed abortions, and far higher numbers of women sought them. By the 1960s, male and female activists sought to get the state government out of the business of regulating human reproduction.

In 1962, the top lawyer for the Texas Medical Association issued a statement that "saving the life of the mother" was the only legally allowable reason its members could perform an abortion. The Texas ban was "stringent and rigidly limited," he said. Women faced a challenge that earlier confronted the supposed unfit. Did they own their bodies or were their reproductive organs subject to state control? Women fought for their bodily autonomy. The *Houston Chronicle* published a story in 1963 based on surveys that estimated about 18,000 abortions were performed in Texas every year "and found an increasing number of doctors backing liberalization" of the state's strict abortion law. In North Texas, the Women's Alliance of the First Unitarian Universalist Church in Dallas formed a subgroup called the Dallas Committee for the Study of Abortion to educate the public about the need for reform, while Dr. Hugh Savage of Fort Worth, the president of the State Association of Obstetricians and Gynecologists, lobbied the Texas Medical Association to draft a statement supporting abortion rights. Savage argued that the existing state law "is in conflict with present medical practice in many reputable hospitals," where doctors loosely interpreted when a patient's life was in danger. In 1969, members of the Texas Medical Association who were surveyed approved liberalization of abortion laws by an overwhelming vote of 4,435 to 536. The Texas legislature even considered loosening abortion restrictions in its 1967 and

1968 sessions. Both efforts failed in spite of support from conservative state senator George Parkhouse and a growing number of churches and physicians. Such efforts eventually culminated in what turned out to be temporary triumph. Texas attorneys Sarah Weddington and Linda Coffee prevailed in the Supreme Court's 1973 *Roe v. Wade* decision, which nationally legalized abortion in the first trimester, allowed some exemptions pertaining to the woman's health up to the quickening, and permitted states to ban such procedures after that point, a decision that stood, with modifications, for almost a half century.[69]

Though the state of Texas never authorized the government to forever surgically alter the bodies of those deemed defective, it did slowly reassert the government's right to control women's reproductive choices. This began in 2003 with passage of the misleadingly named Women's Right to Know Act, which mandated that physicians share misinformation about alleged fetal pain during abortion with women who sought the procedure. *Roe v. Wade* would ultimately be reversed with the 2022 *Dobbs v. Jackson Women's Health Organization* decision in which the Supreme Court decided that women, in fact, do not have a constitutional right to an abortion, and returned to the individual states the decision whether such procedures are legal.[70]

The reversal of *Roe* proved unpopular even in a state as conservative as Texas. Both the sterilization and abortion controversies centered on overlapping issues: the proper size and scope of the government in private matters, self-ownership of the body, and whether individuals had the right to decide whether they wanted a family. Opposition to coerced sterilization in Texas came from across the political spectrum, with some small-government advocates fearful that sterilization laws created a frightening slippery slope whereby allowing the government to sterilize those with blindness or repeat criminal offenders might later give it the power to euthanize the disabled young, the elderly, or even members of certain religious groups. Others saw it as a matter or religious principle. Sterilization opponents believed eugenicists had no right to cause bodily harm to those not guilty of crimes or posing a violent threat to others.

Later, supporters of abortion rights saw the ability of women to chart their own reproductive destiny as a civil right and, like earlier opponents of forced sterilization, saw anti-abortion laws as egregious government overreach. Pro-eugenics Texans obviously never achieved an electoral majority large enough to enact sterilization laws, although such bills often received substantial support in the state legislature. Since the days of Lincecum, however, the opposition to such government power remained strong enough to stop these ideas cold. As of May 2022, Texans were far more united in support of a woman's right to choose, with almost 80 percent backing abortion rights in some circumstances. Anti-abortion voters, however, have consistently shown up in greater numbers on Election Day. As a result, in 2021 the legislature passed a law banning abortions after the sixth week of pregnancy and specified that it would go into effect if and when the US Supreme Court reversed the *Roe* decision, which happened the following year. In 2023, the Texas Supreme Court denied Kate Cox of Dallas the right to end a pregnancy even though her fetus suffered from full trisomy 18, a severe genetic anomaly that guaranteed the child, if it survived pregnancy, might live only minutes. If the pregnancy continued, Cox might have lost the ability to bear children in the future. She fled the state in order to obtain an abortion where the procedure remained legal.[71] The battle over the right of the state to control reproduction once centered on preventing children labeled as dysgenic from being born. By 2023, the state decided it could force women to give birth even when the child had no chance of survival. As of 2023, the two great battles in Texas over government power and bodily integrity since the 1850s, eugenics and abortion, had very different outcomes.

Texas Wields the Purifying Knife

Texans as a group decided they did not want the state to freely wield scalpels on an unwilling population. Prisoners who volunteered were another matter. By 1992, the history of sterilization in Texas had come full circle. Almost 140 years earlier, Gideon Lincecum first called for castrating criminals. Lincecum never fully conceived a modern eugenical program, but his dreams of Americans regulating marriage and encouraging breeding of the "best" to create a super race certainly foreshadowed the major elements of the later movement. However, he began his crusade for the purifying knife with a simpler premise: removing the testicles of male criminals to cure them of their anti-social and often dangerous behavior. In the last decade of the twentieth century, the state's politicians decided to give that idea, stripped of any larger eugenic goals, a shot.

The concept of the "purifying knife" first came back to life in 1992 when Steven Allen Butler, a twenty-eight-year-old African American, requested castration instead of serving a life sentence following conviction in Houston for sexually assaulting a thirteen-year-old girl. Butler was already on probation for an indecency charge involving a seven-year-old girl. A state district judge, Michael McSpadden, agreed to greenlight the procedure in addition to Butler receiving ten years of deferred adjudication. McSpadden publicly supported castration as an alternative to other punishments for sex offenders, which he said did not work. "We're all painfully aware that present laws in Texas and elsewhere neither protect society nor effectively treat sex offenders," McSpadden said. " Here in Harris County, we had 2,500 children raped last year, and those are just reported rapes. If we dare call ourselves a civilized society, we can't tolerate that and other daily violence we see." Many suspected that because of his race, Butler may have been "manipulated, humiliated, intimidated, coerced, and brainwashed" by his attorney and McSpadden to make the suggestion. Civil rights leaders like Jesse Jackson referred to decades of eugenics policies in the United States and condemned the proposed deal, arguing it brought to mind the "social demongrelization schemes devised by eccentric right-wing lunatics and intentionally aimed at African Americans." The bid ultimately failed when no doctor would agree to perform the procedure. Butler instead went on trial and a jury convicted him and handed down a life sentence.[72]

Talk of Lincecum's purifying knife came up again in 1997 when convicted sex offender Larry Don McQuay, who called himself "the scum of the earth," requested castration as a treatment for his pedophilia. McQuay, who was white, claimed he had raped at least 240 children and was serving a sentence for the molestation of a six-year-old boy. He would soon be eligible for parole. He wanted the operation because otherwise he would be "doomed to eventually rape and then murder my poor little victims." McQuay attempted to castrate himself with a razor. He asked for no reduction in sentence as a quid pro quo for the surgery. Texas refused to pay for the castration because it was an elective procedure. Governor George W. Bush suggested crowdfunding the operation. The future president said he supported castration and "thought it could be accomplished without spending any taxpayer funds. There are going to be ample volunteers willing to contribute money to see that it's paid for." *The Fort Worth*

Star-Telegram recoiled, declaring that, "[T]he state has no business castrating him and has no choice, under current law, but to turn him loose . . . Right now he is in the prison psychiatric unit at Rusk. Maybe it would be best if he could stay there." Authorities ultimately released McQuay in 1995 but he was sent back to prison in 1997 when a court convicted him for a different, earlier offense. He had been castrated by the time he was released in 2005. By then, state law allowed repeat offenders to request the Texas Department of Health Services to perform the procedure.[73]

In 1997, Texas finally implemented a surgical castration law though not specifically for eugenic purposes. The legislation, introduced by Senator Teel Bivins, a Republican from Amarillo, limited surgeries to prisoners twenty-one years or older who have been convicted of at least two sex crimes and only after they completed eighteen months of sex offender treatment including "chemical castration" injections that reduce testosterone so the prisoner experienced the bodily changes that come with castration. Bivins insisted that his bill did not violate the constitutional ban on cruel and unusual punishment. "[W]hat's more barbaric?" he said. "Allowing this voluntary surgical treatment or knowing with (some) certainty that an offender is going to molest another child? To me the answer to that question is real simple." Bush signed the law on May 20, 1997, saying "[t]he bill provides a voluntary means—there is no coercion—for people who are obviously sick to cure their illness. Any child we are able to save as a result of this bill makes the bill worthwhile." As of May 2005, three men had completed the procedure.[74]

Wealthy Donors and Stealth Eugenics

The politicians who supported the castration of rapists made no grand eugenic claims. They did not pretend that such occasional surgeries would eliminate future criminality or that such operations represented incremental steps toward a biological paradise. Although many of the elements of the eugenicist worldview in Texas, such as classism, racism, misogyny, homophobia, xenophobia, and biological determinism, still shaped political discourse in the state in the early twenty-first century, the call for a better world through better breeding came almost entirely from the fringe.

The media credited Richard Spencer, who grew up in Dallas's prosperous Preston Hollow neighborhood, with coining the term "alt-right," a

political movement credited with energizing support from white nation-
alists for Donald Trump during his 2016 presidential race. Spencer became
a media darling as a "white collar supremacist" during that campaign,
earning extensive coverage as a dapper and sophisticated product of Dallas's elite St. Mark's School of Texas, a college-preparatory academy. One
St. Mark's classmate described Spencer as making "a bunch of conservative, racially laced comments" even as a teenager. After he left Texas, he
enjoyed a comfortable life at far-right think tanks financed by textile heir
and book publisher William H. Regnery II. In 2016, Spencer came back to
his old stomping grounds, touring college campuses, such as Texas A&M
University. He told students there, "This country belongs to white people
culturally, politically, socially, everything. We define what America is."
Advocating the establishment of a separate white homeland in North
America, Spencer not only called for racial separation but also selective
breeding. He admired Madison Grant, authoring a glowing foreword to a
reprint of Grant's 1933 work *The Conquest of a Continent: Or, the Expansion of the Races in America*, which he called a "great history" advancing a
"grand vision of bio-cultural struggle and evolution, in which demography comes alive." Spencer's moment as a celebrity quickly faded following
a deadly Unite the Right Rally held to defend Confederate monuments in
Charlottesville, Virginia, on August 12, 2017. A neo-Nazi in attendance
rammed his car into an anti-racism counter-protestor named Heather
Heyer, murdering her. When sued, Spencer struggled to find a lawyer. A
jury on November 23, 2021, found him and sixteen other far-right leaders
liable for Heyer's death, ordering them to pay $26 million in damages.[75]

Spencer turned out to be a flash in the pan. Yet the influence of eugenics had not entirely disappeared even at elite institutions in Texas. Through
research grants, a richly endowed modern eugenicist organization sought
to influence academic discourse at the University of Texas. The Pioneer
Fund, based in New York, wanted to definitively prove a relationship
between intelligence and race. The organization hoped proof of this relationship would advance a political agenda: ending affirmative action,
shredding welfare, dismantling educational initiatives like Head Start and
other instituted since the 1950s to reverse the ill effects of racism and dis-
crimination. If Black and Brown Americans were proven to be irredeemably deficient, perhaps society could then consider ways to reduce their
numbers, including coerced sterilization. The Pioneer Fund sought

credibility for its racist theories and recruited university-based scientists to provide them cover. In the 1990s, professors at UT and Texas A&M accepted the organization's grants and did not question whether that largesse was connected to a larger, modern eugenics agenda.

By the 1980s and 1990s, the notion that so-called races represented biologically distinct categories, a necessary underpinning of eugenics theory, had been displaced within the social sciences by the idea that race was a social construct used to sort humans into random, vague, and fluid groups based on the political and economic realities of the time. The social sciences, having largely rejected the idea that race is real, also discarded the notion that there are racial differences in intelligence. At least one academic discipline remained an outlier. A survey of psychologists in the United States conducted in the late 1980s found that around 50 percent believed there were measurable IQ differences between races and that these distinctions were, in part, genetic. A mere 15 percent attributed racial differences in IQ test scores entirely to social factors. This matters, the author Marek Kohn wrote, because "psychologists have a strong influence upon educational practices."[76]

An entire field of psychology, psychometrics, centers on intelligence. Like race, intelligence remains an ill-defined and variable concept. Psychometricians, however, have devoted entire careers to comparing the imagined collective IQs of racial groups. As Kohn notes, "Psychologists tend to base their racial classifications on categories defined socially rather than by physical or biological anthropology. Yet their findings have evidently persuaded them that races are both real and intellectually unequal."[77]

Such was the case in the 1990s at the University of Texas and Texas A&M psychology departments. On December 13, 1994, *The Wall Street Journal* published an open letter signed by fifty-two scholars defending that year's unexpected 845-page bestseller, Richard J. Herrnstein and Charles Murray's *The Bell Curve*. (Bell curves are charts that visually represent the frequency of particular traits, like intelligence among a certain group. Regarding intelligence, the overwhelming majority of humans purportedly cluster in the middle between the extremes of high and low intelligence, forming a bell shape on such graphs.) Murray held a well-compensated position at a right-wing think tank, while Herrnstein, who died shortly before the book reached stores, served as a tenured Harvard psychology professor. *The Bell Curve* contended, among other highly debatable positions, that a fifteen-point mean gap existed between the IQs of whites and African Americans; lower IQ scores meant that Blacks had a higher tendency toward crime, illegitimate births and welfare dependency; those lower IQs stemmed from genetics; and social programs aimed at improving Black life in America could only be exercises in futility because of inherited traits limiting African American achievement. *The Bell Curve* ended with a set of policy recommendations, including calls for an end to affirmative action in college admissions and hiring, the diversion of education funds from programs aimed at helping poor and struggling students to those helping the gifted, and an end to "subsidizing births to anyone rich or poor." The authors suggested that eliminating programs like aid to mothers with dependent children and food stamps might discourage reproduction for the unfit, the proposal most closely linked to eugenicist thinking. They left unanswered what they thought should happen if those they regarded as part of a permanent intellectual underclass became the dominant demographic in American society. Neither Murray nor Herrnstein held expertise in psychometrics.[78]

The book drew heavily from what the *New York Review* called "tainted sources," especially the *Mankind Quarterly*, which obsessively featured articles allegedly proving Black intellectual inferiority. The Pioneer Fund finances publication of the journal. The textile millionaire Wycliffe Draper, who described Madison Grant as "the model" for his life, established the Pioneer Fund in 1937. Draper, who expressed sympathy for the Nazis and eugenics, said he aimed to advance research for the betterment of the white race. One of the Pioneer Fund's first projects was to distribute to American public schools a propaganda film made in Nazi Germany promoting eugenics. Since then, the fund has given preference in grant awards to those "who are deemed to be descended from white persons who settled in the original thirteen states . . . or related stocks." The fund also supports "study and research into the problems of heredity and eugenics in the human race."[79] In addition to backing eugenics, Draper supported the mass deportation of Black people to Africa, and subsidized groups that resisted (sometimes violently) desegregation in the South, like the Mississippi Sovereignty Commission and various White Citizens Councils.[80]

Hidden among more respected works in *The Bell Curve*'s massive bibliography were articles written by seventeen authors who had contributed to the eugenicist *Mankind Quarterly;* ten of those writers at some point served as editor of the white supremacist journal. None of this mattered to the fifty-two signers of the 1994 open letter defending Murray and Herrnstein's book, which included seven signatories from Texas. Insisting that "[i]ntelligence tests are not culturally biased against American blacks or other native-born, English-speaking peoples in the U.S.," the letter argued that "the bell curve for whites is centered roughly around IQ 100 [or average as the letter defined it]; the bell curve for American blacks roughly around 85 [15 points below average and only 15 points above the threshold of mental disability]; and those for different subgroups of Hispanics roughly midway between those for whites and blacks."[81]

The signatories included an infamous neo-eugenicist and psychology professor at the University of Western Ontario, J. Philippe Rushton, who was frequently cited as a credible source in *The Bell Curve*. The Canadian specialist on IQ once claimed that there was an inverse relationship between penis size and intellect. He announced that people of African descent produce more sperm than whites and therefore are dangerously fertile. According to him, Africans and their descendants around the world have smaller brains and are genetically predisposed to crime and poor parenting. "It's a tradeoff, more brains or more penis," Rushton concluded. "You can't have everything." Choosing to associate themselves with Rushton were five scholars from the University of Texas, psychology professors David B. Cohen, Joseph M. Horn, John C. Loehlin, Del Theissen, and Lee Willerman, and two from Texas A&M University, Cecil R. Reynolds of the Department of Educational Psychology and Neuroscience and business professor Lyle F. Schoenfeldt.[82]

All the Texas signatories in the psychology field either received funding from the Pioneer Fund or worked with researchers who had received grants from the racist group. Horn, Willerman, and Loehlin collaborated on the Texas Adoption Project, which explored whether adopted children more closely resembled their custodial or biological parents in terms of intelligence. "For general cognitive ability—general intelligence as assessed by IQ tests—there was evidence that the genes accounted for a larger share of individual differences than did family environments,"

Horn and Loehlin claimed in their 2010 book *Heredity and Environment in 300 Adoptive Families: The Texas Adoption Project.* Genes also accounted for social behaviors such as school success and failure, the authors claimed. The project received a grant from the Pioneer Fund and in *Heredity and Environment*, the authors thanked Philippe Rushton for his help during their research. Horn, Willerman, and Loehlin never closely interrogated the vague concept of intelligence itself, much less "general intelligence," the idea that a person's overall brainpower can be measured by tests that cover only a limited range of mental activities. The Texas Adoption Project's conclusions served a right-wing political purpose. Biology, they claimed, was to a large extent destiny in terms of achievement. Thus, programs that aimed to remediate barriers (such as Head Start) would make minimal impact and were not worth the investment.[83]

In addition to the twins project, Willerman conducted a sloppy study that purported to link brain size to intelligence. He concluded that bigger brains make for smarter people, based on his measurements of only forty test subjects not representative of the general population. Willerman's work argued that men possessed superior intellects to women.[84] Meanwhile, Cecil Reynolds of Texas A&M collaborated on research with Arthur Jensen, a University of California, Berkeley psychologist and a Pioneer Fund recipient who revived interest in supposed IQ differences between racial groups with a 1969 article in the *Harvard Educational Review* that heavily influenced the authors of *The Bell Curve*. Jensen also argued that an intelligence gap existed between whites and African Americans. Jensen entirely dismissed the idea that environment could alter performance on exams.[85]

Loehlin served as coauthor of a 1975 book, *Race Differences in Intelligence*. In spite of all of the certainty he showed by signing the open letter published by the *Wall Street Journal*, he and his collaborators repeatedly conceded in *Race Differences* the vagueness of "intelligence" and "race" as concepts. Intelligence and race have not been defined with any more exactness in the intervening half century.[86] In spite of its white supremacist conclusions, the *Bell Curve* letter published by the *Wall Street Journal* received no press attention and an Austin Unitarian Church even invited Lee Willerman to speak about *The Bell Curve* on March 12, 1995.[87]

The seven academic supporters of *The Bell Curve* did not call at the time of their open letter for selective breeding, state-ordered sterilizations, deportations of those accused of being "inferior," or restricting immigration to the "fit." They had no qualms, however, about accepting the generosity of an organization that embraced such an agenda and might use the data to advance such extreme measures. For almost all scholars in Texas by the dawn of the twentieth century, intellectual respectability required that eugenics be nothing more than subtext buried in lengthy footnotes.

Eugenics and the Alt-Right at Texas Campuses Today

As in the time of Huxley and Muller, eugenics in Texas continued to be to a large degree an import advocated mostly by short-timers in the state. Such was the case with a researcher at the University of Texas funded by right-wing money who openly promoted eugenics almost thirty years after the *Wall Street Journal* published the *Bell Curve* letter. In 2022–23, UT's Salem Center for Policy, established two years earlier as an institution (according to its website) "dedicated to helping students and business leaders better understand the costs, benefits and consequences of policy decisions" and committed to promoting "free enterprise," named Richard Hanania a visiting scholar. Wealthy conservative activists, like far-right Dallas real estate developer Harlan Crow, underwrote the center's establishment. For years, Hanania blogged and authored essays on alt-right (neo-Nazi) websites under the nom de plume Richard Hoste. As Hoste, he advocated eugenics and the sterilization of those with low intelligence. He wrote for *Counter-Currents*, a website that advocates the establishment of a white separatist nation), and *Taki's Magazine*, once edited by Richard Spencer. Under his pseudonym, Hanania wrote that Black people have "low intelligence and impulse control" and, using the claims about African Americans advanced by *The Bell Curve*, lamented that "Telling a race with an IQ of 85 that they can do whatever they set their mind to is cruel." [88]

Hiding under his secret identity, Hanania repeatedly advocated forced sterilization, authoring an essay in *Counter-Currents* titled "Answering Objections to Eugenics," in which he called for the sterilization of anyone with an IQ under ninety. He made another fulsome defense of eugenics on Spencer's website AlternativeRight.com in which he wrote:

> There doesn't seem to be a way to deal with low IQ breeding that doesn't include coercion. Perhaps charities could be formed which

paid those in the 70–85 range to be sterilized, but what to do with those below 70 who legally can't even give consent and have a higher birthrate than the general population? In the same way we lock up criminals and the mentally ill in the interests of society at large, one could argue that we could on the exact same principle sterilize those who are bound to harm future generations through giving birth.[89]

"Hoste" was optimistic about the future of the science of selective breeding. "There is no rational reason why eugenics can't capture the hearts and minds of policy makers the way it did 100 years ago." By the time he earned a JD at the University of Chicago School of Law in 2013, a PhD from UCLA in 2018, and a postdoctoral fellowship at Columbia University, he began authoring essays under his given name published by mainstream publications like the *Washington Post* and the *New York Times* even as he appeared on cable TV programs like Tucker Carlson's highly rated show on *Fox News*. For a while, he mostly railed against "political correctness" and how American colleges and universities supposedly suppressed right-wing views. On his Substack blogging page, however, he continued to share articles that promoted eugenics and mocked feminism. In his own writings, he cited the work of a Holocaust denier, Ron Unz. Posting an article under his real name about "the reality of [B]lack crime," on the social media site then called Twitter, Hanania called for massive surveillance of African Americans as the only way to keep white America safe. He wrote: "I don't have much hope that we'll solve crime in any meaningful way. It would require a revolution in our culture or form of government. We need more policing, incarceration, and surveillance of black people. Blacks won't appreciate it, whites don't have the stomach for it."[90]

The billionaire owner of Twitter, Elon Musk, had a one-word response to Hanania. "Interesting," Musk posted. Even though Hanania had come out of the closet as a believer in Black inferiority and human engineering, he gained a following among others in the ranks of the super-wealthy, such as tech entrepreneur Peter Thiel, 2024 Republican presidential candidate Vivek Ramaswamy and author, US Senator from Ohio, and 2024 Republican vice-presidential nominee J. D. Vance. His many high-tech mogul fans like Musk and Thiel shared with Hanania a belief in "longter-mism," which philosopher and historian Émile Torres described as a "transhumanist vision of creating a superior new race of 'posthumans' . . . eugenics on steroids." (Transhumanists hope for a day that technology can be implanted in bodies to lengthen lifespans, improve health, and increase intelligence.) Believers in longtermism hope to enhance the species through "restrictions on immigration, anti-miscegenation laws and forced sterilizations." Evidence of his open support for eugenics did not prevent him from being appointed by UT's Salem Institute or his planned appointment as a lecturer teaching "Forbidden Courses" at the unaccredited University of Austin founded by former *New York Times* columnist and right-wing provocateur Bari Weiss. (Plans called for the University of Austin to eventually relocate to the state's capital city, but as of early 2024 "UATX" was headquartered in a Harlan Crow-owned office complex called "Old Parkland" in Dallas.)[91]

Hanania seemed to be on an unimpeded path to ever-greater influence until his past as a pseudonymous alt-right activist was exposed by the *HuffPost* on August 4, 2023. By August 10, his name had disappeared from the Salem Center website. The Salem Center did not respond to press inquiries about the appointment, although on social media Hanania complained that, "Of all the cancellation attempts, the best one is University of Texas, where my fellowship already ends before fall (i.e. this month) and I've already received my last pay check [*sic*]. So . . . good luck I guess." Hanania posted a partial mea culpa claiming that once, "I held many beliefs that, as my current writing makes clear, I now find repulsive," but then said that he was being targeted for "cancellation" because "left-wing journalists dislike anyone acknowledging statistical differences between races." Otherwise, the revelation of his interest in selective breeding received little negative response. On September 19, 2023, HarperCollins released his book, *The Origins of Woke: Civil Rights Law, Corporate America, and the Triumph of Identity Politics*. Stanford University, long a font of eugenics thinking, continued to defend its decision to invite Hanania to speak there on October 5, 2023. As of July 27, 2024, he remained listed as a lecturer and his photo still appeared on the University of Austin website for its "Forbidden Courses" program. Neither the University of Texas nor University of Austin endorsed eugenics during this episode but, as in the case of the *Bell Curve* letter writers, there was no specific condemnation of the idea, acknowledgment of its shameful legacy or refutation of a faculty member's belief in Black and Brown inferiority.[92] Hanania earned a brief moment of infamy in the national media but, like the *Bell Curve* signatories, received little attention from the Texas press. Meanwhile, Austin hosted a pro-eugenic "Natal Conference" on December 1, 2023, at the swanky Line Hotel hosted by a far-right, high-tech oriented group charging $1,000 for tickets.[93]

In one sense, Hanania, a Texas outsider, represented a recurring theme in the history of eugenics in the South. Eugenicists in the region remained to a large degree "preachers of a foreign gospel" in a land that if not hostile was at least ambivalent and unconvinced, and their impact remained to a large degree difficult to measure.

One dominant element of the eugenic impulse has never disappeared since the concept of selective breeding ebbed in the 1940s. The fear of the foreign other that obsessed Daniel, Dabney, the 1920s Klan, Box, and Davis returned front and center in Texas politics in the 2020s. The "great replacement theory," a paranoid fantasy once exclusively the domain of the neo-Nazi right, entered the mainstream of state Republican politics. Replacement theory holds that global elites, typically portrayed as rich Jews, have conspired to commit "white genocide" by encouraging wide-open immigration of Black and Brown people. This theory has often been attributed to the French writer Renaud Camus, author of a 2011 book *Le Grand Remplacement*, which has incited racist mass shooters from Christchurch, New Zealand, to El Paso.[94] The theory, in fact, is an old one and, in the United States it merely recapitulates the central thesis of Madison Grant's and Lothrop Stoddard's published works in the early twentieth century: that the "colored" masses around the globe would soon overwhelm the world's white population, threatening extinction for the only race capable of creating and preserving civilization.

In 2021, Texas lieutenant governor Dan Patrick used language almost identical to those who wrote letters a century earlier supporting John Box, the eugenicist US House representative. Like them, Patrick spoke of whites drowning in a sea of color, with unwanted newcomers overthrowing the American way of life through sheer numbers rather than violence. "[T]hey are allowing this year probably 2 million—that is who we apprehended, maybe another million—into this country," Patrick said on the Fox News program *The Ingraham Angle.* Charging the Democratic

Party with conspiring to change the makeup of the electorate in order to push the country politically left, Patrick claimed, "At least in 18 years, even if they all don't become citizens before then and can vote, in 18 years every one of them has two or three children, you're talking about millions and millions and millions of new voters . . . So this is trying to take over our country without firing a shot. That is what is happening."[95]

In the early twentieth century, leading eugenicist Charles Davenport asked, "Can we build a wall high enough around this country, so as to keep out those cheaper races?" and worried that the best the United States could muster would be a "feeble dam." In the 2020s, Governor Greg Abbott sought to make an unscalable wall a reality, and a formidable one, even if it killed people. As of November 2022, about 150 miles of a border wall to keep out "dangerous" Brown people had been constructed along Texas's 1,254-mile border. Since 2021, Abbott repeatedly used the word "invasion" in letters to President Joe Biden to refer to migrant workers crossing the state's southern border. A memo to the state Department of Public Safety and to the Texas National Guard included "Defend Texas Against Invasion" as the alarming subject line. As the *Texas Tribune* reported, on social media Abbott insisted he had "invoked the Invasion Clauses of the U.S. & Texas Constitutions" as the legal basis for his anti-immigration actions. Abbott even ordered "wrecking ball sized" razor-wired buoys placed in the Rio Grande along the US–Mexican border, with one migrant dying after he became entangled in the barrier and drowned.[96]

Like E. E. Davis and his eugenicist peers in California, Abbott suggested that "aliens" carried deadly diseases, blaming them for the spread of COVID.[97] Speaking of his efforts to halt the supposed invasion of the state by Mexican and Central American migrants, Abbott said in a January 5, 2024, radio interview with right-wing host Dana Loesch (a former spokesperson for the National Rifle Association), "The only thing that we're not doing is we're not shooting people who come across the border, because of course, the Biden administration would charge us with murder." Such rhetoric echoed the "Savage Warfare" discourse of the mid-nineteenth century, which encouraged whites to feel ever in peril and rationalized violence against people of color. Abbott never called for eugenics, but his fixation with invaders echoed the obsessions of the eugenic era. Abbott's rhetoric did not repeat the past, but it rhymed.

Straight Lines and Dubious Motives

Moral ambiguity defined the long history of eugenics in Texas. One will not find clear heroes or villains while exploring this story. For instance, Texas eugenicists wanted to shut down immigration from Mexico because they saw the people of that nation as racial pollutants who might lower the collective IQ of the state and taint the whiteness of politically dominant and superior Anglo-Saxons. On the other hand, wealthy employers and politicians who wanted a free flow of poorly compensated migrant workers supported immigration. These advocates were not motivated by sensitivity to the economic needs of these migrants and their families or by appreciation for the hard work, intelligence, and cultural gifts such workers could bring to Texas; they were animated mostly by avarice. The employers of Mexican labor also embraced white supremacy and were certain that alleged Mexican "inferiority" meant such workers represented no threat to white civilization and would passively accept the worst labor conditions.

Texans were spared the tragedy of their government sterilizing thousands of those unlucky enough to be labeled by the state as unfit. The reasons such a ruthless program never became reality, however, had much to do with southern dread of centralized government power. This unease stemmed from the Reconstruction era, when an activist federal government abolished slavery and incorporated African American men and women into civil society, granting them rights that included access to the ballot. An empowered central government posed unpredictable risks to a status quo that so richly benefited Anglo elites.

Texas never developed the cult of the expert that rose in California, one that allowed the most educated men on the West Coast, such as David Starr Jordan, Lewis Terman, and Luther Burbank to oversee the mutilation of the poor, the disabled, and the dark-skinned in assembly-line fashion. For all their education, eugenicists got so much wrong: their belief in racial biological difference and inequality, their simplistic models of human heredity, and their mistaken assumption that abstract personality traits like honesty and a work ethic were physically inherited. Hubris defined the eugenics enterprise in both California and Texas, with scientists making sweeping predictions regarding the destinies of family bloodlines at a time when even the most informed experts barely understood the multi-dimensional nature of human heredity. "These researchers were . . . unaware that most of the traits they were interested in actually result from interactions between genetic and environmental factors, something that confounds predictions of complex disease even today," as the scholar Karen Norrgard wrote.[98]

Skepticism in Texas regarding the highly educated provided a barrier to dangerous theories becoming bloody, widespread practice as it did across much of the rest of the nation. Many academics did often hold the common person in contempt. The poor and working class harbored a well-earned suspicion of scientists like F. E. Daniel and Edgar Odell Lovett, who wanted to subject them to forced vasectomies and hysterectomies. Such skepticism likely played a role in thwarting what was not just a bad idea, as geneticist Elof Carlson put it, but a frankly evil one. Opponents of eugenics in Texas wisely worried that a society defined by eugenical thinking would lack compassion for the unfortunate and might fall into dehumanizing brutality, as eventually unfolded in Nazi Germany.

Yet, the far greater reluctance to embrace eugenics in Texas also stemmed in part from the cynical manipulations of politicians, like the legislators who resisted establishing a public university in Texas in the 1850s and Ma and Pa Ferguson in the early twentieth century. These elected officials presented a false choice between support of public schools or institutions of higher education. Such phony populists worried that the hyper-educated were in fact socialists or worse who might expose the rapacious motives of the ruling class. This led to a long history of poor funding of education in Texas, from preschool to doctoral programs and a self-defeating obsession with pitting "practical" education centered on job skills against the abstract and theoretical.

The Texas population became suspicious of science in general, an attitude sometimes mutating into an anti-intellectualism, which for decades severely hampered the state's ability to maintain a high quality of life by several measures well into the twenty-first century.[99] In some ways, the story of eugenics in Texas offers an affirmation of the scientific method. By 2023 Richard Hanania drew dismay by expressing what had been cutting-edge science one hundred years earlier. The virtual disappearance of the word "eugenics" from high-level academic discourse in the state since the 1950s meant that its most undercooked concepts had been broadly rejected through the process of careful analysis of data, and experimentation and attempted duplication in the emerging field of genetics. A critical mass in the social sciences had also analyzed and rejected eugenics' dubious moral foundations. Done well, science involves extensive self-correction.

The refusal of Texans to adopt eugenics laws, however, had little to do with the accuracy of that science. A straight line runs from the state's rejection of sterilization laws and demands for engaged couples to be subjected to intrusive medical exams to the frequent resistance by women and doctors to the state's strict and expansive abortion bans. Polling suggests that, regardless of policies adopted by the state government, Texans today as a group broadly accept science in the abstract, even on matters as politicized as climate change and COVID policies.[100] One factor, however, has been consistent among white Texans from the height of the eugenics era in the late nineteenth century to the age of COVID in the 2020s.

White supremacist ideology colored both acceptance of and resistance to eugenics measures in Texas throughout its history. The white population accepted as part of the natural order that state and local governments could and should regulate where Black and Brown people lived and attended school, their physical relationships with their white neighbors, if and where they received medical care, rode on a train or a bus, dined, or went to the bathroom.[101] However, straight, cisgendered Anglo men in Texas revolted, rejected, and resisted when asked to submit to similar micromanaging of their lives. Writing of the response to government shutdowns and vaccine and mask mandates during COVID, Patrick Boyle of the American Association of Medical Colleges said, "Where people turn skeptical [regarding science] is when scientists draw conclusions about issues that pluck sensitive chords—namely, telling people what to do."[102] The same was true in Texas among Anglo men regarding sterilization bills and restrictions on marriage during the state's eugenics period.

Millions of Texans accepted the idea that races were unequal, that mental limitations in the general population was widespread, and that the state would be better off with a greater number of "superior" Anglo-Saxons and fewer of everyone else. They rejected, however, granting leaders in Austin the right to regulate their own romantic lives or demand they prove their biological fitness if they wanted to marry.

Texas thus became in many ways an outlier as the eugenics craze elsewhere "made the world go around." The state's exceptionalism typically rested on the worst of motives. Writing of the threat of a new eugenics based on ableism, homophobia, and other hateful attitudes becoming respectable science once more in the future, Calum MacKellar and Christopher Bechtel offered this solution: "To protect humanity from such a prospect, a compassionate civilized society should learn to accept all possible future children in an environment that reflects its unconditional and equal acceptance of the suffering as well as the happy child."[103] There is little in the state's past or present to suggest that future Texans are willing and able to forge such a society.

Notes

Abbreviations Used in Bibliography and Notes

BCAH	Dolph Briscoe Center for American History, University of Texas at Austin, Austin, Texas
BLAC	Nettie Lee Benson Latin American Collection, University of Texas at Austin, Austin, Texas
CSHL	Cold Spring Harbor Laboratory, Cold Spring Harbor, New York
SWC	Southwest Collection/Special Collections Library, Texas Tech University, Lubbock, Texas
TSLAC	Texas State Library and Archives Commission, Austin, Texas
UTA	University of Texas at Arlington Central Library, Arlington, Texas
WRCSC	Woodson Research Center Special Collections, Fondren Library, Rice University, Houston, Texas

Prologue

1. North Texas Agricultural College is now known as the University of Texas at Arlington.

2. See Lewis Meriwether Dabney, *A Memoir and Letters* (New York: privately printed by J. J. Little and Ives Company, 1924).

3. Philippa Levine, *Eugenics: A Very Short Introduction* (Oxford, UK: Oxford University Press, 2017), 1.

4. Edward J. Larson, *Sex, Race, and Science: Eugenics in the Deep South* (Baltimore: Johns Hopkins University Press, 1995), 1.

5. For more on the influence of prophetic religious belief in Texas in the late nineteenth century and the first half of the twentieth century, see Paul Boyer, *When Time Shall Be No More: Prophecy Belief in Modern American Culture* (Cambridge, MA: Belknap Press of Harvard University Press, 1992), 97–99;

Michael Ennis, "Apocalypse Now," *Texas Monthly*, July 2004, accessed July 23, 2018, https://www.texasmonthly.com/articles/apocalypse-now-2/; "Dallas Theological Seminary," *Handbook of Texas Online*, accessed July 26, 2024, https://www.tshaonline.org/handbook/entries/dallas-theological-seminary; and Michael Phillips, *White Metropolis: Race, Ethnicity, and Religion in Dallas, 1841–2001* (Austin: University of Texas Press, 2006). 47–51, 54–56. See also Cyrus Scofield, ed., *The Old Scofield Study Bible* (1917; repr., New York: Oxford University Press, 1996.).

6. Daniel J. Kevles, *In the Name of Eugenics: Genetics and the Uses of Human Heredity* (Cambridge, MA.: Harvard University Press, 1985), 19. xiii, 3–10, 19; Stephen Jay Gould, *The Mismeasure of Man* (New York: W. W. Norton, 1981), 75; Wendy Kline, *Building a Better Race: Gender, Sexuality, and Eugenics from the Turn of the Century to the Baby Boom* (Berkeley: University of California Press, 2001), 13–14; Diane Paul, *Controlling Human Heredity: 1865 to the Present* (Amherst, NY: Humanity Books, 1995), 3. For more on the ideology of whiteness in Brazil, see Sidney Chalhoub, *Cidade Febril: Cortiços e Epidemias na Corte Imperial* (São Paulo: Companhia das Letras, 1996).

7. The historiography of eugenics, an examination of its ethical dimensions and a critique of the movement as an offshoot of the Progressive movement of the early twentieth century, has grown exponentially since the early 1960s partly as a legacy of the civil rights movement of the 1950s and 1960s. In the past sixty years, scholars have begun examining more closely the abusive relationship between the medical community and the poor, Black and Brown people, those with disabilities, and the LGBTQ community. Scholars also have increasingly examined scientists as products of the larger culture, including its racism, misogyny, classism, and ableism, and have come to see supposedly objective scientific tools such as intelligence tests as perhaps irredeemably flawed. "It is not a coincidence that the social and cultural factors that propelled the movement for better breeding in the first decades of the twentieth century re-appeared as the culture wars took place in the last decades of the century," observed David Cullen in his invaluable survey of eugenics scholarship over five decades, "Back to the Future: Eugenics—A Bibliographic Essay," *Public Historian* 29, no. 3 (Summer 2007): 163–175. Publications on eugenics that influenced this work are listed in the select bibliography.

8. For more on Lincecum, see Lois Wood Burkhalter, *Gideon Lincecum, 1793–1874: A Biography* (Austin: University of Texas Press, 1965); Jerry Bryan Lincecum, Edward Hake Phillips and Peggy A. Redshaw, eds., *Science on the Texas Frontier: Observations of Dr. Gideon Lincecum* (College Station: Texas A&M University Press, 1997); and Jerry Bryan Lincecum and Edward Hake Phillips, eds., *Adventures of a Frontier Naturalist: The Life and Times of Dr. Gideon Lincecum* (College Station: Texas A&M University Press, 1994).

9. Gideon Lincecum, to Parson Lancaster, June 12, 1859, Gideon Lincecum Collection, Box 2E363, BCAH; Burkhalter, *Gideon Lincecum*, 93–99.

10. See Stephen S. Kan, "Corporal Punishments and Optimal Incapacitation," *Journal of Legal Studies* 25, no. 1 (January 1996): 123–125.

11. Larson, *Sex, Race and Science,* 26–27.

12. Burkhalter, *Gideon Lincecum,* 93–99.

13. Lois Wood Burkhalter, "Gideon Lincecum," *Handbook of Texas Online,* accessed December 16, 2020, https://www.tshaonline.org/handbook/entries /lincecum-gideon; Lincecum to Lancaster; Burkhalter, *Gideon Lincecum,* 71–73; Paul, *Controlling Human Heredity,* 1.

14. See for example, F. E. Daniel, "Should Insane Criminals, Or Sexual Perverts, Be Allowed to Procreate," *Texas Medical Journal,* August 1893, 255–271, 275.

15. Mark A. Largent, *Breeding Contempt: The History of Coerced Sterilization in the United States* (New Brunswick, NJ: Rutgers University Press, 2011), 8.

16. One can find coverage of such events with "Benefits of Better Babies Contests: Parents Taught How to Improve Their Offspring and Correct Deficiencies," *Dallas Morning News,* November 23, 1913; "Bright Sunshine and Varied Features Bring Big Crowd to The Fair: Better Baby Contest Is Drawing Card," *Dallas Daily Times Herald,* October 28, 1914; and "Y.M.C.A. Does Extensive Work: Community Chest Agency Has Served 6,000 Young Men in One Year," *Dallas Morning News,* April 28, 1924.

17. Essential works on the eugenics movement in California include Miroslava Chávez-García, *States of Delinquency: Race and Science in the Making of California's Juvenile Justice System* (Berkeley: University of California Press, 2012); Natalie Lira, *Laboratory of Deficiency: Sterilization and Confinement in California, 1900–1950s* (Berkeley: University of California Press, 2021); Natalia Molina, *Fit to Be Citizens?: Public Health and Race in Los Angeles, 1879–1939* (Berkeley: University of California Press, 2006); and Alexandra Mina Stern. *Eugenic Nation: Faults and Frontiers of Better Breeding in Modern America* (Berkeley: University of California Press, 2005).

18. For instance, the Dallas school board on March 1, 1926, approved for the district's biology classes the textbook *New Biology* by W. M. Smallwood, Ida L. Reveley, and Guy A. Bailey, and ordered new editions over the years. See Dallas Independent School District Board Minutes, vol. 16, p. 84, Dallas Independent School District Headquarters, Dallas, Texas. See also W. M. Smallwood, Ida L. Reveley, and Guy A. Bailey, *New Biology* (New York: Allyn and Bacon, 1934), 394–395. For more on Huxley, read C. Kenneth Waters and Albert Van Helden, eds., *Julian Huxley: Biologist and Statesman of Science* (College Station: Texas A&M University Press, 1992). James Schwartz, *In Pursuit of the Gene: From Darwin to DNA* (New York: Harper & Row, 2008) provides a compelling examination of Muller's thought and scientific research. Consistently an eccentric, Muller unsurprisingly offered an iconoclastic anti-racist program of eugenics that angered his peers in the movement in *Out of the Night: A Biologist's View of the Future* (New York: Vanguard Press, 1935).

19. There were forty-eight states at the time; Georgia became the last one to adopt a forced sterilization law, in 1937. States that never enacted compulsory sterilization laws in addition to Texas were Arkansas, Colorado, Florida, Illinois, Kentucky, Louisiana, Maryland, Massachusetts, Missouri, New Mexico, Ohio, Pennsylvania, Rhode Island, Tennessee, and Wyoming. See Largent, *Breeding Contempt*, 72.

20. Kevles, *In the Name of Eugenics* 85; Largent, *Breeding Contempt*, 77.

21. Neil Foley explores Texas eugenics in *The White Scourge: Mexicans, Blacks, and Poor Whites in Texas Cotton Culture* (Berkeley: University of California Press, 1997). Jason E. Pierce examines the influence of Social Darwinism and eugenics on the southwestern United States as a whole, though not specifically in Texas, in *Making the White Man's West: Whiteness and the Creation of the American West* (Boulder: University of Colorado Press, 2016). Otherwise, the state is virtually invisible in the historiography of American eugenics. See also the authors' "A Serviceable Villain: Eugenics, the Fear of the 'Underman,' and Anti-Democratic Discourse in Texas Thought and Culture, 1900–1940," *East Texas Historical Journal* 55, no. 2 (Fall 2017): 7–46.

22. Gould, *Mismeasure of Man*, 192–233; Daniel Okrent, *The Guarded Gate: Bigotry, Eugenics, and the Law That Kept Two Generations of Jews, Italians, and Other European Immigrants Out of America* (New York: Scribner, 2019), 247–250, 277, 305, 307; 310, 314, 322, 358; Clarence S. Yoakum and Robert M. Yerkes, *Army Mental Tests* (New York: Henry Holt and Company, 1920); Leila Zenderland, *Measuring Minds: Henry Herbert Goddard and the Origins of American Intelligence Testing* (Cambridge, UK: Cambridge University Press, 2001), 260, 262–263, 281–300, 301, 303, 311–321, 324–325, 348.

23. Kenneth M. Ludmerer, "Genetics, Eugenics, and the Immigration Restriction Act of 1924," *Bulletin of the History of Medicine* 6, no. 1 (January–February 1972): 59–81.

24. Donald K. Pickens, *Eugenics and the Progressives* (Nashville: Vanderbilt University Press, 1968), 213.

25. Paul, *Controlling Human Heredity*, 17–18, 20, 38, 45, 102–103; Martin S. Pernick, *The Black Stork: Eugenics and the Death of 'Defective' Babies in American Medicine and Motion Pictures Since 1915* (New York: Oxford University Press, 1996), 25–27.

26. Robert H. Wiebe, *The Search for Order, 1877–1920* (New York: Hill and Wang, 1967), xiv, 154–157.

27. Hermann J. Muller, "Prepared at Vavilov's, 1936–1937" (typed note), Hermann J. Muller Collection, Series II, Biographical Materials, Memorabilia, 1912–1972, Box 1, Biographical, Folder 1.38, CSHL; Muller, *Out of the Night*, vii.

28. Largent, *Breeding Contempt*, 29, 30; Levine, *Eugenics*, 62; Daniel, "Insane Criminals," 255–271, 275. According to Largent, only eleven states had no known cases of forced sterilizations (Arkansas, Florida, Kentucky, Louisiana, Maryland, Massachusetts, Missouri, New Mexico, Rhode Island, Tennessee, and Wyoming).

29. Levine, *Eugenics*, 60; Pernick, *Black Stork*, 24.

30. Pernick, *Black Stork*, 36–39, 44–46, 98; William S. Bush, *Who Gets a Childhood?: Race and Juvenile Justice in Twentieth-Century Texas* (Athens: University of Georgia Press, 2010), 22–25; "Field Assignments for the 1919 Training Class," *Eugenical News*, September 1919, 72.

31. Jonathan Peter Spiro, *Defending the Master Race: Conservation, Eugenics, and the Legacy of Madison Grant* (Burlington: University of Vermont Press, 2009), 171–173. See also Madison Grant, *The Passing of the Great Race or the Racial Basis of European History* (New York: Charles Scribner's Sons, 1916) and Lothrop Stoddard, *The Rising Tide of Color Against White World Supremacy* (New York: Charles Scribner's Sons, 1920) and *The Revolt Against Civilization: The Menace of the Under Man* (New York: Charles Scribner's Sons, 1922).

32. Grant, *Passing of the Great Race*, xii, 163, 267–293.

33. Grant, *Passing of the Great Race*, 227–229.

34. Grant, *Passing of the Great Race*, 16, 18, 91; Spiro, *Defending the Master Race*, 164.

35. Grant, *Passing of the Great Race*, 49.

36. Okrent, *Guarded Gate*, 270; Foley, *White Scourge*, 5–6; Linda Gordon, *The Second Coming of the KKK: The Ku Klux Klan of the 1920s and the American Political Tradition* (New York: Liveright Publishing Corporation, 2017), 21, 27, 31,41,43, 105, 107, 201, 249; "Imperial Wizard Evans' Great Speech," *Texas 100 Per Cent American*, October 26, 1923, 3–4; Dabney, *Memoir and Letters*, 214; Edward Everett Davis, *The White Scourge* (San Antonio: Naylor, 1940). For more on the Klan's power in 1920s Texas, see David M. Chalmers, *Hooded Americanism: The History of the Ku Klux Klan* (Durham, NC: Duke University Press, 1987), 39–48.

37. George J. Sánchez, *Becoming Mexican American: Ethnicity, Culture, and Identity in Chicano Los Angeles, 1900–1945* (New York: Oxford University Press, 1993), 19.

38. Sánchez, *Becoming Mexican American*, 20, 57–58; Mae M. Ngai, "Nationalism, Immigration Control, and the Ethnoracial Remapping of America in the 1920s," *OAH Magazine of History*, July 2007, 13–14.

39. Levine, *Eugenics*, 47–50, 59–60, 62–63; Stern, *Eugenic Nation*, 6.

40. The *Puck* cover can be seen at the Library of Congress website at https://www.loc.gov/pictures/item/2011649601/, accessed December 17, 2020.

41. Terry D. Jordan, John L. Bean Jr., and Michael M. Holmes, *Texas: A Geography* (Boulder, CO: Westview Press, 1984), 5, 91; Foley, *White Scourge*, 2; Andrew J. Torget, *Seeds of Empire: Cotton, Slavery, and the Transformation of the Texas Borderlands, 1800–1850* (Chapel Hill: University of North Carolina Press), xi–xii.

42. Pekka Hämäläinen, *The Comanche Empire* (New Haven: Yale University Press, 2008), 2, 4.

43. Gary Clayton Anderson, *The Conquest of Texas: Ethnic Cleansing in the Promised Land, 1820–1875* (Norman: University of Oklahoma Press, 2005), 173–174, 359–360.

44. Torget, *Seeds of Empire*, 9–10, 12, 23; Richard Slotkin, *Gunfighter Nation: The Myth of the Frontier in Twentieth-Century America* (Norman: University of Oklahoma Press, 1998), 12–13.

45. Ann Gibbons, "There's No Such Thing as a 'Pure' European—Or Anyone Else," *Science*, May 15, 2017, accessed July 12, 2021, https://www.sciencemag.org/news/2017/05/theres-no-such-thing-pure-european-or-anyone-else; Reginald Horsman, *Race and Manifest Destiny: The Origins of American Anglo-Saxonism* (Cambridge, MA: Harvard University Press, 1981), 301; L. D. Burnett, "In the U.S. Praise for Anglo-Saxon Heritage Has Always Been About White Supremacy," *Washington Post*, April 26, 2021, accessed July 11, 2021, https://www.washingtonpost.com/outlook/2021/04/26/us-praise-anglo-saxon-heritage-has-always-been-about-white-supremacy/.

46. Sam Houston, "Address of Gen. Sam Houston, President Elect, at Houston, November 25, 1841," in *The Writings of Sam Houston, 1813–1863*, ed. Amelia Williams and Eugene Barker (Austin: University of Texas Press, 1938), 392. For an example of Anglo-Saxonism in Texas, see Frank M. Cockrell, *History of Early Dallas* (Chicago: privately published, 1944), 44–46. For more on Sam Houston's Anglo-Saxonism, see Edward Sebesta, "Sam Houston," July 14, 2021, accessed February 17, 2024, https://issuu.com/edwardh.sebesta/docs/20210624_sam_houston_paper.

47. W.W. Newcomb Jr., *The Indians of Texas: From Prehistoric to Modern Times* (Austin: University of Texas Press, 1993), 334, 345; Anderson, *Conquest of Texas*, 15, 129–130, 174, 176; Dorman H. Winfrey, "Mirabeau H. Lamar and Texas Nationalism," *Southwestern Historical Quarterly* 59, no. 2 (October 1955): 193.

48. Anderson, *Conquest of Texas*, 5.

49. Horsman, *Race and Manifest Destiny*, 130–132; Arnoldo De León, *They Called Them Greasers: Anglo Attitudes Toward Mexicans in Texas, 1821–1900* (Austin: University of Texas Press, 1983), 5–6, 8; F. E. Daniel, *Recollections of a Rebel Surgeon (And Other Sketches) Or, In the Doctor's Sappy Days* (Austin: Van Boekmann, Schutze & Co., 1899), 257; Gould, *Mismeasure of Man*, 69–70.

50. De León, *They Called Them Greasers*, 9, 16–17, 73–74.

51. Holly Beachley Brear, *Inherit the Alamo: Myth and Ritual at an American Shrine* (Austin: University of Texas Press, 1995), 36–37; Rodolfo Acuña, *Occupied America: A History of Chicanos* (New York: HarperCollins Publishers, 1988), 11.

52. Slotkin, *Gunfighter Nation*, 12–13.

53. Robert Calvert, Arnoldo De León, and Gregg Cantrell, *The History of Texas*, 6th ed. (Malden, MA: John Wiley & Sons, 2020), 228.

54. Nancy Isenberg provides an excellent history of the concept of the inferior white in *White Trash: The 400-Year Untold History of Class in America* (New York: Viking, 2016).

55. Robert S. Shelton, "On Empire's Shore: Free and Unfree Workers in Galveston, Texas, 1840–1860," *Journal of Social History* 40, no. 3 (Spring 2007): 717.

56. Keri Leigh Merritt, *Masterless Men: Poor Whites and Slavery in the Antebellum South* (New York: Cambridge University Press, 2017), 254; Isenberg, *White Trash*, iv; Shelton, "On Empire's Shore," 726.

57. The best narrative histories of Texas are Calvert, De León, and Cantrell, *History of Texas*, 6th ed.; Randolph B. Campbell, *A History of the Lone Star State* (New York: Oxford University Press, 2003); and Rupert N. Richardson, Cary Wintz, Angela Boswell, and Ernest Wallace, *Texas: The Lone Star State* (New York: Routledge, Taylor, & Francis Group, 2021).

58. For the links among population increase, urbanization, and the rise of eugenicist sentiment, see Garland E. Allen, "'Culling the Herd': Eugenics and the Conservation Movement in the United States, 1900–1940," *Journal of the History of Biology* 46, no. 1 (Spring 2013): 31–72; Katherine Benton-Cohen, *Inventing the Immigration Problem: The Dillingham Commission and Its Legacy* (Cambridge, MA: Harvard University Press, 2018), 83, 145; Matthew Connelly, "Population Control is History: New Perspectives on the International Campaign to Limit Population Growth," *Comparative Studies in Society and History* 45, no. 1 (January 2003): 122–147; Edmund Ramsden, "Social Demography and Eugenics in the Interwar United States," *Population and Development Review* 29, no. 4 (December 2003): 547–593.

59. Frank Hobbs and Nicole Stoops, *Demographic Trends in the 20th Century: Census 2000 Special Reports* (Washington, DC: United States Bureau of the Census, 2002), A-1, A-3, A-20, A-21, A-25, A-26, C-3, Accessed July 3, 2020, https://www.census.gov/prod/2002pubs/censr-4.pdf; United States Bureau of the Census, Population Division, "Table 13. Nativity of the Population, for Regions, Divisions, and States: 1850 to 1990," accessed July 13, 2011, http://www.census.gov/population/www/documentation/twps0029/tab13.html; Robert Calvert and Arnoldo De León, *The History of Texas*, 5th ed. (Malden, MA: Wiley Blackwell, 2014), 26; Terry G. Jordan, "A Century and a Half of Ethnic Change in Texas, 1836–1986," *Southwestern Historical Quarterly* 89, no. 4 (April 1986): 418; Robert McCaa, "Missing Millions: The Human Cost of the Mexican Revolution," Report by the University of Minnesota Population Center (2001), accessed July 13, 2011, http://www.hist.umn.edu/~rmccaa/missmill/mxrev.htm.

60. Foley, *White Scourge*, 58, 136–137.

61. Ty Cashion, *Lone Star Mind: Reimagining Texas History* (Norman: University of Oklahoma Press, 2018), 26.

62. "Charles William Eliot," *History of the Presidency*, accessed December 13, 2020, https://www.harvard.edu/about-harvard/harvard-glance/history-presidency/charles-william-eliot; Adam S. Cohen, "Harvard's Eugenics Era," *Harvard Magazine* March–April 2016, accessed December 13, 2020, https://harvardmagazine.com/2016/03/harvards-eugenics-era; Stern, *Eugenic Nation*, 19, 22–25, 84, 90, 132–133, 208.

63. The underfunding of Texas public schools throughout its history is covered in Patrick L. Cox and Michael Phillips, *The House Will Come to Order: How*

the Texas Speaker Became a Power in State and National Politics (Austin: University of Texas Press, 2010), 12–13, 16, 50, 54, 5–58, 60–62, 64, 82; Frederick Eby, *The Development of Education in Texas* (New York: MacMillan, 1925); John Jay Lane, *History of Education in Texas* (Washington, DC: U.S. Bureau of Education, 1903); Gene B. Preuss, *To Get a Better School System: One Hundred Years of Education Reform in Texas* (College Station: Texas A&M University Press, 2009); Rae Files Still, *The Gilmer-Aikin Bills* (Austin: Steck, 1950); and Stephen Thomas and Billy Don Walker, "Texas Public School Finance," *Journal of Education Finance* 8, no. 2 (Fall 1982): 223–281. Underfunding of higher education in Texas in the first half of the twentieth century and efforts to remedy that deficiency is examined in Carlos Kevin Blanton, "The Campus and the Capitol: John B. Connally and the Struggle over Texas Higher Education Policy, 1950–1970, *Southwestern Historical Quarterly* 108, no. 4 (April 2005): 468–497.

64. The classic work on Texas Progressives' monomania regarding alcohol is Lewis L. Gould's *Progressives and Prohibitionists: Texas Democrats in the Wilson Era* (Austin: Texas State Historical Association, 1992).

65. See Joseph P. Locke, *Making the Bible Belt: Texas Prohibitionists and the Politicization of Southern Religion* (Oxford, UK: Oxford University Press, 2017).

66. Larson, *Sex, Race, and Science*, 8–9.

67. See, for example, "If America Fails," *Baptist Standard*, January 9, 1923, and Jefferson Davis Bragg, review of *The White Scourge* by E. E. Davis, *Journal of American History* 27 (March 1941), 689.

68. Julian Huxley, "The Outlook in Biology: A Course of Three Lectures Delivered in the Physics Amphitheatre of the Rice Institute, September 29 and 30, and October 1, 1924," *Rice Institute Pamphlet*, October 1924, 301; Dabney, *Memoir and Letters*, 215.

Chapter 1

1. Burkhalter, *Gideon Lincecum*, 95.

2. Largent, *Breeding Contempt*, 31; Gideon Lincecum to Parson Lancaster, June 12, 1859, Gideon Lincecum Collection, Box 2E363, BCAH.

3. Burkhalter, *Gideon Lincecum*, 125. See also James Poskett, *Materials of the Mind: Phrenology, Race, and the Global History of Science, 1815–1920* (Chicago: University of Chicago Press, 2019), 1–2, 13, 15, 119, 142, 151, 161, 163; and "Phrenology," *Texian Advocate* (Victoria, TX), November 28, 1850.

4. Burkhalter, *Gideon Lincecum*, 19, 264; Carole E. Christian, "Longpoint, Texas," *Handbook of Texas Online*, accessed July 12, 2021, https://www.tshaonline.org/handbook/entries/longpoint-tx.

5. Largent, *Breeding Contempt*, 11; Gideon Lincecum, "Personal Reminiscences of an Octogenarian," *American Sportsman*, September 12, 1874; Burkhalter, *Gideon Lincecum*, 3, 6, 17, 20, 55; Pat Ireland Nixon, "A Pioneer Texas

Emasculator: A Chapter from the Life of Dr. Gideon Lincecum," *Texas State Journal of Medicine*, May 1940, 34.

6. Lincecum, "Personal Reminiscences."

7. Lincecum, Phillips, and Redshaw, *Adventures of a Frontier Naturalist*, 37–38.

8. See Lincecum, "Personal Reminiscences"; Burkhalter, *Gideon Lincecum*, 209–213; Lincecum, Philips, and Redshaw, *Science on the Texas Frontier*, 18–27; Lincecum and Phillips, *Adventures of a Frontier Naturalist*, 38–39.

9. Lincecum and Phillips, *Science on the Texas Frontier*, 18–29.

10. For more on Lincecum's atheism, see Burkhalter, *Gideon Lincecum*, 105–107.

11. Burkhalter, *Gideon Lincecum*, 55, 93. For more on the brutal nature of nineteenth-century medicine, see John Duffy, *From Humors to Medical Science: A History of American Medicine* (Urbana: University of Illinois Press, 1993), 69–71.

12. Burkhalter, *Gideon Lincecum*, 56–57.

13. Susan E. Cayleff, *Nature's Path: A History of Naturopathic Healing in America* (Baltimore: Johns Hopkins University Press, 2016), 32–34.

14. Deidre Cooper Owens, *Medical Bondage: Race, Gender, and the Origins of American Gynecology* (Athens: University of Georgia Press, 2017), 34–40; Charles Sellers, *The Market Revolution: Jacksonian America, 1815-1846* (Oxford, UK: Oxford University Press, 1991), 256–257; Harriet Washington, *Medical Apartheid: The Dark History of Medical Experimentation on Black Americans from Colonial Times to the Present* (New York: Doubleday, 2006), 61–70.

15. Burkhalter, *Gideon Lincecum*, 55, 93.

16. Burkhalter, *Gideon Lincecum*, 93, 95.

17. Burkhalter, *Gideon Lincecum*, 94.

18. Lincecum to Lancaster, June 12, 1859, Gideon Lincecum Papers; Nixon, "Pioneer Texas Emasculator," 37.

19. Burkhalter, *Gideon Lincecum*, 94; Lincecum to Lancaster, June 12, 1859, Gideon Lincecum Papers.

20. Gideon Lincecum to W. Richardson, 1874, Gideon Lincecum Collection, Box 2E365, Folder 4, Letters from 1873–1899, BCAH.

21. Burkhalter, *Gideon Lincecum*, 96.

22. Burkhalter, *Gideon Lincecum*, 96, 99–100; Nixon, "Pioneer Texas Emasculator," 37.

23. Lincecum to Lancaster, June 12, 1859, Gideon Lincecum Papers; Burkhalter, *Gideon Lincecum*, 103; Lincecum Diary, Lincecum Papers Box 2E363, Folder 1, Diary—1867 (BCAH.)

24. Lincecum to Lancaster, June 12, 1859, Gideon Lincecum Papers; Burkhalter, *Gideon Lincecum*, 100; Lincecum Diary, 1859, Gideon Lincecum Papers, Box 2E363, Folder 1, Diary—1867, BCAH.

25. Burkhalter, *Gideon Lincecum*, 96.

26. F. H. Merriman, to Gideon Lincecum, July 13, 1856, Gideon Lincecum Collection, Box 2E363, Folder 3, BCAH.

27. Merriam to Lincecum, July 13, 1856, Gideon Lincecum Collection.

28. Josiah Higgerson to Gideon Lincecum, March 2, 1856, Gideon Lincecum Collection, Box 2E363, Folder 3, BCAH.

29. Burkhalter, *Gideon Lincecum*, 97–99.

30. Burkhalter, *Gideon Lincecum*, 101–102; Largent, *Breeding Contempt*, 14.

31. Lincecum Diary, August 29, 1867, Gideon Lincecum Papers.

32. Lincecum and Phillips, *Adventures of a Frontier Naturalist*, xxiii–xxiv.

33. Burkhalter, *Gideon Lincecum*, 102.

Chapter 2

1. Daniel, *Recollections of a Rebel Surgeon*, 252, 256.

2. Violet M. Baird, "Nineteenth Century Medical Journalism in Texas, with a Journal Checklist," *Bulletin of the Medical Library Association* 60 (July 1972): 376–377, 380.

3. Courtney Shah, "The Woman's Department: Maternalism and Feminism in the Texas Medical Journal," *Historian* 64, no. 1 (Fall 2001): 83–84, 85–86.

4. Both Wiebe, *Search for Order* and Nell Irvin Painter, *Standing at Armageddon: The United States, 1877–1919* (New Work: W. W. Norton, 1987) provide critical insights on the zeitgeist of the Progressive Era, roughly from the 1890s to 1920.

5. Alan Dawley, *Struggles for Justice: Social Responsibility and the Liberal State* (Cambridge, MA: Harvard University Press, 1991), 160–161.

6. Wiebe, *Search for Order*, xiv, 154–157.

7. A thoughtful and fascinating discussion of the relationship between the suffrage movement and white supremacy can be found in Rachel Gunter, "More Than Black and White: Woman Suffrage and Voting Rights in Texas, 1918–1923" (PhD diss., Texas A&M University, 2017), 11–22.

8. Gould, *Progressives and Prohibitions*, 286; F. E. Daniel, "Elements of Decay in American Civilization," *Texas State Journal of Medicine* 4 (December 1908): 196.

9. Daniel, "Elements of Decay in American Civilization," 197.

10. Shah, "Woman's Department," 83; "Transactions of the Texas State Medical Ass'n, 1887," *Daniel's Texas Medical Journal* 3, no. 7 (January 1888): 394.

11. Largent, *Breeding Contempt*, 5–6.

12. Chandler Davidson, *Race and Class in Texas Politics* (Princeton, NJ: Princeton University Press, 1990), 21–23.

13. "The Texas Sterilization Bill," *Lancet-Clinic*, May 3, 1913, 467.

14. Daniel, *Recollections of a Rebel Surgeon*, 7–8.

15. Merritt, *Masterless Men*, 310–311; Daniel, *Recollections of a Rebel Surgeon*, 9, 39, 45.

16. Daniel, *Recollections of a Rebel Surgeon*, 39, 45.

17. Daniel, *Recollections of a Rebel Surgeon* 108; Shah, Woman's Department," 84; Daniel, "Elements of Decay in American Civilization," 195.

18. Shah, Woman's Department," 85–86.

19. Daniel, *Recollections of a Rebel Surgeon*, 108, 238–239.

20. Daniel, "Elements of Decay in American Civilization," 195.

21. Daniel, "Elements of Decay in American Civilization," 196–197.

22. Dora Costa, "Health and Economy in the United States, from 1750 to the Present," *Journal of Economic Literature* 53 (September 2015), accessed July 20, 2022, https://www.ncbi.nlm.nih.gov/pmc/articles/PMC4577070/; Okrent, *The Guarded Gate*, 142.

23. Daniel, "Sentiment and Science" *Texas State Journal of Medicine* 1 (February 1906), 267.

24. "On Preventing Immigration," *Galveston Daily News*, September 3, 1893.

25. Alan M. Kraut, *Silent Travelers: Germs, Genes, and the "Immigrant Menace"* (Baltimore: Johns Hopkins University Press, 1994), 65–66, 107–109, 136–137, 145; "For Quarantines Against Trachoma," *Fort Worth Record and Register*, January 16, 1908; "Danger from Diseased Immigrants," *Brownsville Herald*, May 21, 1907.

26. "For Protection Against Insane: Congress to Enact Stringent Exclusion Laws," *Fort Worth Record and Register*, February 27, 1901.

27. Sarah C. Sitton, *Life at Texas State Lunatic Asylum, 1857–1997* (College Station: Texas A&M University Press, 1999), 3–5, 10–11, 14, 16; Dan L. Creson, "Mental Health," *Handbook of Texas Online*, accessed July 26, 2024, https://www.tshaonline.org/handbook/entries/mental-health; Jennifer Hopkins, "Abilene State School," *Handbook of Texas Online*, accessed July 26, 2024, https://www.tshaonline.org/handbook/entries/abilene-state-school.

28. Sitton, *Life at Texas State Lunatic Asylum*,20–21, 24, 29, 33–34.

29. M. L. Graves, "The Care of the Insane," *Bulletin of the University of Texas*, June 15, 1905, 4, 11, 12.

30. Graves, "Care for the Insane," 15.

31. Philip R. Reilly, *The Surgical Solution: A History of Involuntary Sterilization in the United States* (Baltimore: Johns Hopkins University Press, 1991), 9–10.

32. Calvert and De León, *History of Texas*, 5th ed., 241; Thomas C. Henthorn, "A Nation's Need—Good and Well-Trained Mothers: Gender, Charity, and the New Urban South," *Frontiers: A Journal of Women Studies* 32, no. 1 (2011): 76.

33. Texas history has been defined by migration and the fluidity of its population. The authors, therefore, do not confine their definition of "Texan" to those born in the state. For simplicity, the authors define "Texans" as those who have made residence within the state for a part of their life relevant to the period covered in the narrative.

34. United States Census Bureau, *Religious Bodies: 1906* (Washington, DC: Government Printing Office, 1910), 17, 43; John W. Storey and Mary L. Kelly,

Twentieth Century Texas: A Social and Cultural History (Denton: University of North Texas Press, 2008), 136.

35. Bryan Edward Stone, *The Chosen Folks: Jews on the Frontiers of Texas* (Austin: University of Texas Press, 2010), 76, 78, 80–83.

36. Bryan Edward Stone, "On the Frontier: Jews without Judaism," in Hollace Ava Weiner and Kenneth D. Roseman, *Lone Stars of David: The Jews of Texas* (Waltham, Mass.: Brandeis University Press, 2007), 30; Hollace Ava Weiner, introduction to Weiner and Roseman, *Lone Stars of David*, 13–14; Hollace Ava Weiner, *Jewish Stars in Texas: Rabbis and their Work* (College Station: Texas A&M University Press, 1999), 29.

37. Ernest B. Speck, "Texas Siftings," *Handbook of Texas Online*, accessed July 27, 2024, https://www.tshaonline.org/handbook/entries/texas-siftings; Michael Dubkowski, "American Anti-Semitism: A Reinterpretation," *American Quarterly* 29, no. 2 (Summer 1977): 174; William Linneman, "Immigrant Stereotypes: 1880–1900," *Studies in American Humor* 1, no. 1 (1974): 32.

38. Linneman, "Immigrant Stereotypes," 35–36.

39. Campbell Gibson and Kay Jung, "Historical Census Statistics on Population Totals by Race, 1790–1990 for the United States, Regions, and States," Table 58, Texas—Race and Hispanic Origin: 1850–1990 (Washington, DC: United States Census Bureau, September 2002), 76, accessed July 23, 2022, https://www.census.gov/content/dam/Census/library/working-papers/2002/demo/POP-twps0056.pdf; Stanley Solamillo, "From Half a World Away: The First Chinese in Dallas, 1873–1940," *Legacies* 19, no. 2 (Fall 2007): 16–17.

40. Solamillo, "From Half a World Away," 18–19; "'The Chinese Must Go'!: Making War on the First Ward Bagnios," *Dallas Morning News*, July 18, 1886. The authors owe thanks to Stephanie Drenka, the one-time communications director for Dallas Truth, Racial Healing, and Transformation, the founder of *Visible* Magazine, and co-founder of the Dallas Asian American Historical Society, for generously sharing these sources and her insights into the Asian American experience in north central Texas.

41. James C. Mohr, *Abortion in America; The Origins and Evolution of National Policy* (New York: Oxford University Press, 1978), 3–4; 6–7; Ralph Frasca, "Abortion in the Early American Press: Secular and Catholic Approaches to the Pre-Born Child," *U.S. Catholic Historian* 34, no. 1 (Winter 2016): 44; Leslie J. Reagan, *When Abortion Was a Crime: Women, Medicine, and Law in the United States, 1867–1973* (Berkeley: University of California Press, 1997), 16–19.

42. Mohr, *Abortion in America*, 46–73.

43. Mohr, *Abortion in America*, 161, 163, 168–169, 177–179; Reagan, *When Abortion Was a Crime*, 22, 25; Ryan Johnson, "A Movement for Change: Horatio Robinson Storer and Physicians' Crusade Against Abortion," *James Madison Undergraduate Research Journal* 4, no. 1 (2017): 16–17.

44. Reagan, *When Abortion Was a Crime*, 22.

45. David Garrow, *Liberty and Sexuality: The Right to Privacy and the Making of Roe v. Wade* (Berkeley: University of California Press, 1994), 564, 863; Eleanor Klibanoff, "Not 1925: Texas' Law Banning Abortion Dates Back to Before the Civil War," *Texas Tribune*, August 17, 2022, accessed August 22, 2022, https://www.texastribune.org/2022/08/17/texas-abortion-law-history/; "Arrested on Grave Charge," *Fort Worth Record and Register*, November 2, 1899; "Prisoner Fatally Wounded: Dr. Jenkins Was on Trial for Murder Through Abortion of Mary Wheat," *Houston Daily Post*, December 19, 1899; "General News," *Laredo News*, December 20, 1899.

46. "Highest State Courts: Synopses of Decisions Entered at the Austin Term," *Galveston Daily News*, June 16, 1892.

47. Reagan, *When Abortion Was a Crime*, 70–71.

48. "Induced Abortion to Relieve Vomiting of Pregnancy," *Daniel's Medical Journal*, August 1885, 74, 77.

49. "Transactions Texas State Medical Association for 1887," *Daniel's Medical Journal*, September 1887, 101; "The Kidder Electro-Medical Apparatus," and "Dr. F. T. Paine," *Daniel's Medical Journal*, January 1888, 306–307; "How to Use Electricity in Extra Uterine Pregnancy," *Daniel's Medical Journal*, March 1888, 395. For more on the fascination with electricity in late nineteenth-century American medicine, see Rebecca Herzig, "Subjected to the Current: Batteries, Bodies, and the Early History of Electrification in the United States," *Journal of Social History* 41, no. 4 (Summer 2008): 867–885.

50. "Proceedings of the Terrell Medical Society," *Daniel's Medical Journal*, October 1887, 134–135.

51. "Proceedings of the Terrell Medical Society," 135.

52. W. C. Fisher, "Pelvis Peritonitis," *Daniel's Texas Medical Journal*, June 1888, 505.

53. Fisher, "Pelvis Peritonitis," 505.

54. Spiro, *Defending the Master Race*, 99.

55. Largent, *Breeding Contempt*, 12–14.

56. See Alan Hunt, "The Great Masturbation Panic and the Discourse of Moral Regulation in Nineteenth- and Early-Twentieth Century Britain," *Journal of the History of Sexuality* 8, no. 4 (April 1998): 575–615.

57. Byrne Fone, *Homophobia: A History* (New York: Picador USA, 2000), 274–275.

58. Sellers, *Market Revolution*, 245–246.

59. Sellers, *Market Revolution*, 250–251, 253.

60. Thomas W. Laqueur, *Solitary Sex: A Cultural History of Masturbation* (New York: Zone Books, 2003), 185, 202, 242, 257, 265, 280–281, 289; Robert Darby, "The Masturbation Taboo and the Rise of Routine Male Circumcision: A Review of the Historiography," *Journal of Social History* 36, no. 3 (Spring 2003): 739.

61. Geoffrey P. Miller, "Law, Pollution, and the Management of Social Anxiety," (working paper, New York University School of Law Public Law and Legal Theory, 1999), 3.

62. Ronald Goldman, *Circumcision, the Hidden Trauma: How an American Cultural Practice Affects Infants and Ultimately Us All* (Boston: Vanguard Publications, 1997), 2, 58–59.

63. Hans Peter Mareus Neilsen Gammel, *The Laws of Texas, 1822–1897* (Austin: Gammel Book Company, 1898), 4:97.

64. Kline, *Building a Better Race*, 8; F. E. Daniel, "Should Insane Criminals, Or Sexual Perverts, Be Allowed to Procreate?," *Texas Medical Journal* 27 (April 1912): 370–371; Melissa Norelle Stein, "Embodying Race: Gender, Sex, and the Sciences of Difference" (PhD diss., Rutgers University, 2008), 253.

65. Daniel, "Insane Criminals," 370, 375–376; Fone, *Homophobia*, 348.

66. Daniel, "Insane Criminals," 371.

67. Daniel, "Insane Criminals, 370.

68. Daniel, "Insane Criminals," 377.

69. Daniel, "Insane Criminals," 377.

70. Daniel, "Insane Criminals," 380.

71. Daniel, "Insane Criminals,: 380–381.

72. Daniel, "Insane Criminals," 380–381.

73. Reilly, *Surgical Solution*, 29; "An Outrage," *Texas Medical Journal* 10 (October 1894): 186; Dean T. Collins, "Children of Sorrow: A History of the Mentally Retarded in Kansas," *Bulletin of the History of Medicine*, January–February 1965, 60–61, 69.

74. "The State Lunatic Asylum," *Texas Medical Journal* 10, no. 4 (October 1894): 189.

75. Cohen, "Harvard's Eugenic Era." At North Texas Agricultural College, Professor H. B. Carroll taught a course in 1938, "History of Civilization," which included the textbook *Heredity and Eugenics*. That work included an essay, "Inheritance of Physical and Mental Traits," by Charles Davenport, still the head of the Eugenics Record Office in Cold Spring Harbor, New York. Contrasting the family pedigrees of the accomplished and prominent with those of the criminal and insane, Davenport wrote, "These studies of inheritance of mental defect inevitably raise the question how to eliminate the mentally defective. This is a matter of great importance because . . . it is now coming to be recognized that mental defect is at the bottom of most of our social problems." See Syllabus for History of Civilization, First Semester, by H. B. Carroll, E. E. Davis Papers, Box 12, Folder 258–12–8, UTA.

76. Preuss, *To Get a Better School System*, 13, 15, 16.

77. Charles R. Matthews, *Higher Education in Texas: Its Beginnings to 1970* (Denton: University of North Texas Press, 2018), 20–21.

78. Dudley G. Wooten, *A Comprehensive History of Texas, 1685–1897* (Dallas: William G. Scarff, 1898), 2:411, 442–444; Ronnie Dugger, *Our Invaded Universities:*

Form, Reform, and New Starts (New York: W. W. Norton, 1974), 4–5; Roger A. Griffin, "To Establish a University of the First Class," *Southwestern Historical Quarterly* 86, no. 2 (October 1982): 136–138.

79. Mark Odintz, "Bryan," *Handbook of Texas Online,* accessed July 27, 2024, https://www.tshaonline.org/handbook/entries/bryan-tx; Mark Odintz, "College Station," *Handbook of Texas Online,* accessed July 27, 2024, https://www.tshaonline .org/handbook/entries/college-station-tx; Paul Burka, "Did You Hear the One about the New Aggies?" *Texas Monthly,* April 1997, accessed January 29, 2022, https://www.texasmonthly.com/news-politics/did-you-hear-the-one-about-the -new-aggies/; Griffin, "To Establish a University of the First Class," 141; Kenneth E. Hendrickson Jr., *The Chief Executives of Texas: From Stephen F. Austin to John B. Connally, Jr.* (College Station: Texas A&M University Press, 1995). 105–108.

80. Burka, "Did You Hear the One about the New Aggies"; Henry C. Dethloff, *A Centennial History of Texas A&M University, 1876–1976* (College Station, Texas A&M University Press 1975), 409.

81. Dethloff, *A Centennial History of Texas A&M University,* 42.

82. John A. Adams Jr., *Keepers of the Spirit: The Corps of Cadets at Texas A&M University, 1876–2001* (College Station: Texas A&M University Press, 2001), 65, 71–73. Burka, "Did You Hear the One about the New Aggies."

83. Robert Lewis Dabney, *A Defence of Virginia (and Through Her, of the South) in Recent and Pending Contests against the Sectional Party* (New York: E. J. Hale, 1867), 166; Daniel A. Penick, "Robert Lewis Dabney, *Handbook of Texas Online,* accessed July 27, 2024, https://www.tshaonline.org/handbook/entries /dabney-robert-lewis; Dabney, *A Memoir and Letters,* 13; Charles Reagan Wilson, *Baptized in Blood: The Religion of the Lost Cause, 1865–1920* (Athens: University of Georgia Press, 1980), 52, 66, 69; Griffin, "To Establish a University of the First Class," 141–142, 151–152; Wooten, *A Comprehensive History of Texas,* 445, 449–450: Thomas Cary Johnson, *The Life and Letters of Robert Lewis Dabney* (Carlisle, PA: Banner of Truth Trust, 1903), 396–398, 437–438.

84. Frank Vandiver, "John William Mallett and the University of Texas," *Southwestern Historical Quarterly* 53, no. 4 (April 1950): 437–438.

85. Dugger, *Our Invaded University,* 8; Vandiver, "John William Mallett and the University of Texas," 435–437.

86. Dugger, *Our Invaded University,* 8–9.

87. Gould, *Progressives and Prohibitionists,* 286.

88. "Crazy Headed Legislation," *Austin Statesman,* April 12, 1906.

89. See Ella K. Dearborn, "Would Slay Criminals, Insane, Incurably Ill, And Degenerates," *Fort Worth Telegram,* August 27, 1905, and "Euthanasia Again," *Fort Worth Telegram,* November 29, 1906.

90. F. E. Daniel, *The Strange Career of Dr. Bruno* (New York: Guarantee Publishing, 1906), 26, 55–56, 108, 146–147.

91. Daniel, *Strange Career of Dr. Bruno,* 121, 122, 124, 184, 190, 199–201, 212.

92. Largent, *Breeding Contempt,* 3.

93. Daniel, *Strange Case*, 35–38.

94. Daniel, *Strange Career of Dr. Bruno*, 39; Texas Department of Criminal Justice, "Death Row Information," accessed August 21, 2022, https://www.tdcj .texas.gov/death_row/dr_facts.html.

95. Daniel, *Strange Career of Dr. Bruno*, 39–47.

96. "Scheme to Have Condemned Criminals Turned Over to Science," *Texas Medical Journal* 22, no. 6 (December 1906): 236–237.

97. Reilly, *Surgical Solution*, 13–14, 26.

98. Elof Axel Carlson, *The Unfit: A History of a Bad Idea* (Cold Spring Harbor, NY: Cold Spring Harbor Laboratory Press, 2001), 209–221; Largent, *Breeding Contempt*, 72.

99. "Castration for Rape," *Texas Medical Journal* 22, no. 10 (April 1907): 393–394.

100. "The Scientific Basis of Eugenics," *Texas Medical Journal*, October 1, 1912; "Theodore Young Hull," *Handbook of Texas Online*, accessed July 27, 2024, https://www.tshaonline.org/handbook/entries/hull-theodore-young.

101. Reilly, *Surgical Solution*, 38.

102. Shah, "Woman's Department," 87, 91.

103. Laura Mondt, "An Act to Prevent Procreation of Confirmed Criminals: The Origins of Sterilization in Indiana," *Historia* 20 (2011): 58; Diana J. Kleiner, "Ferdinand Eugene Daniel," *Handbook of Texas Online*, accessed July 27, 2024, https://www.tshaonline.org/handbook/entries/daniel-ferdinand-eugene.

Chapter 3

1. "Prof. Bramlette Says Blind Are Not Defectives," *Austin Stateman*, August 20, 1916.

2. "Prof. Bramlette Says Blind Are Not Defectives."

3. Pernick, *Black Stork*, 18; Sarah F. Rose, *No Right to Be Idle: The Invention of Disability, 1840s–1930s* (Chapel Hill: University of North Carolina Press, 2017), 69–75. Disability history is one of the most exciting new scholarly fields. In addition to Rose's ground breaking work, see also Douglas C. Baynton, *Defectives in the Land: Disability and Immigration in the Age of Eugenics* (Chicago: University of Chicago Press, 2020) and Kim Neilsen, *A Disability History of the United States* (Boston: Beacon Press, 2012).

4. "Prof. Bramlette Says Blind Are Not Defectives."

5. Edwin Black, *War against the Weak: Eugenics and America's Campaign to Create a Master Race* (New York: Thunder's Mouth Press, 2003), 149–150.

6. Carlson, *The Unfit*, 235–237; Levine, *Eugenics*, 16; Kevles, *In the Name of Eugenics*, 46–47, 54–55.

7. Garland E. Allen, "The Eugenics Record Office at Cold Spring Harbor, 1910–1940: An Essay in Institutional History," *Osiris* 2 (1986): 240–241; Gould,

Mismeasure of Man, 98–99; Black, *War against the Weak*, 52–55, 58, 98, 388; Carlson, *The Unfit*, 241.

8. Black, *War against the Weak*, 52.

9. Black, *War against the Weak*, 58, 60; Carlson, *The Unfit*, 242.

10. "One Out of Every Ten Children in Public Schools Show Physical Defects or Disease," *Fort Worth Record*, July 10, 1910.

11. Mark Odintz, "Calvert, Tx.," *Handbook of Texas Online*, accessed July 27, 2024, https://www.tshaonline.org/handbook/entries/calvert-tx; "Daniel F. Parker," Legislative Reference Library of Texas, accessed August 26, 2022, https://lrl.texas .gov/legeLeaders/members/memberDisplay.cfm?memberID=2870&searchparams =chamber=~city=~countyID=0~RcountyID=~district=~first=~gender=~last =Parker~leaderNote=~leg=33~party=~roleDesc=~Committee=; "The Parker Sterilization Bill . . . ," *Marshall Messenger*, March 11, 1913; "Senate Kills Bill," *Fort Worth Star-Telegram*, January 29, 1913; William Lewis Hill, Legislative Reference Library of Texas, accessed August 26, 2022, https://lrl.texas.gov/legeLeaders /members/memberDisplay.cfm?memberID=2699&searchparams=chamber =H~city=~countyID=0~RcountyID=~district=~first=~gender=~last=Hill%20 ~leaderNote=~leg=33~party=~roleDesc=~Committee=; "William Benjamin Goodner," Legislative Reference Library of Texas, accessed August 26, 2022, https:// lrl.texas.gov/legeLeaders/members/memberDisplay.cfm?memberID =2839&searchparams=chamber=H~city=~countyID=0~RcountyID=~district =~first=~gender=m~last=Goodner~leaderNote=~leg=33~party=Democrat ~roleDesc=~Committee=; UT Southwestern Texas Physicians Historical Biographical Database, accessed August 26, 2022, https://library.utsouthwestern.edu /main/doctors.aspx?alpha=G; "Senate Committees Busy: Number of Bills of General Interest are Favorably Reported," *Austin Daily Statesman*, March 19, 1913.

12. "Kills Sterilization Bill," *Houston Post*, March 29, 1913; "Wright Chalfant Morrow," Legislative Reference Library of Texas, accessed August 27, 2022, https:// lrl.texas.gov/legeLeaders/members/memberDisplay.cfm?memberID =2643&searchparams=chamber=S~city=~countyID=0~RcountyID=~district =~first=~gender=~last=Morrow~leaderNote=~leg=33~party=~roleDesc =~Committee=; "Ed Westbrook," Legislative Reference Library of Texas, accessed August 27, 2022, https://lrl.texas.gov/legeLeaders/members/memberDisplay.cfm ?memberID=2122&searchparams=chamber=S~city=~countyID=0~RcountyID =~district=~first=~gender=~last=Westbrook~leaderNote=~leg=33~party =~roleDesc=~Committee=; "Clinton West Nugent," Legislative Reference Library of Texas, accessed August 27, 2022, https://lrl.texas.gov/legeLeaders/members /memberDisplay.cfm?memberID=2644&searchparams=chamber=S~city =~countyID=0~RcountyID=~district=~first=~gender=~last=Nugent ~leaderNote=~leg=33~party=~roleDesc=~Committee=; "Homer Platte Brelsford," Legislative Reference Library of Texas, accessed August 27, 2022, https://lrl .texas.gov/legeLeaders/members/memberDisplay.cfm?memberID=2632

&searchparams=chamber=S~city=~countyID=0~RcountyID=~district=~first
=~gender=m~last=Brelsford~leaderNote=~leg=33~party=~roleDesc
=~Committee=; "The Texas Sterilization Bill," *Lancet-Clinic*, May 3, 1913.

13. "The Texas Sterilization Bill."

14. Betsy L. Nies, "Defending Jeeter: Conservative Arguments against Eugenics in the Depression Era South," in Susan Currell and Christina Cogdell, eds., *Popular Eugenics: National Efficiency and American Mass Culture in the 1930s* (Athens: Ohio University Press, 2006), 123–124, 136; Edwin L. Cobb, "Representation Theory and the Flotorial District: The Case of Texas," *Western Political Quarterly* 22, no. 4 (December 1969): 792, 797.

15. Larson, *Sex, Race, and Science*, 17.

16. Larson, *Sex, Race, and Science*, 17.

17. Largent, *Breeding Contempt*, 72.

18. Largent, *Breeding Contempt*, 72, 77–78; Stern, *Eugenic Nation*, 84.

19. Pierce, *Making the White Man's West*, 79.

20. Pierce, *White Man's West*, 83.

21. Stern, *Eugenic Nation*, 84.

22. Stern, *Eugenic Nation*, 84–86.

23. Stern, *Eugenic Nation*, 86, 107.

24. Black, *War Against the Weak*" 73–74.

25. Smallwood, Reveley, and Bailey, *New Biology*, 416. The board approved this text March 1, 1926. See the Dallas Independent School District School Board Minutes, vol. 16, p. 84, Dallas Independent School District Headquarters. The board ordered the 1934 edition on March 23, 1937. See the Dallas Board Minutes, vol. 24, p. 172.

26. Smallwood, Reveley, and Bailey, *New Biology*, 416.

27. Gould, *Mismeasure of Man*, 168–171.

28. Smallwood, Reveley, and Bailey, 392–393, 394.

29. Black, *War Against the Weak*, 75–76; "Alexander Caswell Ellis," *Handbook of Texas Online*, accessed July 27, 2024, https://www.tshaonline.org/handbook/entries/ellis-alexander-caswell.

30. Alexander Caswell Ellis, "Suggestions for a Philosophy of Education," (PhD diss., Clark University 1897), 2–3.

31. Ellis, "Suggestions for a Philosophy of Education," 3; Alexander Caswell Ellis, "World Peace Through Education," n.d., Alexander Caswell Ellis Papers, Box 2P62, BCAH.

32. Walter F. Pilcher, "Keasbey, Lindley Miller, "*Handbook of Texas Online*, accessed July 27, 2024, https://www.tshaonline.org/handbook/entries/keasbey-lindley-miller; Paul Meadows, "Achille Loria: Agrarian Determinist," *American Journal of Economics and Sociology* 10 (January 1951): 175–184.

33. Pilcher, "Keasbey, Lindley Miller"; Lindley M. Keasbey, "Competition," *Bulletin of the University of Texas*, January 15, 1908, 23.

34. Pilcher, "Keasbey, Lindley Miller."

35. Edward T. Downer, "A. Caswell Ellis," *Skyline: A Quarterly of Cleveland College*, 13, no. 4 (May 1940), 19–20, Ellis Papers, Box 2P23, BCAH; "Alexander Caswell Ellis," *Handbook of Texas Online.*

36. Notecards, Speeches Folder, Ellis Papers, Box 2P62.

37. "At the Crystal," advertisement, *Dallas Morning News*, August 31, 1917; Black, *War Against the Weak*, 252–254; Pernick, *Black Stork*, 11–12, 49.

38. *The Black Stork*, directed by Leopold Wharton and Theodore Wharton (1917; Whartons' Studio), accessed October 10, 2022, https://www.youtube.com /watch?v=9rWkGCsEuxY,; Pernick, *Black Stork*, 53.

39. "'The Black Stork' Based on Eugenics, At Texas," *Austin American*, October 24, 1917; "'The Black Stork" Coming to the Texas Theater," *Austin American*, October 24, 1917.

40. Queen Theatre advertisement, *Fort Worth Star-Telegram*, September 7, 1917; Queen Theatre advertisement, *Fort Worth Record*, September 11, 1917; Queen Theatre advertisement, *Fort Worth Record*, November 4, 1917; Strand Theater advertisement, *Laredo Weekly Times*, November 11, 1917.

41. Kevles, *In the Name of Eugenics*, 61–62.

42. "Better Babies' Show for Texas Mothers: Contest for the Entire Southwest to Be Held in Fort Worth November 22–29," *Dallas Morning News*, August 3, 1913; Ramona Hopkins, "Was There a 'Southern' Eugenics? A Comparative Case Study of Eugenics in Texas and Virginia, 1900–1940" (master's Thesis, University of Houston, 2009), 64–66; "Better Babies Show," advertising copy, *Dallas Daily Times Herald*, October 11, 1914; "Prizes Offered for The Baby Show," *Dallas Daily Times Herald*, October 26, 1914; "Wednesday Is Big Day For Baby Contest," *Dallas Daily Times Herald*, October 27, 1914; "Bright Sunshine And Varied Features Bring Big Crowd To The Fair: Better Baby Contest Is Drawing Card," *Dallas Daily Times Herald*, October 28, 1914. The details on the finger and hair measurements came from "Averaged 95.5 Per Cent in Baby Show Contest: Dallas Can Boast of Being 'Corking Good Community'; City Makes Unusual Record of Physical Conditions of Children in Recent Contest," *Dallas Morning News*, May 24, 1914. The comparison of baby to animal contests at fairs comes from Chip Berlet and Matthew N. Lyons, *Right-Wing Populism in America: Too Close for Comfort* (New York: The Guilford Press, 2000), 94. For more on such contests in Dallas, see Nancy Wiley, *The Great State Fair of Texas: An Illustrated History* (Dallas: Taylor Publishing Company, 2000), 73.

43. "Benefits of Better Babies Contests: Parents Taught How to Improve Their Offspring and Correct Deficiencies," *Dallas Morning News*, November 23, 1913; "'Better Babies' Show for Texas Mothers: Contest for the Entire Southwest to Be Held in Fort Worth November 22–29," *Dallas Morning News*, August 3, 1913.

44. "'Fitter Families' Campaign Object: Mrs. Mary T. Watts in Dallas for Work in Eugenics at State Fair," *Dallas Morning News*, October 7, 1924.

45. "Guinea Pigs Used in Fitter Families Contest at Fair," *Dallas Morning News*, October 14, 1925.

46. Wiley, *Great State Fair of Texas*, 25; "State Fair Grounds Extra Attraction: Millie Christine," advertisement, *Dallas Morning News*, October 21, 1906; "State Fair of Texas," advertisement, *Dallas Morning News*, October 21, 1906.

47. "State Fair Shows: Something About Attractions to be Seen on Amusement Row This Year," *Dallas Morning News*, August 18, 1907.

48. "Tribe of Igorrotes: Members of One of the Most Primitive Races in Philippines Will Be Seen Here in Original Savage State," *Dallas Morning News*, August 5, 1905; Claire Prentice, "The Igorrote Tribe Traveled the World for Show And Made These Two Men Rich," *Smithsonian Magazine*, October 14, 2014, accessed July 12, 2017, http://www.smithsonianmag.com/history/igorrote-tribe-traveled-world-these -men-took-all-money-180953012/.

49. "Texas State Fair: A Continuance of Good Weather and a Large Attendance Passed through the Gates," *Dallas Morning News*, October 31, 1894; "State Fair Shows"; Nancy Wiley, *Great State Fair*, 33, 56.

50. For a notice for an appearance of the Sells-Floto Circus in Dallas, see "Sells-Floto Shows," *Dallas Morning News*, August 29, 1907; Robert Bogdan, *Freak Show: Presenting Human Oddities for Amusement and Profit* (Chicago: University of Chicago Press, 1988), 2, 8, 84–85, 105.

51. "Texas State Fair: The Auspicious Opening of the Ninth Annual Fair," *Dallas Morning News*. October 21, 1894.

52. Michele Mitchell, *Righteous Propagation: African Americans and the Politics of Racial Destiny After Reconstruction* (Chapel Hill: University of North Carolina Press, 2004), 79–81, 87–88, 95, 187–188.

53. On Du Bois's socialist ideology and his late membership in the Communist Party USA, see Sterling Stuckey, *Slave Culture: Nationalist Theory and the Foundations of Black America* (New York: Oxford University Press, 1987), and David Levering Lewis, *W. E. B. Du Bois: The Fight for Equality and the American Century, 1919–1963* (New York: Henry Holt and Company, 2000), 567.

54. W. E. B. Du Bois, "The Talented Tenth," in *The Negro Problem: A Series of Articles by Representative American Negroes of Today* (New York: James Pott, 1903), 33.

55. W. E. B. Du Bois, *The Philadelphia Negro: A Social Study* (Philadelphia: University of Pennsylvania, 1899), 311.

56. Gregory Michael Dorr and Angela Logan, "'Quality, Not Mere Quantity, Counts,' Black Eugenics and the NAACP Baby Contests," in *A Century of Eugenics in America: From the Indiana Experiment to the Human Genome Era*, ed. Paul A. Lombardo (Bloomington and Indianapolis: Indiana University Press, 2011), 68–75, 82–87.

57. "Passing for White," *Dallas Express*, April 18, 1925.

58. "Not So Complimentary To the Nordics," *Dallas Express*, March 21, 1925.

59. "Scientist Says Negroes Completed Dead Gas Tests," *Dallas Express*, April 18, 1925.

60. "Scientist Says Negroes Completed Dead Gas Tests."

61. "White Moron Admits Assault on Little Negro Girl," *Dallas Express*, October 3, 1925. For more on Henry Goddard's role in creating modern intelligence tests and his support for the eugenics movement, see Leila Zenderland, *Measuring Minds: Henry Herbert Goddard and the Origins of American Intelligence Testing* (Cambridge, UK: Cambridge University Press, 1998).

62. United States Census Bureau, "Table 1—Color or Race, Nativity, Parentage for the State and Urban And Rural Population, 1920, 1910, 1900," in *Fourteenth Census of the United States Taken in the Year 1920, Volume III: Population, 1920—Composition and Characteristics of the Population By State* (Washington, DC: Government Printing Office, 1923), 984.

63. From 1882–1930, Texas ranked third nationally in the number of lynchings behind only Mississippi and Georgia. Texas lynch mobs murdered 492 Texans, including 143 whites and 349 blacks. See Jacquelyn Dowd Hall, *Revolt Against Chivalry: Jessie Daniel Ames and the Women's Campaign Against Lynching* (New York: Columbia University Press, 1993), 134–135.

64. "A Baby in Your Arms," and "Childless Marriages Explained," advertisement, *Dallas Express*, January 10, 1925.

65. "The *Dallas Express* Better Baby Contest," *Dallas Express*, June 26, 1920.

66. Dorr and Logan, "'Quality, Not Mere Quantity, Counts,'" 76.

67. Finnie D. Coleman, *Sutton E. Griggs and the Struggle Against White Supremacy* (Knoxville: University of Tennessee Press, 2007), v, 5. After being largely overlooked by contemporary readers and ignored by scholars, Griggs's thought and art has recently received overdue attention. In addition to Coleman's work, see John Cullen Gruesser's thoughtful new biography *A Literary Life of Sutton E. Griggs: The Man on the Firing Line* (Oxford, UK: Oxford University Press, 1922); Randolph Meade Walker, *The Metamorphosis of Sutton E. Griggs: The Transition from Back Radical to Conservative, 1913–1933* (Memphis: Walker Publishing, 1991) and Tess Chakkalakal and Kenneth W. Warren, eds., *Jim Crow, Literature and the Legacy of Sutton E. Griggs* (Athens: University of Georgia Press, 2013). A biographical sketch of Griggs, "Sutton E. Griggs: A Black Son of Texas Lifts His Pen," appears in William Loren Katz, *Black People Who Made the West* (Trenton, NJ: Africa World Press, 1992).

68. Carter Woodson, *The Miseducation of the Negro* (1933: Trenton, NJ: Africa World Press, 1990), xii–21.

69. Coleman, *Sutton E. Griggs*, 5.

70. Coleman, *Sutton E. Griggs*, 93.

71. Sutton E. Griggs, *Imperium in Imperio: A Study of the Negro Race* (1899; Sioux Falls, SD: Greenbook Publications, 2010), 71–79.

72. Gruesser, *A Literary Life of Sutton E. Griggs*, 20, 203.

73. Kenneth W. Warren, "Perfecting the Political Romance: The Last Novel of Sutton Griggs" in Chakkalakal and Warren, *Jim Crow Literature*, 266; Gruesser, *A Literary Life*, 75.

74. See Walker, *Metamorphosis of Sutton E. Griggs*, 40.

75. Warren, "Perfecting the Political Romance," 279.

76. Theodorus Laboure, "The Morality and Lawfulness of Vasectomy," *Ecclesiastical Review*, May 1911, 575.

77. Laboure, "The Morality and Lawfulness of Vasectomy," 575. Information on Laboure's career can be found in the *Official Catholic Directory* (New York: P. J. Kenedy & Sons, 1935), 864.

78. Christine Rosen, *Preaching Eugenics: Religious Leaders and the American Eugenics Movement* (Oxford, UK: Oxford University Press, 2004), 48.

79. "Contraception," in *New Catholic Encyclopedia* (Farmington Hills, MI: Gale Research, 2002); "Birth Control," in *HarperCollins Encyclopedia of Catholicism*, (San Francisco: HarperSanFrancisco, 1995); Rosen, *Preaching Eugenics*, 15, 20–21,118, 141–144.

80. Samuel B. Hesler and Presnall H. Wood, "Baptist Standard," *Handbook of Texas Online*, accessed July 27, 2024, https://www.tshaonline.org/handbook /entries/baptist-standard; Keith E. Whittington, "American Political Thought," accessed September 4, 2022, https://global.oup.com/us/companion.websites /fdscontent/uscompanion/us/static/companion.websites/9780199338863 /whittington_updata/ch_8_batten_new_world_order.pdf; Samuel Zane Batten, *If America Fail: Our National Mission and Our Possible Future* (Philadelphia: Judson Press, 1922), 87.

81. Rosen, *Preaching Eugenics*, 120–121, 124; Spiro, *Defending the Master Race*, 187.

82. Pamela Bleisch, "Spoilsmen and Daughters of the Republic: Political Interference in the Texas State Library during the Tenure of Elizabeth Howard West, 1911–1925," *Libraries and the Cultural Record* 45, no. 4 (2010): 387.

83. A. F. Cunningham, "Eugenics or the Young Man Foursquare," American Eugenics Society Papers, Folder 575.06:Am3, American Philosophical Society, Philadelphia.

84. Cunningham, "Eugenics or the Young Man Foursquare."

85. Rosen, *Preaching Eugenics*, 124, 168–169.

86. Gunter, "More Than Black and White," 33; Black, *War Against the Weak*, 127–133, 135–137, 139, 143–144, 156. Black points out how the modern "pro-life" movement manipulatively focuses on Sanger's support for eugenics and her leadership of Planned Parenthood, a group that advocates abortion rights, to discredit the pro-choice movement as racist.

87. "Death of Rev. J. R. Smith," *Atlanta Constitution*, December 10, 1895; Carrie Weaver Smith, "Andrew's Raid: A Ballad," *Railway and Locomotive Historical Society Bulletin*, October 1943, 41–42; Michael Phillips and Betsy Friauf, "Carrie Weaver Smith, *Handbook of Texas Online*, accessed July 27, 2024, https://www.tshaonline.org/handbook/entries/smith-carrie-weaver; Chelsea Hodge, "'Deserting the Broad and Easy Way,' Southern Methodist Women, the Social Gospel, and the New Deal State, 1909–1939" (PhD diss., University of Arkansas, 2020), 71–72.

88. Hodge, "'Deserting the Broad and Easy Way,'" 72, 75; Smith, "Andrew's Raid," 42.

89. Bush, *Who Gets a Childhood?*, 24.

90. Allison Leigh Hughes, "Turning Bad Girls into Ladies: Female Juvenile Delinquency in Texas in the Twentieth Century" (master's thesis, Texas State University at San Marcos, 2012), 51; Robert Perkinson, *Texas Tough: The Rise of America's Prison Empire* (New York: Picador, 2010), 159, 162, 167, 179–181; Carrie Weaver Smith. letter to Elizabeth Ring, "A Woman's Reformatory for Women," ca. 1921, Ring Papers, 1913–1931, Box 2G 445. BCAH.

91. Bush, *Who Gets a Childhood?*, 22–25; Carrie Weaver Smith, "The Unadjusted Girl," *Social Hygiene*, October 1920, 401.

92. Bush, *Who Gets a Childhood?*, 22–25.

93. William I. Thomas and Dorothy Swaine Thomas, *The Child in America: Behavior Problems and Programs* (New York: Alfred K. Knopf, 1928), 111.

94. Smith, "The Unadjusted Girl," 402–403; Smith, "The Elimination of the Reformatory," in *Proceedings of the National Conference of Social Work* (Chicago: University of Chicago Press, 1921), 127; "Field Assignments for the 1919 Training Class," *Eugenical News*, September 1919, 72; Michael A. Rembis, *Defining Deviance: Sex, Science, and Delinquent Girls, 1890–1960* (Urbana: University of Illinois Press, 2011), 168.

95. "Field Assignments for the 1919 Training Class."

96. "Indian-White Blood," *Eugenical News*, March 1922, 48.

97. Sharon Bice Endelman, "Elizabeth L. Fitzsimmons Ring," *Handbook of Texas Online*, accessed July 27, 2024, https://www.tshaonline.org/handbook /entries/ring-elizabeth-l-fitzsimmons; Paul M. Lucko, "Texas Committee on Prisons and Prison Labor," *Handbook of Texas Online*, accessed July 27, 2024, https:// www.tshaonline.org/handbook/entries/texas-committee-on-prisons-and-prison -labor; Richard T, Fleming, "Daniel James Moody, Jr." *Handbook of Texas Online*, accessed July 27, 2024, https://www.tshaonline.org/handbook/entries/moody -daniel-james-jr; J. K. Jaffray to Ring, August 29, 1921,; Sarah King to Jaffray, December 20, 1921,; Jaffray to King, December 21, 1921; King to Ring, March 15, 1922; Elizabeth M. Speer to Survey Committee of Texas Committee on Prisons and Prison Labor, August 7, 1924; Ruby Neale Long to Ring, May 19, 1924, Ring Papers, Correspondence, 1–20–12–30, BCAH; Paul M. Lucko, "Counteracting Reform: Lee Simmons and the Texas Prison System," *East Texas Historical* Journal 30, no. 2 (1992), 20.

98. "Training School Head Criticized; Dallas Women Protest against Striking Out of Appropriations," *Dallas Morning News*, February 5, 1921; "Purl Renews Fight on Parole System on State Girls School; Said Matter to Be Offered to Solons," *Dallas Morning News*, February 1, 1925; "Committee Votes Strike Out Appropriations for Girls Training School: Fight Over Fence Cause for Action," *Dallas Morning News*, February 4, 1925; "Political League of Women Assails Action on Girls' Institution," *Dallas Morning News*, February 6, 1925; "Eleemosynary Bill Now in

Conference: Measure Amended Monday in Senate and Finally Passed, Girl's School Saved," *Dallas Morning News*, February 17, 1925; "Shytles Declines Job in Austin Hospital," *Dallas Morning News*, July 18, 1925; Carrie Weaver Smith, "Self[-]Expression is Stressed as Means of Coping with the Problems of Delinquent Girls," *Dallas Morning News*, August 10, 1925; "Carrie Weaver Smith Asks That Poor Girl Who Errs Get Equal Right with Rich," *Dallas Morning News*, December 14, 1925.

99. "First Lady is Hostess to 70 Girl Inmates," *Marysville (California) Appeal-Democrat*, May 16, 1936; "Dr. Carrie Weaver Smith Dies; Center of School Controversy," *Washington Evening Star*, May 23, 1942.

100. Bush, *Who Gets a Childhood?*, 25; "Dr. Carrie Weaver Smith Dies."

101. Spiro, *Defending the Master Race*, xii; Largent, *Breeding Contempt*, 72.

102. Spiro, *Defending the Master Race*, 102.

103. Spiro, *Defending the Master Race*, 115, 138–139, 155.

104. Dabney's career and his works quoted here are also discussed in Phillips, *White Metropolis*, 65–66, 72.

105. Dabney, *A Memoir and Letters*, ix, 12, 16–17, 22–24, 196.

106. Dabney, *A Memoir and Letters*, 194.

107. Dabney, *A Memoir and Letters*, 195–196.

108. United States Bureau of the Census, Population Division, "Nativity of the Population, for Regions, Divisions, and States: 1850 to 1990"; Calvert and De León, *History of Texas*, 5th ed., 186; Benjamin Heber Johnson, *Revolution in Texas: How a Forgotten Rebellion and its Bloody Suppression Turned Mexicans in Americans* (New Haven: Yale University Press, 2003), 26; Jordan, "Century and a Half of Ethnic Change in Texas," 418; McCaa, "Missing Millions."

109. Dabney, *A Memoir and Letters*, 104–106; David Montejano, *Anglos and Mexicans in the Making of Texas, 1836–1986* (Austin: University of Texas Press, 1987), 122–123.

110. Robert Prince, *A History of Dallas from a Different Perspective* (Dallas: Nortex Press,, 1993), 68; Alan B. Govenar and Jay Brakesfield, *Deep Ellum and Central Track: Where the Black and White Worlds of Dallas Converged* (Denton: University of North Texas Press, 1998), xv, xix; Lee Ballard, "The Rise and Decline of Deep Ellum," *Westward*, September 25,1983, 30; Sister Mary Paul Valdez, *Hispanic Catholics in The Diocese of Dallas, 1890–1990* (Dallas: n.d.), 5–7,12–15; United States Bureau of the Census, *Twelfth Census of the United States, Taken in the Year 1900: Census Reports*, Volume II, Population Part II (Washington DC: United States Census Office, 1902), 784, 787; United States Bureau of the Census, *Fourteenth Census of the United States, 1920*, Volume II, Population, General Report and Analytical Tables, 732–733, Accessed January 1, 2020, https://www2.census.gov/library/publications/decennial/1920/volume-2/41084484v2cho8.pdf.

111. Dabney, *A Memoir and Letters*, 224. Rabbi William Henry Greenberg of Temple Emanu-El, George Bannerman Dealey, vice president and general

manager *Dallas Morning News* in 1926, and Cesar Lombardi, president of the A. H. Belo Corporation, parent company of the newspaper, established the Dallas Critic Club in 1908 to provide a private setting for key leaders in the city to discuss not just local issues but controversies facing the country and the world. See Michael V. Hazel, "The Critic Club: Sixty Years of Quiet Leadership," *Legacies* 2, no. 2 (Fall 1990): 9–17.

112. Dabney, *A Memoir and Letters*, 147.

113. Dabney, *A Memoir and Letters*, 228.

114. Dabney, *A Memoir and Letters*,177.

115. Dabney, *A Memoir and Letters*, 215.

116. Dabney, *A Memoir and Letters*, 215–217.

117. Dabney, *A Memoir and Letters*, 218.

118. Dabney, *A Memoir and Letters*,220–221.

119. Dabney, *A Memoir and Letters*, 217.

120. *Dabney, A Memoir and Letters*, 232.

121. Dabney, *A Memoir and Letters*, 269.

122. Chalmers, *Hooded Americanism, 39–48*; Phillips, *White Metropolis*, 85, 88–90, 91–92.

123. Spiro, *Defending the Master Race, 171.*

124. Thomas Pegram, *One Hundred Percent American: The Rebirth and Decline of the Ku Klux Klan in the1920s* (Chicago: Ivan R. Dee, 2011), 207, 209–211.

125. E. M. Dealey, "Neff Says Texas Breeding Lunatics: Expects to Make Most Unpopular Speech Ever Made by Governor," *Dallas Morning News*, April 29, 1922.

Chapter 4

1. John B. Boles, *The Education of a University President: Edgar Odell Lovett and the Opening of the Rice Institute* (Houston: Rice Historical Society, 2000), 5–6, 21, 50, 69–70; Fabiola López-Durán and Adrienne Rooney, "Unveiling the Layers: Interview with the Racial Geography Project," Rice Design Alliance, May 16, 2022, accessed December 8, 2022, https://www.ricedesignalliance.org/racialgeographyproject-interview; Frances Ortega, "Hidden Symbols and Secrets at Rice University," *Houston Chronicle*, August 18, 2015, accessed December 8, 2022, https://www.chron.com/life/slideshow/Hidden-symbols-and-secrets-at-Rice-University-115444.php; John B. Boles, "Rice University," *Handbook of Texas Online*, accessed July 27, 2024, https://www.tshaonline.org/handbook/entries/rice-university; Clay Bailey, "Edgar Odell Lovett," *Handbook of Texas Online*, accessed July 27, 2024, https://www.tshaonline.org/handbook/entries/lovett-edgar-odell.

2. "Rice University Task Force on Segregation, Slavery, and Injustice," June 2021, 2, 5, accessed June 7, 2022, https://rice.app.box.com/s/724h7kq3gj3g6d-4khj52mmouxtqidq1e; Lucio Vasquez, "Statue of Rice Founder to be Relocated After Criticism of the University's Racist Past," Houston Public Media,

January 26, 2022, accessed December 7, 2022, https://www.houstonpublicmedia
.org/articles/news/education-news/2022/01/26/417683/statue-of-rice-founder-to
-be-relocated-in-response-to-criticism-regarding-universitys-lack-of-diversity/;
Boles, "Rice University."

3. Boles, *Education of a University President*, 5; C. Kenneth Waters, introduction to., *Julian Huxley: Biologist and Statesman of Science*, ed. C. Kenneth Water
and Albert Van Helden (College Station: Texas A&M University Press, 1992), 1, 4,
5–6; Alison Bashford, *The Huxleys: An Intimate History of Evolution* (Chicago:
University of Chicago Press, 2022), 25–26–27, 89, 107–108.

4. "Religion Not Yet Routed," *Houston Chronicle*, undated newspaper clip-
ping, Julian S. Huxley Papers, General Correspondence, 1916, Box 5, Folder 14,
WRCSC.

5. For more on anti-Darwinism in early twentieth-century Texas and legislative attempts to limit how the theory of evolution could be taught in the state's
classrooms, see David Stricklin, "Fundamentalism," *Handbook of Texas Online*,
accessed July 27, 2024, https://www.tshaonline.org/handbook/entries/fundamen-
talism; "Anti-Evolution Engrossed in House," *Dallas Morning News*, March 4,
1923; Norman D. Brown, *Hood, Bonnet, and Little Brown Jug: Texas Politics, 1921–
1928* (College Station: Texas A&M University Press, 1984), 147–148; "Rep.
Roundtree Won in Parliamentary Struggle in Austin," *Bryan Weekly Eagle*,
March 1, 1923; Kyle Wilkison, "The Evils of Socialism: The Religious Right in
Early Twentieth-Century Texas," in David O'Donald Cullen and Kyle G.
Wilkison, *The Texas Right: The Radical Roots of Lone Star Conservativism* (Col-
lege Station: Texas A&M University Press, 2014), 43; Thomas F. Glick, *Darwinism
in Texas: An Exhibition in the Texas History Center, April 1972* (Austin: Texas
History Center, 1972), 20–21.

6. Waters, introduction, 5–6; Ashford, *Huxley*, 26–27, 89, 107–108; Hermann
Muller, "Autobiographical Notes Requested of the National Academy of Sci-
ences," Hermann J. Muller Collection, Series II, Box 1, Biographical, Folder 1.38,
Carnegie Library, CSHL; Kevles, *Name of Eugenics*, 187.

7. Julian Huxley, "The Outlook in Biology: A Course of Three Lectures
Delivered in the Physics Amphitheatre of the Rice Institute, September 29 and
30, and October 1, 1924," *Rice Institute Pamphlet*, October 1924.

8. Huxley, "Outlook in Biology," 301.

9. Larson, *Science, Race, and Sex*, 17.

10. Edward L. Ayers, *The Promise of the New South: Life After Reconstruction*
(New York: Oxford University Press, 1992), 154–157. The Lynching in Texas database, which covers the years 1882–1945, draws from the records of investigations
by the National Association for the Advancement of Colored People, and various
newspapers across the country such as the *Chicago Tribune* and can be found at
https://lynchingintexas.org, accessed January 8, 2023. Jeffrey L. Littlejohn of Sam
Houston State University is the driving force behind this vital resource.

11. Johnson, *Revolution in Texas*, 113, 115, 119, 176; "History of Racial Violence on the Mexico-Texas Border," accessed January 8, 2023, https://refusingtoforget .org/the-history/.

12. L. B. De Pontes, "The Burning at the Stake," *Houston Post*, September 6, 1901.

13. See, for example, "Squirrel Hunt Shot: Negro Mistaken for Rapist and Killed by Beaumont Contractor" and "Beaumont Girl Victim of Negro," in *Austin Statesman*, July 15, 1908; "Steve Walton on Trial for Criminal Assault: Alleged Negro Rapist Faces a Jury in the District Court," *Austin Statesman*, February 12, 1903; "Want Him Returned: The Corsicana People Want the Negro Rapist," *Austin Daily Statesman*, March 10, 1901; "Colonization is the Solution of the Race Problem," *Wichita Falls Times*, November 23, 1907; "The Negro Problem: Rev. William Hayne Leavell to Preach on Subject Sunday," *Houston Post*, December 16, 1904; "Without Saloons, No Negro Problem," *Fort Worth Record*, January 8, 1908; Ayers, *Promise of the New South*, 154–155.

14. Stern, *Eugenic Nation*, 22.

15. Stern, *Eugenic Nation*, 18–19, 96–97.

16. Stern, *Eugenic Nation*, 100–101; Stern, "From Legislation to Lived Experiences: Eugenic Sterilization in California and Indiana, 1907–1979," in Lombardo, *A Century of Eugenics*, 97–101; E. Wilson Lyon, review of *David Starr Jordan: Prophet of Freedom*, by Edward McNall Burns, *American Historical Review* 59, no. 3 (April 1954): 651–652.

17. "Many School Children Held to Be Defective by Bureau of Hygiene," *Ferguson Forum*, June 11, 1925; "Hospitals for Insane Crowded," *Ferguson Forum*, April 13, 1933; "Public Health Nurses Have Unique Exhibit at Dallas State Fair," *Ferguson Forum*, October 29, 1925.

18. Andrea Ivey Webb, "Katie Litty Daffan," *Handbook of Texas Online*, accessed July 27, 2024, https://www.tshaonline.org/handbook/entries/daffan -katie-litty; Katie Daffan, "Blood, The Tell-Tale," *Ferguson Forum*, May 28, 1919; Larson, *Sex, Race, and Science*, 73–79.

19. John Lundberg, "The Great Texas 'Bear Fight,': Progressivism and the Impeachment of James E. Ferguson," in *Impeached: The Removal of Texas Governor James E. Ferguson*, ed. Jessica Brannon-Wranosky and Bruce A. Glasrud (College Station: Texas A&M University Press, 2017) 19–20; Pamela Bleisch, "Spoilsmen and Daughters of the Republic: Political Interference in the Texas State Library During the Tenure of Elizabeth Howard West, 1911–1925," *Libraries and the Cultural Record* 45, no. 4 (2010): 387.

20. Lundberg, "The Great Texas 'Bear Fight,'" 19–21; Ronnie Dugger, *Our Invaded Universities: Form, Reform, and New Starts* (New York: W. W. Norton & Company, 1974), 14–16.

21. Lundberg, "The Great Texas 'Bear Fight,'" 22–23.

22. Lundberg, "The Great Texas 'Bear Fight,'" 26–27; Dugger, *Our Invaded Universities*, 16–17.

23. Lundberg, "The Great Texas 'Bear Fight,'" 26–27; Dugger, *Our Invaded Universities*, 16–17.

24. Dugger, *Our Invaded Universities*, 20–21; Walter F. Pilcher, "Lindley Miller Keasbey," *Handbook of Texas Online*, accessed July 27, 2024, https://www.tshaonline.org/handbook/entries/keasbey-lindley-miller.

25. Charles Ramsdell to Roy Gittinger, October 4, 1917, Charles Ramsdell Papers, Box 2L463, General Correspondence, 1917, BCAH; Ramsdell to James Edmund, Ramsdell Papers, Box 2L463, General Correspondence, 1918, BCAH.

26. "Political Professors," *Ferguson Forum*, January 10, 1918; "Aims of the University," *Ferguson Forum*, January 31, 1918; "The Teacher who Teaches . . . ," *Ferguson Forum*, January 10, 1924.

27. Eugene Barker to Ramsdell, August 19, 1921, Ramsdell Papers, Box 2L465, General Correspondence, January-May 1921, BCAH; Eugene Barker to Robert Vinson, February 3, 1921, Eugene C. Barker Papers, Box 2B97, General Correspondence, January to March, 1921, BCAH; Barker to Robert E. Vinson, November 22, 1921, Barker Papers, Box 2B97, BCAH; Ramsdell to Walter Prescott Webb, July 11, 1923, General Correspondence, January–July 1923, BCAH; Ramsdell to Charles S. Boucher, July 16, 1923, Ramsdell Papers, Box 2L466, General Correspondence, January–July 1923, BCAH.

28. Dugger, *Our Invaded Universities*, 22–23.

29. Susan M. Schweik, *The Ugly Laws: Disability in Public* (New York: New York University Press, 2009), 1–2, 16.

30. Schweik, *Ugly Laws*, 104–105, 158.

31. "Mrs. Wilmans' Eugenics Bill Killed in House," *Dallas Morning News*, March 2, 1925, p. 11; Kevles, *In the Name of Eugenics*, 99–100.

32. Edith Moriarity, "With the Women of Today," *Wichita Falls Record News*, April 27, 1923; "Legislative Sidelights," *The Austin Statesman*, January 12, 1923; Nancy Baker Jones and Ruthe Winegarten, *Capitol Women: Texas Female Legislators, 1923–1999* (Austin: University of Texas Press, 2000), 76–77; "Triumvirate Gets Hearty Ovations," *Galveston Daily News*, September 7, 1922.

33. "Mrs. Wilmans' Eugenics Bill"; "Eugenics Measure Lost," *El Paso Herald*, March 5, 1923; "Legislative Sidelights," *Austin Statesman*, January 12, 1923. The cost of the examinations required in Wilmans's bill would be about $257 in 2023 dollars.

34. "Mrs. Wilmans' Eugenics Bill."

35. "Mrs. Wilmans' Eugenics Bill"; "Woman Loses Fight," *El Paso Herald*, March 2, 1923; *Journal of the House of Representatives of the Regular Session of the Thirty Eighth Legislature Begun and Held at the City of Austin, January 9, 1923* (Austin: Von Boeckmann-Jones, 1923), 47–48, 311, 1,078–1,080.

36. Jones and Winegarten, *Capitol Woman*, 78.

37. Larson, *Science, Race, and Sex*, 100–101.

38. Gould, *Mismeasure of Man*, 146–148.

39. Gould, *Mismeasure of Man*, 148–149, 151–153; J. Blaine Hudson, "Scientific Racism: The Politics of Tests, Race and Genetics," *Black Scholar* 25, no. 1 (Winter 1995): 3–10.

40. Gould, *Mismeasure of Man*, 156–157.

41. Gould, *Mismeasure of Man*, 157.

42. Larson, *Science, Race, and Sex*, 80–81.

43. Larson, *Science, Race, and Sex*, 64–65.

44. Larson, *Science, Race, and Sex*, 101–103.

45. Anne W. Hooker, "John Calvin Box," *Handbook of Texas Online*, accessed July 27, 2024, https://www.tshaonline.org/handbook/entries/box-john-calvin; John C. Box, "Are We to Poison the Lifeblood of the Nation?," *Dearborn Independent*, December 25, 1920.

46. David Redles, "The Turning Point: *The Protocols of the Elders of Zion* and the Eschatological War between Aryans and Jews" in *The Paranoid Apocalypse: A Hundred Year Retrospective on the* Protocols of the Elders of Zion, ed. Richard Landes and Steven T. Katz (New York: New York University Press, 2012), 114, 115.

47. Deborah Lipstadt, "*The Protocols of the Elders of Zion* on the Contemporary American Scene" in Landes and Katz, *Paranoid Apocalypse*, 173–174; Leo P. Ribuffo, "Henry Ford and the 'International Jew,'" *American Jewish History* 69, no. 4 (June 1980): 447–453.

48. Neil Baldwin, *Henry Ford and the Jews: The Mass Production of Hate* (New York: Public Affairs, 2001), 50–53, 170; Leonard Dinnerstein, *Anti-Semitism in America* (New York: Oxford University Press, 1994), 82.

49. Okrent, *Guarded Gate*, 220–223.

50. Box, "Are We to Poison the Lifeblood of the Nation?"

51. Box, "Are We to Poison the Lifeblood of the Nation?"

52. John Kifner, "Armenian Genocide of 1915: An Overview," *New York Times*, December 7, 2007; Shlomo Lambroza, "The Tsarist Government and the Pogroms of 1903–1906," *Modern Judaism* 7 (October 1987)" 287.

53. Box, "Are We to Poison the Lifeblood of the Nation?"

54. Gould, *Progressives and Prohibitionists*, 247; Leah LaGrone, "A Woman's Worth: Wages, Race, and Respectability in Twentieth-Century Texas" (PhD diss., Texas Christian University, 2021), 115–116.

55. Kelley Marie Reidt, "The Texas Cyclone: The Life of Educator-Activist Anna J. H. Pennybacker" (PhD diss., University of Texas at Austin, 2006), 340–341.

56. "Clarence Stone Yoakum," University of Michigan Staff Memoirs and Memories, accessed January 31, 2023, https://apps.lib.umich.edu/staff-memoir /apps.lib.umich.edu/staff-memoir/about-project.html.

57. C. S. Yoakum, *Care of the Feeble-Minded and Insane in Texas* (Austin: Bulletin of the University of Texas, 1914), 11–13.

58. Yoakum, *Care of the Feeble-Minded and Insane in Texas*, 18–22.

59. Yoakum, *Care of the Feeble-Minded and Insane in Texas*, 81.

60. Yoakum, *Care of the Feeble-Minded and Insane in Texas*, 143.

61. Yoakum, *Care of the Feeble-Minded and Insane in Texas*, 81–82.

62. Yoakum, *Care of the Feeble-Minded and Insane in Texas*, 82; Black, *War Against the Weak*, 38.

63. Yoakum, *Care of the Feeble-Minded and Insane in Texas*, 109–112.

64. Yoakum, *Care of the Feeble-Minded and Insane in Texas*, 80; George P. Huckaby, "Oscar Branch Colquitt," *Handbook of Texas Online*, accessed July 27, 2024, https://www.tshaonline.org/handbook/entries/colquitt-oscar-branch; Sheri-lyn Brandenstein, "Austin State School," *Handbook of Texas Online*, accessed July 27, 2024, https://www.tshaonline.org/handbook/entries/austin-state-school.

65. Larson, *Science, Race, and Sex*, 79, 84.

66. Gould, *Mismeasure of Man*, 192–193; Anne C. Rose, "An American Science of Feeling: Harvard's Psychology of Emotion During the World War I Era," *Journal of the History of Ideas* 73, no. 3 (July 2012): 495, 498.

67. Gould, *Mismeasure of Man*, 194, 199–200. Washington was the first US president and Adams the second. Matthewson was a star pitcher for the New York Giants.

68. Gould, *Mismeasure of Man*, 194, 201–204.

69. Gould, *Mismeasure of Man*, 196–197.

70. Spiro, *Defending the Master Race*, 208–209, 210, 232; Kristopher Allerfeldt, "'And We Got Here First': National Origins and Self-Interest In the Immigration Debates of the 1920s," *Journal of Contemporary History* 45, no. 1 (January 2010): 18; Pegram, *One Hundred Percent American*, 52. The tests themselves, and a description of the theories behind the tests and how they were administered can be found in Clarence S. Yoakum and Robert M. Yerkes, eds., *Army Mental Tests* (New York: Henry Holt and Company, 1920.

71. Gould, *Mismeasure of Man*, 197, 219–200, 224–233; Okrent, *Guarded Gate*, 320; "The Figures on Ourselves," *Granbury News*, March 31, 1922; Spiro, *Defending the Master Race*, 232; Franz Samelson and Leon J. Kamin, "On the Science and Politics of the IQ," *Social Research* 42 (Autumn 1975): 472; Kenneth M. Ludmerer, "Genetics, Eugenics, and the Immigration Restriction Act of 1924," *Bulletin of the History of Medicine* 46, no. 1 (January–February 1972): 59–81; Roy L. Garis, "America's Immigration Policy," *North American Review*, September 1924, 63–77. Samelson and Kamin feel the impact of the US Army IQ tests has been overstated but they, in turn, ignore the degree to which the results influenced the Harding administration, which supported the 1924 law.

72. Okrent, *Guarded Gate*, 340; "Texas Solon Praised," *Austin American*, February 10, 1924; John C. Box, "Immigration Control," *Eugenical News*, September 1927, 118–119.

73. Roger Daniels, *Guarding the Golden Door: American Immigration Policy and Immigrants Since 1882* (New York: Hill and Wang, 2004), 61.

74. Largent, *Breeding Contempt*, 72, 77–78.

75. Natalia Molina, *Fit to Be Citizens: Public Health and Race in Los Angeles, 1879–1939* (Berkeley: University of California Press, 2006), 119; "Steel is Coming," *Wichita Falls Times Record News*, February 20, 1924.

76. Alexander Caswell Ellis, Typed note, Ellis Papers, Box 2P62.

77. Elmer V. Eyman, *Report of the Texas Mental Hygiene Survey, 1924: Psychiatric Study of Public School Children in Eleven Counties, Children in State and County Institutions for Delinquents and Dependents, [and] Inmates of Eleven County Poor Farms Inmates of Eighteen County Jails* (New York: National Committee for Mental Hygiene, December, 1924). A copy of the Eyman report can be found in the Alexander Caswell Ellis Papers, Box 2P49, BCAH. This material is also discussed in Michael Phillips, "Texan By Color: The Racialization of the Lone Star State," in Cullen and Wilkison, *Texas Right*, 22.

78. Eyman, *Report of the Texas Mental Hygiene Survey*, 19, 53, 55.

79. Eyman, *Report of the Texas Mental Hygiene Survey*, 53.

80. M. E. Haggerty, L. M. Terman, E. L. Thorndike, G. M. Whipple, and R. M. Yerkes, "National Intelligence Test, Scale B, Form 1," Alexander Caswell Ellis Papers, Box 4P347, BCAH.

81. Calvert and De León, 5th ed., *History of Texas*, 277–278.

82. Carpenter's legislative efforts are also discussed in Phillips, "Texan by Color."

83. *Journal of the House of Representatives of the Regular Session of the Thirty Eighth Legislature*, 587–588, 614, 643.

84. Foley, *White Scourge*, 55.

85. Marshall Roderick, "'The 'Box Bill': Public Policy, Ethnicity, and Economic Exploitation in Texas" (master's thesis, Texas State University, 2011), 2; Foley, *White* Scourge, 50; Montejano, *Anglos and Mexicans*, 189–190.

86. Roderick, "'The 'Box Bill,'" 2, 9; Mark Reisler, "Always the Laborer, Never the Citizen: Anglo Perceptions of the Mexican Immigrant during the 1920s," *Pacific Historical Review* 45, no 2 (May 1976): 233.

87. Foley, *White Scourge*, 54–57.

88. Arthur E. Knolle to John C. Box, February 4, 1928, typescript copy, Box 2, Folder 12, Oliver Douglas Weeks Collection, Nettie Lee Benson Latin American Library, University of Texas, BLAC.

89. Knolle to Box, February 4, 1928; E. E. Davis, Letter to John C. Box, February 4, 1928, Oliver Douglas Weeks Collection, Box 2, Folder 8, BLAC.

90. Hooker, "John Calvin Box"; "Foley, *White Scourge*, 46–47, 50, 54–56, 59; Katherine Benton-Cohen, *Inventing the Immigration Problem: The Dillingham Commission and its Legacy* (Cambridge, MA: Harvard University Press, 2018), 238; W. M. Branch, MD, to John C. Box, August 3, 1926, Oliver Douglas Weeks Collection, Box 2, Folder 3, BLAC; Branch to John C. Box, June 2, 1926, Oliver Douglas Weeks Collection, Box 2, Folder 17, BLAC; W. C. McDonald to John C. Box, April 9, 1928, Oliver Douglas Weeks Collection, Box 2, Folder 17, BLAC.

91. Foley, *White Scourge*, 58.

92. "Shutting Out the Mexicans," *Austin American*, December 12, 1924.

93. C. L. Wallis to John C. Box, January 23, 1924, Oliver Douglas Weeks Collection, Box 2, Folder 2, BLAC; Roderick, 42–43.

94. Daniels, *Guarding the Golden Door*, 61–62; Foley, *White Scourge*, 58–59.

95. Roderick, "'The 'Box Bill,'" 87, 105; "Martin Dies Lead Over John C. Box is 5,730," *Fort Worth Star-Telegram*, July 29, 1930.

96. Robert R. McKay, "Mexican Americans and Repatriation," *Handbook of Texas Online*, accessed July 27, 2024, https://www.tshaonline.org/handbook/entries/mexican-americans-and-repatriation; Manuel G. Gonzales, *Mexicanos: A History of Mexicans in the United States* (Bloomington: Indiana University Press, 2009), 164; John S. Huntington, *Far-Right Vanguard: The Radical Roots of Modern Conservatism* (Philadelphia: University of Pennsylvania Press, 2021), 50.

97. Garland E. Allen, "Julian Huxley and the Eugenical View of Human Evolution," in Waters and Van Helden, *Julian Huxley*, 196–199, 206–207.

98. Hermann J. Muller, typed note, "Prepared at Vavilov's, 1936–1937, Hermann J. Muller Collection, Series II, Biographical Materials, Memorabilia, 1912–1972, Box 1, Biographical, Folder 1.38, Cold Spring Harbor Library, CSHL.

99. Muller, typed note, "Prepared at Vavilov's, 1936–1937."

100. Hermann Muller, "Autobiographical Notes Requested of the National Academy of Sciences." Hermann J. Muller Collection, Series II, Box 1, Biographical, Folder 1.38, CSHL; Kevels, *Name of Eugenics*, 187.; Schwartz, *In Pursuit of the Gene*, 210.

101. Muller, "Prepared at Vavilov's," 1936–1937; Schwartz, *In Pursuit of the Gene*, 226; Bentley Glass, "Geneticists Embattled: Their Stand against Rampant Eugenics and Racism in America during the 1920s and 1930s," *Proceedings of the American Philosophical Society* 130, no. 1 (March 1986): 139, 148–149. Glass received his bachelor's degree from Baylor and his PhD in biology under the guidance of Muller. Like Muller, Glass also became a critic of scientific racism. See Frank C. Erk, "Remembering Bentley Glass (1906–2005)," *Quarterly Review of Biology*, Vol. 80, no. 2 (June 2005): 166.

102. Muller, "Prepared at Vavilov's, 1936–1937"; Hermann Joseph Muller, *Out of the Night: A Biologist's View of the Future* (New York: Vanguard Press, 1935), vii.

103. Muller, *Out of the Night*, ix–x.

104. "Herman Joseph Muller, 1890–1967," *Yearbook of the American Philosophical Society* (reprint, 1967), Hermann J. Muller Collection, Series II: Biographical Materials/Memorabilia, 1912–1972, Box 2, Folder 2.23, BCAH; Schwartz, *In Pursuit of the Gene*, 234–251; Muller, *Out of the Night*, 113–114, 120.

105. Kevels, *In the Name of Genetics*, 187; Schwartz, *In Pursuit of the Gene*, 256–257; Hermann Joseph Muller to Edgar Altenburg, December 15, 1935, Hermann J. Muller Collection, Series II, Biographical Materials, Memorabilia, 1912–1972, Box 1, Correspondence Folder 1.3, BCAH.

106. "Muller Gets Extension," *Austin American*, September 10, 1935; Schwartz, *In Pursuit of the Gene*, 262–266; "Noted Prof Quits UT; To Remain in Russia," *Austin American*, April 28, 1936.

107. Largent, *Breeding Contempt*, 72, 78.

108. Nancy Leys Stepan, *"The Hour of Eugenics": Race, Gender, and Nation in Latin America* (Ithaca, NY: Cornell University Press, 1991), 16–17, 145–146. See also the foundational essay by Alan Knight, "Racism, Revolution, and *Indigenismo*: Mexico, 1910–1940," *The Idea of Race in Latin America, 1870–1940*, ed. Richard Graham (Austin: University of Texas Press, 1990) and Edward Telles and Tianna Paschel, "Who is Black, White, or Mixed Race?: How Skin Color, Status and Nation Shape Racial Classification in Latin America," *American Journal of Sociology* 120, no. 3 (November 2014): 864–907.

109. "Horosa Distincion Al Sabio Mexicano Sr. Manuel Gamio," *La Prensa de San Antonio*, October 4, 1920. The authors thank Margarita Birnbaum for her generous translation assistance and for sharing her knowledge of how colloquial Spanish has changed over the decades.

110. Stepan, *"Hour of Eugenics,"* 17.

111. Stepan, *"Hour of Eugenics,"* 36, 41–42, 55.

112. Stepan, *"Hour of Eugenics,"* 55–57, 102–103, 128–133; Office of the High Commissioner for Human Rights, United Nations, "The Hashtag That Went Around the World," December 20, 2022, March 13, 2023, https://www.ohchr.org/en/stories/2022/12/hashtag-went-around-world.

113. "Practica Muy Antigua," *El Paso Times*, September 20, 1916.

114. "En Pro De La Raza," *El Paso Times*, August 6, 1915; "Matrimonio Futuro," *El Paso Times*, May 3, 1915.

115. "En Pro De La Raza."

116. Reilly, *Surgical Solution*, 113, 115.

117. Larson, *Sex, Race, and Science*, 167–168.

Chapter 5

1. "Platform of Arthur P. Duggan, Candidate for Congress in the New 19th Congressional District of Texas, 1931," Arthur P. Duggan Sr. Papers, 1860–1942, Box S 275 2, Folder 1, Southwest Collection/Special Collections Archive, SWC; Alice Duggan Gracy, "Arthur Pope Duggan, *Handbook of Texas Online*, accessed July 27, 2024, https://www.tshaonline.org/handbook/entries/duggan-arthur-pope.

2. Arthur P. Duggan, Sr. Collection Finding Aid, Texas Tech University, accessed February 27, 2023, https://txarchives.org/ttusw/finding_aids/00180.xml; "Platform of Arthur P. Duggan," Duggan Papers.

3. "Platform of Arthur P. Duggan," Duggan Papers.

4. Arthur P. Duggan, undated notes for speech, Duggan Papers.

5. "Duggan's Bill Being Watched," *Lubbock Avalanche-Journal*, February 10, 1935.

6. Claude Teer to Arthur Duggan November 5, 1934, James V. Allred Papers, Sterilization Bill Folder 1985/024–42, TSLAC; Dick Smith, "Board of Control,"*Handbook of Texas Online*, accessed July 27, 2024, https://www.tshaonline .org/handbook/entries/board-of-control.

7. "Sterilization Law," *Dallas Morning News*, January 18, 1935.

8. "Upper House Soon to Take Action." In *Buck v. Bell*, the court upheld the constitutionality of a Virginia coerced sterilization law, with Justice Oliver Wendell Holmes Jr. defending the statute. In the majority opinion he authored, he referenced the family of Carrie Buck, a woman contesting an order that she undergo a tubal ligation, infamously declaring, "Three generations of imbeciles are enough." See Black, *War Against the Weak*, 116–122.

9. "Upper House Soon to Take Action on Sterilization Bill; Opposition Is Expected, but Author Believes It Will Survive Vote," *Dallas Morning News*, February 19, 1935; "Duggan's Bill Being Watched," *Lubbock Avalanche-Journal*, February 10, 1935; "Senate Committee Votes Sterilization Measure," *Austin American*, February 8, 1935; "Sterilization Bill Cause of House Fight," *Marshall Morning News*, February 2, 1935; "Sterilization Bill Is Called Vicious Move at Hearing; Tie Is Voted on Test Ballot and Measure is Sent to Subcommittee," *Dallas Morning News*, February 1, 1935.

10. Pope Pius XI, *Casti Connubii* ("On Christian Marriage,") 1930, Papal Encyclicals Online, accessed February 28, 2023, https://www.papalencyclicals .net/pius11/p11casti.htm.

11. "Un Ataque En Contra Del Paganismo," *El Heraldo de Brownsville*, May 24, 1935; "Texas Should Not Resort to the Practice of Sterilization," *Southern Messenger*, January 3, 1935; Robert E. Wright, "Catholic Church," *Handbook of Texas Online*, accessed July 27, 2024, https://www.tshaonline.org/handbook /entries/catholic-church.

12. Letters supporting and opposing Duggan's sterilization bill can be found in James V. Allred Papers, Sterilization Bill Folder 1985/024–42, 306–21, TSLAC.

13. Harry H. Laughlin to Gov. James V. Allred, March 1, 1935; C. R. Miller to Harry H. Laughlin, March 7, 1935, Allred Papers, Sterilization Bill Folder 1985/024–42, TSLAC.

14. *Texas Senate Journal, Forty-fourth Legislature, Regular Session* (Austin: Texas Senate, 1935), 339, 367; Bart Alvara, "Olan Rogers Van Zandt," *Handbook of Texas Online*, accessed July 27, 2024, https://www.tshaonline.org/handbook /entries/van-zandt-olan-rogers. Van Zandt represented Cooke, Fannin, and Grayson County in far northeast Texas along the Oklahoma border.

15. "Arthur Duggan, Member of State Senate, Is Dead; Littlefield Man Dies on Visit to Relatives at Gonzales, Old House," *Dallas Morning News*, September 7, 1935; Alice Duggan Gracy, "Arthur Pope Duggan," *Handbook of Texas Online*, accessed January 13, 2016, https://tshaonline.org/handbook/online /articles/fduo8; "Duggan Mourned as One of Littlefield Builders," *Fort Worth Star-Telegram*, September 7, 1935.

16. *Journal of the House of Representatives of the Regular Session of the Forty-Fifth Legislature of the State of Texas, Begun and Held at the City of Austin, January 12, 1937*, Volume 1. (Austin: Capital Printing Company, 1937), 429.

17. *Journal of the House of Representatives of the Regular Session of the Forty-Fifth Legislature of the State of Texas*, 1937,752; "Sterilization Bill Passage Favored," *Dallas Morning News*, March 3, 1937.

18. "Prefers Horse and Buggy for This Kind of Trip," *Dallas Morning News*, March 6, 1937.

19. "Eugenics Measure Urged by Texas Control Board," *Vernon (Texas) Daily Record*, May 11, 1937; "Contemporary Comment: Sterilization," *Wichita Falls News*, March 5, 1937.

20. Larson, *Science, Race, and Sex*, 131–136.

21. "Contemporary Comment."

22. E. E. Davis to Will H. Mayes, May 12, 1939, University of Texas at Arlington Office of the President Records, Dean E. E. Davis Folder 258–12–3, UTA; Gerald D. Saxon, *Transitions: A Centennial History of the University of Texas at Arlington, 1895–1995* (Arlington: UTA Press, 1995), 53; Samuel B. Hamlett, "University of Texas at Arlington." *Handbook of Texas Online*, accessed July 27, 2024, https://www.tshaonline.org/handbook/entries/university-of-texas-at-arlington. Post was perhaps the most important business leader in the national movement for anti-union "right to work" laws. For more on this, see Chad E. Pearson, *Capital's Terrorists: Klansmen, Lawmen and Employers in the Long Nineteenth Century* (Chapel Hill: University of North Carolina Press, 2022), 183–185, 198, 205. His fascinating book details American businesses' frequent use of violence as a means of labor control from Reconstruction to the Progressive Era.

23. William M. Pearce, "Charles William Post," *Handbook of Texas Online*, accessed July 27, 2024, https://www.tshaonline.org/handbook/entries/post-charles-william; Paul M. Lucko, "Post, Tx.," *Handbook of Texas Online*, accessed January 27, 2024, https://www.tshaonline.org/handbook/entries/post-tx; Jan Reid, "C. W. Post," *Texas Monthly*, March 1987, accessed October 22, 2022, https://www.texasmonthly.com/news-politics/c-w-post/; Brian C. Wilson, *Dr. John Harvey Kellogg and the Religion of Biologic Living* (Bloomington: Indiana University Press, 2014), xi, 46–49, 73, 79, 114, 125–132, 148–171, 175.

24. C. W. Post, *The Modern Practice: Natural Suggestion, or Scientia Vitæ* (Battle Creek, MI.: La Vita Inn Company, 1894), [unpaginated].

25. Charles Dudley Eaves, "Colonization Efforts of Charles William Post," *Southwestern Historical Quarterly* 43, no. 1 (July 1939): 73; C. W. Post, Speech, April 27, 1909, C. W. Post Papers, Speeches, Pamphlets, and Publications, 1909, 3–13, C.W. Post Papers, Bentley Historical Library, University of Michigan; Dan Flores, *Caprock Canyonlands* (repr.; College Station: Texas A&M University Press, 2010), 38; Reid, "C. W. Post"; Willis L. Moore telegram, n.d., C.W. Post Papers; "Artificially Made Rain is Discredited," *Rapid City Journal*, July 25, 1912; "C. W. Post A Suicide in California Home," *New York Times*, May 10, 1914.

26. Saxon, *Transitions*, 53–54.

27. E. E. Davis to Will H. Mayes, May 12, 1939, University of Texas at Arlington Office of the President Records, Dean E. E. Davis, Folder 258–12–3, UTA; Saxon, *Transitions*, 53–54; Hamlett, "University of Texas at Arlington."

28. Saxon, *Transitions*, 54–57; R. O. Peterson, to E. E. Davis, February 6, 1936, Box 2, Folder 258–2-7, E. E. Davis, Presidents' Papers, UTA.

29. *Junior Aggie Yearbook* (Arlington: North Texas Agricultural College, 1936); Darwin Payne, *Big D: Triumphs and Troubles of an American Supercity in the 20th Century* (Dallas: Three Forks Press, 1994), 85–109; Charles Alexander, "Kleagles and Cash: The Ku Klux Klan as a Business Organization," *Business History Review* 39, no. 3 (Autumn 1965): 360.

30. Foley, *White Scourge*, 6.

31. Foley, *White Scourge*, 36.

32. E. E. Davis to George Witte, March 26, 1941, E. E. Davis Papers, Folder 258–20–1, UTA.

33. Foley, *White Scourge*, 42, 62; Davis, *White Scourge*, ix.

34. E. E. Davis to H. L. Pritchett, October 7, 1935, E. E. Davis Papers, Box 4, Folder 258–4-12, UTA.

35. E. E. Davis to W. B. Bizzell, January 23, 1936, E. E. Davis Papers, Box 4, Folder 258–4-13, UTA; W. B. Bizzell to E. E. Davis, January 27, 1936, E. E. Davis Papers, Box 4, Folder 258–4-13, UTA.

36. Davis, *White Scourge*, x, 31.

37. Davis, *White Scourge*, 1, 3, 52, 53.

38. Davis, *White Scourge*, 70, 98, 116.

39. Davis, *White Scourge*, 26, 29, 43, 60. Also see Jeffrey Weinstock, "Circumcising Dracula," *Journal of the Fantastic in Arts* 12, no. 1 (2001): 90–102, and Frederic Cople Jaher, *A Scapegoat in the Wilderness: The Origins and Rise of Anti-Semitism in America* (Cambridge, MA: Harvard University Press, 1994), 226–227.

40. Davis, *White Scourge*, 58, 63.

41. Davis, *White Scourge*, 58–59.

42. Davis, *White Scourge*, 61, 117–118.

43. Davis, *White Scourge*, 146.

44. Bragg, review of Davis, *White Scourge*, 689.

45. Hamlett, "University of Texas at Arliington"; Michael Phillips arid Betsy Friauf, "Opinion: Hereford isn't the Only Problematic Figure from UTA's Past," *Shorthorn*, October 12, 2018, accessed March 10, 2023, https://www.theshorthorn.com/opinion/opinion-hereford-isn-t-the-only-problematic-figure-from-uta-s-past/article_1cbafd46-cc29–11e8–8874–730caca3fb8d.html; Cole Kembel, Samantha Knowles and Chongyang Zhang, "A History of How the University Administration Building Lost Its Name," *Shorthorn*, May 10, 2021, accessed March 10, 2023, https://www.theshorthorn.com/news/a-history-of-how-the-university-administration-building-lost-its-former-namesake/article_5981d77e-b031–11eb-9634-fff2695c70f1.html; Teik C. Lim, "E. E. Davis Hall to be Renamed University

Administration Building," May 6, 2021, accessed March 10, 2023, https://www.uta
.edu/enews/email/2021/05–06-president-davis-hall.html; Simone Carter, "Students
Fight to Change 2 Building Names at UT Arlington," *Dallas Observer*, February 28,
2023, accessed March 10, 2023, https://www.dallasobserver.com/news/university-of
-texas-at-arlington-students-fight-for-change-of-buildings-named-after-hereford
-woolf-16026389

46. Largent, *Breeding Contempt*, 81.

47. Largent, *Breeding Contempt*, 72–78. See also Keith L. Bryant Jr., "Organized
Labor, and Social Justice in Oklahoma During the Progressive Era," *Journal of
Southern History* 35, no. 2 (May 1969): 145–46, and James R. Green, *Grassroots
Socialism: Radical Movement in the Southwest* (Baton Rouge: Louisiana State
University Press, 1978).

48. Victoria F. Nourse, *In Reckless Hands: Skinner v. Oklahoma and the Near
Triumph of American Eugenics* (New York: W. W. Norton, 2008), 19–21.

49. Nourse, *In Reckless Hands*, 39, 41, 44, 73, 84–85; Largent, *Breeding Contempt*, 79.

50. Largent, *Breeding Contempt*, 79–80; Johanna Schoen, "Reassessing Sterilization: The Case of North Carolina," in Lombardo, *A Century of Eugenics*,
149–150.

51. Black, *War Against the Weak*, 393–395.

52. Schoen, "Reassessing Sterilization," 147–148.

53. Nourse, *In Reckless Hands*, 131–132.

54. Stern, *Eugenic Nation*, 127; Spiro, *Defending the Master Race*, 267–293,
389–390.

55. Gregory Michael Dorr, "Protection or Control? Women's Health Sterilization Abuse and *Relf v. Weinberger*" in Lombardo, *A Century of Eugenics*, 175.

56. Levine, *Eugenics*, 105–107; Maxwell J. Mehlman, "Modern Eugenics and
the Law," in Lombardo, *A Century of Eugenics*, 231.

57. Nourse, *In Reckless Hands*, 163; See also, for example, Lawrence K. Altman,
"Scientists See a Link Between Alcoholism and a Specific Gene," *New York Times*,
April 18, 1990, accessed March 13, 2023, https://www.nytimes.com/1990/04/18/us
/scientists-see-a-link-between-alcoholism-and-a-specific-gene.html; Marta
Zaraka "The Genes of Left and Right: Our Political Attitudes May be Written in
our DNA," *Scientific American*, May 1, 2016, accessed March 13, 2023, https://www
.scientificamerican.com/article/the-genes-of-left-and-right/; Helen Zhao and Meg
Perret, "The Search for Gay Genes: Should Queer People Support It?" *Ms. Magazine*, November 14, 2021, accessed March 13, 2023, https://msmagazine.com/2021
/11/14/gay-genes-is-homosexuality-a-choice/; Nicholas Wade, "The Evolution of
the God Gene," *New York Times*, November 14, 2009, accessed March 13, 2023,
https://www.nytimes.com/2009/11/15/weekinreview/12wade.html.

58. Kali Holloway, "Modern-day Eugenics? Prisoners Sterilized for Shorter
Sentences," *Salon*, July 28, 2017, March 13, 2023, https://www.salon.com/2017/07
/28/modern-day-eugenics-prisoners-sterilized-for-shorter-sentences_partner/.

59. Derek Hawkins, "California Once Forcibly Sterilized People by the Thousands. Now the Victims May Get Reparations," *Washington Post*, July 9, 2021; Bill Chappell, "California's Prison Sterilizations Reportedly Echo Eugenics Era," National Public Radio, July 9, 2013, accessed March 13, 2023, https://www.npr.org/sections/thetwo-way/2013/07/09/200444613/californias-prison-sterilizations-reportedly-echoes-eugenics-era; Adam Beam, "California Tries to Find and Compensate Victims of Forced Sterilization Program," KQED, January 7, 2023, accessed March 13, 2023, https://www.kqed.org/news/11937272/california-tries-to-find-and-compensate-victims-of-forced-sterilization-program.

60. Eric Mennel, "Payments Start for N.C. Eugenics Victims, But Many Won't Qualify," National Public Radio, October 31, 2014, accessed March 13, 2023, https://www.npr.org/sections/health-shots/2014/10/31/360355784/paymentsstart-for-n-c-eugenics-victims-but-many-wont-qualify.

61. "Virginia Eugenics Victims Compensated for Sterilization," BBC, February 27, 2015, March 13, 2023, https://www.bbc.com/news/world-us-canada-31654546.

62. Jon Evans, "Congress Passes Bill to Protect Eugenics Victims," WECT, September 27, 2016, March 13, 2023, https://www.wect.com/story/33264080/congress-passes-bill-to-protect-eugenics-victims/.

63. "Sexologia," *La Prensa* (San Antonio), August 21, 1958.

64. "Una Voz de Mujer," *El Puerto de Brownsville*, August 27, 1955.

65. Sitton, *Life at the Texas State Lunatic Asylum*, 126–127.

66. See, for instance, "Tarrant County Inmate's 'Unnecessary Death' Spotlights Mental Health Crisis in Jails Nationwide," *Texas Standard*, August 18, 2023, accessed August 22, 2023, https://www.texasstandard.org/stories/tarrant-county-tx-inmate-death-spotlights-mental-health-crisis-jails/.

67. In addition to Leslie Reagan's *When Abortion Was a Crime*, cited above, some of the most important works on the government attempts to regulate reproduction include Laura Briggs, *Reproducing Empire: Race, Sex, Science, and U.S. Imperialism in Puerto Rico* (Berkeley: University of California Press, 2002); Elena Gutiérrez, *Fertile Matters: The Politics of Mexican-Origin Women's Reproduction* (Austin: University of Texas Press, 2008); Peggy Pascoe, *What Comes Naturally: Miscegenation Law and the Making of Race in America* (Oxford, UK: Oxford University Press, 2010); Dorothy Roberts, *Killing the Black Body: Race, Reproduction, and the Meaning of Liberty* (New York: Vintage Books, 1997); and Alicia Gutiérrez-Romine, *From Back Alley to the Border: Criminal Abortion in California* (Lincoln: University of North Carolina Press, 2020).

68. See Bruce A. Glasrud, "Jim Crow's Emergence in Texas," *American Studies* 15, no. 1 (Spring 1974): 52; Larry D. Barnett, "Anti-Miscegenation Laws," *Family Life Coordinator* 13., no. 4 (October 1964): 95–97; Barbara C. Cruz and Michael J. Berson, "The American Melting Pot? Miscegenation Laws in the United States," *OAH Magazine of History*, Summer 2001, 83.

69. Garrow, *Liberty and Sexuality*, 288, 296, 302, 305, 325–326, 405.

70. Sergio Martínez-Beltrán, "Texas Lawmakers Have Been Working to Ban Abortion for Decades. Their Mission is Almost Complete," KERA, June 16, 2022, accessed February 22, 2023, https://www.keranews.org/texas-news/2022–06–16/texas-lawmakers-have-been-working-to-ban-abortion-for-decades-their-mission-is-almost-complete; Nina Totenberg and Sarah McCammon, "Supreme Court Overturns *Roe v. Wade*, Ending Right to Abortion Upheld for Decades," National Public Radio, June 24, 2022, accessed August 22, 2024, https://www.npr.org/2022/06/24/1102305878/supreme-court-abortion-roe-v-wade-decision-overturn.

71. Eleanor Klibanoff, "Kate Cox's Case Reveals How Far Texas Intends to Go to Enforce Abortion Laws," *Texas Tribune*, December 13, 2023, accessed February 25, 2024, https://www.texastribune.org/2023/12/13/texas-abortion-law suit/. For more on Texans' views on abortion, see Garrow, *Liberty and Sexuality*, 368; Reese Oxner, "78 Percent of Texas Voters Think Abortion Should Be Allowed in Some Form, UT Poll Shows," *Texas Tribune*, May 4, 2022, accessed August 22, 2023, https://www.texastribune.org/2022/05/04/texas-abortion-ut-poll/; Jolie McCullough, "After Pursuing an Indictment, Starr County District Attorney Drops Murder Charge Over Self-Induced Abortion," *Texas Tribune*, April 10, 2022, accessed August 22, 2023, https://www.texastribune.org/2022/04/10/starr-county-murder-charge/; Eleanor Klibanoff, "Texas Isn't Ready to Support More Parents and Kids in a post-*Roe* World," *Texas Tribune*, May 9, 2022, accessed August 22, 2023, https://www.texastribune.org/2022/05/09/texas-abortion-law-medicaid-contraception/; Ariana Perez-Castells, Eleanor Klibanoff and Erin Douglass, "Abortions Up to Six Weeks of Pregnancy Can Temporarily Resume In Texas, Judge Rules," *Texas Tribune*, June 28, 2022, accessed February 28, 2024, https://www.texastribune.org/2022/06/28/texas-abortion-resume/#:~:text=While%20some%20abortion%20access%20has,even%20know%20they%20are%20pregnant.

72. Tamar Lewin, "Texas Court Agrees to Castration for Rapist of 13-Year-Old Girl," *New York Times*, March 7, 1992; "Rapist Who Requested Castration Gets Life Term," *Orlando Sentinel*, August 7, 1992; Largent, *Breeding Contempt*, 144.

73. Largent, *Breeding Contempt*, 144; "Medical, Legal Experts Debate Merits of Castration Legislation," *Tyler Morning Telegraph*, May 8, 1997; "Grim Conundrum," *Fort Worth Star-Telegram*, April 5, 1996.

74. "Medical, Legal Experts Debate Merits of Castration Legislation"; "New Law Lets Molesters Volunteer for Castration," *Austin American Statemen*, May 12, 1997; Joseph Bui, "Chemical and Surgical Castration for Sex Offenders," FindLaw.com, accessed March 12, 2023, https://www.findlaw.com/criminal/criminal-charges/chemical-and-surgical-castration.html.

75. See James Cook, "U.S. Election: Trump and the Rise of the Alt-Right," BBC, accessed August 26, 2023, https://www.bbc.com/news/election-us-2016–37899026; Michael Phillips, "The Elite Roots of Richard Spencer's Racism," *Jacobin*,December

29, 2016, accessed February 24, 2023, https://jacobin.com/2016/12/richard-spencer-alt-right-dallas-texas/; Clay Risen, "William H. Regnery II, 80, Dies; Bankrolled the Rise of the Alt-Right," *New York Times*, July 16, 2021, accessed August 24, 2023, https://www.nytimes.com/2021/07/16/obituaries/william-h-regnery-ii-dead.html; Alexandra Mina Stern, "Navigating the Dark Web of American Racism," Literary Hub, July 17, 2019, accessed August 24, 2023, https://lithub.com/navigating-the-dark-web-of-american-racism/; Denise Lavoie, "Jury Awards $26M in Damages for Unite the Right Violence," AP News, November 23, 2021, accessed July 19, 2024, https://apnews.com/article/violence-lawsuits-race-and-ethnicity-charlottesville-01d9437ec28ed71b4bae293d7e0d815d.

76. Marek Kohn, *The Race Gallery: The Return of Racial Science* (London: Vintage, 1995), 19.

77. Kohn, *Race Gallery*, 19.

78. Richard J. Herrnstein and Charles Murray, *The Bell Curve: Intelligence and Class Structure in American Life* (New York: The Free Press, 1994), 191–201, 235–251, 276–283, 289, 298–303, 311, 473–474; Quinn Slobodian and Stuart Schrader, "The White Man Unburdened: How Charles Murray Stopped Worrying and Learned to Love Racism," *Baffler*, July–August 2018; William H. Tucker, *The Funding of Scientific Racism: Wycliffe Draper and the Pioneer Fund* (Urbana and Chicago: University of Illinois Press, 2002), 1–2.

79. Tucker, *Funding of Scientific Racism*, 43–44; Haroon Kharem, *A Curriculum of Oppression: A Pedagogy of Racial History in the United States* (New York: Peter Lang, 2006), 129–130; Kohn, *The Race Gallery*, 111–112.

80. Tucker, *Funding of Scientific Racism*, 71; 119, Angela Saini, *Superior: The Return of Race Science* (Boston: Beacon Press, 2019), 64; Spiro, *Defending the Master Race*, 265; Kharem, *Curriculum of Oppression*, 129–130; Kohn, *Race Gallery*, 111–112.

81. Tucker, *Funding of Scientific Racism*, 1–2; "Mainstream Science on Intelligence," *Wall Street Journal*, December 13, 1994, accessed July 19, 2024, https://www1.udel.edu/educ/gottfredson/reprints/1994WSJmainstream.pdf.

82. Eric Alterman, *What Liberal Media?: The Truth About Bias and the News* (New York: Basic Books, 2003), 100–101; "Mainstream Science on Intelligence."

83. Joseph M. Horn and John C. Loehlin, *Heredity and Environment in 300 Adoptive Families: The Texas Adoption Project* (New Brunswick, NJ: Aldine-Transaction, 2010), viii, 144, 148–151;

84. Kohn, *Race Gallery*, 134–135.

85. Tucker, *Funding of Scientific Racism*, 2; Elaine Woo, "Arthur Jensen Dies at 89; His Views on Race Caused a Furor," *Los Angeles Times*, November 2, 2012, accessed March 15, 2023, https://www.latimes.com/local/obituaries/la-me-arthur-jensen-20121102-story.html; Cecil R. Reynolds and Arthur R. Jensen, "WISC-R Subscale Patterns of Abilities of Blacks and Whites Matched on Full Scale IQ," *Journal of Educational Psychology*, Vol. 75, no. 2 (1983): 207–214.

86. John C. Loehlin, Gardner Lindzey, and J.H. Spuhler, *Race Difference in Intelligence* (San Francisco: W. H. Freeman and Company, 1975), 20–33, 49–50. In 2007, one of the authors had a conversation with a signatory of the "Mainstream Science on Intelligence" open letter. The signatory was asked how he defined racial categories when he analyzed IQs of African Americans. He said the categories were self-reported. When asked if this lacked the proper precision necessary to quality science, he said of African Americans, "I know one when I see one."

87. "Unitarian," *Austin American-Statesman*, March 11, 1995.

88. Christopher Mathias, "Richard Hanania, Rising Right-Wing Star, Wrote for White Supremacist Sites Under Pseudonym," *Huffpost*, August 4, 2023, accessed August 24, 2023, https://www.huffpost.com/entry/richard-hanania -white-supremacist-pseudonym-richard-hoste_n_64c93928e4b021e2f295e817; Zak Cheney-Rice, "Our Journey Into Extremism: The Revealing Case of the Anti-Woke Crusader Richard Hanania," *New York Magazine Intelligencer*, August 12, 2023, accessed August 25, 2023, https://nymag.com/intelligencer/2023/08/richard -hanania-racist-message.html; "Texas McCombs Salem Center: About Us," Salem Center, accessed August 24, 2023, https://salemcenter.org/about/; "New Salem Center for Policy," Medium, accessed August 24, 2023, https://medium.com/texas -mccombs-news/new-salem-center-for-policy-4d7da0c25ca3.

89. Mathias, "Richard Hanania."

90. Matthias, "Richard Hanania."

91. Mathias, "Richard Hanania"; Robin McKie, "No Death and Enhanced Life: Is the Future Transhumanism?" *Guardian*, May 6, 2018, accessed September 16, 2023, https://www.theguardian.com/technology/2018/may/06/no-death -and-an-enhanced-life-is-the-future-transhuman; Noah Rawlings, "An American Education: Notes from UATX," *New Inquiry*, February 19, 2024, accessed February 25, 2024, https://thenewinquiry.com/an-american-education-notes -from-uatx/. Beginning in 2020, Elon Musk bought 281 acres in rural Bastrop County, about thirty-three miles southeast of Austin, and a total of 3,500 acres near the state capital. He opened a warehouse for his Space X company in Bastrop County, as well as a headquarters for the Boring Co. (a drilling firm), a bodega, a salon, a pub, and a housing complex. Like C. W. Post, he hopes to construct "a sort of Texas utopia along the Colorado [River], where his employees could live and work." He calls his planned company town Snailbrook. His Texas enterprises have already been accused of dumping wastewater in the nearby Colorado River, in addition to causing serious soil erosion and other environmental damage.

After buying and renaming Twitter "X," Musk has used this platform to promote "race science" popular among eugenicists from a century earlier, amplifying social media posts that purportedly prove that African Americans are less intelligent than whites and people of Asian descent and far more prone to violence. Dr. Sasha Gusev, a statistical geneticist and associate professor at Harvard, and others have noted how popular white supremacist concepts are in the high-tech industry, a phenomena that has led to X's saturation with racism and neo-eugenicist ideas. The "tech bro" fascination with supposed racial differences in IQ and the blessings of selective breeding has granted these long-discredited notions a new aura of respectability. "There's a kind of fusion between old-school gutter racism that everyone can recognize and this new-school Silicon Valley, data-driven analysis. And I think that this is very confusing to people," said Gusev. "They don't know what to do with it. They say, 'Hey, there's this thing that I recognize as ugly, and then there's somebody posting a hundred charts that seem to support it.'" See Paris Marx, "Elon Musk's New Baby's Name Is Actually Less Absurd Than His Anti-Democratic, Quasi-Eugenicist Views," *Jacobin*, May 7, 2020, accessed April 8, 2024, https://jacobin.com/2020/05/elon-musk-grimes -baby-population-democracy; "Elon Musk is Building a Town in Bastrop County," KVUE, March 10, 2023, accessed April 8, 2024, https://www.kvue.com/article /money/economy/boomtown-2040/elon-musk-town-snailbrook-bastrop /269–8b9adab4–4fdf-4dcd-8c8d-42dab00e504b; Arianna Coghill and Garrison Hayes, "Elon Musk Keeps Spreading and Very Specific Kind of Racism," *Mother Jones*, March 13, 2024, accessed April 8, 2024, https://www.motherjones.com /politics/2024/03/elon-musk-racist-tweets-science-video/; Alexandra Tremayne-Pengelly, "Elon Musk is Facing Environmental Backlash From Rural Texas Neighbors," *Texas Observer*, May 30, 2023, https://observer.com/2023/05/elon-musk -facing-environmental-backlash-rural-texas-neighbors/; Jane Turchi, Fields to Factories: Elon Musk-led Companies Spur Transformation of Bastrop Landscape," *Community Impact*, April 2, 2024, accessed April 8, 2024, https:// communityimpact.com/austin/bastrop/development/2024/04/02/fields-to -factories-elon-musk-led-companies-spur-transformation-of-bastrop-landscape /#:~:text=Since%20moving%20his%20startup%20The,bodega%20and%20a%20 housing%20complex.

92. Matthias, "Richard Hanania"; Ryan Quinn, "After Racist Writings Revealed, Scholar's Link to Texas Center Erased," *Inside Higher Ed*, August 10, 2023, accessed August 25, 2023, https://www.insidehighered.com/news/faculty -issues/academic-freedom/2023/08/10/hananias-name-gone-ut-austin-center -after-expose; "Forbidden Courses," University of Austin, accessed August 25, 2023, https://www.uaustin.org/forbidden-courses; web page for Richard Hanania, *The Origins of Woke: Civil Rights Law, Corporate America, and the Triumph of Identity Politics* (New York: Broadside Books, 2023), accessed February 25, 2024, https://www.harpercollins.com/products/the-origins-of-woke-richard -hanania?variant=41004650528802.

93. For the limited examples of Texas coverage on the Hanania matter, see "Editorial: The University of Texas Must Cut Ties With White Supremacist Richard Hanania," *San Antonio Express-News* August 9, 2023, accessed August 25, 2023, https://www.expressnews.com/opinion/editorial/article/texas-white-supremacist -richard-hanania-18286953.php, and Bryant Bingamon, "New Report Reveals UT

Austin Scholar Wrote for White Supremacist Publications," *Austin Chronicle*, August 9, 2023, accessed August 25, 2023, https://www.austinchronicle.com/daily /news/2023–08–09/new-report-reveals-ut-austin-scholar-wrote-for-white -supremacist-publications/print/. For more on the Natal Conference, see Jason Wilson, "Revealed: Pro-Birth Conference's Links to Far-Right Eugenicists," *Guardian*, September 4, 2023, accessed September 16, 2023, https://www.theguardian .com/us-news/2023/sep/04/natal-conference-austin-texas-eugenics; Louis T. March, "At Last, At Long Last, They've Got the Message: The World Is Running Out of People," *Mercator*, December 18, 2023, accessed February 25, 2024, https:// www.mercatornet.com/at_last_at_long_last_they_ve_got_the_message_the _world_is_running_out_of_people.

94. Renaud Camus, *Le Grande Remplacement* (Paris: David Reinharc: 2011); "Christchurch Shooting: Gunman Tarrant Wanted to Kill 'As Many as Possible,'" BBC August 24, 2020, accessed June 15, 2021, https://www.bbc.com/news/world -asia-53861456; Nicholas Bogel-Burroughs, "'I'm the Shooter': El Paso Suspect Confessed to Targeting Mexicans, Police Say," *New York Times*, August 9, 2019, accessed June 9, 2021, https://www.nytimes.com/2019/08/09/us/el-paso-suspect -confession.html; Robert Moore and Mark Berman, "El Paso Suspect Said He Was Targeting 'Mexicans,' Told Police He Was Shooter," *Washington Post*, August 9, 2019, accessed June 9, 2021, https://www.washingtonpost.com/national /el-paso-suspect-said-he-was-targeting-mexicans-told-officers-he-was-the -shooter-police-say/2019/08/09/ab235e18-bac9–11e9-b3b4–2bb69e8c4e39_story .html.

95. Justin Baragona, "Texas Lt. Guv Spews Racist 'Great Replacement' Theory on Fox: 'A Revolution Has Begun,'" *Daily Beast*, September 21, 2021, accessed February 25, 2024, https://www.thedailybeast.com/texas-lt-gov-dan-patrick-spews -racist-great-replacement-theory-on-fox-news.

96. William Melhado, "Gov. Greg Abbott Embraces "Invasion" Language About Border, Evoking Memories of El Paso Massacre," *Texas Tribune*, November 18, 2022, accessed March 16, 2023, https://www.texastribune.org/2022/11/18 /texas-greg-abbott-immigration-invasion-el-paso/; Justin Miller, "Records Shed Light on Abbott's Secretive Border Wall Boondoggle," *Texas Tribune*, November 7, 2022, accessed March 16, 2023, https://www.texasobserver.org/abbott-border-wall -texas-facilities-commission/; "Battle Grows over Buoys, Razor Wire on US-Mexico Border," *Al Jazeera*, July 24, 2023, accessed February 25, 2024, https://www .aljazeera.com/gallery/2023/7/24/photos-battle-grows-over-buoys-razor-wire-on -us-mexico-border; J. David Goodman and Edgar Sandoval, "Body of Migrant Found in Texas' Buoy Barrier in Rio Grande," *New York Times*, August 3, 2023, accessed February 25, 2024, https://www.nytimes.com/2023/08/03/us/texas-border -buoys-bodies.html.

97. Noah Higgins-Dunn, "Texas Gov. Abbott Blames Covid Spread on Immigrants, Criticizes Biden's 'Neanderthal' Comment," CNBC, March 4, 2021, accessed March 16, 2023, https://www.cnbc.com/2021/03/04/texas-gov-abbott

-blames-covid-spread-on-immigrants-criticizes-bidens-neanderthal-comment
-.html.

98. Karen Norrgard, "Human Testing, the Eugenics Movement, and IRBs," *Nature Education* 1, no. 1 (2008), accessed August 27, 2023, https://www .nature.com/scitable/topicpage/human-testing-the-eugenics-movement-and -irbs-724/.

99. See Michael Karliss, "Study: Texas Ranks As the State With the Lowest Quality of Life," *San Antonio Current*, July 17, 2023, accessed August 26, 2023, https://www.sacurrent.com/news/study-texas-ranks-as-the-state-with-nations -lowest-quality-of-life-32196575.

100. See Ross Ramsey, "Texans Say climate Change is Happening, But It's a Highly Partisan Issue, UT/TT Poll Finds," *Texas Tribune*, November 6, 2019, accessed August 27, 2023, https://www.texastribune.org/2019/11/06/texans-say -climate-change-happening-highly-partisan-issue-uttt-poll/, and Dan Solomon, "What Do Texans Want? Progressive Policies and Conservative Politicians," *Texas Monthly*, February 4, 2022, accessed August 27, 2023, https://www.texasmonthly .com/news-politics/texas-primary-election-2022-polling/.

101. Alwyn Barr, *Black Texans: A History of African Americans in Texas, 1528–1995* (1973; Norman: University of Oklahoma Press, 1996), 140–143.

102. Patrick Boyle, "Why Do So Many Americans Distrust Science?," AAMC, May 4, 2022, accessed August 27, 2023, https://www.aamc.org/news/why-do-so -many-americans-distrust-science.

103. Calum MacKellar and Christopher Bechtel, *The Ethics of the New Eugenics* (New York: Berghahn, 2014), 193.

Select Bibliography

Archival Sources and Government Reports

Barker, Eugene. Letter to Robert Vinson, February 3, 1921, Eugene C. Barker Papers, Box 2B97, General Correspondence, January to March, 1921. BCAH.

———. Letter to Charles Ramsdell, August 19, 1921. Ramsdell Papers, Box 2L465, General Correspondence, January–May 1921. BCAH.

———. Letter to Robert E. Vinson, November 22, 1921, Barker Papers, Box 2B97, General Correspondence, November to December 1921. BCAH.

Bizzell, W. B. Letter to E. E. Davis, January 27, 1936, E. E. Davis Papers, Box 4, Folder 258-4-13. UTA.

Branch, W. M. Letter to John C. Box, August 3, 1926, Oliver Douglas Weeks Collection, Box 2, Folder 3. BLAC.

———. Letter to John C. Box, June 2, 1926. Oliver Douglas Weeks Collection, Box 2, Folder 17. BLAC.

Cunningham, A. F. "Eugenics or the Young Man Foursquare." American Eugenics Society Papers, Folder 575.06:Am3. American Philosophical Society, Philadelphia, Pennsylvania.

Dallas Independent School District Board Minutes, Volumes 16 and 24. Dallas Independent School District Headquarters, Dallas, Texas.

Davis, E. E. Letter to John C. Box, February 4, 1928, Oliver Douglas Weeks Collection, Box 2, Folder 8. BLAC.

———. Letter to H. L. Pritchett, October 7, 1935, E. E. Davis Papers, Box 4, Folder 258-4-12. UTA.

———. Letter to W. B. Bizzell, January 23, 1936, E. E. Davis Papers, Box 4, Folder 258-4-13. UTA.

———. Letter to Will H. Mayes, May 12, 1939, University of Texas at Arlington Office of the President Records, Dean E. E. Davis, Folder 258-12-3. UTA.

———. Letter to George Witte, March 26, 1941, E. E. Davis, Folder 258-20-1. UTA.

Downer, Edward T. "A. Caswell Ellis." In *Skyline: A Quarterly of Cleveland College*, May 1940. Alexander Caswell Ellis Papers, Box 2P23. BCAH.

Duggan, Arthur P. Undated notes for Speech, Arthur P. Duggan Papers, Southwest Collection, Box S 275 2, Folder 3. SWC.

Ellis, Alexander Caswell. Notes for "World Peace Through Education" (speech), Alexander Caswell Ellis Papers, Box 2P62. BCAH.

Evans, Griffin C. Letter to Julian Huxley, March 24, 1913, Julian S. Huxley Papers, General Correspondence, 1904–1919, Box No. 5, Folder 10 (Correspondence - 1913). WRCSC.

Eyman, Elmer V. *Report of the Texas Mental Hygiene Survey, 1924: Psychiatric Study of Public School Children in Eleven Counties, Children in State and County Institutions for Delinquents and Dependents, [and] Inmates of Eleven County Poor Farms Inmates of Eighteen County Jails.* New York: National Committee for Mental Hygiene, December, 1924. BCAH.

Haggerty, M. E., L. M. Terman, E. L. Thorndike, G. M. Whipple, and R. M. Yerkes. "National Intelligence Test, Scale B, Form 1." Alexander Caswell Ellis Papers, Box 4P347. BCAH.

"Herman Joseph Muller, 1890–1967," *Yearbook of the American Philosophical Society* (reprint, 1967). Hermann J. Muller Collection, Series II: Biographical Materials/Memorabilia, 1912–1972, Box 2, Folder 2.23. BCAH.

Higgerson, Josiah. Letter to Gideon Lincecum, March 2, 1856, Gideon Lincecum Collection, Box 2E363, Folder 3. BCAH.

Hobbs, Frank, and Nicole Stoops. *Demographic Trends in the 20th Century: Census 2000 Special Reports.* Washington, DC: United States Bureau of the Census, 2002. Tables A-1, A-3, A-20, A-21, A-25, A-26, C-3. Available online at https://www.census.gov/prod/2002pubs/censr-4.pdf.

Huxley, Julian. "Eugenics and Eugenicists." *Athenaeum*, December 31, 1920. WRSCS.

Jaffray, J. K. Letter to "Elizabeth" L. Ring, August 29, 1921, Mrs. Henry F. "Elizabeth" L. Ring Papers, 1913–1931, Box 2G 445. BCAH.

———. Letter to Sarah King, December 21, 1921, Ring Papers, Correspondence, 1-20-12-30. BCAH.

Journal of the House of Representatives of the Regular Session of the Thirty Eighth Legislature Begun and Held at the City of Austin, January 9, 1923. Austin: Von Boeckmann-Jones Co., 1923.

Journal of the House of Representatives of the Regular Session of the Forty-Fifth Legislature of the State of Texas, Begun and Held at the City of Austin, January 12, 1937, Volume 1. Austin: Capital Printing Company, 1937.

Junior Aggie Yearbook. Arlington: North Texas Agricultural College, 1936.

Knolle, Arthur E. Letter to John C. Box, February 4, 1928, Oliver Douglas Weeks Collection Box 2, Folder 12, Oliver Douglas Weeks Collection. BLAC.

Laughlin, Harry H. Letter to Governor James V. Allred, March 1, 1935, James V. Allred Papers, Sterilization Bill Folder 1985/024-42, 306-21. TSALC.

Lincecum, Gideon. Letter to Parson Lancaster. June 12, 1859, Gideon Lincecum Papers, Box 2E363. BCAH.

———. Journal. Entry for January 11, 1864, Lincecum Collection, Box 2E363, Folder 1. BCAH.

———. Diary. Lincecum Papers Box 2E363, Folder 1, Diary—1867. BCAH.

———. "Personal Reminiscences of an Octogenarian." *American Sportsman*, September 12, 1874. Lincecum Collection, Folder 2010–253, Box 2E514. BCAH.

———. Letter to W. Richardson. 1874, Gideon Lincecum Collection, Box 2E365, Folder 4, Letters from 1873–1899. BCAH.

King, Sarah. Letter to J. K. Jaffray, December 20, 1921, Mrs. Henry F. Ring Papers, 1913–1931, Box 2G 445, Correspondence, 1–20–12–30. BCAH.

———. Letter to Mrs. Henry F. "Elizabeth" L. Ring, March 15, 1922. Ring Papers, 1913–1931, Box 2G 445, Correspondence, 1–20–12–30. BCAH.

Long, Ruby Neale. Letter to Mrs. Henry F. "Elizabeth" L. Ring, May 19, 1924. Ring Papers, Correspondence, 1–20–12–30. BCAH.

McCaa, Robert. "Missing Millions: The Human Cost of the Mexican Revolution." Report by the University of Minnesota Population Center (2001), http://www.hist.umn.edu/~rmccaa/missmill/mxrev.htm.

McDonald, W. C. Letter to John C. Box, April 9, 1928, Oliver Douglas Weeks Collection, Box 2, Folder 17. BLAC.

Merriman, F. H., Letter to Gideon Lincecum, July 13, 1856, Gideon Lincecum Collection, Box 2E363, Folder 3. BCAH.

Miller, C. R., Letter to Harry H. Laughlin, March 7, 1935, Allred Papers, Sterilization Bill Folder 1985/024–42. TSLAC.

Muller, Herman J. "Prepared at Vavilov's, 1936–1937" (typed note). Hermann J. Muller Collection, Series II, Biographical Materials, Memorabilia, 1912–1972, Box 1, Biographical, Folder 1.38, Carnegie Library. CSHL.

———. "Autobiographical Notes Requested of the National Academy of Sciences." Hermann J. Muller Collection, Series II, Box 1, Biographical, Folder 1.38. CSHL.

———. Letter to Edgar Altenburg, December 15, 1935, Hermann J. Muller Collection, Series II, Biographical Materials, Memorabilia, 1912–1972, Box 1, Correspondence Folder 1.3. BCAH.

Peterson, R. O. Letter to E. E. Davis, February 6, 1936, Box 2, Folder 258-2-7, E. E. Davis, Presidents' Papers, University of Texas at Arlington Central Library, Special Collections. UTA.

"Platform of Arthur P. Duggan, Candidate for Congress in the New 19th Congressional District of Texas, 1931." Arthur P. Duggan Sr. Papers, 1860–1942, Box S 275 2, Folder 1. SWC.

Ramsdell, Charles. Letter to Roy Gittinger, October 4, 1917, Charles Ramsdell Papers, Box 2L463, General Correspondence, 1917. BCAH.

———. Letter to James Edmund, Charles Ramsdell Papers, Box 2L463, General Correspondence, 1918. BCAH.

———. Letter to Walter Prescott Webb, July 11, 1923, General Correspondence, January-July 1923. BCAH.

———. Letter to Charles S. Boucher, July 16, 1923, Charles W. Ramsdell Papers, Box 2L466, General Correspondence, January–July 1923. BCAH.

"Religion Not Yet Routed," *Houston Chronicle*, n.d., Julian S. Huxley Papers, General Correspondence, 1916, Box 5, Folder 14. WRCSC.

Smith, Carrie Weaver. "The Elimination of the Reformatory." In *Proceedings of the National Conference of Social Work*. Chicago: University of Chicago Press, 1921. BCAH.

———. Letter to Elizabeth Ring. "A Woman's Reformatory for Women," ca. 1921, Mrs. Henry F. "Elizabeth" L. Ring Papers, 1913–1931, Box 2G 445. BCAH.

Speer, Elizabeth M. Letter to Survey Committee of Texas Committee on Prisons and Prison Labor, August 7, 1924, Ring Papers, 1913–1931, Box 2G 445, Correspondence, 1–20–12–30. BCAH.

Terr, Claude. Letter to Arthur Duggan, November 5, 1934, James V. Allred Papers, Sterilization Bill Folder 1985/024–42. TSL.

Texas Senate Journal, Forty-Fourth Legislature, Regular Session. Austin: Texas Senate, 1935.

United States Bureau of the Census. *Twelfth Census of the United States, Taken in the Year 1900*. Census Reports, Volume II, Population Part II. Washington, DC: United States Census Office, 1902.

———. *Fourteenth Census of the United States, 1920*. Volume II, Population, General Report and Analytical Tables.

———. "Table 1—Color or Race, Nativity, Parentage for the State and Urban and Rural Population, 1920, 1910, 1900," *Fourteenth Census of the United States Taken in the Year 1920, Volume III: Population, 1920—Composition and Characteristics of the Population by State*. Washington, DC: Government Printing Office, 1923.

———, Population Division. "Table 13. Nativity of the Population, for Regions, Divisions, and States: 1850 to 1990." Nativity of the Population, for Regions, Divisions, and States: 1850 to 1990," http://www.census.gov/population/www/documentation/twps0029/tab13.html.

Dissertations and Theses

Ellis, Alexander Caswell. "Suggestions for a Philosophy of Education." PhD diss., Clark University, 1897.

Gunter, Rachel. "More Than Black and White: Woman Suffrage and Voting Rights in Texas, 1918–1923." PhD diss., Texas A&M University, 2017.

Hodge, Chelsea. "'Deserting the Broad and Easy Way,' Southern Methodist Women, the Social Gospel, and the New Deal State, 1909–1939." PhD diss., University of Arkansas, 2020.

Hopkins, Ramona. "Was There a 'Southern' Eugenics? A Comparative Case Study of Eugenics in Texas and Virginia, 1900–1940." Master's thesis, University of Houston, 2009.

Hughes, Allison Leigh. "Turning Bad Girls into Ladies: Female Juvenile Delinquency in Texas in the Twentieth Century." Master's thesis, Texas State University at San Marcos, 2012.

LaGrone, Leah. "A Woman's Worth: Wages, Race, and Respectability in Twentieth-Century Texas." PhD diss., Texas Christian University, 2021.

Roderick, Marshall. "The 'Box Bill': Public Policy, Ethnicity, and Economic Exploitation in Texas." Master's thesis, Texas State University, 2011.

Periodicals

Austin Chronicle
Austin Daily Statesman
Austin Statesman
Baptist Standard (Dallas)
Dallas Daily Times Herald
Dallas Express
Dallas Morning News
Dallas Observer
El Paso Herald
El Paso Times
Eugenical News (Cold Spring Harbor, NY)
Ferguson Forum (Temple, TX)
Fort Worth Record
Fort Worth Star-Telegram
Galveston Daily News
Granbury News
El Heraldo de Brownsville
Houston Post
Lancet-Clinic (Cincinnati)
Laredo Weekly Times
Marshall Messenger
La Prensa de San Antonio
Marysville (California) Appeal-Democrat
Marshall Morning News
El Puerto de Brownsville
Shorthorn University of Texas at Arlington)
Southern Messenger (San Antonio)
Texas 100 Per Cent American (Dallas)
Texas Tribune

Texian Advocate
Tyler Morning Telegraph
Vernon Daily Record.
Washington Evening Star
Washington Post
Wichita Falls Record News
Wichita Falls News
Wichita Falls Times

Books, Journal Articles, and Other Published Sources

Acuña, Rodolfo. *Occupied America: A History of Chicanos*. New York: Harper-Collins Publishers, 1988.

Adams, John A., Jr. *Keepers of the Spirit: The Corps of Cadets at Texas A&M University, 1876–2001*. College Station: Texas A&M University Press, 2001.

Allen, Garland E. "The Eugenics Record Office at Cold Spring Harbor, 1910–1940: An Essay in Institutional History." *Osiris* 2 (1986): 225–264.

———. "Julian Huxley and the Eugenical View of Human Evolution." In *Julian Huxley: Biologist and Statesman of Science*, ed. Kenneth Waters and Albert Van Helden, 193–222. College Station: Texas A&M University Press, 1992.

Anderson, Gary Clayton. *The Conquest of Texas: Ethnic Cleansing in the Promised Land, 1820–1875*. Norman: University of Oklahoma Press, 2005.

Ayers, Edward L. *The Promise of the New South: Life After Reconstruction*. New York: Oxford University Press, 1992.

Baird, Violet M. "Nineteenth Century Medical Journalism in Texas, With a Journal Checklist." *Bulletin of the Medical Library Association*, July 1972.

Barr, Alwyn. *Black Texans: A History of African Americans in Texas, 1528–1995*. Norman: University of Oklahoma Press, 1996.

Bashford, Alison. *The Huxleys: An Intimate History of Evolution*. Chicago: University of Chicago Press, 2022.

Benton-Cohen, Katherine. *Inventing the Immigration Problem: The Dillingham Commission and Its Legacy*. Cambridge, MA: Harvard University Press, 2018.

Berlet, Chip, and Matthew N. Lyons. *Right-Wing Populism in America: Too Close for Comfort*. New York: The Guilford Press, 2000.

Black, Edwin. *War Against the Weak: Eugenics and America's Campaign to Create a Master Race*. New York: Thunder's Mouth Press, 2003.

Bogdan, Robert. *Freak Show: Presenting Human Oddities for Amusement and Profit*. Chicago: University of Chicago Press, 1988.

Boles, John B. *The Education of a University President: Edgar Odell Lovett and the Opening of the Rice Institute*. Houston: Rice Historical Society, 2000.

Box, John C. "Are We to Poison the Lifeblood of the Nation?" *Dearborn Independent*, December 25, 1920.

———. "Immigration Control." *Eugenical News*, September 1927.

Bradford, and T. N. Campbell. "Journal of Lincecum's Travels in Texas, 1835." *Southwestern Historical Quarterly* 53 (October 1949): 180–201.

Brear, Holly Beachley. *Inherit the Alamo: Myth and Ritual at an American Shrine.* Austin: University of Texas Press, 1995.

Brown, Norman D. *Hood, Bonnet, and Little Brown Jug: Texas Politics, 1921–1928.* College Station: Texas A&M University Press, 1984.

Burka, Paul. "Did You Hear the One About the New Aggies?" *Texas Monthly,* April 1997, https://www.texasmonthly.com/news-politics/did-you-hear-the-one -about-the-new-aggies/.

Burkhalter, Lois Wood. *Gideon Lincecum, 1793–1874: A Biography.* Austin: University of Texas Press, 1965.

Burnett, L. D. "In the U.S. Praise for Anglo-Saxon Heritage Has Always Been About White Supremacy," *Washington Post,* April 26, 2021, https://www .washingtonpost.com/outlook/2021/04/26/us-praise-anglo-saxon-heritage -has-always-been-about-white-supremacy/.

Bush, William S. *Who Gets a Childhood? Race and Juvenile Justice in Twentieth-Century Texas.* Athens: University of Georgia Press, 2010.

Carlson, Elof Axel. *The Unfit: A History of a Bad Idea.* Cold Spring Harbor, NY: Cold Spring Harbor Laboratory Press, 2001.

Cashion, Ty. *Lone Star Mind: Reimagining Texas History.* Norman: University of Oklahoma Press, 2018.

Cayleff, Susan E. *Nature's Path: A History of Naturopathic Healing in America.* Baltimore: Johns Hopkins University Press, 2016.

Chalmers, David M. *Hooded Americanism: The History of the Ku Klux Klan.* Durham, NC: Duke University Press, 1987.

Chávez-García, Miroslava. *States of Delinquency: Race and Science in the Making of California's Juvenile Justice System.* Berkeley: University of California Press, 2012.

Cohen, Adam S. "Harvard's Eugenics Era." *Harvard Magazine,* March–April 2016, https://harvardmagazine.com/2016/03/harvards-eugenics-era.

Coleman, Finnie D. Sutton *E. Griggs and the Struggle Against White Supremacy.* Knoxville: University of Tennessee Press, 2007.

Cullen, David O'Donald. "Back to the Future: Eugenics—A Bibliographic Essay." *Public Historian* 29, no. 3 (Summer 2007): 163–175.

Dabney, Lewis Meriwether. *A Memoir and Letters.* New York: privately printed by J. J. Little and Ives Company, 1924.

Daniel, F. E. "Should Insane Criminals, Or Sexual Perverts, Be Allowed to Procreate," *Texas Medical Journal,* August 1893.

———. *Recollections of a Rebel Surgeon (And Other Sketches) Or, In the Doctor's Sappy Days.* Austin: Von Boeckmann, Schutze & Co., 1899.

Daniels, Roger. *Guarding the Golden Door: American Immigration Policy and Immigrants Since 1882.* New York: Hill and Wang, 2004.

Davidson, Chandler. *Race and Class in Texas Politics.* Princeton, NJ: Princeton University Press, 1990.

Davis, Edward Everett. *The White Scourge*. San Antonio: Naylor, 1940.

Dethloff, Henry C. *A Centennial History of Texas A&M University, 1876–1976*. College Station, Texas A&M University Press 1975.

De León, Arnoldo. *They Called Them Greasers: Anglo Attitudes Toward Mexicans in Texas, 1821–1900*. Austin: University of Texas Press, 1983.

Dorr, Gregory Michael Dorr, and Angela Logan. "'Quality, Not Mere Quantity, Counts,' Black Eugenics and the NAACP Baby Contests." In *A Century of Eugenics in America: From the Indiana Experiment to the Human Genome Era*, ed. Paul Lombardo, 68–94. Bloomington and Indianapolis: Indiana University Press, 2011.

———. "Protection or Control? Women's Health Sterilization Abuse and Relf v. Weinberger." In Lombardo, *Century of Eugenics in America*; 161–192.

Du Bois, W. E. B. *The Philadelphia Negro: A Social Study*. Philadelphia: University of Pennsylvania, 1899.

———. "The Talented Tenth," in *The Negro Problem: A Series of Articles by Representative American Negroes of Today*. New York: James Pott, 1903.

Duffy, John. *From Humors to Medical Science: A History of American Medicine*. Urbana: University of Illinois Press, 1993.

Dugger, Ronnie. *Our Invaded Universities: Form, Reform, and New Starts*. New York: W. W. Norton, 1974.

Foley, Neil. *The White Scourge: Mexicans, Blacks, and Poor Whites in Texas Cotton Culture*. Berkeley: University of California Press, 1997.

Friedman, J. M. "Eugenics and the 'New Genetics.'" *Perspectives in Biology and Medicine* 35, no. 1 (Autumn 1991): 145–154.

Galton, David J. "Greek Theories on Eugenics." *Journal of Medical Ethics* 24 (1998): 263–267.

Gibbons, Ann. "There's No Such Thing as a 'Pure' European—Or Anyone Else." *Science*, May 15, 2017, https://www.sciencemag.org/news/2017/05/theres-no-such-thing-pure-european-or-anyone-else.

Glass, Bentley. "Geneticists Embattled: Their Stand against Rampant Eugenics and Racism in America during the 1920s and 1930s." *Proceedings of the American Philosophical Society* 130, no. 1 (March 1986): 130–154.

Glick, Thomas F. *Darwinism in Texas: An Exhibition in the Texas History Center, April 1972*. Austin: Texas History Center, 1972.

Gould, Lewis L. *Progressives and Prohibitionists: Texas Democrats in the Wilson Era*. Austin: Texas State Historical Association, 1992.

Gould, Stephen Jay. *The Mismeasure of Man*. New York: W. W. Norton, 1981.

Grant, Madison. *The Passing of the Great Race or the Racial Basis of European History*. New York: Charles Scribner's Sons, 1916.

Griggs, Sutton E. *Imperium in Imperio: A Study of the Negro Race*. 1899; Sioux Falls, SD: Greenbook Publications, LLC, 2010.

Gruesser, John Cullen. *A Literary Life of Sutton E. Griggs: The Man on the Firing Line*. Oxford, UK: Oxford University Press, 2022.

Hall, Jacquelyn Dowd. *Revolt Against Chivalry: Jessie Daniel Ames and the Women's Campaign Against Lynching*. New York: Columbia University Press, 1993.

Hämäläinen, Pekka. *The Comanche Empire*. New Haven: Yale University Press, 2008.

Herrnstein, Richard J. and Charles Murray. *The Bell Curve: Intelligence and Class Structure in American Life*. New York: Free Press, 1994.

Horn, Joseph M., and John C. Loehlin. *Heredity and Environment in 300 Adoptive Families: The Texas Adoption Project*. New Brunswick, NJ: AldineTransaction, 2010.

Horsman, Reginald. *Race and Manifest Destiny: The Origins of American Anglo-Saxonism*. Cambridge, MA: Harvard University Press, 1981.

Houston, Sam. "Address of Gen. Sam Houston, President Elect, at Houston, November 25, 1841." In *The Writings of Sam Houston, 1813–1863*, ed. Amelia Williams and Eugene Barker, 391–397. Austin: University of Texas Press, 1938.

Hudson, J. Blaine. "Scientific Racism: The Politics of Tests, Race and Genetics." *Black Scholar* 25, no. 1 (Winter 1995): 3–10.

Huxley, Julian. "The Outlook in Biology: A Course of Three Lectures Delivered in the Physics Amphitheatre of the Rice Institute, September 29 and 30, and October I, 1924." *Rice Institute Pamphlet*, October 1924.

Isenberg, Nancy. *White Trash: The 400-Year Untold History of Class in America*. New York: Viking, 2016.

Johnson, Benjamin Heber. *Revolution in Texas: How a Forgotten Rebellion and its Bloody Suppression Turned Mexicans in Americans*. New Haven: Yale University Press, 2003.

Jordan, Terry G., John L. Bean Jr., and Michael M. Holmes. *Texas: A Geography.*. Boulder, CO: Westview Press, 1984.

Jordan, Terry G. "A Century and a Half of Ethnic Change in Texas, 1836–1986." *Southwestern Historical Quarterly* 89 (April 1986): 385–422.

Keasbey, Lindley M. "Competition." *Bulletin of the University of Texas*, January 15, 1908.

Kevles, Daniel J. *In the Name of Eugenics: Genetics and the Uses of Human Heredity*. Cambridge, MA: Harvard University Press, 1985.

Kline, Wendy. *Building a Better Race: Gender, Sexuality, and Eugenics from the Turn of the Century to the Baby Boom*. Berkeley: University of California Press, 2001.

Knight, Alan. "Racism, Revolution, and Indigenismo: Mexico, 1910–1940." n *The Idea of Race in Latin America, 1870–1940*, ed. Richard Graham, 71–113. Austin: University of Texas Press, 1990.

Kohn, Marek. *The Race Gallery: The Return of Racial Science*. London: Vintage, 1995.

Laboure, Theodorus. "The Morality and Lawfulness of Vasectomy." *Ecclesiastical Review*, May 1911.

Largent, Mark A. *Breeding Contempt: The History of Coerced Sterilization in the United States*. New Brunswick, NJ: Rutgers University Press, 2011.

Larson, Edward J. *Sex, Race, and Science: Eugenics in the Deep South.* Baltimore: Johns Hopkins University Press, 1995.

Leon, Sharon M. In *the Image of God: The Catholic Struggle with Eugenics.* Chicago: University of Chicago Press, 2013.

Levine, Philippa. *Eugenics: A Very Short Introduction.* Oxford, UK: Oxford University Press, 2017.

Lewis, David Levering. *W. E. B. Du Bois: The Fight for Equality and the American Century, 1919–1963.* New York: Henry Holt and Company, 2000.

Lincecum, Gideon. "The Cutting Ant of Texas: Oecodoma, Texana Buckley." *Proceedings of the Academy of Natural Sciences of Philadelphia* 19 (1867); 24–31.

Lincecum, Jerry Bryan, and Edward Hake Phillips, eds. *Adventures of a Frontier Naturalist: The Life and Times of Dr. Gideon Lincecum.* College Station: Texas A&M University Press, 1994.

———, Edward Hake Phillips, and Peggy A. Redshaw, eds. *Science on the Texas Frontier: Observations of Dr. Gideon Lincecum.* College Station: Texas A&M University Press, 1997.

Lira, Natalie. *Laboratory of Deficiency: Sterilization and Confinement in California, 1900–1950s.* Berkeley: University of California Press, 2021.

Locke, Joseph P. *Making the Bible Belt: Texas Prohibitionists and the Politicization of Southern Religion.* Oxford, UK: Oxford University Press, 2017.

Loehlin, John C., Gardner Lindzey, and J. H. Spuhler. *Race Difference in Intelligence.* San Francisco: W. H. Freeman and Company, 1975.

López-Durán, Fabiola, and Adrienne Rooney. "Unveiling the Layers: Interview with the Racial Geography Project," Rice Design Alliance, May 16, 2022, https://www.ricedesignalliance.org/racialgeographyproject-interview.

Lucko, Paul M. "Counteracting Reform: Lee Simmons and the Texas Prison System." *East Texas Historical Journal* 30, no. 2 (1992): 19–29.

Ludmerer, Kenneth M. "Genetics, Eugenics, and the Immigration Restriction Act of 1924." *Bulletin of the History of Medicine,* January–February 1972.

Lundberg, John R. "The Great Texas 'Bear Fight': Progressivism and the Impeachment of James E. Ferguson." In *Impeached: The Removal of Texas Governor James E. Ferguson,* ed. Jessica Brannon-Wranosky and Bruce A. Glasrud, 13–52. College Station: Texas A&M University Press, 2017;.

"Mainstream Science on Intelligence." *Wall Street Journal,* December 13, 1994, https://www1.udel.edu/educ/gottfredson/reprints/1994WSJmainstream.pdf.

Matthews, Charles R. *Higher Education in Texas: Its Beginnings to 1970.* Denton: University of North Texas Press, 2018.

MacKellar, Calum, and Christopher Bechtel. *The Ethics of the New Eugenics.* New York: Berghahn, 2014.

Mehlman, Maxwell J. "Modern Eugenics and the Law." In Lombardo, *Century of Eugenics in America,* 219–240.

Merritt, Keri Leigh. *Masterless Men: Poor Whites and Slavery in the Antebellum South.* New York: Cambridge University Press, 2017.

Mitchell, Michele. *Righteous Propagation: African Americans and the Politics of Racial Destiny After Reconstruction.* Chapel Hill: University of North Carolina Press, 2004.

Molina, Natalie. *Fit to Be Citizens?: Public Health and Race in Los Angeles, 1879–1939.* Berkeley: University of California Press, 2006.

Montejano, David. *Anglos and Mexicans in the Making of Texas, 1836–1986.* Austin: University of Texas Press, 1987.

Muller, Hermann Joseph. *Out of the Night: A Biologist's View of the Future.* New York: Vanguard Press, 1935.

Newcomb, W. W., Jr. *The Indians of Texas: From Prehistoric to Modern Times.* Austin: University of Texas Press, 1993.

Ngai, Mae M. "Nationalism, Immigration Control, and the Ethnoracial Remapping of America in the 1920s." OAH Magazine of History, July 2007.

Nies, Betsy L. "Defending Jeeter: Conservative Arguments Against Eugenics in the Depression Era South." In *Popular Eugenics: National Efficiency and American Mass Culture in the 1930s,* ed. Susan Currell and Christina Cogdell, 10–139. Athens: Ohio University Press, 2006.

Nixon, Pat Ireland. "A Pioneer Texas Emasculator: A Chapter from the Life of Dr. Gideon Lincecum," *Texas State Journal of Medicine,* May 1940.

Nourse, Victoria F. *In Reckless Hands: Skinner v. Oklahoma and the Near Triumph of American Eugenics.* New York: W. W. Norton, 2008.

Okrent, Daniel. *The Guarded Gate: Bigotry, Eugenics, and the Law That Kept Two Generations of Jews, Italians, and Other European Immigrants Out of America.* New York: Scribner, 2019.

Ortega, Frances. "Hidden Symbols and Secrets at Rice University," *Houston Chronicle,* August 18, 2015, https://www.chron.com/life/slideshow/Hidden-symbols-and-secrets-at-Rice-University-115444.php.

Paul, Diane. *Controlling Human Heredity and The Politics of Heredity: Essays on Eugenics, Biomedicine, and the Nature-Nurture Debate.* Albany: State University Press of New York, 1995.

———. *Controlling Human Heredity: 1865 to the Present.* Amherst, NY: Humanity Books, 1998.

———. "The Value of Diversity in Huxley's Eugenics," in Waters and Van Helden, *Julian Huxley;* 223–229.

Perkinson, Robert. *Texas Tough: The Rise of America's Prison Empire.* New York: Picador, 2010.

Pernick, Martin S. *The Black Stork: Eugenics and the Death of "Defective" Babies in American Medicine and Motion Pictures Since 1915.* New York: Oxford University Press, 1996.

Pickens, Donald K. *Eugenics and the Progressives.* Nashville: Vanderbilt University Press, 1968.

Pierce, Jason E. *Making the White Man's West: Whiteness and the Creation of the American West.* Boulder: University of Colorado Press, 2016.

Poskett, James. *Materials of the Mind: Phrenology, Race, and the Global History of Science, 1815–1920*. Chicago: University of Chicago Press, 2019.

Prentice, Claire. "The Igorrote Tribe Traveled the World for Show and Made These Two Men Rich," Smithsonian Magazine, October 14, 2014, http://www .smithsonianmag.com/history/igorrote-tribe-traveled-world-these-men-took -all-money-180953012/.

Preuss, Gene B. *To Get a Better School System: One Hundred Years of Education Reform in Texas*. College Station: Texas A&M University Press, 2009.

Reagan, Leslie. *When Abortion Was a Crime: Women, Medicine, and Law in the United States, 1867–1973*. Berkeley: University of California Press, 1997.

Reilly, Philip R. *The Surgical Solution: A History of Involuntary Sterilization in the United States*. Baltimore: Johns Hopkins University Press, 1991.

Reynolds, Cecil R., and Arthur R. Jensen. "WISC-R Subscale Patterns of Abilities of Blacks and Whites Matched on Full Scale IQ." *Journal of Educational Psychology*, 75, no. 2 (1983): 207–214.

Rose, Sarah F. *No Right to Be Idle: The Invention of Disability, 1840s–1930s*. Chapel Hill: University of North Carolina Press, 2017.

Rosen, Christine. *Preaching Eugenics: Religious Leaders and the American Eugenics Movement*. Oxford, UK: Oxford University Press, 2004.

"Rice University Task Force on Segregation, Slavery, and Injustice." June 2021, https://rice.app.box.com/s/724h7kq3gj3g6d4khj52mmouxtqidq1e.

Saini, Angela. *Superior: The Return of Race Science*. Boston: Beacon Press, 2019.

|Samelson, Franz and Leon J. Kamin. "On the Science and Politics of the IQ." *Social Research* 42, no. 3 (Autumn 1975); 467–492.

Sánchez, George J. *Becoming Mexican American: Ethnicity, Culture, and Identity in Chicano Los Angeles, 1900–1945*. New York: Oxford University Press, 1993.

Saxon, Gerald D. *Transitions: A Centennial History of the University of Texas at Arlington, 1895–1995*. Arlington: The UTA Press, 1995.

Schoen, Johanna. "Reassessing Sterilization: The Case of North Carolina." In Lombardo, *Century of Eugenics in America*, 141–160.

Schwartz, James. *In Pursuit of the Gene: From Darwin to DNA*. New York: Harper & Row, 2008.

Schweik, Susan M. *The Ugly Laws: Disability in Public*. New York: New York University Press, 2009.

Shah, Courtney. "The Woman's Department: Maternalism and Feminism in the Texas Medical Journal," *Historian* 64, no. 1 (Fall 2001): 81–98.

Shelton, Robert S. "On Empire's Shore: Free and Unfree Workers in Galveston, Texas, 1840–1860." *Journal of Social History* 40, no. 3 (Spring 2007): 717–730.

Slobodian, Quinn, and Stuart Schrader. "The White Man Unburdened: How Charles Murray Stopped Worrying and Learned to Love Racism." *Baffler*, July–August 2018.

Slotkin, Richard. *Gunfighter Nation: The Myth of the Frontier in Twentieth-Century America*. Norman: University of Oklahoma Press, 1998.

Smallwood, W. M., Ida L. Reveley, and Guy A. Bailey. New Biology. New York: Allyn and Bacon, 1934.

Smith, Carrie Weaver. "The Unadjusted Girl." Social Hygiene, October 1920.

——. "Andrew's Raid: A Ballad." Railway and Locomotive Historical Society Bulletin, October 1943.

Spiro, Jonathan Peter. Defending the Master Race: Conservation, Eugenics, and the Legacy of Madison Grant. Burlington: University of Vermont Press, 2009.

Stepan, Naney Leys. "The Hour of Eugenics": Race, Gender, and Nation in Latin America. Ithaca, NY: Cornell University Press, 1991.

Stern, Alexandra Mina. Eugenic Nation: Faults and Frontiers of Better Breeding in Modern America. Berkeley: University of California Press, 2005.

Stoddard, Lothrop. The Rising Tide of Color Against White World Supremacy. New York: Charles Scribner's Sons, 1920.

——. The Revolt against Civilization: The Menace of the Under Man. New York: Charles Scribner's Sons, 1922.

Stuckey, Sterling. Slave Culture: Nationalist Theory and the Foundations of Black America. New York: Oxford University Press, 1987.

Tucker, William H. The Funding of Scientific Racism: Wickliffe Draper and the Pioneer Fund. Urbana: University of Illinois Press, 2002.

Vasquez, Lucio. "Statue of Rice Founder to be Relocated After Criticism of the University's Racist Past." Houston Public Media, January 26, 2022, https://www.houstonpublicmedia.org/articles/news/education-news/2022/01/26/417683/statue-of-rice-founder-to-be-relocated-in-response-to-criticism-regarding-universitys-lack-of-diversity/

Walker, Randolph Meade. The Metamorphosis of Sutton E. Griggs: The Transition from Back Radical to Conservative, 1913–1933. Memphis: Walker Publishing, 1991.

Warren, Kenneth W. "Perfecting the Political Romance: The Last Novel of Sutton Griggs." In Jim Crow, Literature and the Legacy of Sutton E. Griggs, ed. Tess Chakkalakal and Kenneth Warren, 254–282. Athens: University of Georgia Press, 2013.

Waters, C. Kenneth and Albert Van Helden. Preface to Waters and Van Helden, Julian Huxley; v–vii.

Wiebe, Robert H. The Search for Order, 1877–1920. New York: Hill and Wang, 1967.

Wiley, Nancy. The Great State Fair of Texas: An Illustrated History. Dallas: Taylor Publishing Company, 2000.

Wilkison, Kyle. "The Evils of Socialism: The Religious Right in Early Twentieth-Century Texas." in The Texas Right: The Radical Roots of Lone Star Conservatism, ed. David O'Donald Cullen and Kyle G. Wilkison, 34–50. College Station: Texas A&M University Press, 2014.

Woodson, Carter. The Miseducation of the Negro. 1933; Trenton, NJ: Africa World Press, 1990.

Yoakum, Clarence S. and Robert M. Yerkes. *Army Mental Tests*. New York: Henry Holt and Company, 1920.

Yoakum, Clarence Stone. "Care of the Feeble-Minded and Insane in Texas." *Bulletin of the University of Texas*, November 5, 1914.

Zenderland, Leila. *Measuring Minds: Henry Herbert Goddard and the Origins of American Intelligence Testing*. Cambridge, MA: Cambridge University Press, 2001.

Index

ableism, 1, 2, 4, 8, 9, 14, 74–75, 90–92, 138, 172, 211

abortion: acceptance of, 53–55, 193–195, 210; African American opposition to, 92; and anti-abortion politics in the United States, 53–54; ban in Texas, 53–54; and the Catholic Church, 53; and the *Dobbs* decision, 194; eugenicists and, 38, 55–56, 192–193; the S.M. Jenkins murder trial and, 54–55; racism and, 53–56; *Roe v. Wade* and, 194; the sexual double standard and, 57; Texas opposition to, 54, 56–57, 193–195; and the Texas Medical Association, 193–194. *See also* Black eugenics; Catholic Church; Daniel, Ferdinand Eugene (F. E.)

African American population in Texas, 94, 129–130

allopathy, 31–32, 53

Allred, James, 174–175

American Eugenics Society, 83, 88, 99–100; and the *Eugenics Catechism*, 99; and the eugenics sermon contest, 99–100

Anglo-Saxonism, 19–21

anti-Blackness, 5, 15, 20–21, 26, 37, 40; 45–46, 51, 53, 57, 66, 90–92, 129–130, 132, 153, 178, 180, 188, 198, 200, 204, 208, 210. *See also* Bell Curve, *The*; Daniel, Ferdinand Eugene (F. E.); Davis, Edward Everett; Hanania, Richard; Lincecum, Gideon; Rice Institute; Rushton, Philippe J.; State Fair of Texas; University of Texas at Austin

anti-Darwinism, 67–68, 127–128. *See also* University of Texas at Austin

anti-intellectualism, 209

anti-miscegenation" laws, 193, 205

Army IQ tests, 143–145. *See also* Yerkes, Robert; Yoakum, Clarence Stone

Austin State Hospital, 190

Baptist Standard, 98–99

Barker, Eugene, 135, 137

Bell Curve, The: support by Texas academics, 199, 201–202, 253; summary, 199–201. *See also* Cohen, David B.; Draper, Wycliffe; Herrnstein, Richard; Horn, Joseph M.; Loehlin, John C.; Murray, Charles; Reynolds, Cecil R.; Schoenfeldt, Lyle F.; Willerman, Lee better baby and fitter family contests, 88–89

Binet, Alfred: and his concerns about use of his intelligence tests, 143; and invention of intelligence tests, 142–143; and skull measurements, 142; and the Stanford-Binet test, 143

Black eugenics, 92–92; and baby contests, 93–95; *Dallas Express* and, 93–94; W.E.B. Du Bois and, 92–93; and homosexuality, 92; and masturbation, 92. *See also* Griggs, Sutton R.

Black Stork, The, 87–88

Boas, Franz, 168

Box, John C.: antisemitism of, 51, 146–148; and Armenians, 147–148; background of, 146; *Dearborn Independent* column by, 146–148; and Edward Everett Davis, 16, 169; and the Johnson-Reed Act, 10, 144, 154; and literacy requirements for immigrants, 148; and Mexican immigration quotas, 144, 153–155, 158–159–162; and political supporters of, 158; xenophobia of, 2, 144–145, 147, 155, 167, 206. *See also* Davis, Edward Everett

Bramlette, E. F., 74–75

Brumby, William, 47

Buck v. Bell, 173, 190, 246

Burbank, Luther, 82–83, 147, 208

Bush, George W., 196–197

California: esteem of education in, 9, 64, 83,129, 131; eugenics in 9–10, 71, 73, 82, 131–133, 137, 165, 188–189, 208; reparations for eugenics victims in, 189; science leadership in, 82; and sterilization laws, 132–133, 188–189; and white supremacist ideology in,

82. *See also* Davis, Gray; Ehrlich, Paul; Jordan, David Starr; Popenoe, Paul; Terman, Lewis

Carnegie Institute, 13, 76, 187

Carpenter, Rep. Lewis, 157–158

castration of prisoners, 195–197

Catholic Church: and abortion, 53, 97; and anti-Catholicism, 43, 98, 160; and anti-eugenics activism, 98, 167, 169, 174, 192; and birth control, 97–98; and doctrine on eugenics, 73, 97–98, 173–174; and growth in Texas, 50–51, 174. *See also* Laboure, Theo

Chinese immigrants, 16, 47, 52–53, 147

Cohen, David B., 200. See also *Bell Curve, The*; University of Texas at Austin

Cook, W.G., 78

Crow, Harlan, 203, 205

Cunningham, A.F.: James Ferguson nomination of, 135; sermon on eugenics, 99–100

Dabney, Lewis Meriwether: anti-Mexican racism of, 108–109; antisemitism of, 109; background of, 107; classism of, 5, 107, 11; contempt for democracy of, 107–108, 110; death of, 111; eugenics beliefs of, 109–111, and higher education, 109; influence of, 236–237; Lothrop Stoddard's influence on, 110; Madison Grant's influence on, 16, 106–107; racial classifications of, 110; on religion, 107; and Robert Dabney, 66; xenophobia of, 2, 107, 109. 206. *See also* Grant, Madison; Stoddard, Lothrop

Daffan, Katie: and eugenics, 133–134; and women's clubs, 133–134. *See also*

Ferguson, James "Jim"; Ferguson, Miriam "Ma"

Dallas Morning News: coverage of "Better Baby" contests, 89; and coverage of "freak shows," 91–92; support for eugenics, 172–173

Daniel, Ferdinand Eugene (F. E.): ableism of, 38; abortion and, 38, 55–56, 192–193; advice to doctors, 39; and capital punishment, 61, 68–70; and Confederate military service, 44; death of, 42, 71, 73, 149; eugenics beliefs of, 39, 41–42, 46–47, 50, 60, 69; homophobia of, 38, 58, 60–61; human medical experimentation and, 69–70; influence of, 38, 58; on marriage laws, 60; and masturbation, 61–62; as a medical journalist, 2, 39–40, 42; opposition to democracy and, 5, 46; personality of, 39–40, 44, 61; poor whites and, 45, 209; Progressive politics of, 5, 40–42; racism of, 5, 44–47, 61, 71; and *Recollections of a Rebel Surgeon*, 39; and the "Sanitary Utopia," 62; and secession, 44; and slavery, 44; and sterilization, 2, 8, 41–43, 61–62, 72–73, 78–80; Texas Medical Association and, 42, 72; and *The Strange Case of Dr. Bruno*, 68–70; xenophobia of, 38, 45–46, 206. *See also* abortion; Daniel, Josephine; homosexuality; Progressives

Daniel, Josephine, 72. *See also* Daniel, Ferdinand Eugene (F. E.)

Davenport, Charles, 4, 13, 76, 83, 99, 104, 152, 178, 207, 226. *See also* Eugenics Records Office; Kellogg, John Harvey; Smith, Carrie Weaver

Davis, Edward Everett: anti-Black racism of, 178, 180, 182;
anti-democratic sentiments of, 183–184; anti-Mexican racism of, 2, 160, 167, 178, 180, 182, 184, 206–207; antisemitism of, 51, 182–183; background of, 177; and John C. Box, 16, 160, 169; and C. W. Post, 177–178; classism of, 5, 178–179, 182; cotton industry and, 179–182; and David Starr Jordan, 182; eugenics belief of 12, 16, 181–182; genocidal discourse of, 184; and Lothrop Stoddard, 16, 160; and Madison Grant, 16; and North Texas Agricultural College, 2, 5, 12, 179; removal of his name from University of Texas at Arlington administrative building, 184–185; reputation of, 180, 184; and sterilization, 184; and *The White Scourge*, 180–184. *See also* Box, John C.; Grant, Madison; North Texas Agricultural College; Jordan, David Starr; Post, C. W.; Stoddard, Lothrop

Davis, Gray, 189. *See also* California

Dies, Martin, 162. *See also* Box, John C.

Dougherty, W. F., 74–75

Draper, Wycliffe, 200. See also *Bell Curve, The*; Herrnstein, Richard; Horn, Joseph M.; Loehlin, John C.; Murray, Charles; Pioneer Fund; Willerman, Lee

Duggan, Arthur: background of, 171; on crime, 170–172; death of, 175; on education, 171; and the poor, 171; his sterilization bill, 171–172, 192

Ehrlich, Paul, 188. *See also* California

Eliot, Charles Williams, 25. *See also* Harvard University and eugenics

Ellis, Alexander Caswell: and better baby contests, 89; as eugenics popularizer, 2, 86–87, 155–156; firing by the University of Texas, 135; hiring by the University of Texas, 85; on human evolution, 85; on immigrants, 144; and IQ tests, 105, 155–156; philosophy of education and, 85; and the Texas Committee on Prisons and Prison Labor, 105; and the Texas State Society of Social Hygiene, 72. *See also* Ferguson, James "Jim"; fitter family and better baby contests; Progressives; Texas Mental Health Agency; University of Texas at Austin

Emergency Quota Act of 1921, 153, 158

eugenics: in Alabama, 81; as an anti-democratic discourse, 5, 11–12, 36, 43, 63, 183–184; as an apocalyptic discourse, 4–5, 14–15, 146–147, 170, 183–184; in Arkansas, 186, 216; in Arizona, 82; and biological determinism, 7–8, 143, 189; in Brazil, 6; and class politics, 2–4, 5, 8, 11–12, 16–17, 24, 28, 38, 40, 43, 47–48, 63, 73, 80–81, 110–111, 130, 140–142, 149, 159–161, 170–172, 175, 178, 182, 188–189, 200, 209; ; in Colorado, 216; in Connecticut, 71, 138; and crime, 2–3, 8, 28, 33–34, 38, 50, 61, 71, 76, 83, 98, 189; critics of, 168–169; and "defectives," 2, 4, 6, 46, 58, 61, 70, 74, 76–78; defined, 3, 6; and eugenic segregation, 150; in Finland, 17; and the First International Eugenics Conference, 25; flawed reasoning in, 208–209; in Florida, 216; in France, 17; in Georgia, 12, 165, 176; in Germany, 6, 17; in Great Britain, 6; Holocaust and, 6, 187; and homophobia, 58, 92, 175; in Idaho, 155; in Illinois, 216; in Indiana, 7, 13, 28, 70–71; in Iowa, 68; in Italy, 17; in Japan, 6, 17; in Kentucky, 216; in Louisiana, 186, 216; in Mexico, 6, 17, 165–167; in Maine, 155; marriage laws and, 3, 10, 70–71, 77, 138–140; in Maryland, 216; in Massachusetts, 216; in Michigan, 71; in Minnesota, 155; in Missouri, 216; in Nebraska, 81; in New Jersey, 71; in New Mexico, 81, 186, 216; in New York, 71; in North Carolina, 81, 189; and neo-eugenics, 187–189; in Ohio, 216; in Oregon, 81; in Pennsylvania, 216; in Poland, 17; in Puerto Rico, 71; "race suicide" and, 12, 46, 53–54, 57; in Rhode Island, 216; in South Carolina, 165; in South Dakota, 81; in the Southern United States, 3–4, 22, 26, 80–81, 129, 140, 144, 150, 169, 176, 185, 206; in the Southwestern United States 81–82; in the Soviet Union, 17; in Switzerland, 17; in Tennessee, 216; in Turkey, 17; ubiquity of, 6, 8–10, 13; in Utah, 155; and utopian hopes for, 4, 6–7, 13; in Vermont, 165; in Virginia, 165, 189; and "visual defects," 74–76; in Wyoming, 216. *See also* Black eugenics; Eugenics Records Office

Eugenics Records Office: and Carrie Weaver Smith, 14, 104; and David Starr Jordan, 132; and the *Eugenical News*, 14; and eugenics field workers, 104; impact of the Holocaust on, 187; and Robert Yerkes, 152; and "visual defect," 75; work of, 14, 76–77. *See also* Davenport, Charles; Jordan, David Starr; Smith; Carrie Weaver; Yerkes, Robert

euthanasia, 6, 13, 68

Evans, Hiram Wesley, 106, 111. *See also* Ku Klux Klan

Ferguson, James "Jim": and attitudes towards higher education, 128, 136–140, 142, 209; and eugenics, 133–134; as governor, 135–136; impeachment of, 136; the University of Texas and, 25, 133–137. *See also* University of Texas at Austin

Ferguson, Miriam "Ma": and attitudes towards higher education, 128, 142, 209; University of Texas and, 25, 133, 140. *See also* University of Texas at Austin

fitter family and better baby contests, 9, 88–90, 92, 94, 133, 168

Ford, Henry, 146–147. *See also* Box, John C.; Jews

Gainesville (Tex.) School for Girls, 14, 73, 77, 102–105. *See also* Smith, Carrie Weaver

Galton, Francis, 6, 37

Gamio, Manuel, 166. *See also* Mexicans and Mexican-Americans

Garner, John Nance, 160

Goddard, Henry H., 83, 94, 143. *See also* Army IQ tests; Binet, Alfred; Yerkes, Robert; Yoakum, Clarence Stone

Graham, Sylvester, 59

Grant, Madison: antisemitism of, 15; on democracy, 107; ideology of, 12; 106; influence in Texas, 14, 106–107, 110–112; and influence in the United States, 16, 106, 135, 200; and racial classifications, 14–15, 106–107; and support for euthanasia and genocide, 15. *See also* Dabney, Lewis Meriwether; Davis, Edward Everett; Ku Klux Klan

Graves, M. L., 49

"great replacement theory," 206–207; echoed by Gov. Greg Abbott, 207; echoed by Lt. Gov. Dan Patrick, 206–207; history of, 206

Griggs, Sutton R.: and Black history, 95–96; elitism of, 95–97; and eugenics in his novels, 96–97. *See also* Black eugenics

Hanania, Richard: as an "alt-right" activist, 203–204; eugenics and, 203–204; influence of, 204–205; as a lecturer at the University of Austin, 205; and racism of, 203–204; and Richard Spencer, 203; as a visiting scholar at the University of Texas, 203, 205. *See also* Spencer, Richard; University of Texas at Austin; Weiss, Bari

Harvard University and eugenics, 14, 25, 53, 62–64, 76, 85, 147, 152, 153, 199–200. *See also* Davenport, Charles; Eliot, Charles; Herrnstein, Richard; Howe, Lucien; Stoddard, Lothrop; Ward, Lester; Yerkes, Robert

Herrnstein, Richard, 199–200. See also *Bell Curve, The*; Murray, Charles; Pioneer Fund; Harvard University and eugenics

Hogg, James, 61, 71

Hogg, Will, 135

homeopathy, 31, 40

homosexuality: as an "atavism," 59–60; and eugenics, 32, 175; as a health threat, 59, 92; as an identity, 58; laws against, 58, 60; terms for, 58. *See also* Daniel, Ferdinand Eugene (F. E.); Lincecum, Gideon

Horn, Joseph M., 200–203. See also *Bell Curve, The*; Horn, Joseph M.; The Texas Adoption Project; Pioneer Fund; University of Texas at Austin; Willerman, Lee

Houston, Sam: and Anglo-Saxonism, 21; and attitudes towards higher education, 64

Howe, Lucien, 76. *See also* Harvard University and eugenics

Hull, Theodore Young, 72. *See also* the Texas State Society of Social Hygiene

humoral theory of disease, 29

Huxley, Julian: beliefs about race, 162–163; on the Comstock Act,128; on democracy, 129–130; and the hiring of Hermann Joseph Muller, 128; mental health struggles of, 127; the religious beliefs of, 127–128; reputation of, 133, 162; at the Rice Institute, 9, 127, 129, 203; socialism of, 128. *See also* Muller, Hermann Joseph

immigrants: and disease, 43, 47–48, 147; and intelligence, 10, 132, 141, 152, 153, 156; and mental illness, 48; and racialization, 43, 45–47, 147, 153, 156; and supposed radicalism, 43, 47; and restrictions on entry into the United States, 145, 147, 153; and xenophobia, 144, 147, 150, 154, 178

intelligence tests, 10, 77, 131, 141–144, 152–153, 155–157

Jensen, Arthur, 202

Jews: and antisemitism in Texas, 2, 48, 51, 109, 18–183, 206; and antisemitism in the United States, 144, 146 183; and the *Dearborn Independent*, 146–148; and the "Galveston Plan," 51; and the "great replacement theory," 206; and *The Protocols of the Elders of Zion*, 146. *See also* Box, John C.; Dabney, Lewis Meriwether; Davis, Edward Everett; *Dearborn Independent*; "great replacement theory"

Johnson-Reed or National Origins Act (1924), 10, 112, 144, 154; John C.

Box's role in, 10, 144, 154; Mexican immigrants not included in, 17, 145, 157–158, 160–161; impact of, 112. *See also* Army IQ tests; Binet, Alfred; Yerkes, Robert; Yoakum, Clarence Stone

Jordan, David Starr: and pessimism during World War I, 168; presidency of Stanford University, 131; prestige and influence of, 25, 83, 131, 133, 135–136, 147, 208; in *The White Scourge*, 182. *See also* California and *The White Scourge*

"Jukes" family, 50

"Kallikak" family, 83, 88

Keasby, Lindley M.: and eugenics, 86; and socialism, 86, 136; firing of, 136. *See also* Ferguson, James "Jim"; University of Texas at Austin

Kellogg, John Harvey, 177–178. *See also* Post, C. W.

Ku Klux Klan: embrace of eugenics, 111–112; Madison Grant's influence on, 16, 106, 111–112; and immigration, 153, 206. *See also* Wilmans, Edith

LaBoure, Theo, 97–98, 169. *See also* Catholic Church

Lamarkism, 166

Laughlin, Harry Hamilton, 76–77, 168–169, 174–175. *See also* Eugenics Records Office

Lincecum, Gideon: and allopathy, 31; and ant "slavery," 30; arrival in Texas, 29; and capital punishment; 8, 33, 35; and castration, 2, 7, 28–29, 32–34, 36–37, 195; and Charles Darwin, 30–31; and Edmund J. Davis, 37; embarrassment over his education, 30; ; and Erasmus Darwin, 30–31; and homeopathy, 31;

limited influence of, 8, 37; on marriage, 34; and his "Memorial," 28, 33–34; and opposition to his eugenics proposals, 33, 35–36; proto-eugenics theories of, 6–8, 28–29, 31–32; racism of, 33, 37; religious skepticism of, 30–31; scientific contributions of, 6; on sex, 32; support for, 35–36, 37; utopianism of, 7, 28, 34. *See also* allopathy, homeopathy; homosexuality; humoral theory of disease; phrenology; slavery

Loehlin, John C., 200–203. See also *Bell Curve, The*; Horn, Joseph P.; the Texas Adoption Project; Pioneer Fund; University of Texas at Austin; Willerman, Lee

Lovett, Edgar Odell: admiration for Francis Galton, 126; background of, 126; and class politics, 209; eugenics and, 9, 126, 131, 162; and the hiring of Julian Huxley, 127; as president of reputation of, 133; Rice Institute, 9, 126–128, 131. *See also* Galton, Francis; Huxley, Julian; Muller, Hermann Joseph; Rice Institute

lynching, 23, 92, 129–130

masturbation: as an "atavism," 59–60; and eugenics, 38, 71, 92; as a "health threat," 58–59; suppression of, 59, 62. *See also* Black eugenics

Mendelism, 166

Mexicans and Mexican-Americans: and anti-Mexican racism, 21–22, 25, 90–91, 108–109, 132, 144–145, 153–161, 178, 180, 182, 184, 188, 198, 210; and anti-Mexican violence, 129–130, 162; eugenics views of, 165–168, 190–191; as portrayed in *The White Scourge*, 182, 184; and repatriation and deportation in the Great

Depression, 162, 192; and their role as workers, 47–48, 73, 131, 144–145, 158–159, 160–161, 180, 192; as viewed by Anglo eugenicists, 132, 144, 159–160. *See also* Box, John C. and Davis, Edward Everett

Muller, Hermann Joseph: anti-racism of, 163; background of, 163; communism and, 163–164; departure from UT and, 164–165; eugenics views of, 13, 163–164; Nobel Prize won by, 163, and *Out of the Night*, 164; reputation of, 133, 163; at the Rice Institute, 9, 127–129; in the Soviet Union, 164–165; at the University of Texas, 163–165, 203. *See also* Lovett, Edgar Odell; Huxley, Julian

Murray, Charles, 199–200. See also *Bell Curve, The*; Herrnstein, Richard; Pioneer Fund

Musk, Elon: and "longtermism," 204–205; and Richard Hanania, 204; and "race science," 253–254; in Texas, 253. *See also* Hanania, Richard

Native Americans, 18–22, 26; 104, 166, 188

Neff, Pat, 112

North Texas Agricultural College, 179, 184–185. *See also* Davis, Edward Everett

Obama, Barack, 189

Oklahoma: eugenics in, 165, 186; Progressive politics in, 186; *Skinner* decision and its impact, 186–187

phrenology, 29

Pickens, William P., 93. *See also* Black eugenics

Pilcher, Hoyt, 62

Pioneer Fund: history of, 198, 200–201; and Texas academia, 198–201

poor whites: political unreliability and racialization of, 1, 3, 5, 20, 22–23

Popenoe, Paul, 9, 83. *See also* California

populism, 9, 23, 63, 133, 141

Post, C.W.: background of, 177; and Edward Edwin Davis, 177–178; and his death, 178; and depression, 177; and "enfoldment," 178; and eugenics, 178; and Fort Worth, 177; and health foods, 177; and John Harvey Kellogg, 177–178; and Post, Texas, 177–178; and rainmaking, 178; and workers, 247; and xenophobia, 178. *See also* Davis, Edward Everett; Kellogg, John Harvey

Progressives: and class identity, 1, 81; and democracy, 5, 40–41; and eugenics, 5, 12, 40–41, 176; and political priorities in Texas, 25, 40–42, 185–186; racism of, 40; and suffrage, 40. *See also* Daniel, Ferdinand Joseph; Daniel Josephine; Ellis, Alexander Caswell; Wilmans, Edith; women's clubs

psychology and racism, 199

"race suicide," 12, 46, 53, 55–57, 192. *See also* "great replacement theory"; Roosevelt, Theodore

Ramsdell, Charles, 136

reparations for sterilizations, 13, 189. *See also* California

Reynolds, Cecil R., 200, 202–203. See also *Bell Curve, The*; Jenson, Arthur; Texas A&M University

Rice Institute: eugenics and, 9; founding of, 126–127; and Julian Huxley, 127–129; and Hermann Joseph Muller, 128, 163–164; racism in the history of, 126–127. *See also* Huxley, Julian, Muller; Lovett, Edgar Odell; Muller, Hermann Joseph

Rice University. *See* Rice Institute

Rice, William Marsh, 126–127

Rockefeller, John D, 76

Roosevelt, Theodore, 12, 54, 57, 192. *See also* "race suicide"

Rushton, Phillipe J., 201–202

Sanger, Margaret, 100

"savage warfare" myth, 21–22, 207. *See also* "great replacement theory"; "race suicide"

Schoenfeldt, Lyle F., 201. *See also* Texas A&M University

Sharp, Henry Clay, 71

Sims, Marion, 32

slavery, 11, 18–20, 23, 29, 32–33, 36, 37, 40, 44–45, 66, 92–93, 126–127, 208. *See also* African American population in Texas; Black eugenics

Smith, Carrie Weaver: background, 101; and corporal punishment, 101–103; and the Eugenic Records Office, 14, 104; death of, 106; eugenics beliefs, 2, 12, 103–104; firing by Texas Board of Control, 105; and the Gainesville School for Girls, 73, 102–105; and the Goree Farm, 102; influence of, 100–103; and the Johnson Home and Training School, 101; and Native Americans, 104; opposition to: 103, 105; and sex education, 103, 105; support from feminists, 105; in Washington, D.C., 105–106. *See also* Davenport, Charles; Eugenics

Records Office; Native Americans; Texas Board of Control

Southern Baptists: and eugenics, 26; and their influence in Texas, 98–99

Spencer, Richard: background, 197–198; and Richard Hanania, 203; support for eugenics, 198; and the "Unite the Right" rally, 198. *See also* Hanania, Richard

State Fair of Texas: ableism and, 90–92; eugenics and, 8–9, 88–89; racism and, 90

sterilization: advocacy for, 7, 8, 15, 16, 26, 29, 32–34, 37–40, 58, 71–73, 76–77, 78–80, 132, 144, 169, 171–173, 176–177; and techniques, 42, 173. *See also* Dabney, Meriwether Lewis; *Dallas Morning News*; Daniel, Ferdinand Eugene (F. E.); Davis, Edward Everett; Duggan, Arthur; Lincecum, Gideon

Stoddard, Lothrop: influence of, 14–16, 110, 147, 159. *See also* Dabney, Meriwether Lewis; Davis, Edward Everett; Grant, Madison; Harvard University and eugenics

Storer, Horatio, 53. *See also* abortion

Teer, Claude, 172. *See also* Texas Board of Control

Terman, Lewis: impact of, 83, 132, 135; and intelligence testing, 132, 143; reputation of, 208; at Stanford, 132. *See also* California

Texas: antisemitism in, 48, 51, 144; and attitudes towards education, 24–26, 63–65, 81, 109, 192; and the "Bible Belt," 25–26, 127–128; demographics of, 24; 38, 43, 47, 50–51, 108–109, 112, 129, 131, 142, 157, 165; English-only requirements in public schools in, 148; eugenics beliefs in, 191–192,

194–195; eugenics curriculum in, 9, 83–85, 150; eugenics legislation in, 9–10, 28, 34–36, 43, 49, 71–72, 76, 78–80, 131, 138–141, 150–151, 168, 171–176, 206, 208; and eugenic segregation, 149; IQ panic in, 141–145, 149, 156, 172; mental health care in, 38, 48–50, 73, 131, 148–150, 171–172, 186, 192; as a racial borderland, 18–19, 129; and the rural-urban divide, 25, 64, 81, 134–136, 142; xenophobia in, 47–48, 129, 141, 144, 148, 154

Texas Adoption Project, 201–202

Texas A&M University: establishment of, 65; limited curriculum of, 65–66; racism at, 198; reputation of, 65–66; Richard Spencer visits, 198. *See also* Spencer, Richard

Texas Board of Control, 105, 172, 176. *See also* Smith, Carrie Weaver; Teer, Claude

Texas Committee on Prisons and Prison Labor, 105

Texas Medical Journal, 2, 5, 8, 39–40, 42, 55–56, 60, 62, 70, 72, 80. *See also* Daniel, Ferdinand Eugene (F. E.); Daniel, Josephine

Texas Mental Health Agency. 156

Texas Mental Hygiene Society. 180

Texas Siftings: antisemitism and, 51–52; xenophobia and, 52

Texas State Society of Social Hygiene, 72

Theil, Peter, 204–205. *See also* Hanania, Richard

Theissen, Del, 200. *See also* University of Texas at Austin

"Ugly" Law, 10, 138

University of Texas at Arlington. *See* North Texas Agricultural College

University of Texas at Austin: academic freedom at, 66–68, 86, 163–164; ban on hiring atheists at, 137; as "elitist," 63; eugenics at 85–87, 136, 155–156, 163; the Fergusons and, 131, 133, 135, 209; funding of, 66–67; and Pioneer Fund, 198–199; Progressives at, 135; racism at, 66, 111, 198–199; reputation of, 68; as "unpatriotic," 136. *See also* Ellis, Alexander Caswell; Ferguson, James "Jim,"; Ferguson, Miriam "Ma"; Keasby, Lindley M.; Muller, Hermann Joseph

Van Zandt, Olan Rogers, 175. *See also* Duggan, Arthur
Vasconcelos, José, 166. *See also* Mexicans and Mexican-Americans

Ward, Lester, 168–169. *See also* Harvard University and eugenics
Weiss, Bari, 205. *See also* Hanania, Richard
Willerman, Lee, 200–203. *See also* Horn, Joseph M; Loehlin, John C.; the Texas Adoption Project; Pioneer Fund; University of Texas at Austin
Wilmans, Edith: and the Ku Klux Klan, 138; anti-communism of, 139; background of, 139; her legislative record, 139; and her marriage bill, 10, 138–140. *See also* Ku Klux Klan; Progressives; women's clubs
women's clubs: and eugenics, 133–134, 148; xenophobia in, 148. *See also* Progressives; Wilmans, Edith

Yerkes, Robert: and the Army IQ tests, 143–145, 153; background of, 152; and Charles Davenport, 152; and Clarence Stone Yoakum, 143. *See also* Army IQ tests; Davenport, Charles; Terman, Lewis; Yoakum, Clarence Stone
Yoakum, Clarence Stone: and the Army IQ tests, 10, 144–145, 152–153; and the Austin State School 150; and eugenic segregation, 150; and *Care of the Feeble-Minded and Insane in Texas*, 149; on the intelligence of immigrants, 144, 152; on the futility of mass sterilization, 144, 149–150; and state asylums, 2, 10, 144, 149, 192; and Lewis Terman, 152; at the University of Texas, 143, 149–151; and Robert Yerkes, 152–153. *See also* Army IQ tests; Terman, Lewis; Yerkes, Robert; University of Texas at Austin

The manufacturer's authorized representative in the EU for
product safety is Mare Nostrum Group B.V., Mauritskade 21D,
1091 GC Amsterdam, The Netherlands
email: gpsr@mare-nostrum.co.uk